Lecture Notes in Computer Sci

Commenced Publication in 1973
Founding and Former Series Editors:
Gerhard Goos, Juris Hartmanis, and Jan van Leeuwe

T0230267

Editorial Board

Daniel Amyot   Alan W. Williams (Eds.)

System Analysis
and Modeling

4th International SDL and MSC Workshop, SAM 2004
Ottawa, Canada, June 1-4, 2004
Revised Selected Papers

 Springer

Volume Editors

Daniel Amyot
Alan W. Williams
University of Ottawa
800 King Edward, Ottawa, ON K1N 6N5, Canada
E-mail: {damyot, awilliams}@site.uottawa.ca

Library of Congress Control Number: 2004118419

CR Subject Classification (1998): C.2, D.2, D.3, F.3, C.3, H.4

ISSN 0302-9743
ISBN 3-540-24561-8 Springer Berlin Heidelberg New York

Springer is a part of Springer Science+Business Media

springeronline.com

© Springer-Verlag Berlin Heidelberg 2005
Printed in Germany

Typesetting: Camera-ready by author, data conversion by Scientific Publishing Services, Chennai, India
Printed on acid-free paper   SPIN: 11386100   06/3142   5 4 3 2 1 0

Preface

The SDL and MSC (SAM) workshop, held every two years, provides an open discussion arena on topics related to the modelling and analysis of reactive systems, distributed systems, and real-time systems (e.g., telecommunications, automotive, aerospace, and Web-based applications). The SAM workshop is a place for intensive discussions enabling the unfolding of ideas for the future development and application of SDL and MSC, and of related languages: ASN.1, eODL, TTCN, UML, and URN.

The fourth instance of this workshop was held at the University of Ottawa, Canada, from June 1 to June 4, 2004 (http://www.site.uottawa.ca/sam04/). It was co-organized by the University of Ottawa, the SDL Forum Society, and the International Telecommunication Union (ITU-T). SAM 2004 was also sponsored by SOLINET, SAFIRE-SDL, and Telelogic AB. The workshop welcomed 60 participants from 10 different countries, including SDL Forum members, tool vendors, standardizers, industrial users, and researchers.

In 2004, the program was composed of 21 papers, two panel sessions, one tutorial, several posters, and the third edition of the SDL design contest. The papers were selected by the Program Committee from 46 submissions. After postworkshop revisions, a second round of review led to the selection of 19 papers for publication in this volume of Lecture Notes in Computer Science.

Since the theme proposed for 2004 was *Security Analysis and Modelling*, the workshop started with a full-day tutorial on black-box security protocols, given by Sjouke Mauw and Cas Cremers. This tutorial introduced the basics of security protocols (which are "three-line programs that people still manage to get wrong") and ways of preventing many types of attacks based on a security model, verification, and formal modelling and analysis. Many of the models were expressed as message sequence charts annotated with security properties.

The invited talk on Model-Driven Software Engineering, given by Bran Selic (Distinguished Engineer, IBM Rational Software), emphasized that in the hype surrounding MDA, *platform independence* does not mean *platform ignorance*. Bran noted that engineering is "design with constraints," and the models need to incorporate those constraints. The characteristics of the underlying platform or machinery need to be taken into consideration early in the design process to address quality-of-service (QoS) issues. The challenge is to introduce technology-independent specifications of required and offered QoS in our models.

These proceedings contain 19 papers, presented in six different sessions:

1. SDL and eODL
2. Evolution of Languages
3. Requirements and MSC
4. Security
5. SDL and Modelling
6. Experience

Some of these contributions are likely to influence the evolution of ITU-T languages. In particular:

- Rick Reed presents his contribution on the ASN.1 data encoding for SDL in Z.104.
- Markus Scheidgen presents a metamodel for SDL-2000 in the context of metamodelling ITU-T languages. The idea of metamodels for ITU-T languages gains more and more support, especially with the current trend related to the development of UML 2.0 profiles for these languages, starting with SDL (i.e., Z.109).
- Øystein Haugen presents a comparison between UML 2.0 interactions and MSC-2000, where he discusses the many commonalities between the two languages, as well as aspects where one language is more advanced than the other. Three scenarios are envisioned by Haugen: (1) MSC/SDL and UML both prevail; (2) UML fails; (3) UML succeeds more.

During the workshop, the most active and heated discussions focused on the future of SDL, especially with these three presentations, followed by a panel session chaired by Alan Williams:

- Edel Sherratt presented new potential areas of application for SDL. She emphasized the importance of new trends such as ubiquitous and pervasive computing, ad hoc networking, and grid computing, and she discussed the influence of UML 2.0.
- William Skelton presented SIMPL-T (SDL intended for management and planning of tests), a simple test language for SDL specifications, where he argued for the use of SDL with minor extensions as a test language to test SDL models. These extensions include the organization and management of tests, the checking of responses (e.g., with "Input Via" and matching mechanisms), and the assigning and handling of verdicts.
- Andreas Prinz reported on the activities and suggestions of the SDL Task Force on the "simplest useful enhanced SDL-subset." The need for such a subset and its nature led to much discussion, which is still continuing on the SDL Forum and SDL Task Force mailing lists.

The second panel session, chaired by Ostap Monkewich, focused on Security Analysis and Modelling. Together with the three papers presented in the Security session and included in this volume, several challenges and opportunities regarding security modelling and ITU-T languages were presented, especially in the context of security vulnerabilities in the IP world.

Again this year, SOLINET/SAFIRE-SDL sponsored an SDL design contest, this time using an electronic access control system as the problem description (http://www.safire-sdl.com/sam_04.htm). Three contestants presented their solutions, and the workshop participants voted for the best one. For the second year in a row, Alkis Yiannakoulias (National Technical University of Athens) won the contest. Christian Webel (University of Kaiserslautern) finished second, followed by Keith Moss (Open University, UK) in third place.

Overall, the 2004 edition of SAM was a success, thanks to many people involved in this event, including the Local Organization Committee, Program Committe members, reviewers, speakers, invited speaker (Bran Selic), session and panel chairs, panellists, tutorial speakers, and contest participants and organizers. We hope you will enjoy our selection of papers. We are especially grateful to Jacques Sincennes for his help and technical support, and to Richard van de Stadt for making his CyberChair software (http://www.cyberchair.org) available to us.

The workshop presentations are also available online at the following Web site: http://www.site.uottawa.ca/sam04/.

November 2004   Daniel Amyot and Alan Williams

Organization

Organization Committee

Workshop Co-chairs

Daniel Amyot (SITE, University of Ottawa, Canada)
Alan Williams (SITE, University of Ottawa, Canada)

SDL Forum Society

Chairman: Rick Reed (TSE Ltd., UK)
Treasurer: Uwe Glässer (Simon Fraser University, Canada)
Secretary: Andreas Prinz (Agder University College, Norway)

ITU-T

B. Georges Sebek (TSB Councellor to ITU-T Study Group 17)

Local Organization Committee

Edna Braun
Bo Jiang
Jacques Sincennes
Yang Sun
Yong Xiang Zeng

Program Committee

Daniel Amyot, University of Ottawa, Canada
Rolv Bræk, Norwegian University of Science and Technology, Norway
Laurent Doldi, TransMeth Sud-Ouest, France
Olivier Dubuisson, France Telecom R&D, France
Anders Ek, Telelogic AB, Sweden
Joachim Fischer, Humboldt-Universität zu Berlin, Germany
Uwe Glässer, Simon Fraser University, Canada
Reinhard Gotzhein, University of Kaiserslautern, Germany
Susanne Graf, Verimag, France
Peter Graubmann, Siemens AG, Germany
Ferhat Khendek, Concordia University, Canada
Øystein Haugen, University of Oslo, Institute for Informatics, Norway
Dieter Hogrefe, Georg August University, Göttingen, Germany
Clive Jervis, Motorola, USA

Martin von Löwis, Hasso Plattner Institute, Germany
Nikolai Mansurov, Klocwork, Canada
Sjouke Mauw, Eindhoven University of Technology, The Netherlands
Arve Meisingset, Telenor, Norway
Ostap Monkewich, NCIT, Canada
Anders Olsen, Cinderella, Denmark
Andreas Prinz, Agder University College, Norway
Rick Reed, TSE Ltd., UK
Amardeo Sarma, NEC, Germany
Ina Schieferdecker, Fraunhofer FOKUS, Germany
Edel Sherratt, University of Wales, Aberystwyth, UK
William Skelton, SOLINET, Germany
Ken Turner, Stirling University, UK
Thomas Weigert, Motorola, USA
Alan Williams, University of Ottawa, Canada

Additional Reviewers

Harald Böhme	Knut Eilif Husa	Toby Neumann
Francis Bordeleau	Xiaoming Fu	Michel Piefel
Humberto Castejón	Andreas Kunert	Rene Soltwisch
Robert G. Clark	Ramiro Liscano	Andreas Ulrich
Cas Cremers	Christophe Lohr	Erik de Vink
Peter Deussen	Bill Mitchell	Frank Weil
George Din	Arjan J. Mooij	Constantin Werner
Michael Ebner	Bertram Neubauer	Dirk Westhoff

Sponsoring Organizations

Table of Contents

Security

SDL and Modelling

Experience

Author Index

Deployment and Configuration of Distributed Systems

Andreas Hoffmann[1] and Bertram Neubauer[2]

[1] Fraunhofer-Institut FOKUS, Kaiserin-Augusta-Allee 31,
10589 Berlin, Germany
a.hoffmann@fokus.fraunhofer.de
[2] Humboldt-Universität zu Berlin, Institut für Informatik,
Rudower Chaussee 25, 12489 Berlin, Germany
neubauer@informatik.hu-berlin.de

Abstract. In order to ease the development and handling of complex software systems, component models and distributed object technologies have been developed that allow the decomposition of systems and the use of software components in a distributed processing environment. While modelling and development of components is well supported, the deployment and configuration of component-based distributed systems lacks proper model reflection and is still a time consuming and difficult task. Hence, several approaches for supporting the deployment and configuration of component-based distributed systems at the modelling level have been developed recently and exist in parallel today. In this paper, the main concepts for deployment and configuration of three of those approaches are investigated and compared. It turns out that each of them focuses on different aspects. The approaches considered are ITU-eODL, UML 2.0 and the Deployment and Configuration Specification of the OMG. The ultimate goal is to identify the core concepts in this area in order to facilitate integration with the Unified Language Family of the ITU (ITU-ULF).

1 Introduction

In order to cope with an increasing software complexity on one hand and the rise of requirements on the development and usage of such software on the other hand, component technologies have been developed. The introduction of components allows the decomposition of systems on almost all levels, including design, specification, implementation and runtime level. When using distributed object technologies, reusable software components can be distributed over a network of computing nodes. Examples for appropriate technologies are the CORBA Component Model [7], Enterprise Java Beans and Microsoft .NET. In parallel to the introduction of component technologies, the Model Driven Architecture (MDA) [6] initiative from the Object Management Group (OMG) succeeded in introducing a new methodology for software development. Although the basic idea of MDA is not new, it was given a new shape, new terminology and appropriate

D. Amyot and A.W. Williams (Eds.): SAM 2004, LNCS 3319, pp. 1–16, 2005.

underlying technologies, like UML [2, 3] and MOF [5]. The basic idea is to focus the development of software systems on the abstract modelling of such systems rather than on their concrete implementation. Thus system design information can be decoupled from implementation technologies, which have shown to suffer from shorter lifecycles than general modelling concepts. The existence of different models on different levels of abstraction allows the distinction between a Platform Independent Model (PIM) on one hand and a Platform Specific Model (PSM) on the other. The transformation of models is done with strong tool support, at best in an automatic manner. This way, different PSMs can be used to derive different concrete implementations from the same common PIM.

Although modelling and development of components is well supported, deployment and configuration of component based distributed systems is not. Deployment and configuration of large-scale distributed systems is still a time consuming and difficult task. In order to allow better integration within the software development process, several approaches for modelling the deployment and configuration of component-based distributed systems have been developed. In this paper, the main concepts for deployment and configuration of three approaches are investigated and compared. In the sense of OMG MDA, each approach comprises a platform independent language, mainly based on component concepts. Thus it can be seen as an attempt to identify common concepts for platform independent modelling of application deployment. With respect to language integration and ITU-ULF, it should be the aim to find a language that is compliant or can be aligned with all relevant approaches or standards in order to serve as an MDA PIM.

2   Deployment and Configuration

In the scope of this paper, the term *deployment and configuration* addresses the deployment and configuration of component-based distributed applications. Given a concrete runtime environment, it designates the process that results in a running application ready to be used according to the application's specification. Obviously, this process has some requirements including information about the specific runtime environment, the application topology and concrete implementations of components. The provision of this information determines the degree of possible automation of the process, which is desired in general. In the context of component-based applications, deployment and configuration includes

1. the mapping of the application's topology in terms of interconnected component instances onto the runtime environment's network of computing nodes,
2. the installation of component implementations,
3. the creation of component instances and
4. the set-up of connections as well as the configuration of component properties.

Actual requirements of the components respecting their implementing artifacts have to be taken into account. They have to be met by the specific properties of the actual target environment where the application's components are to be deployed. As depicted in figure 1, for each of the application's components, a proper artifact implementing this component is to be selected and to be installed at a particular node that matches the artifact's specific deployment requirements (such as operating system, etc.). When the application is started, the deployment system instantiates the component instances by loading the proper artifacts into the runtime, and connects and configures them.

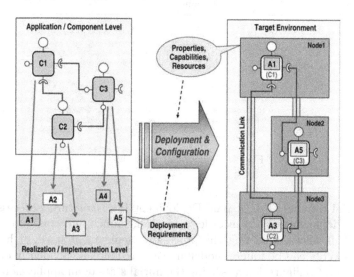

Fig. 1. Deployment process overview

Deployment and configuration can be seen as a mapping of the application from the specification level onto the runtime level. Therefore, appropriate reflection of the application on one hand and the target runtime environment on the other hand, are with dedicated deployment points of view required. As to be seen in figure 2, modelling of applications and target environments can in general be divided into two dimensions: the specification and the runtime. For each deployment related point of view a set of common modelling concepts can be identified. The Application/Component Modelling comprises concepts for component definition, component realization, and a composition or topology of components as application and its initial configuration. Target Environment Modelling comprises concepts for the modelling of computing nodes and communication links between nodes. Finally the Distribution Modelling allows giving up the distribution transparency of computational modelling by mapping a component topology onto a target environment.

While on the specification level, modelling is based on abstract concepts representing information, on the runtime level, the application and environment are reflected by runtime instances. The Application Representation allows the representation and management of running applications. The Deployment Data

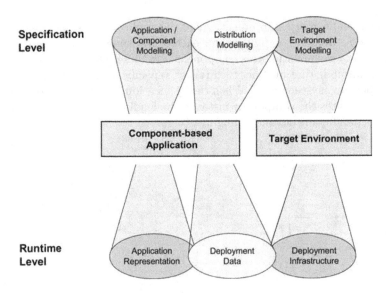

Fig. 2. Deployment modelling

reflect special formats of data. The Deployment Infrastructure is necessary to process the deployment data in order to install, launch and configure the application. This allows reflecting the process of deployment itself. If here also common concepts can be found, modelling can be done independently of a concrete platform. Configuration as setting the initial state of an application can be easily modelled with static specifications. Reconfiguration in contrast to configuration is the dynamic change of an existing configuration at runtime. It imposes stronger requirements on its specification, triggering and processing and is not in the scope of this paper.

In the area of deployment and configuration of distributed component-based applications, some different specifications were recently developed in and are available today in parallel. When looking for a common modelling in this area, each approach should be considered. Therefore, the respective specifications are listed subsequently.

2.1   eODL

ITU-eODL is a language for platform independent specification of component-based distributed systems. It provides several different viewpoints reflecting different but somehow related aspects of a system. Each viewpoint is connected with dedicated abstraction concepts, which can be used for specific modelling goals. The central viewpoint is the computational view point for modelling of components. Here a component concept is introduced that has the ability to define ports for operational, signal-based and stream interactions. These ports are directed and allow the composition of components to applications. eODL only allows the definition of black-box components and does not permit recursive composition of components. Besides the component modelling, the other major aspect is the deployment and configuration of component-based, distributed applications. In fact, originally a separate language called Deployment and Configuration Language (DCL) was planned, but this was later integrated into eODL. It includes three additional viewpoints. The implementation viewpoint covers the modelling of component realizations, including the specification of requirements on a runtime environment. The target environment viewpoint covers the modelling of the target environment. The deployment viewpoint covers the deployment mapping. With eODL there is no modelling of the runtime level. The language itself is based on a MOF metamodel definition, which allows defining arbitrary notations.

2.2   UML 2.0

UML in general is a language family for graphical modelling purposes. It can be used for visualization or specification of arbitrary systems, where different aspects are modelled with different sublanguages. Each sublanguage defines a separate set of modelling concepts and offers different graphical diagrams for notation. UML is standardized by the OMG, and version 2.0 was recently adopted. UML 2.0 is a major revision of the language, introducing a wide range of changes and advanced concepts in comparison to former versions. This includes the definition of new concepts for the modelling of components like provided and used interfaces and ports that can be used for the composition of components. In UML 2.0, components can be specified as black-box or white-box. The decomposition of components is possible so that a component-based application is a component in turn. From the viewpoint of deployment and configuration of component-based applications, essential concepts are defined for modelling the realization of components, i.e. their implementation, the target environment and the deployment mapping. With UML 2.0 there is no modelling of the runtime management of components. The language is based on a metamodel definition aligned with MOF 2.0. UML is widely accepted and also for version 2.0 a variety of tools will be available.

2.3   OMG Deployment and Configuration Specification (DnC)

In parallel with UML 2.0 and especially for the purpose of deployment and configuration of component-based applications, the Deployment and Configuration of Component-based Distributed Applications Specification (DnC) was adopted by the OMG in 2003. This specification is strictly structured according to the OMG MDA approach. Thus it separates between platform independent and platform specific modelling. The core of this specification is a MOF-compliant platform independent metamodel (PIM) for deployment and configuration of component-based distributed applications. In this model the definitions of a component and its implementing artifacts are aligned with the respective definitions of UML 2.0. Thus the OMG DnC specification can be seen as an extension of UML 2.0. The OMG DnC specification also defines a UML profile supporting the specification of applications made up from components as well as the modelling of the application's target environments. This UML profile can be seen as a concrete syntax for the abstract deployment concepts defined by the PIM.

While eODL and UML2.0 strongly focus on the development phase of component-based applications, the OMG's DnC specification does not cover this phase in the application's life cycle. How an application is created is out of scope of this specification. The starting point for the DnC is a complete (implemented) specification of an application as a result from the development phase. The reason for this is that one of the major objectives of the DnC specification is that it shall be applicable to any application in a wide range of domains developed by different methodologies. The major precondition is that the application is based on distributed component technology. The DnC specification also defines an interoperable deployment machinery. This includes the definition of a deployment architecture with well-defined interfaces and interchange formats. Both can be automatically derived from the PIM, since the DnC specification also defines proper mapping rules.

Beside the platform independent metamodel, one example of a metamodel for platform specific modelling is enclosed. This is the metamodel for the CCM platform to be used for specification of CCM applications. In order to transform a platform independent model into a model for CCM, transformation rules are defined for automatic processing. From the deployment point of view of component based applications, concepts for modelling component implementations, component assemblies, target environments and application deployment are provided. In addition to the modelling of these data, there is also a modelling of deployment processing and infrastructure. The metamodels for platform independent as well as platform specific models are based on MOF. Thus each used concept is provided as a MOF model.

2.4   Platform Specific Component Technologies

Platform independent modelling languages can hardly be used for the implementation of appropriate applications. In order to implement a component-based application, its technology dependent specification, for instance based on CCM, EJB or .NET, is required at least. When following the MDA approach this means that each concept used in an appropriate platform independent specification of an application has to be mapped to elements of the technology, which is chosen for the implementation of the application, including its deployment and runtime management. In consequence, it is vital for the metamodel of the platform independent specification, that its concepts are to be aligned with possible target technologies. This fact justifies having a look at the concepts of specific technologies in general. The support for deployment and configuration of component-based applications is reflected in different technologies to very different extents. The most comprehensive support is provided by CCM, which provides a framework for the development and deployment of CORBA components. In this paper there is no further study on these technologies.

3   Comparison of Common Concepts

Subsequently the approaches of eODL, UML 2.0 and OMG Deployment and Configuration Specification (DnC) are examined for its reflection of some selected vital concepts for deployment and configuration. For each such concept the respective modelling elements have to be compared in order to assess the expressiveness and usability in a PIM.

3.1   Component and Component-Based Application

A component-based application is an application that is realized by a composition of components. Obviously in this context the concept of component is the central modelling concept. In general terms it represents a modular part of a system that encapsulates its contents and whose implementation is replaceable within its environment. Moreover a component allows the modelling of composition by defining interaction ports for provided and required interfaces. Thus connections between components can be modelled by connecting required and provided ports determining interaction kind and direction. Components can be reused in different applications. This general concept of component is to be found in all three languages. As to be seen there are huge differences in the extent of additional component concepts. Nevertheless there is a set of common concepts like component, port, interface, connection so that the different representations of applications can be mapped to each other.

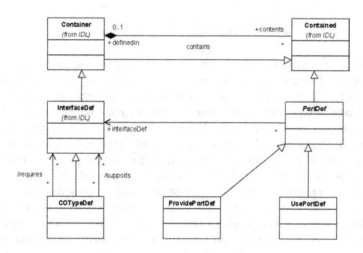

Fig. 3. Component definition in eODL

In eODL, a component is represented by COTypeDef. Since eODL is based on OMG IDL the reflection of the contained relationship is covered by the concepts of Container and Contained. A COTypeDef is a Container that may contain several Contained elements, including PortDef. A PortDef is a Contained and can be a ProvidePortDef or a UsePortDef. It has a relation to an InterfaceDef. As already said, components in eODL are only black-boxes. The modelling of internal structures of a component is not possible. This means that component-based applications made as assemblies of components cannot be modelled as a component, but require an additional concept. This concept is AssemblyDef, which comprises information about the topology of the component assembly, required component instances and connections between them.

In UML 2.0, a component is represented by the class Component. It may provide or require interfaces and inherits the concepts of ports and connections from the Class EncapsulatedClassifier. A component in UML 2.0 can be modelled as black-box or white-box. UML 2.0 provides a very sophisticated component model, where internal structures can be modelled with the concept of part and connections between parts. Thus, here a component based application is a component, that in turn results in a recursive decomposition.

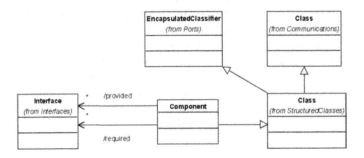

Fig. 4. Component definition in UML 2.0

In DnC, a component specification is represented by the modelling element ComponentInterfaceDescription. In contrast to eODL and UML the modelling of components is only based on the reflection of component and port. It is not integrated with a type system or other component concepts. Instead, it is fully based on strings in order to refer to identifiers for interfaces and types, modelled outside the deployment and configuration model. This approach on one hand prevents a close integration of component modelling and deployment modelling, since relations are not reflected by associations between model elements but by comparison of attribute values. On the other hand, it provides the opportunity to apply modelling of deployment and configuration to arbitrary component models, given that they support the concepts of interface and named ports as required by DnC. Of course components can this way only be modelled as black-boxes, and a component based application requires another concept for its reflection. In DnC an application is modelled as the implementation of a component. Using the alternative concepts of MonolithicImplementationDescription or ComponentAssemblyDescription, the implementation can be monolithic or recursive, respectively, see figure 6. Recursive implementation means, that the component is implemented by an assembly of other components. In fact, the independency of the implementation description from the component specification

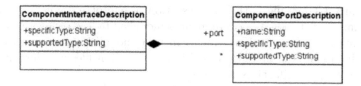

Fig. 5. Component definition in DnC

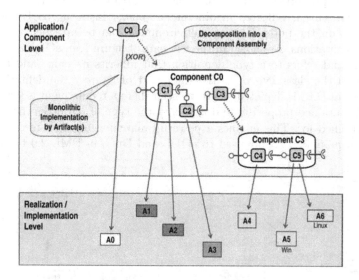

Fig. 6. Application definition in DnC

would allow to have an implementation structure that differs from a possibly given white-box component specification, like with UML 2.0. Actually, in such cases the implementation structure would be derived from the component structure.

3.2 Realization of Components

In order to be deployed and instantiated as part of an application, components have to be implemented and the appropriate information concerning the implementation, such as the name of the implementation files, and their dependencies and requirements has to be reflected in the model. All three approaches allow modelling of component realization in a quite similar way that makes an alignment of concepts for component realization possible. A component, potentially together with other components, is implemented by a software artifact. This is according to the specification of components in [8]. Unfortunately, the concept of Artifact is to be found in all models with different meanings. In eODL, a components realization is modelled by the concept of SoftwareComponentDef. The concept of Artifact is used here to reflect the implementation structure in form of implementation classes. In UML 2.0, the concept of Artifact as the representation of an arbitrary file is the manifestation of one or more components. In DnC, the implementation of a component is modelled by the concept of ComponentImplementationDescription, which can be a monolithic implementation or an assembly of components. The actual implementation files are then modelled by ImplementationArtifactDescriptions.

Very important for the determination of the distribution of component implementations on a target environment is the availability of proper information concerning the properties of the implementation artifacts needed to derive their requirements. This is reflected in different manners. In both eODL and DnC requirements on the potential target environment can be attached to component implementations. As shown in the left part of figure 7, in eODL a property has a value and refers to a type definition that inherits its name and type attributes from the class Typed. In the right part of figure 7 the definition of a requirement in DnC is depicted. As to be seen there a requirement is structured by several contained properties and typed by the type of resources the requirement is specified for. This enables a powerful matching mechanism during the distribution mapping. As opposed to eODL and DnC, in UML 2.0 there is no

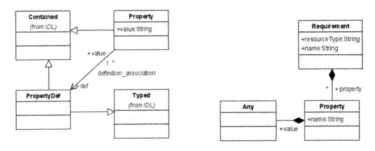

Fig. 7. Deployment requirements in eODL (left) and DnC (right)

special concept defined supporting the definition of deployment requirements. Instead, one can use the general-purpose annotation mechanism of UML to add untyped property-value pairs to classes in the deployment diagram stereotyped with «artifact». This means, that without profiling, no further semantics for the specification of requirements is provided.

3.3   Target Environment Description

UML does not define explicitly the term target environment. It basically provides the concept of Nodes and CommunicationPath connecting nodes. Nodes have processing capabilities and may be nested. UML defines the concept of Devices allowing better substructering of nested nodes. An ExecutionEnvironment allows the execution of specific types of components. The connecting feature of CommunicationPath is achieved implicitly by inheritance. The concepts of Node and CommunicationPath can be used in so-called deployment diagrams providing a simple notation for static mapping of component implementations (artifacts) to selected nodes. Static mapping means that in the current UML 2.0 version it is not really anticipated to support the distribution mapping of component's implementations to different arbitrary target environments by a generic requirement-property matching mechanism.

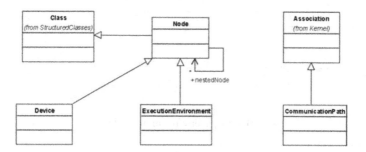

Fig. 8. Target environment in UML

As depicted in figure 9, in eODL a target environment is composed of nodes and links connecting nodes (NodeLink). This model is fairly simple. However, as opposed to UML it allows the direct attachment of properties (type-name-value triple) to nodes and links between nodes. This is achieved by inheritance from the Container class (figure 9) that inherits in turn the ability of having properties from the Contained class (see figure 3 and figure 7).

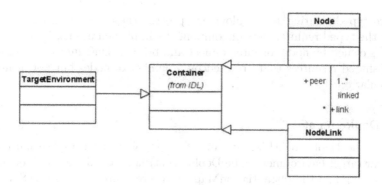

Fig. 9. Target environment in eODL

In DnC a target environment is called a domain. As depicted in figure 10, it is composed of nodes, bridges and interconnects. Nodes are connected by interconnects providing a shared communication path. Bridges are representations for routers and switches connecting interconnects. Nodes provide processing capabilities. They are the target for executing deployed component implementations. Features of nodes as well as interconnects and bridges are modelled by resources

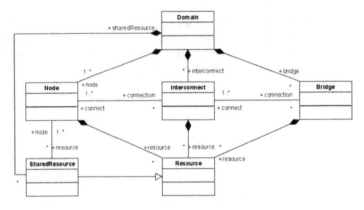

Fig. 10. Target environment in DnC

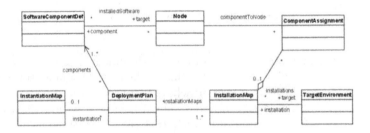

Fig. 11. Deployment plan in eODL

that are typed. During the deployment process these resources are matched against the typed requirements of component's implementations. In addition to resources owned by nodes or interconnect and bridges, DnC introduces the concept of shared resources that are used by a number of nodes but not owned by a particular one.

3.4 Deployment

In eODL the DeploymentPlan specifies the mapping of an application onto a particular target environment. The DeploymentPlan basically consists of the InstallationMap and the InstantiationMap. It also refers to one or more SoftwareComponentDefs that are involved in the DeploymentPlan. The InstallationMap contains a number of ComponentAssignments defining what software components are to be installed at what node. An InstantiationMap specifies what component instances are to be instantiated at what node. Figure 11 provides a brief overview on eODL's concept of a DeploymentPlan. The subsequent diagrams explaining the InstallationMap and InstanceMap in more details have been omitted due to the limited paper space.

In contrast to eODL, UML does not provide a concept for a general deployment plan but only allows modelling of an assignment of artifacts to deployment targets. It is a quite simple model. Deployment targets are mainly Nodes, but also Parts inheriting from Properties and InstanceSpecifications can be targets for deployment. Each deployment target owns a set of deployments reflecting the installation of artifacts or instances of artifacts. Furthermore (not shown in figure 12), there is the possibility to give additional artifacts containing deployment related information as configuration values, etc., by using the class DeploymentSpecification.

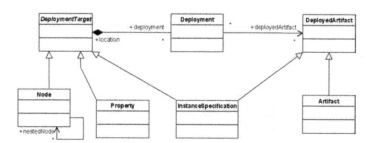

Fig. 12. Deployment definition in UML

As in eODL, the central concept in the DnC Specification for Distribution Mapping is the DeploymentPlan. This is a complex structure referring to the descriptions of the application on one hand, and to an actual target environment that the application has been mapped to on the other hand. Mapping an application into a domain (see figure 10) includes, in particular, the mapping of component implementations to nodes and connections between component instances to bridges and interconnects. All requirements of the application's components need to be met as a result of this mapping process. The DeploymentPlan records all these deployment decisions. In more detail, the MonolithicDeploymentDescription specifies the deployment of a particular component. It references at least one ArtifactDeploymentDescription, which specifies that a particular artifact has to be installed on a selected target node as part of the component deployment. It also contains execution parameters needed for loading the artifact into runtime. The application's initial topology in terms of instances to be created and connected is described by the InstanceDeploymentDescription and PlanConnectionDescription. Finally, the DeploymentPlan allows the specification of dependencies to other applications that must have been deployed prior to the application the DeploymentPlan is for. The DeploymentPlan also references the ComponentInterfaceDescription describing a component's set of required and provided interfaces.

3.5 Runtime Management

As already mentioned, the DnC specification is the only one of the three compared approaches that provides a model for executing a deployment specification, i.e. for installing and launching a distributed application in its dedicated target

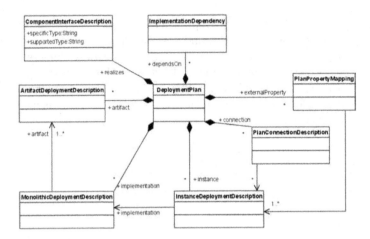

Fig. 13. Deployment plan in DnC

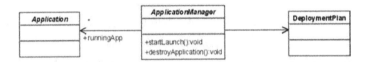

Fig. 14. Runtime management overview in DnC

environment according to the deployment specification. Figure 14 just shows the ApplicationManager as an integral part of the deployment infrastructure as specified by DnC. The ApplicationManager manages the complete installation and bootstrapping of the application as specified by the DeploymentPlan.

4   Summary

The examination of the languages eODL, UML 2.0 and OMG DnC from the perspective of modelling deployment and configuration of component-based applications has shown that these languages are different, but based on a set of common concepts. These concepts unfortunately are reflected by different modelling elements, but could be aligned. In order to have a common language for modelling deployment and configuration of component-based applications, especially with respect to build a uniform language family, this set of concepts has to be identified in detail. Within this paper an overview was given. Figure 15 shows the comparison of modelling elements of the three languages.

It should be no option to develop a new language but instead adapt and use one of the existing ones. It is essential for the usability of such a language that it should cover as much as possible of the concepts used in this area. Furthermore, mappings to other languages, either platform independent or platform dependent, must be possible. Since all three languages have a MOF-based metamodel,

	eODL	UML 2.0	OMG DnC
Application / Component Modelling	COTypeDef	Component	ComponentInterfaceDescription
	PortDef	Port	ComponentPortDescription
	AssemblyDef	(nested) Component	AssemblyDescription
	SoftwareComponentDef	Artifact	ComponentImplementationDescription, MonolithicImplementationDescription, ComponentAssemblyDescription
	Property (name-type-value)	*(name-value annotation)*	typed Requirement
Target Environment Modelling	TargetEnvironment	-	Domain
	Node	Node	Node
	NodeLink	CommunicationPath	Interconnect, Bridge
	Property	*(name-value annotation)*	typed Resource and SharedResource
Distribution Modelling	DeploymentPlan	(deployment diagram)	DeploymentPlan
	InstallationMap, ComponentAssignment	Deployment	ArtifactDeploymentDescription
	InstantiationMap	InstanceSpecification	InstanceDeploymentDescription
	<Properties of SoftwareComp. meet TargetEnv. Properties>	-	<typed Resources meet typed Requirements>
Run-time Management	-	-	ApplicationManager, Application (Target-,Node-,ExecutionManager)

Fig. 15. Concept comparison

mappings can be easily done on this basis. It is hard to determine which language should be taken as a common language for the considered purpose and the choice probably will depend on the context. In the context of ITU-T, the adoption and further development of eODL would be a good choice, since it is already an ITU-T language. From the perspective of usability and publicity on the other hand UML (2.0) is wide spread and prepared to be extended by its build-in feature of profiles. The specification of UML 2.0 explicitly states, that the Deployment package supports a streamlined model of deployment that is deemed sufficient for the majority of modern applications. Where more elaborate deployment models are required, it can be extended through profiles or metamodels to model specific hardware and software environments. Also the DnC could serve as a base for a common language. Due to its relative independence of the used component model, it can easily be combined with a variety of models. Furthermore DnC already provides a mapping to CCM, one of the most advanced component technologies. Since technology mappings are very important for the MDA-approach they will play a key role for the acceptance of a common PIM.

References

1. ITU-T: Recommendation Z.130 (07/03), Extended Object Definition Language (eODL). International Telecommunication Union, Geneva.
2. OMG: UML 2 Superstructure Specification. OMG document ptc/03-08-02.
3. OMG: UML 2 Infrastructure Specification. OMG document ptc/03-09-15.
4. OMG: Deployment and Configuration of Component-based Distributed Applications Specification. OMG document ptc/03-07-08.

5. OMG: MOF 2.0 Core Final Adopted Specification. OMG document ptc/03-10-04.
6. OMG: MDA Guide Version 1.0.1. OMG document formal/03-06-01.
7. OMG: CORBA Component Model. Version 3.0. OMG document formal/2002-06-65.
8. Szyperski, C.: Component Software - Beyond Object-Oriented Programming. ACM Press Books, 1999.
9. W3C: Extensible Markup Language (XML) 1.0 (Second Edition). World Wide Web Consortium, 2000.

eODL and SDL in Combination for Components

Harald Böhme and Joachim Fischer

Humboldt-Universität zu Berlin
{boehme, fischer}@informatik.hu-berlin.de
http://www.informatik.hu-berlin.de/~boehme

Abstract. Today's software development is component-oriented. We show how well-established techniques like SDL and component development can be combined. This approach will keep the strength of well-founded formal languages to improve the specification of components. Moreover, an abstract model notation (eODL) of component based applications (assemblies) is shown. A first proof of concept is done by a realisation on top of a standardised component middleware platform of the OMG (CCM). For the integration of different model abstractions we use the OMG adopted MDA technology. An overview of the resulting development process will complete the picture of the proposed approach.

1 Introduction

The process of software development has been changing over the time to react to current needs and inventions of software design. One important force for the improvement of the software development process is the search for a better reuse of already developed and existing software. In the beginning this was done with libraries. For a long time they were used at linkage stage only. Later, compiler languages were enhanced by notations for multiple compilation units, where the library approach was extended in that direction, too. Until recently, the linkage library solution was the only widespread method for software reuse. Meanwhile, computer languages have been progressed further, in particular object-oriented concepts were introduced. On the one hand the use of those languages adds to the improvement of the software design at all, but on the other hand this does not really support the reuse. Today the paradigm of component-orientation is meant to solve the reuse problem. In this perspective component-orientation elevates the aspect of reuse to the level of software design. This is a big step forward, because already the designer can pay attention to software reuse. As a result it is now possible to reuse software components at design level and not only at engineering level.

For the enforcement of the component-oriented paradigm in the design stage the availability of suitable design languages is important. eODL [5] is an ITU language. Its roots are the TINA [15] context, where the language ODL [4] had introduced concepts for component description for the first time. Like many other modelling techniques on the abstract level eODL too deals only with structural

D. Amyot and A.W. Williams (Eds.): SAM 2004, LNCS 3319, pp. 17–32, 2005.

aspects of the software system. Elements to model behavioural aspects are missing. But the behavioural aspects belong to the basic system design as well as the structure and should also persist across development iterations and technological changes. However, utilities for the preservation of the behavioural aspects at design level are needed.

One practically used language dealing with behavioural aspects is SDL [3]. Our paper will show in section 3, that the combination of the two description techniques will overcome the lack of behavioural description for component development at abstract level (s. Figure 2).

But the software development process will not stop with abstract models, real implementations have to be produced. For the transition from abstract to implementation-oriented models an existing method has to be applied. The Model Driven Architecture (MDA) [8] defined by the OMG propose such a general method for model transformation. This approach is used in our paper to map models from abstract to implementation level. More detailed information on MDA is given in section 2. The mapping to implementation level is shown in section 4. To illustrate several steps of used model transformation and model enrichment a simple example "Hello World" is given.

2   Model Driven Architecture (MDA)

The Model Driven Architecture is a new software engineering approach developed and published by the Object Management Group (OMG). One fundamental observation in the evolution of living software systems over the years is that their basic design models are mostly unchanged. Most changes to evolving software systems take place only at engineering level, forced by the introduction of new technologies and platforms.

MDA promotes simply the usage of models for the whole software system development. To capture the problem of technology evolution MDA defines two classes of models. The first one is for abstract modelling of the software systems at the design level. This model class is called Platform Independent Model (PIM). The second class is related to specific platforms and/or technologies. It contains mainly engineering aspects of the software system and is called Platform Specific Model (PSM). Between these two classes of models MDA defines a relation in form of several mappings, which insure the structural equivalence of PIM and PSM (see Fig. 1).

Another key issue of MDA is a technology framework for different kinds of model handling (storage, exchange, mapping of models, etc.). The Meta Object Facility [7] is convenient for this purpose. Historically modelling languages are defined by abstract grammars. MOF instead defines modelling languages on the base of so called metamodels. Metamodels are models (instances) of built-in MOF concepts. Using this framework the developer can focus more on the definition of mappings between models rather than having to struggle with ordinary model handling. This is due to the fact that MOF comes with a method for the definition of model classes (metamodels) and for the exchange of models using

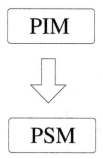

Fig. 1. Relation between PIM and PSM

the XML Metadata Interchange (XMI) [6]. In addition, MOF provides mappings of metamodels to repository interfaces as well. Such a repository holds all necessary information about model instances.

2.1   Component Model

For the development of component-oriented software a common understanding of what a component is has to be achieved first. This must be supported by a component model. Component models are used during the whole development process from design over implementation until deployment. Components in general are selfcontained software units, which export their functionality with the help of *provided* interfaces to their environment. The functionality required from the environment of a component is expressed by *used* interfaces of that component.

A software system based on such a component model can be seen as a configuration of components. The interaction of the single components in this configuration combines their individual functionalities and performs the complex system functionality. Thus, the division of functional aspects is a main issue in the software development process.

A component model contains all structural information for the system design, especially component type with their interfaces and relations, number and types of component instances and interconnection between component instances.

2.2   Overview on Applied Model Techniques

The MDA approach offers only a road-map for the software development process and is not connected a priori with component development. That's why MDA does not contain a predefined component model. So we have to identify or adapt modelling techniques and/or languages for component development which are convenient for PIM and PSM descriptions.

In Figure 2 we give an overview on the languages used in the approach proposed by the authors. At the PIM level of design eODL is used in combination with SDL. This gives us the strength of a component-oriented technique (eODL)

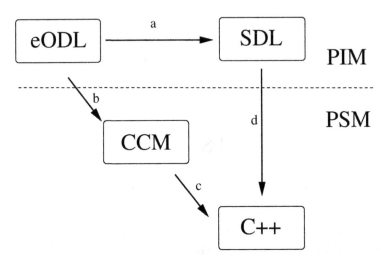

Fig. 2. Mappings between involved languages

as well as the power of behavioural description (SDL). Furthermore, SDL has a formal semantics, which may be very useful to analyse and test at an abstract design level. The mapping **a** in Figure 2 is part of the component modelling at PIM level and results in corresponding model structures in SDL.

As component model for PSM we choose the CORBA Component Model (CCM) [9]. CCM offers a metamodel for components based on MOF. A more detailed description is given in section 4.1. The following section describes mapping **a** of Figure 1.

An alternative language for PIM could be UML 2.0. For the PSM other established component platforms like EJB and .NET are possible.

3   eODL-SDL Mapping

In specialisation of the MDA approach the authors use an eODL-SDL combination for the description of components at the PIM level. Because eODL is defined with a MOF metamodel it is well suited for a realisation of the MOF approach. Furthermore, eODL provides a human-readable notation and a feature for the model exchange between different eODL-tools based on XMI. The core modelling concepts of eODL are grouped by different *view points*[1]:

- *computational view point,*
- *implementation view point,*
- *deployment view point,*
- *target environment view point.*

---

[1] *view point* means here the same as in ODP.

For the PIM level only the computational view point is relevant. All structural aspects of components belong to the computational design. Examples for structural concepts are component (in eODL called CO-Type) and interface. Further computational concepts of eODL are *port* and *provided/used*.

3.1   Z.130 eODL-SDL Mapping

eODL as pure component technique deals only with structural aspects of components, behavioural aspects are not covered. To overcome the lack of behavioural description we propose the usage of SDL in combination with eODL. SDL is well suited for the description of behaviour of reactional systems. Components themselves with their *provided* interfaces act like reactive subsystems. Signal and RPC interaction from eODL have corresponding built-in concepts in SDL. The inheritance relation is covered in SDL as well. eODL has its own data type system. The data type system of SDL provides other concepts as eODL, but is powerful enough to build adequate data types for the needed kinds of interaction in eODL. For behaviour SDL uses the concept of extended state machines, which is defined by a transition graph.

Starting point of the SDL part of components are SDL structures, which are generated from the originating eODL structures.

The concept of **used port** in eODL is a mechanism that enables a **CO** to store interface references of other **CO**s.

This concept is mapped onto a set of remote procedures that are declared in the configuration interface of the **CO**.

A **used port** `foo` of type `bar` is mapped onto the remote procedure `link_foo` that takes an reference to `bar` as **parameter**. If the **port** is of attribute **single** and there is already a reference stored at this **port**, the predefined **exception** `AlreadyConnected` is raised. Moreover, a remote procedure `unlink_foo` is declared that removes the stored reference from **port** `foo`. If there is no reference stored at `foo`, the predefined **exception** `NotConnected` is raised. If the **port** is of attribute **multiple**, a sequence of references is stored. The **exception** is `AlreadyConnected` never raised.

...

This mapping defined by Z.130 is able to handle all eODL concepts of all different view points. In the example above a computational concept is identified, but the mapping covers concepts from other view points, too. The main disadvantage of that mapping is the hardwired relation to CCM. This shows up especially through the usage of RPC in combination with predefined exceptions. Moreover, the mapping results in an unneeded complexity of the resulting SDL structures. That's why in this paper a new mapping is proposed which will only cover concepts of the computational view point of eODL.

The concepts of the other view points are taken care of by other technology dependent mappings as shown in Figure 3. Here mapping d' as technology de-

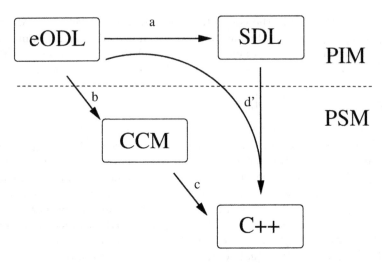

Fig. 3. New mappings between involved languages

pendent mapping use not only information from the SDL-model (computational) additional information from other view points in the eODL-model are obtained.

3.2   Principles of a Revised eODL-SDL Mapping

Now we are able to postulate some requirements for a revised version of the eODL to SDL mapping:

1. The resulting SDL has to be platform independent.
2. The resulting SDL should be in a shape to be executable for simulation, test and usage.
3. The mapping should be defined on the base of MOF.

The third requirement assumes definitions of the source (eODL) and target language (SDL) to use the MOF approach. For eODL such a definition already exists by the standard. In [12] an ongoing work for a SDL-metamodel is described. This metamodel is used in the definition of the mapping rules. To give an outline of the nature of the new mapping rules an example[2] is presented:

Rule: For each element in the eODL model of type `COTypeDef` (**A**) there is an element of type `Agent_type_definition` (**A'**) in SDL with the same name. If the `COTypeDef` (**A**) is a specialisation of another `COTypeDef` (**B**) than also the `Agent_type_definition` (**A'**) in SDL is a specialisation of the other resulting `Agent_type_definition` (**B'**).

---

[2] It should be remarked that all mappings of the eODL standard are of informal nature.

The rule above refers to concepts of both metamodels, in our case `COTypeDef` and `Agent_type_definition`. This is necessary, because model modifications in the development process should be reflected in both directions. If for instance the name of a `COTypeDef` in eODL is changed also the corresponding name in SDL for the `Agent_type_definition` has to be modified.

```
interface Hello {
    void say ();
};

interface Manage {
    void init ();
};

/* operational state is entered after init() */

CO Callee {
    provides Hello the_hello;
    provides Manage the_manage;
};

CO Caller {
    use Hello hi;
};
```

Listing 1.1. eODL example

Another aspect demonstrated by the rule is the fact that there is no 1:1 relation between all non-abstract concepts in eODL and SDL. The mapping rule defines a relation between the concrete concept `COTypeDef` and the abstract concept `Agent_type_definition` of SDL. But models of SDL do not contain instances of `Agent_type_definition` as such. While establishing the relation between eODL and SDL model elements, it has to be decided which actual concept will be used for `Agent_type_definition`. For the metamodel of SDL this could be either `Block_agent_type_definition` or `Process_agent_type_definition`, which both are concrete specialisations of `Agent_type_definition`. This is illustrated by example listings 1.1 and 1.2. In the eODL specialisation in 1.1 we define two `COTypeDef`, which are mapped to SDL in listing 1.2. In the process of mapping the user and/or the mapping tool has to decide which concrete concept in the target metamodel should be used. In our example here we use in both cases `Process_agent_type_definition` as target concept.

```
interface Hello;
    procedure say;
endinterface;

interface Manage;
    procedure init;
endinterface;
```

```
process type Calle;
gate the_hello in with interface Hello;
gate the_manage in with interface Manage,
exported as << interface Hello>> say procedure say;
endprocedure;
exported as << interface Manage>> init procedure init;
endprocedure;
endprocess type;

process type Caller;
gate hi out with interface Hello;
endprocess type;
```

Listing 1.2. SDL structures generated from eODL example

However, not for all concepts of the computational view point of eODL exist simple mappings to SDL. This shows up if you try to establish a relation between `InterfaceDef` and a corresponding concept in SDL. Although SDL contains interface as a language element this is not a first class concept, it is only a short hand. So the semantical foundation for interfaces does not exist and the relation can not be built up[3]. It would be much more in line with actual used communication infrastructures to have interface as first class communication concept in SDL.

3.3   Component Model Enrichment by Behaviour Description

The final step of the development of a PIM related component model is the enrichment of the generated SDL model by a behavioural description. Using our eODL-SDL mapping we get agent types with well-defined interfaces. All signatures of signals and remote procedures are generated too. Now the design can start to fill out behavioural description in the SDL specification. That means it has to define all exported procedures, the state machine and the internal structure of all agent types. In our example (listing 1.3) this is only suggested by an introduction of a state-oriented behaviour. The enriched model is based on listing 1.2.

```
interface Hello;
    procedure say;
endinterface;

interface Manage;
    procedure init;
endinterface;

process type Calle;
```

---
[3] Note that example listing 1.2 is textual notation for SDL, which contains short hands

```
gate the_hello in with interface Hello;
gate the_manage in with interface Manage;
exported as << interface Hello>> say procedure say;
    start;
        task 'say hello ';
        return;
endprocedure;
exported as << interface Manage>> init procedure init;
    start;
        task 'do init stuff ';
        return;
endprocedure;
    start;
        nextstate ini;
    state ini;
        input init;
        nextstate running;
    endstate ini;
    state running;
        input say ;
            nextstate -;
    endstate running;
    state *;
        input init reject;
            nextstate -;
        input say reject;
            nextstate -;
    endstate;
endprocess type;

process type Caller;
gate hi out with interface Hello;
endprocess type;
```

Listing 1.3. Enriched SDL specification

A so enriched component model has all information for an automated code generation, which is described in section 4, where CCM is used as target platform.

The advantage of an enriched SDL model is obvious. A now possible simulation of the computational model can give important indications for computational problems of the component. This leads to feedback for detecting wrong structural layout in the eODL model and to the improvement of the behavioural description in SDL. With an iterative process of doing simulation and changes to the eODL and SDL model the quality of the computational description can be advanced.

4   CCM as PSM

Following the MDA approach not only a PIM related component model is necessary, also one for the PSM has to be provided. In our proposal we use CCM as component model for PSM in the development process. More precisely we select CCM in combination with C++ as target implementation language. Another candidate for the CCM implementation language is Java. For a better understanding a short introduction in CCM is given in the next section.

4.1   CORBA Component Model (CCM)

The CORBA Component Model [9] is a standard published by the OMG. It provides the metamodel for CORBA Components and the technology and runtime environment for components developed using that model. It is based on mature CORBA technologies like the GIOP protocol[4] and language bindings for implementation languages.

The component model of CCM defines two kinds of interactions for components. There is a RPC-like interaction with request/response and a signal-like one with events. For each of these interaction kinds components can declare the usage or the provision.

For the notation of models CCM extends the IDL2[5] syntax by rules for components. CCM also contains a mapping from IDL3 (IDL2 + components) to the older IDL2. This was introduced for a compatibility with older, not component-aware CORBA clients.

An implementation of CCM components in a target language like C++ is supported by further mappings defined by CCM: The set of interfaces provided by a component is mapped to *local* interfaces[6]. By defined language bindings of plain CORBA these *local* interfaces are than translated to C++. Now the developer can use the same approach to implement the component in the implementation language as he did with plain interfaces in CORBA.

The runtime environment of CCM covers two parts. The deployment process and deployment infrastructure belong to the first part. File formats for packages containing component implementations or whole software systems are defined here. The meta information in the packages make them selfcontained and provide additional information about the system structure. This means, it defines the number and type of component instances which participate in the initial configuration of the software system. The deployment infrastructure provides interfaces for the deployment process itself. There are operations to move packages to nodes of the runtime environment and to build containers, homes and instances.

The second part of the CCM runtime environment is the runtime functionality for the component instances. So-called containers are the execution environment for all components. They provide functionality through context interfaces

---

[4] The General Inter ORB Protocol defines the exchange of requests and replies for RPC interaction.

[5] IDL2 is the 2.x version of the Interface Definition Language standardised by the OMG.

[6] *local* interfaces are used by IDL to express the locality of an interface implementation, it can be seen as abstract notation for a class.

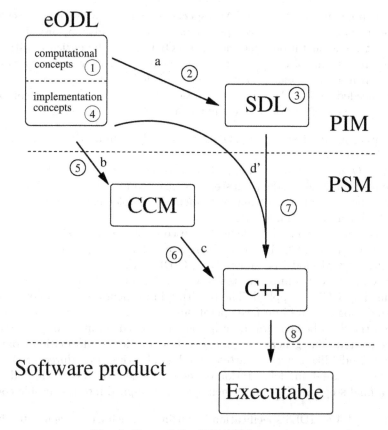

Fig. 4. Steps of the PIM-PSM mapping

to the components. Components can use this functionality during their execution.

With the support of two interaction kinds CCM is a good choice as a target platform for components designed with eODL. Stream interaction as the third interaction kind of eODL will be supported by CCM extensions in future [14].

4.2 PIM-PSM Mapping

With the availability of a concrete PIM in terms of eODL and SDL on one hand side and a concrete PSM in terms of CCM and C++ on the other hand side a mapping from PIM to PSM can be defined. As stated in section 4.1 CCM covers most of the computational concepts of eODL. A simple mapping from the components in eODL to the components in CCM can be done, even the *port* concept from eODL has a counter-part in CCM. In realisation of that mapping we get an 1:1 relation between the PIM and PSM concepts (see example listing 1.4). This mapping is called **b** in Figure 4. The usage of the IDL type-system in eODL is of great help in order to map interfaces from eODL to IDL3.

The mapping from eODL to CCM respects all identified view points of eODL. Now we no longer deal with computational concepts only, we are aiming at component implementation. The model in eODL has to be enriched with new information in terms of concepts of the implementation view point. Names for the implementation artefacts[7] have to be provided by the developer, because they are needed by the C++ implementation. Figure 4 describes the complete scenario of the developer of components as a sequence of following steps.

1. Components are described in eODL, where only computational concepts are considered.
2. These eODL concepts are mapped onto corresponding ones in SDL.
3. The resulting SDL model from step 2 is enriched by behavioural description.
4. With the introduction of model element for implementation concepts the PIM modelling is completed.
5. The computational and implementation concepts from the eODL model are mapped onto the CCM model. There are different representations for the resulting CCM model possible (IDL3, CIDL[8], XML).
6. The CCM model is implemented in C++. Therefore the language mapping defined by CCM is applied. The resulting implementation does not contain business logic for all interface operations.
7. From the SDL behavioural description the needed business logic for step 6 is generated. The generation process takes additional information from the eODL model like names for artefacts (class libraries, procedures, etc.). Now a complete C++ implementation of the component has been achieved.
8. As a final step the C++ implementation is compiled into executable code.

In listing 1.4 an IDL3 specification is outlined, which can be generated from listing 1.1.

```
interface hello {
    void say ();
};

interface manage {
    void init ();
};

component Callee {
    provides hello the_hello;
    provides manage the_manage;
};
```

---

[7] artefact is a concept from the implementation view point, which is used to denote implementation language constructs. Here we understand an artefact as a programming language class.

[8] The Component Implementation Description Language is defined by CCM and helps the developer to express structural aspects for the component implementations.

```
home CalleeHome manages Callee { };

component Caller {
    uses Hello hi;
};

home CallerHome manages Caller { };
```

Listing 1.4. eODL example mapped to IDL3

4.3   Implementation of the PIM-PSM Mapping

The authors did experiments with the Qedo [11] implementation for CCM. This is a C++ implementation of the CCM standard of the OMG. The code generation from IDL3/CIDL to C++ (see step 6 in Fig. 4) produces skeleton classes for the implementation of provided interfaces. This code contains large sections of pre-implemented code. On selected places *user sections* are located: they are marked areas in the code where the developer has to insert application specific code fragments to complete the implementation. The contents of *user sections* will remain unchanged over multiple runs of the code generation. From a CCM/Qedo perspective the developer is in charge of providing the behavioural implementation of the component. The reason for this is that there are no other sources of information for the behavioural description in the plain CCM development model.

As proposed in our paper a full behavioural description of the component in SDL can be used to fill the *user sections*. This has to be done by mapping d' from Figure 4. The authors have expert knowledge for code generation from SDL to C++ resulting from the development of the SITE tool environment [13][1] for SDL. As said before, components can always be seen as reactive systems, like SDL agents too. So providing the behavioural implementation for the component as an behavioural description in SDL is not a great challenge. The core part of the generated code is always a dispatch function. This function triggers the different transitions, based on the current state of the Agent and the signal input. For the usage of the dispatch function in the context of CCM two main tasks have to be realised:

– *Datatype conversion* The data types used in the stimuli of the SDL agent have to match the types used by the CCM implementation. This problem is easily solved. We get the basic structure of the SDL agent from the eODL model and eODL uses IDL types. This means the types in the generated code from SDL will always correspond to IDL types.
– *Inheritance of transition graphs* The inheritance of agent types in SDL has an impact to transition graph definition. This means transitions can be redefined in the specialisation. The generated dispatch function have two options to reflect this kind of redefinitions here: flatten the whole graph over all inheritance steps or usage of inheritance concepts from the target programming language. SITE use the later approach. Therefore a language construct,

which supports inheritance has to be used for the realisation of the dispatch function in the business logic of CCM.

As mentioned above the code generation from SDL to C++ fullfilled by the SITE tool environment can be adapted for the use in the approach proposed by this paper. This gives the developer the strength of automatic code generation. With that on hand the source of many errors are eliminated.

5   Deployment of Components

As shown in Figure 5 not only development is part of the life cycle of a software system. The usage phase is at least from the perspective of the end user the most important phase. Here the components building the software systems have to be moved to action. According to the selected PSM technology CCM two tasks have to be done:

– Packaging
– Distribution

5.1   Packaging

The *Packaging* in CCM is the process of producing selfcontained software packages for later distribution. They contain the implementation of components and meta information. The implementation could be gained from the step 8 Figure 4. The meta information has to be obtained from the eODL model. The matching concepts in eODL belong to the deployment view point. A mapping for this kind of information onto the meta information has to be defined in future work.

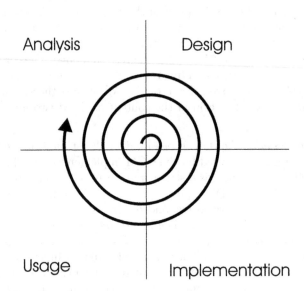

Fig. 5. Basic software life cycle

5.2   Distribution

After producing packages distribution of the software system is only a compulsory exercise. The infrastructure of the CCM runtime provides necessary interfaces on each node in the computing environment for distribution and building of initial component instances. The deployment tool will extract the metainformation from the packages distribute the needed packages. Later initial component instances are builded on the determined nodes and are interconnected following the plan contained in the metainformation.

5.3   Open Issues

The connection between the deployment process and the needed informations from the eODL model has to be investigated. Moreover, the whole part of information concerning the target environment has to be worked out. Concepts for these are already defined in the target environment view point of eODL, but the relation with the selected PSM technology has to be investigated.

6   Conclusion

The application of eODL in combination with SDL for the modelling of components enables the behavioural description at design level. Both languages together are good candidates for the PIM level of MDA. However, this has to be supported by a mapping for the structure of the component to SDL. The standardised mapping from eODL to SDL is too complex and technology dependent on CCM. A revised and flexible mapping is proposed. This mapping enables analysis, test and implementation of components. The provision of a metamodel based SDL definition will simplify the combination further. It is proposed that the interface concept should become a first class communication concept in the metamodel of SDL, because it is a fundamental concept for components. The PIM-PSM mapping identifies several working tasks for structural and behavioural concepts. More research on the deployment of components realised with our approach has to be done.

References

1. Böhme, H.: Objektorientierte Codegenerierung für SDL'92. Diploma thesis, Humboldt-Universität zu Berlin,
   http://www.informatik.hu-berlin.de/sam/diplom/boehme97.ps (1997).
2. Fischer, J., Piefel, M., Scheidgen, M.: A Metamodel for SDL2000 in the Context of Metamodeling ULF. Amyot, D., Williams, A. (Eds.) Fourth SDL and MSC Workshop. Volume 3319 of Lecture Notes in Computer Science (2004) 205–230.
3. ITU-T: Recommendation Z.100 (08/02), Specification and Description Language (SDL). International Telecommunication Union, Geneva (2002).
4. ITU-T: Recommendation Z.130 (02/99), ITU Object Definition Language (ODL). International Telecommunication Union, Geneva (1999).

5. ITU-T: Recommendation Z.130 (07/03), Extended Object Definition Language (eODL). International Telecommunication Union, Geneva (2003).
6. Object Management Group: XML Metadata Interchange (XMI) version 1.1. OMG document, formal/00-11-02 (2000).
7. Object Management Group: Meta Object Facility, Version 1.3. OMG document, formal/00-11-02 (2000).
8. Object Management Group: Model Driven Architecture, OMG document, omg/00-11-05 (2000).
9. Object Management Group: CORBA Components, v3.0 full specification, OMG document, formal/02-06-65 (2002).
10. Pischel, E.: Extended Object Definition Language. Diploma thesis, Humboldt-Universität zu Berlin,
http://www.informatik.hu-berlin.de/sam/diplom/pischeldip02.pdf (2002).
11. Qedo-Team: QoS enabled distributed objects. Open source CCM implementation (2000-2004).
12. Scheidgen, M.: Metamodelle für Sprachen mit formaler Syntaxdefinition, am Beispiel von SDL-2000. Diploma thesis, Humboldt-Universität zu Berlin (2004).
13. SITE-Team: SDL Integrated Tool Environment. Software project, Humboldt-Universität zu Berlin,
http://www.informatik.hu-berlin.de/SITE (1996-2003).
14. Stoinski, F.: The CORBA Component Model Streaming Extension. Proceedings of IASTED International Conference on Software Engineering 2004, Innsbruck, Österreich (2004).
15. TINA-C: http://www.tinac.com

Applying eODL and SDL-Patterns for Developing TMN Managed Systems

Margarita de Cabo and Manuel Rodríguez

Departamento de Teoría de la Señal, Comunicaciones e Ingeniería Telemática,
University of Valladolid, Spain
{marcab, manrod}@tel.uva.es

Abstract. This paper presents how eODL, in combination with SDL-patterns, helps to enhance the ITU-T framework for defining CORBA-based TMN systems. This proposal consists in utilizing eODL, instead of CORBA IDL, incorporating behavior using SDL-patterns. This leads to the following advantages: first, eODL models are described from several points of view, giving more information about the system modeled. Second, the models obtained can be deployed on any Distributed Platform Environment (DPE), not only on CORBA. Third, SDL is a formal language, which is very powerful for modeling the behavior of a system. Furthermore, SDL-patterns provide a more systematic way of describing solutions to a concrete problem than *ad hoc* SDL. The feasibility of this work is presented with an example.

1 Introduction

Nowadays, there is a strong trend towards combining ITU-T languages and defining design methods based on metamodels that can be mapped into various implementation languages and different target environments. The main idea is to offer a common environment where all the key concepts for developing distributed systems appear [4]. From this common environment, mappings to concrete implementation languages and/or target platforms must be supplied to deploy the system. Furthermore, the representation of the metamodel can be achieved by means of several notations, still implementation-independent.

The ITU-T Rec. Z.130 [16], extended Object Definition Language (eODL) follows this philosophy. eODL is used for a component-oriented development of distributed systems. Nevertheless, eODL is not designed either for code implementation or for behavior description of the components. Code implementation implies that a standardized target platform will be needed. Without that, it is not possible to obtain a generic model that can be translated into concrete code for a target platform, such step being completely dependent on the kind of target platform. Behavior cannot be expressed with eODL, because it lacks the necessary constructs. Therefore, for this topic, we consider another ITU-T language, Specification and Description Language (SDL) [15]. We propose joining these

D. Amyot and A.W. Williams (Eds.): SAM 2004, LNCS 3319, pp. 33–49, 2005.
© Springer-Verlag Berlin Heidelberg 2005

two ITU languages, eODL and SDL, for improving the ITU framework that defines interfaces for CORBA-based Telecommunication Management Network (TMN) systems [8].

The paper is organized as follows: Section 2 gives a brief explanation about eODL and SDL-2000. Section 3 presents the CORBA-based TMN framework. Then, Sect. 4 deals with the steps to obtain the eODL model from the ITU-T CORBA-IDL interfaces and how to add pattern-based SDL behavior to this model. In Sect. 5, an example is given in order to obtain a better view of how to apply eODL and SDL-patterns. Finally, in Sect. 6, some conclusions are drawn.

2   ITU-T Languages for the Development of Distributed Applications

2.1   eODL

eODL is a language standardized by ITU-T for developing component-oriented distributed systems. It provides a model-driven approach with a well-defined metamodel, and defines the concept space using MOF (Meta Object Facility) technology [17].

One advantage of the approach is that it allows the use of MOF-related tools to support the automation of model transitions between the different software development phases. Another benefit is the ability to instantiate concrete models from the metamodel, which can be represented by existing languages, so an integration of different design methods can be achieved. The concept space is built from different conceptual views [1]: computational, implementation, deployment and target environment.

eODL can be used for describing a single component or a whole system, but it does not constrain the deployment of the components to a concrete target platform. As we said before, eODL cannot be used for behavior specification so we propose the use of SDL-2000.

2.2   SDL-2000

ITU-T Rec. Z.130 includes a representation of eODL-relevant concepts into SDL. The use of SDL-2000 is presented as an alternative way of obtaining a real running system in [2].

This alternative has been chosen due to two main reasons. First, SDL has proven its usefulness regarding behavior modeling. SDL is a formal description technique that allows simulation and validation of specifications without building a prototype. SDL does not restrict the target platform, and specifications can be automatically translated into code using existing tools. The code has to follow the restrictions imposed by eODL deployment and target environment views. Second, SDL can be used for defining patterns of behavior.

When comparing with use of SDL *ad-hoc* descriptions or SDL descriptions using inheritance and specialization, SDL-patterns improve reuse and sharing of expertise gained in other projects [5]. Furthermore, SDL-patterns are *formalized reuse artifacts* They are formalized because they are described by a formal description technique, SDL; and they can be reused because they are not a concrete SDL specification but the guidelines to obtain a context-dependent description which follows the rules given by each pattern template. This template represents the generic form of some kind of behavior that has to be adapted to the concrete context.

There is a need for supporting the description of such artifacts, since SDL alone is not sufficient to describe generic solutions, which depend on the context of application. Pattern Annotated-SDL (PA-SDL) appears as the notation for describing syntactically incomplete SDL components and for capturing genericity in a flexible way [6]. In the case that a collaboration structure also appears, it can be represented using CoSDL (Collaborative SDL) [18].

3   Field of Application: Developing TMN Systems

A Telecommunication Management Network (TMN) [8] is an infrastructure, standardized by ITU-T, which provides interfaces for interconnection between various types of Operation Systems (OSs) and/or telecommunications equipment to manage telecommunication networks and services. The management information is exchanged through those standard interfaces.

The TMN architecture consists of three components: the *Functional Architecture*, referring to the distribution of TMN functionality into categories of "function blocks" interconnected via "reference points"; the *Information Architecture* based on the ISO systems management model and defined using GDMO [13]; and the *Physical Architecture*, which maps combinations of functional blocks to physical blocks based on non-functional requirements such as performance, ownership etc.

To deal with the complexity of telecommunications management, management functionality may be considered to be partitioned into logical layers. The Logical Layered Architecture (LLA) is a concept for the structuring of management functionality which organizes the functions into groupings called "logical layers" and describes the relationship between layers. A logical layer reflects particular aspects of management arranged by different levels of abstraction [8].

At each level, there is an Operation Systems Function (OSF) block. OSFs processes information related to the telecommunications management for the purpose of monitoring/coordinating and/or controlling telecommunication functions including management functions (i.e. the TMN itself). The grouping of management functionality implies grouping OSF function blocks into layers. A specialization of OSF function blocks based upon different layers of abstraction is: Business, Service, Network and Element. These layers of abstraction are depicted in Fig. 1, (this figure is extracted from [8]).

The element management layer manages each network element on an individual or group basis and supports an abstraction of the functions provided by the network element layer. The network management layer has the responsibility for

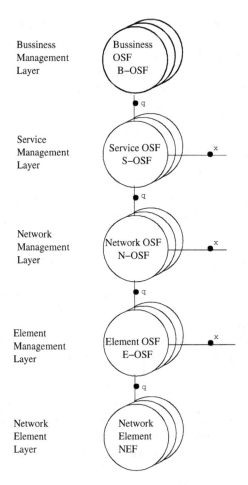

Fig. 1. Suggested model for layering of TMN management functions

the management of a network as supported by the element management layer. Service management is concerned with, and responsible for, the contractual aspects of services that are being provided to customers or available to potential new customers. The business management layer has responsibility for the total enterprise, and it comprises proprietary functionality.

A telecommunication network is, in essence, distributed, so there was a trend to bring together TMN and middleware principles, specially CORBA ones. The result was the definition of a framework for CORBA-based TMN systems.

Such framework consists of several ITU-T recommendations: TMN guidelines for defining CORBA managed objects (Rec. X.780) [14], CORBA-based TMN services (Rec. Q.816) [12], and CORBA generic network and network element level information model (Rec. M.3120) [9].

This framework presents two main limitations. First, it is constrained to the use of CORBA as target platform. Second, it does not give a formal description of the behavior of the elements managed. We hence propose addressing these limitations using eODL and SDL. eODL gives the advantage of having a description with a well-defined metamodel. This description can be mapped to several notations -the most useful in each case- and can be deployed on any target platform, including component-oriented ones. SDL will be used for formally describing the behavior and applied by means of SDL-patterns developed for managed systems. Those patterns can be stored and organized in a pool to make it easier to find out which patterns are adequate for a concrete situation. SDL-patterns can be improved from experience as long as projects are developed using the pattern pool. Deficiencies or new cases can be detected while using the patterns, so they have to be re-engineered [6].

This work starts from the CORBA-based TMN framework, not from the original TMN infrastructure, because the former defines CORBA-IDL interfaces, which are easily translated into eODL. Furthermore, we focus on the information model at network element level [9], and its technology-independent hierarchical structure of the network managed objects, see Fig. 2.

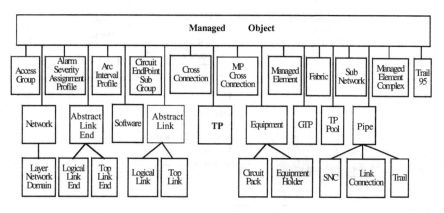

Fig. 2. Hierarchical organization of managed objects (excerpt)

Any new network managed object must be defined as a specialization of some object of this hierarchical structure. At least it has to specialize *Managed Object (MO)*, offering all the MO features and may add new ones that are not included in other object of the presented hierarchy. This way, managed objects may share certain features, and they can be dealt with in a similar way, with at least a group of identical functionalities. Indeed, it is possible to add new ones as necessary. This organization gives a suitable structure to apply our SDL-patterns. For instance, if a managed object is a specialization of Termination Point (TP) object, it will inherit all the characteristics (interfaces and behavior) from MO and TP objects, therefore SDL-patterns for MO and TP have to be applied. Then, its particular characteristics will be added.

4   Improving ITU-T Framework by Means of eODL and SDL-Patterns

4.1   Overview

This proposal consists in reusing and improving the ITU framework for defining CORBA-based TMN systems, such that the framework allows development of TMN managed systems that can be deployed on any platform. The new framework will include formally specified behavior. An overall view of the steps involved is presented in Fig. 3.

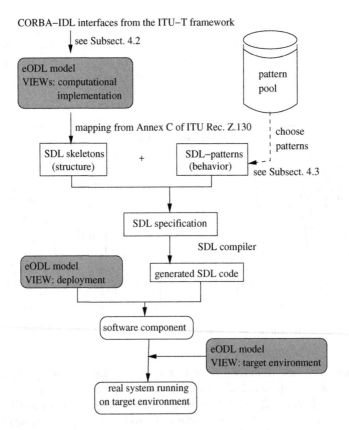

Fig. 3. Steps of the proposed design procedure

The first step is to map the defined ITU-T CORBA-IDL interfaces into eODL, see Subsect. 4.2. The second step is to use the mapping defined in Annex C of Rec. Z.130, to obtain SDL skeletons (structural aspects) corresponding to the mapping of eODL definitions. The third one is to enrich these skeletons with the SDL-patterns presented in the pattern pool, see Subsect. 4.3.

Once the complete SDL specification (structural and behavioral parts) is finished, the last step is to create the software components. The SDL specification must be translated into code, taking into account the eODL deployment view [2]. The software components obtained must be deployed in the target environment in order to have a real system running on the chosen platform. The eODL target environment view provides the modeling concepts that allow the description of the topology and properties of the target environment.

4.2   Translating CORBA-IDL into eODL

Mapping the elements that appear in the CORBA-IDL definition into eODL is straightforward, because all data types and constructs (operations, attributes, exceptions and interface types) of CORBA-IDL are part of the eODL metamodel. In order to complete the eODL definition, other constructs that do not appear in CORBA-IDL, have to be added. These are: *Computational Object type* (COs), for the structural view, and the *artifact* concept for the eODL implementation view; the deployment and target environment views are not supported in CORBA-IDL.

The concept of CO type is used to specify the functional decomposition of a system. The instances of a CO type (COs) are autonomous interacting entities, which encapsulate state and behavior. COs interact with their environment via well defined interfaces. The artifact is used to describe a programming language context in a model. The instances of the concept artifact implement the behavior of COs. They therefore provide the business logic of CO types.

We propose the following steps to obtain an eODL model, involving several interfaces and classes as defined in the ITU-T framework:

1. Mapping CORBA-IDL data types and constructs into eODL concepts, obtaining operations, attributes, exceptions and interface types;
2. Defining one CO for every class as it appears in any of the recommendations given by ITU-T [9, 14, 11, 10]. This CO will support every interface of the class, as stated by the ITU framework, and will require any other interface it has to use for the foreseen interactions. Every CO will be implemented by as many artifacts as interfaces it provides;
3. Defining one artifact for each interface. This artifact will implement all the interaction elements (operations and signal exchange) of the interface.

Deployment and target environment views cannot be derived from the initial CORBA-IDL interfaces. They come from the actual needs of the concrete system to be developed. The designer has to decide how to compose the software components with the COs obtained (deployment view), and how to model the installation and environment where the model is going to be used (target environment view).

The eODL definition is then mapped to SDL-2000 skeletons, following the guidelines given in Annex C of ITU Rec. Z.130 [16].

4.3   Applying SDL-Patterns

The mapping from an eODL model to a SDL-2000 skeleton produces several SDL agent types that are empty or half complete: these are mainly coming from the mapping of artifacts. eODL does not support any way to model that behavior, as we said before, so the obtained agent types do not offer this feature either. This is the behavior that an SDL-pattern pool will help to construct.

SDL-patterns help to specify the behavior of the artifacts corresponding to management CORBA-IDL interfaces defined by ITU-T for a TMN system. These patterns allow the development of a complete SDL model (interfaces and formally-defined behavior) of a TMN system compliant with the ITU-T framework. Some advantages of using SDL-patterns are:

1. Development is less error-prone, because the pattern gives the schema of a well-know solution, and the rules for applying it;
2. Development is less time-consuming, the elements required for specifying the behavior are already provided; there is only a need to add and customize them to the specific context;
3. When applying patterns, it is known what other related patterns have to be applied, so the related behavior cannot be skipped by a mistake;
4. Patterns are easily reused and adapted to construct our own system.

We are developing a pattern pool for storing the obtained patterns with the aim of having a central repository from where it is easy to find and choose the adequate patterns for the managed system being modeled. At this time, the pool is only populated with the generic-MO and the ARC patterns, (see [3] for a description of them). Patterns are being constructed from the generic functionalities for the objects defined in Rec. M.3120. This recommendation gives the characteristics that generic objects at network and network element level must offer, including optional features like Alarm Reporting Control. These characteristics have to be adapted to every concrete object and context. Therefore, the generic functionalities are mapped to SDL-patterns. These will guarantee the functionalities when implementing the SDL specification of a concrete object into a concrete context. The pattern template will restrict the way the pattern can be customized in order not to lose the generic functions described by the pattern that the concrete object must offer.

Patterns are described by means of PA-SDL and are depicted using a pattern template [7]. The template shows how the pattern has to be used, and in which cases it can be applied and how. Therefore, it is easy to determine whether a pattern is useful in any given situation.

5   Applying eODL and SDL-Patterns to a Generic TMN Managed Object Class

This section presents a brief example of how to apply eODL and SDL-patterns for defining a generic MO (Managed Object) with the ARC (Alarm Reporting Control) feature [11]. A generic MO, as defined in [14], is the simplest class that can appear in a managed system. The example will show how the IDL definition of MO can be translated into an eODL definition, and how this leads to SDL skeletons. The skeletons are completed with behavior using SDL-patterns. As an example of the use of patterns, the *ARC pattern* has been chosen. This is the pattern that adds the ARC feature to a generic MO. Once the patterns related to generic behavior of an MO are applied, the ARC pattern can be easily used to add this feature to the MO. Then we have to choose an adequate tool that transforms SDL into code following the deployment view of eODL definition.

5.1   Translating Generic MO CORBA-IDL Interface into eODL

This section presents how to translate the generic MO CORBA-IDL interface and the ARC feature into eODL. The deployment and target environment views are not taken into account, because they have only sense in a full specification. In that particular case, there are several objects that interact with each other, and there is a need for specifying how they are going to be assembled to render software components, and where they have to be deployed. In this simple example, there is only one object, so different software components cannot be constructed, and we are not taking into account any target environment restrictions regarding where to deploy our single object.

The original IDL is shown in Fig. 4, and the eODL obtained can be seen in Fig. 5.

In this simple case, one CO is defined *o_MOARC*.

This CO supports *interface i_MO*, which represents the CORBA-IDL generic MO interface, and *interface i_ARC*, which represents the ARC feature.

We are defining a generic MO, so the corresponding CO does not use any other interface. When modeling several MOs with different needs, they may require

/* Value types and exceptions no included for the sake of simplicity*/

/**Managed Object interface, Rec. X.780*/

    interface ManagedObject{

        NameType nameGet() raises (ApplicationError);

        ...

        void destroy() raises (ApplicationError, DeleteError);

    }; //end of interface MO

/** The following are additional operations for an interface that supports
    the ARC function. Rec. M.3120*/

    void arcManagementRequestedIntervalSet (in ArcTimeType time)
        raises (ApplicationError,NOarcPackage);

        ...

    boolean arcControl (in ArcControlRequest request)
        raises (ApplicationError,NOarcPackage);

Fig. 4. IDL definition of MO and ARC feature (excerpt)

```
module itut_x780{
        /*Data types and exceptions not included for the sake of simplicity.*/
                ...
        /*Definition of the interface, as defined in X.780 (excerpt)*/
        interface i_MO{
                NameType nameGet() raises (ApplicationError);

                ...

                void destroy() raises (ApplicationError);
        };
        /*Definition of the artefact corresponding to the implementation of the
        generic MO*/
        artefact a_MOImpl{
                nameGet implements supply i_MO::nameGet;
                        ...
                destroy implements supply i_MO:destroy;
        };
        interface i_ARC {
                boolean arcControl() raises (ApplicationError, NOarcPackage);
                        ...
                void arcManagementRequestedIntervalSet( in ArcTimeType time)
                        raises (ApplicationError, NOarcPackage);
        };
        artefact a_ARCImpl{
                arcControl implements supply i_ARC::arcControl;
                        ...
                arcManagementRequestedIntervalSet implements supply
                        i_ARC::arcManagementRequestedIntervalSet;
        };
        /*Computational object definition for generic MO with ARC feature*/
        CO o_MOARC{
                supports i_MO, i_ARC;
                provide i_MO mo;
                provide i_ARC arc;
                /*requires nothing*/
                implemented by a_MOImpl with Singleton, a_ARCImpl with Singleton;
        };


};
```

Fig. 5. eODL definition for MO with ARC feature

other interfaces; this condition will appear in the CO definition, (*requires* clause).
Furthermore, CO *o_MOARC* provides two ports for accessing the interfaces, *mo*

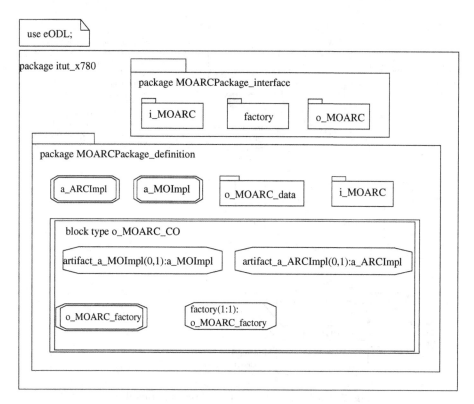

Fig. 6. SDL skeleton for eODL definition of MO with ARC feature

and *arc*. Every interface is supposed to be implemented by one artifact, so we define such artifacts, *a_MOImpl* and *a_ARCImpl*, respectively.

The eODL definition leads to the SDL skeleton in Fig. 6 by applying the rules in Annex C of Rec. Z.130 [16].

In this example, automatically generated code, as explained in Sect. C.8 of [16], has not been chosen. Our choice allows defining artifact *artifact_a_MOImpl* and *artifact_a_ARCImpl* as separate processes at block type *o_MOARC_CO* level, so they are concurrently executed. This concurrency is mandatory; while the MO is executing its generic behavior, it has to manage alarms at the same time. With automatically generated code, these artifacts should be inside a process type, *o_MOARC*, therefore they will be executed interleaved.

5.2   Applying SDL-Patterns to Provide MO Skeletons with Behavior

In our example, we assume that the patterns giving MO its generic behavior have already been applied. Now, Alarm Reporting Control (ARC) functionalities are going to be added, as defined in [11, 9]. Therefore, we present our ARC specification based on patterns. The specification consists in several related pat-

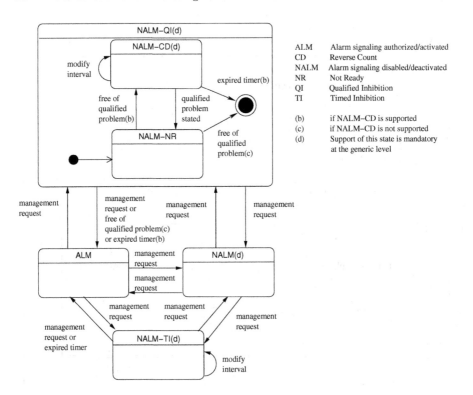

Fig. 7. UML state diagram for ARC functionality

terns. They specify the way of using them to add the desired characteristics of ARC functionality to the non-ARC behavior of such MO. The ARC specification formally defines the behavior of ARC functionality, including all the optional features. The specification is customizable to fit the behavior of any MO that is going to offer ARC.

The generic MO can easily offer ARC by applying our patterns. We are not going to present how to add the rest of the MO behavior, but the steps are similar using the relevant patterns.

The full process of designing the pattern is not explained here, because it is quite complex, and we are mainly interested in its application. In a nutshell, we started from the UML state diagram for ARC (see Fig. 7) [11].

We obtained four possible SDL composite states, one for each state in the UML diagram: ALM (ALarM), NALM (No ALarM), NALM-TI (No ALarM-Time Inhibited) and NALM-QI (No ALarM-Qualified Inhibited).

Depending on what state the MO is in, the behavior is different. The alarm control is executed while the MO is sending notifications, changing its state, simply living. So, the ARC pattern is modeled, in a first stage, as an SDL process in order to provide concurrency with the behavior of the MO without ARC. The set of all four states is not mandatory; MO has to incorporate at least two of

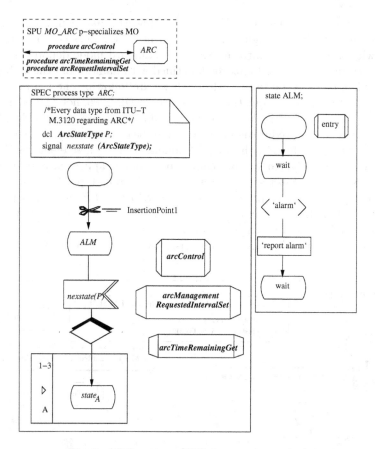

Fig. 8. ARC pattern (SDL fragment, excerpt)

them, one of them being the ALM state. Each MO has to add to its behavior the corresponding ARC states that it will support.

The main body of the ARC functionality has been separated from the optional states, putting each one into a different pattern (*ARC, NALM, NALM-TI* and *NALM-QI* patterns). So, to obtain an MO with ARC, it is necessary to apply at least two of the patterns related to ARC: one for the main functionality, *ARC* pattern that includes ALM state by default, and one of the others. This is clearly stated in the pattern template. This way, the overall complexity of MO's behavior and the complexity of the model is reduced.

Figure 8 presents an excerpt of the generic ARC solution defined by the SDL-pattern: *ARC pattern*. The excerpt is taken from the *SDL fragment*, the syntactical part of the design solution defined by the pattern, and shows the context and the specification of the ARC process.

Solid symbols denote design elements that are added to the context specification as a result of the pattern application.

As a general rule, names may be changed. However, names in italics must be new, they refer to fresh design elements for which the names can be arbitrarily chosen when applying the pattern. Names in standard mode denote the role of existing design elements and must be identified with names from the embedding context when being instantiated. Although we are following the template given by [7], it has to be pointed out that we are using SDL-2000, not SDL96 as in [6].

Because we are following the ITU recommendations, there are some data types, variable names and procedure names that cannot be renamed, in order to maintain compatibility of interfaces with ITU recommendations. These elements that are new when applying the pattern but cannot be renamed appear in bold-italics.

SPU (Structural Process Unit) refers to a diagram type that can contain agents of type process, as process type ARC; *SPEC (SPECific)* indicates that the state machine has to be in a specific diagram type, process type in this case.

Scissor symbols indicate the possibility of refinements, for instance by adding further actions to a transition, without disrupting the control flow.

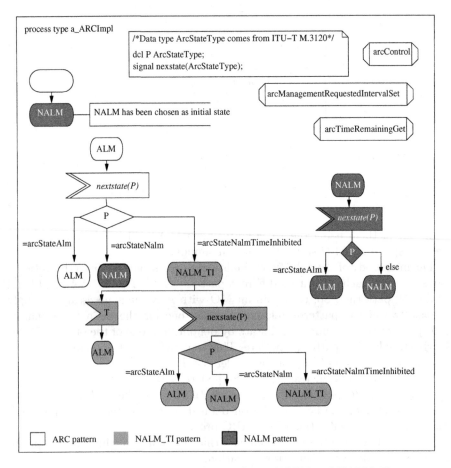

Fig. 9. Example application: ARC with ALM, NALM and NALM-TI states

The box named A is a *border symbol*, an annotation denoting replications. The direction is given by the arrow, the number of replications is specified by the multiplicity. It gives an opportunity to add up to three new states to ARC pattern, those deriving of ARC-related patterns: NALM, NALM-TI and NALM-QI.

The shadowed decision symbol denotes a *cascade symbol*, it may be substituted by a cascade of decisions.

Finally, the three procedures are defined in [9] as part of the interface for ARC feature. They are exported remote procedures called by an external entity, the manager that controls the MO. They are used by the manager to change the ARC state of the MO, *arcControl*, to set the timers internally used, *arcManagementRequestedIntervalSet*, or to inquire the remaining time of a timer, *arcTimeRemainingGet*. To apply a pattern, the context has first to be identified. In case of the ARC pattern, the embedding context is a generic MO, because the *SPU MO_ARC p-specializes* this kind of SDL agent. The *block type o_MOARC_CO*, see Fig 6, represents the MO, so this block is the context of the ARC pattern. Furthermore, the ARC pattern is the behavior of process *artifact_a_ARCImpl*.

The added process type has to be adapted, renaming the elements that can be renamed, choosing the correct decisions for the cascade symbol, and deciding if any other transition is inserted at *insertionPoint1*. Further refinement is also needed to replace the comments 'alarm' and 'report alarm' in the ALM state with a real variable that is set when an alarm is produced, and a real mechanism to report this alarm, according to the designer's needs. The application of the ARC pattern, plus the NALM and NALM-TI patterns, yields the SDL process type shown in Fig. 9.

6   Conclusions

The proposal of mapping the ITU-T CORBA-IDL interfaces for TMN systems into eODL offers the advantage of defining the concept space using MOF (Meta Object Facility) technology. That allows the use of MOF-related tools to support the automation of model transitions between the different software development phases. Another benefit is the ability to instantiate concrete models from the metamodel, which can be represented by existing languages, so an integration of different design methods can be achieved. Such approach allows one to obtain managed systems according to the ITU-T standards for distributed management systems, in addition to the means of deploying them into any target environment, not only CORBA. Furthermore, this proposal lets designers define behavior in a formal way without doing all the work from scratch, but using syntactically incomplete generic solutions (SDL-patterns). Using SDL as the description language offers a formal specification of behavior. In addition, SDL-patterns improve reuse and sharing of expertise gained in other projects, when comparing with use of SDL *ad hoc* descriptions or SDL descriptions using inheritance and specialization. SDL-patterns are not closed solutions, they are flexible and powerful enough to really simplify the development of new management systems. They allow the addition of business logic to the eODL artifacts in a semi-automatic way. SDL-patterns are *formalized reuse artifacts*.

The main shortcoming of the eODL to SDL-2000 mapping proposed in Rec. Z.130 is the lack of flexibility for expressing concurrent behavior within a CO. The automatic translation forces the alternating execution of the artifacts which implement the interfaces of the CO. So as to maintain the automatic translation, more flexibility to choose between concurrent and alternating behavior would be desirable.

New rules for mapping would be needed, they should allow choosing the insertion of SDL agents into the most appropriate context (process inside process or inside blocks). These changes have to be included while providing a smooth transition between the two languages.

There is another drawback as well: the current lack of tools for the automatization of the described process. Automatizing the overall process of obtaining a complete SDL description and then generating code to achieve real software components and a running system on a platform, involves two main steps. First, eODL translation into SDL-2000. Second, choosing and customizing SDL-patterns. This process heavily relies on the development of adequate tools. These tools may mix the information given by eODL deployment and target environment views, with the ability of integrating them with SDL specifications, obtained from SDL-patterns customization, and generating code from all the information given to the tool.

References

1. Böhme, H.: Z.130 Extended ODL. http://www.omg.org/docs/telecom/02-04-05.pdf (2002).
2. Böhme, H.: Integrated Application of eODL. ITU-T Integrated Application of Formal Languages Workshop, Geneva (2003) http://www.itu.int/ITU-T/worksem/iafl/documents/iafl_006.ppt.
3. de Cabo, M., Rodríguez M.: The generic-MO and the ARC patterns. http://www.rest.tel.uva.es/~marcab/technicalReports/patterns.pdf.
4. Dubois, F., Born, M., Böhme, H., Fischer, J., Holz, E., Kath, O., Neubauer, B., Stoinski, F.: Distributed Systems: From Models to Components. Reed, R., Reed, J. (Eds.), 10th SDL Forum. Volume 2078 of Lecture Notes in Computer Science, Springer (2001) 250–267.
5. Geppert, B., Rößler, F., Gotzhein, R.: Pattern Application vs Inheritance in SDL. IFIP, International Conference on Fomal Methods for Open Object-Based Distributed Systems, FMOODS'99 (1999).
6. Geppert, B.: The SDL Pattern Aproach. A Reuse-Driven SDL Methodology for Designing Communication Software Systems. PhD thesis, Fachbereich Informatik der Universität Kaiserslautern, Germany (2001).
7. Geppert, B., Rößler, F.: The SDL pattern approach - a reuse-driven SDL design methodology. Computer Networks **35** (2001) 627–645.
8. ITU-T: Recommendation M.3010 (02/00), Principles for a Telecommunications Management Network. International Telecommunication Union, Geneva (2000).

9. ITU-T: Recommendation M.3120 (02/00), CORBA Generic Network and Network Element Level Information Model. International Telecommunication Union, Geneva (2000).
10. ITU-T: Recommendation M.3100 (07/95), Generic Network Information Model. International Telecommunication Union, Geneva (1995).
11. ITU-T: Recommendation M.3100 (1995), Amendment 3 (08/01) Definition of the management interface for a generic alarm reporting control (ARC) feature. International Telecommunication Union, Geneva (2001).
12. ITU-T: Recommendation Q.816 (01/01), CORBA-based TMN Services. International Telecommunication Union, Geneva (2001).
13. ITU-T: Recommendation X.722 (01/92), Information Technology - Open Systems Interconnection - Structure of Management Information: Guidelines for the Definition of Managed Objects. International Telecommunication Union, Geneva (1992).
14. ITU-T: Recommendation X.780 (01/01), TMN Guidelines for Defining CORBA Managed Objects. International Telecommunication Union, Geneva (2001).
15. ITU-T: Recommendation Z.100 (08/02), Specification and Description Language (SDL). International Telecommunication Union, Geneva (2002).
16. ITU-T: Recommendation Z.130 (07/03), Extended Object Definition Language (eODL): Techniques for distributed software component development - Conceptual foundation, notations and technology mappings. International Telecommunication Union, Geneva (2003).
17. Object Management Group: Meta-Object Facility (MOF), version 1.4 (2002).
18. Rößler, F.: Collaboration-Based Design of Communicating Systems with SDL. PhD thesis, University of Kaiserslautern, Germany (2002).

SPT – The SDL Pattern Tool*

Jörg Dorsch[1], Anders Ek[2], and Reinhard Gotzhein[3]

[1] joerg.dorsch@web.de
[2] Telelogic AB, Malmø, Sweden
anders.ek@telelogic.com
[3] Computer Science Department, University of Kaiserslautern
Postfach 3049, D-67653 Kaiserslautern, Germany
gotzhein@informatik.uni-kl.de

Abstract. In 1997, the SDL pattern approach, consisting of a specific design process, notation for the definition of generic design fragments, rules for the definition of patterns, and a pattern pool, has been introduced. While the approach is now consolidated and has been applied in industry, a major issue still is the provision of tool support. In this paper, we present SPT, the SDL Pattern Tool, which focuses on the application of a selection of SDL patterns. SPT is fully integrated with TTD G2 (Telelogic Tau Developer Generation 2), the new tool environment from Telelogic, which supports UML 2.0 as well as an SDL profile.

1   Introduction

Reuse of project results and developer know-how are receiving growing attention both in industry and academia. There is a broad range of reuse approaches, which can be classified according to the artefacts – e.g., frameworks, patterns, components – they are based on. In previous work, we have introduced and consolidated the *SDL pattern approach* [4][5][6]. SDL patterns combine the traditional advantages of the well-known design patterns [3] – reduced development effort, quality improvements, and orthogonal documentation – with the precision of a formal design language for pattern definition and pattern application.

Recently, the SDL design pattern approach has been applied and evaluated in an industrial environment, the development of a UMTS call processing system [8]. In the course of this work, we have analysed a substantial part of the available SDL design, and have discovered eight SDL patterns that capture and document the most frequent design decisions. We have then assessed the benefits of these project-specific SDL patterns by evaluating a large number of trouble reports raised during project development and maintenance. As it turned out, 37% of these trouble reports could have been avoided by correctly applying six of the

* This work has been supported by the Deutsche Forschungsgemeinschaft (DFG) as part of Sonderforschungsbereich (SFB) 501, *Development of Large Systems with Generic Methods*, and by Telelogic AB in Malmo/Sweden.

D. Amyot and A.W. Williams (Eds.): SAM 2004, LNCS 3319, pp. 50–64, 2005.

project-specific SDL patterns, and that up to 47% could have been avoided by adding further patterns to the pool. These figures correspond to a reduction of the total development effort by 4.7% and 6%, respectively. We note that this is a conservative estimate, since defects discovered after deployment, which are particularly expensive in terms of rework, have not been available at the time of the evaluation.

In subsequent discussions, it has been an important concern to what degree these benefits are achievable. In particular, given the project-specific SDL patterns, what can be predicted about their correct application by system developers? In order to find an answer to this question, we have conducted a controlled experiment with a group of 18 students, forming six development teams [15]. Prior to the experiment, the participants had attended a course about protocol engineering, where they were introduced to SDL and the SDL pattern approach. As it turned out, the teams working with the SDL pattern approach avoided 59% of the design errors where suitable patterns were available. This is remarkable, in particular since the participants hat no practical experience with SDL, SDL patterns or the SDL tool environment when the experiment started. We conclude that experienced developers in industry who are familiar with SDL, SDL tools, and the SDL pattern pool will outperform these results. Also, in the industrial environment, pattern-specific checklists to be used in design reviews were provided in addition, which should further improve the correct application of SDL patterns.

Our industrial partners pointed out that to fully exploit the benefits of the SDL pattern approach, and to fully incorporate it into development projects, graphical tool support is indispensable. Tool support should address the definition and application of SDL patterns on the one hand, and the documentation of pattern applications on the other hand. Furthermore, it should be integrated with tool environments that are used in industry. In a previous effort, we have developed a tool called SPEEDI, a pattern-enhanced SDL editor [1] [14]. While SPEEDI provided complete functionality for pattern application, documentation, and navigation, it was still based on SDL-PR, which turned out to be a major obstacle to a broader dissemination.

In a recent effort, we have developed another tool called *SPT*, the *SDL Pattern Tool*. SPT has a graphical user interface, and is fully integrated with TTD G2 (Telelogic Tau Developer Generation 2), the new tool environment from Telelogic, which supports UML 2.0 as well as an SDL profile. Currently, SPT supports three SDL patterns from two different pattern categories, namely architecture and interaction patterns. The results clearly show the feasibility of the tool concept.

The paper is structured as follows. In Section 2, we briefly summarize the SDL pattern approach. Section 3 identifies and details areas of tool support for SDL patterns. In Section 4, we present SPT, the SDL Pattern Tool, and illustrate how SPT supports the application of SDL patterns. Section 5 addresses implementation issues of SPT, in particular, the integration into TTD G2, the new tool chain from Telelogic. Status and outlook are reported in Section 6.

2   Survey of the SDL Pattern Approach

The SDL pattern approach [4][5][6] consists of the SDL *pattern design process*, a notation for the description of generic SDL fragments called PA-SDL (*Pattern Annotated SDL*), a *description template* and *rules* for the definition of SDL patterns, and an *SDL pattern pool* for distributed systems in general, and communication systems in particular. The approach has been applied successfully to the engineering and reengineering of several communications systems (cf. [6] for further references). In [8], results of an industrial application are reported.

An *SDL pattern* is a reusable software artefact that represents a generic solution for a recurring design problem with SDL as the design language. The main argument for this choice is that SDL [10] is one of the few formal description techniques that are widely used in industry, with commercial tool support being readily available. SDL patterns are collected in a pattern pool, which can be seen as a repository of experience from previous projects that has been analyzed and packaged.

The definition of SDL patterns is organized following a *description template* (cf. [8]). In an informal part, the intent of and the motivation for the pattern are explained. Structure and message scenarios identify the involved design components and their relationships, and specify typical generic behavior. The syntactical part of the design solution is captured by the SDL fragment together with syntactical embedding rules. A specific notation called PA-SDL (Pattern Annotated SDL) is used to constrain the context in which the pattern may be applied, and describes some of the modifications resulting from its application. Further entries are refinement, cooperative usage and known uses.

The *SDL pattern design process* is part of an overall development process, and may be integrated in methodologies such as SOMT [17], SDL+ [12] or TIMe [1]. The starting point for the communication system design activity is a set of communication requirements, which is partitioned into a sequence of subsets. For each of these subsets, several steps are performed. Firstly, an analysis of the requirements is executed. This leads to an analysis model, consisting of a structural part and a set of collaborations described by message scenarios. Based on this analysis model, the designer searches the SDL pattern pool for suitable SDL patterns, which he then selects, adapts, and composes into an embedding context. The selection step is supported by the definition of SDL patterns, which contains a generic analysis model. Adaptation is restricted by constraints on the SDL context, and by renaming and refinement rules in the pattern definition. Finally, the pattern instance is embedded into the context specification, leading to a may modified SDL specification. Note that patterns may be applied simultaneously and/or sequentially.

3   Areas of Tool Support for SDL Patterns

To fully exploit the benefits of the SDL pattern approach, pattern-directed tool support is required. This tool support can be classified according to the pattern-related activities addressed in the following subsections.

3.1   Definition of SDL Patterns

SDL patterns are the result of analyzing system designs with the objective to identify and document frequent generic design decisions. They form part of a full-scale, evolutionary product-line experience base, improving the quality of the system design and reducing the loss of know-how inflicted by staff fluctuation.

The definition of SDL patterns follows a description template, which determines the items as well as the rules of pattern definitions (see Section 2). Tool support should provide special-purpose editors for each of these items, aggregation of items into pattern definitions, and the management of pattern definitions in a repository including versioning. As different description techniques are used to define structure (UML class diagrams), message scenarios (MSC), and SDL fragments (SDL, PA- SDL), a major effort is needed to integrate these fragments into a homogeneous document.

3.2   Application of SDL Patterns

The application of SDL patterns consists of several steps. Firstly, an SDL pattern is selected from a pattern pool. The selection is based on the concrete analysis model resulting from the analysis of the communication requirements, the generic analysis model of the SDL pattern, and background knowledge of the system developer. It may be assisted by a tool that reduces the choice of patterns to those that are compatible with the concrete analysis model, and by an interactive resolution in case of alternatives.

Once the pattern has been selected, the design context where the pattern instance is to be embedded is identified. This is usually an interactive process, which may take advantage of information from the pattern selection step. For instance, the involved design components may appear in the concrete analysis model. Further constraints are expressed in the pattern definition and are to be enforced by the tool.

Next, the (generic) SDL pattern is adapted to the (concrete) design context. As before, choices may be resolved automatically, based on the analysis model and the design context determined before. Any remaining choices are then resolved interactively. Again, constraints are to be enforced by the tool.

Finally, the resulting pattern instance is embedded into the design context, i.e., into the SDL specification. Before this, all variation points have been resolved, so the embedding of a pattern instance can be automated, yielding a modified SDL design. It should be noted that pattern-based design steps have to be mixed with ad-hoc design steps. As a general requirement, the pattern-oriented tool support therefore has to be integrated with the ad-hoc tool support for editing SDL specifications.

3.3   Documentation of SDL Pattern Applications

The application of SDL patterns leads to an orthogonal structure of the system design. Application of an interaction pattern, for instance, modifies the state graph of different SDL components. Furthermore, it represents a particular abstract design decision. The pattern application history thus becomes an important part of the design documentation, because this information can not be retrieved from the SDL design afterwards. Tool support for the documentation of SDL pattern applications can range from a simple pattern application log up to labelling individual language elements such that the complete design history can be reconstructed. Furthermore, individual pattern instances may be highlighted by suitable coloring, and navigation support between pattern instance fragments may be provided.

3.4   Generation of Tool Support

It is expected that pattern-oriented tool support will be partially independent of individual SDL patterns. For instance, pattern definitions all follow the same description template and all use the same notations, therefore, it suffices to have one pattern editor. However, application of SDL patterns is highly pattern-specific. Therefore, it is necessary to integrate each SDL pattern individually into existing general-purpose SDL editors, especially in cases where syntactical embedding rules are expressed in natural language. To improve this situation, portions of the tool code may be derived automatically on the basis of PA-SDL constructs, and from the knowledge about the steps of applying SDL patterns.

4   The SDL Pattern Tool SPT

SPT – the SDL Pattern Tool – has been developed with the support of Telelogic. It is fully integrated with Telelogic Tau Developer Generation 2 (TTD G2), the new tool environment from Telelogic, which in the future will replace the former Telelogic Tau SDL Suite [16]. SPT is focused on the application of SDL patterns (see Section 3). Currently, SPT supports the application of three SDL patterns from two different pattern categories, namely architecture patterns and interaction patterns, and produces a simple pattern application log. Furthermore, the generation of pattern application scripts from pattern definitions has been studied. We will illustrate the results in this section.

At this point, we note that TTD G2 is primarily targeted to UML 2.0 users. However, SDL-2000 and UML 2.0 are converging on a conceptual level [9]. To cover SDL, TTD G2 offers several SDL packages that can be included on a case by case basis. As TTD G2 provides a flexible tool developer interface that supports the integration of pattern-oriented functionality, we have converted the SDL pattern pool to UML 2.0 – which has been straightforward –, and have implemented the tool support accordingly. In the following, we will sometimes refer to SDL patterns, although they are illustrated using the syntax of UML 2.0 in this section.

4.1   SDL Pattern Selection

In Section 3, it has been pointed out that the selection of SDL patterns can be sup- ported, e.g., by reducing the choice of patterns to those that are compatible

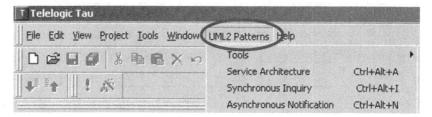

Fig. 1. Menu bar of the TTD G2 screen with entry "UML2 Patterns" and pull-down menu

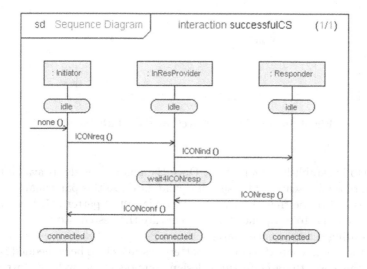

Fig. 2. Sequence diagram "successful connection setup"

with the analysis model. As this option has not yet been implemented, pattern selection is per- formed autonomously by the system designer, who then enters his choice by marking the pattern in a pull-down menu. For this purpose, an entry "UML2 Patterns" has been added to the menu bar of the TTD G2 screen (see Fig. 1). When clicking this entry, a pull-down menu with a list of all supported patterns appears. Furthermore, the menu offers a list of pattern-specific editing tools.

4.2   Identification of the Design Context

Following the SDL pattern design process (cf. Section 2), an analysis of the require- ments is performed, leading to a concrete analysis model that consists of a structural part and a set of collaborations. The sequence diagram shown in Fig. 2 and taken from the pattern-based development of the InRes-system [6] is part of an analysis model for the connection setup. It identifies the involved de- sign components – Initiator, InRes- Provider, Responder – and their interaction

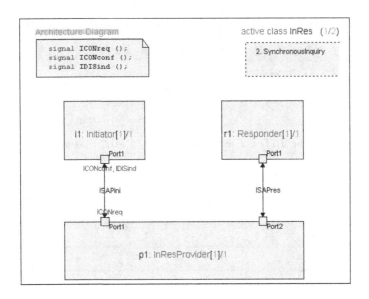

Fig. 3. Intermediate architecture of the InRes-system

to successfully establish a connection. Once the analysis model is available, the SDL pattern pool is searched for suitable candidates. In this particular case, it is straightforward to see that the SYNCHRONOUSINQUIRY pattern [7] is a suitable candidate, and has to be applied twice to capture the nested two-way handshake detected during requirements analysis.

Next, the design context where the pattern instance is to be embedded is identified. In this case, the architectural design components as well as start states already appear in the sequence diagram, and can be associated with the corresponding components in the SDL design. To enter this information into SPT, a sequence of user dialogues (see Figs. 4-6) is initiated, based on the selected pattern. We assume the architectural context shown in Fig. 3, resulting from the previous application of patterns SERVICEARCHITECTURE and SYNCHRONOUS-INQUIRY (first instance).

Firstly, the inquiry automaton[1] is selected by clicking on the corresponding design element, the statechart diagram of InResProvider in the model view of TTD G2 (see Fig. 4).

Next, the trigger of the confirmed interaction – in this case the input signal ICONreq – is marked, which also defines the outgoing state. Following is a user dialogue to determine the reply automaton (Fig. 5) as well as the sender and the receiver ports (Fig. 6). Note that this context information appears in the

---

[1] The SYNCHRONOUSINQUIRY pattern introduces a confirmed interaction between two automata. After a trigger, the InquiryAutomaton sends an inquiry and is blocked until receiving a reply. This signal is eventually received by the ReplyAutomaton, which sends a reply finally releasing the InquiryAutomaton from its waiting state.

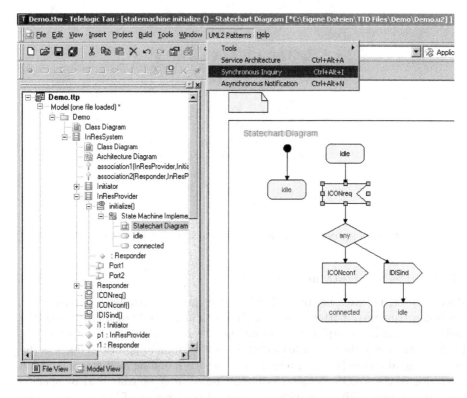

Fig. 4. SYNCHRONOUSINQUIRY pattern: context identification (InquiryAutomaton)

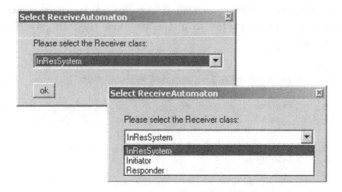

Fig. 5. SYNCHRONOUSINQUIRY pattern: context identification(ReplyAutomaton)

sequence diagram in Fig. 2 and in the architecture diagram in Fig. 3, and could therefore be extracted automatically in a more advanced version of SPT.

Fig. 6. SYNCHRONOUSINQUIRY pattern: context identification (ports)

4.3   Pattern Adaptation

Once the design context has been identified, the (generic) SDL pattern is adapted, yielding a (concrete) pattern instance. In particular, the SDL fragments of the design solution are completed by resolving all variation points as expressed in PA-SDL. In case of the SYNCHRONOUSINQUIRY pattern, adaptation concerns the input of signal names (inquiry, reply1..n), the corresponding next states, and the resolution of the generic decision symbol. Choices may be restricted by specific annotations, prescribing, for instance, that all occurrences of "name" are to be replaced uniquely, or that a "fresh" name is to be used. SPT offers a pattern-specific sequence of user dialogues to enter this information, and immediately checks whether all constraints are satisfied (see Fig. 7). In an advanced version, this information may be extracted from the sequence diagram, which is part of the analysis model.

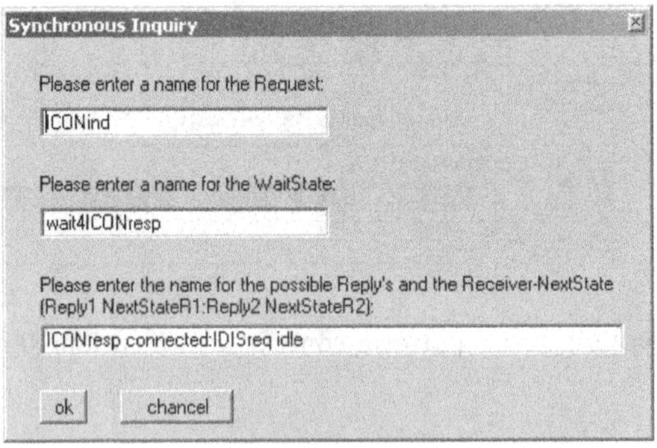

Fig. 7. SYNCHRONOUSINQUIRY pattern: adaptation

4.4   Embedding into the Design Context

Finally, the resulting pattern instance is embedded into the design context. In SPT, this step is automated, as all variation points have been resolved interactively in the previous steps (context identification and pattern adaptation).

Figs. 8 and 9 show the statecharts of InResProvider and Responder after the second application of the SYNCHRONOUSINQUIRY pattern, which completes the connection setup phase. In comparison to the design context in Fig. 4, the

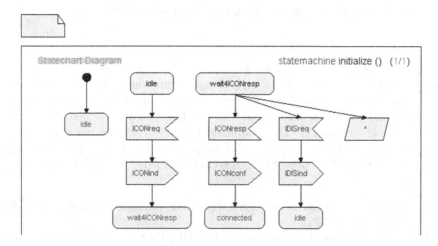

Fig. 8. SYNCHRONOUSINQUIRY pattern: embedding (InResProvider)

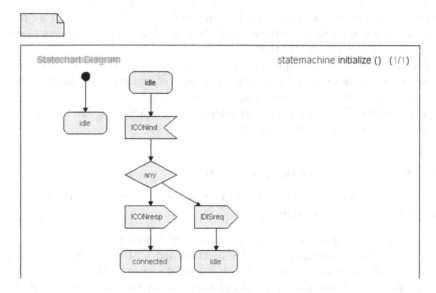

Fig. 9. SYNCHRONOUSINQUIRY pattern: embedding (Responder)

non-deterministic choice expressed by "any" has been replaced by interaction with Responder, where ICONind, ICONresp, and IDISreq substitute the generic signal names inquiry, reply1 and reply2 of the generic SDL fragment in the pattern definition, respectively.

5   Implementation of SPT

In this section, we give a brief overview of the current implementation of SPT (Section 5.1), and outline future extensions (Sections 5.2 and 5.3).

5.1   Overview

SPT is based on a tool developer API – called *basic API* – of TTD G2, which provides flexible access to SDL design elements and their graphical representation. For instance, model and diagram elements may be created, modified, or deleted, and tool bars, menus and dialogue boxes may be added. Since this basic API is written in Tcl (Tool command language [11]), we have decided to implement SPT by pattern- specific Tcl scripts that are interpreted under the control of TTD G2. The code of SPT is collected in a Tcl file with the following structure:

- *Include part*: inclusion of packages with basic dialogue support and basic commands (basic API)
- *Menu part*: code for the menu bar item "UML2 Patterns" and the pull-down menu (s. Fig. 1)
- *Menu procedures*: common procedures for the creation of SPT menus
- *Dialogue procedures*: common procedures for SPT user dialogues
- *Pattern procedures*: common Tcl procedures that are used to structure pattern scripts, e.g., to properly arrange SDL symbols that are added in the course of a pattern application
- *Pattern scripts*: Tcl scripts for the application of SDL patterns. Pattern scripts are structured according to the phases of a pattern application, i.e., context identification, adaptation, and embedding.
- *Tool scripts*: Tcl scripts for user support tools (arrangement of symbols, management of the pattern log etc.)

5.2   Enhancements of the Basic API

TTD G2's basic API can be used to define further abstractions for the development of SDL pattern tool support:

- *Basic user dialogues.* The application of an SDL pattern consists of several steps, including design context identification and pattern adaptation, which require intensive interaction with the system designer. It should be possible to base this interaction on graphical dialogues of the model view and the representation view, in addition to text dialogues (edit fields, combo boxes).

In particular, it should be possible to navigate in the model and to select model elements during a user dialogue. Furthermore, the dynamic update of combo boxes based on intermediate user input should be supported.

- *Auto-layout.* The application of SDL patterns leads to extensions and/or modifications of the SDL context specification. Syntactically, this amounts to adding graphical and textual SDL symbols. These extra symbols should be laid out automatically, with some possibilities for adjustments according to specific project guidelines.
- *Automatic refresh of the representation view.* When an SDL pattern instance is embedded into the context specification, all open diagrams that are affected should be refreshed automatically. Currently, these diagrams have to be closed and reopened manually in order to visualize the embedding.
- *Abstract manipulation of the model view and the representation view.* Manipulation of the model view and the representation view should be based on larger units, and should maintain consistency between these views automatically. E.g., creation of an input symbol should be defined relative to a particular state, without having to deal with connectors, layout, and model elements.
- *Search functionalities for the model view and the representation view.* Some basic search operations in order to support the user dialogues are needed. E.g., it should be possible to find all parts and ports reachable through connectors from a given part. Or, it should be straightforward to collect all ports where a given signal may potentially be delivered.
- *Addition of object attributes.* The application of SDL patterns yields an orthogonal structure of the design specification. Additionally, design decisions are made explicit. To preserve this knowledge, pattern applications have to be documented by the development tool, which requires additional object attributes.
- *Dynamic coloring of SDL symbols.* To make SDL pattern applications visible, some highlighting of SDL symbols is needed. This can be achieved by providing coloring of SDL symbols, as supported, e.g., by SDT. To be flexible, it should be possible to couple coloring to object attributes, and to switch it on and off dynamically.
- *Navigation support.* The application of SDL design patterns may lead to modifications and extensions of the design specification in several places. To find these places and to move back and forth, basic navigation support will be needed.
- *SDL pattern view.* To visualize system designs, TTD G2 currently offers a model and a representation view. These views can be augmented by an SDL pattern view (another tab in the work space) that visualizes the pattern application history and the design elements addressed by each pattern application, and serves as a user interface for quick navigation.

5.3   Provision of an SDL Pattern Command Package

With the additional features of the basic API described in Section 5.2, it will be feasible to define an *SDL pattern command package* providing high-level support for the development of tool support for SDL pattern application and documentation. In particular, the SDL pattern command package may provide the following functionalities:

- *Generic user dialogues for the selection of SDL patterns.* Selection of SDL patterns can be based on an additional menu bar item, possibly hierarchical, to show the pattern categories and, on the next level, the patterns in that particular category. Selection of a pattern triggers its application.
- *Generic high-level user dialogues for the application of SDL patterns.* Context identification and pattern adaptation can be based on the analysis model that captures the involved design units as well as typical message scenarios. This may be assisted by user dialogues, if the analysis model leaves choices, e.g., which portions of a message scenario to cover by applying a particular pattern. Graphical user dialogues, based on the model view and the representation view, would simplify these steps significantly. For instance, it should be possible to navigate in the model and to select model elements during a user dialogue.
- *Developer guidelines to conceive and implement tool support for SDL patterns.* Tool support for SDL patterns is based on the SDL pattern command package. Guidelines could be supplied how to use this command package and how to conceive and implement tool support for a particular pattern. In particular, script templates for specific PA-SDL constructs (e.g., generic trigger symbol, generic decision symbol, border symbol) may be defined.
- *Dynamic coloring of SDL design pattern instances.* With basic coloring features of SDL symbols being available, aggregated features to support the documentation and highlighting of SDL pattern instances can be conceived and implemented.
- *Generic high-level navigation support for SDL patterns.* Basic navigation support is aggregated to obtain pattern-specific, still generic, support.
- *Generic features for the management of the SDL pattern view.* The SDL pattern view (another tab in the work space) is derived from the documentation of SDL pattern applications. It visualizes the pattern application history, and serves as a user interface for quick navigation. Further functionality, e.g., an undo-function, is conceivable in a future release.

6   Status and Outlook

In this paper, we have presented *SPT, the SDL Pattern Tool.* SPT has a graphical user interface, and is fully integrated with TTD G2, the new tool environment from Telelogic. Currently, SPT supports three SDL patterns: SERVICEARCHITECTURE, ASYNCHRONOUSNOTIFICATION, and SYNCHRONOUSINQUIRY. In [6], these patterns have been applied manually during the pattern-based development of the InRes- service. With SPT, we have been able to repeat this development, which provides evidence for the feasibility of the tool concept.

The development of SPT has been triggered by our industrial partners, who pointed out the need for graphical tool support in order to fully exploit the benefits of the SDL pattern approach. Tool support should address the definition and application of SDL patterns on the one hand, and the documentation of pattern applications on the other hand. Furthermore, it should be integrated with existing tool environments. The development of SPT shows that these requirements can be met. However, there is still a lot of room for improvements. In particular, an SDL pattern command package should be provided, with suitable abstractions for the development of SDL pattern tool support as well as guidelines to conceive and implement tool support for project-specific SDL. This will enable development teams to define and maintain their own, project-specific SDL pattern pool and customized tool support.

The SDL pattern approach has been introduced in 1997, and has been improved, applied, consolidated and transferred to industry since. These activities have so far been driven by a small group of people from academia, in cooperation with industry. With this experience being available, the future development of the approach and, in particular, the definition of a set of standard SDL patterns, should be pursued by an SDL pattern task force with broad membership, to trigger wider discussion and exposure.

References

1. R. Bræk, Ø. Haugen: Engineering Real Time Systems. Prentice Hall, 1993.
2. D. Cisowski, B. Geppert, F. Rößler, M. Schwaiger: Tool Support for SDL Patterns. Y. Lahav, A. Wolisz, J. Fischer, E. Holz (Eds.), Proceedings of the 1st Workshop on SDL and MSC (SAM'98), Berlin, 1998.
3. E. Gamma, R. Helm, R. Johnson, J. Vlissides: Design Patterns: Elements of Reusable Object-Oriented Software. Addison-Wesley, Reading, Massachusetts, 1995.
4. B. Geppert, R. Gotzhein, F. Rößler: Configuring Communication Protocols Using SDL Patterns. A. Cavalli, A. Sarma (Eds.), SDL'97 – Time for Testing, Proceedings of the 8th SDL Forum, Elsevier, Amsterdam, 1997, pp. 523-538.
5. B. Geppert: The SDL Pattern Approach – A Reuse-Driven SDL Methodology for Designing Communication Software Systems. Ph.D. Thesis, University of Kaiserslautern, 2000.
6. R. Gotzhein: Consolidating and Applying the SDL Pattern Approach: A Detailed Case Study. Journal of Information and Software Technology, Vol. 45, Issue 11 (727-741), Elsevier Sciences, 2003.
7. R. Gotzhein: .The SDL Design Pattern Approach – A Tutorial. SFB 501 Report 07/2003, Technical University of Kaiserslautern, Germany, 2003.
8. R. Grammes, R. Gotzhein, C. Mahr, P. Schaible, H. Schleiffer: Industrial Application of the SDL Pattern Approach in UMTS Call Processing Development – Experience and Quantitative Assessment. R. Reed and J. Reed (Eds.), SDL 2003: System Design, Volume 2708 of Lecture Notes in Computer Science, Springer, 2003, pp. 102-116.
9. R. Grammes, R. Gotzhein: Towards the Harmonisation of UML and SDL – Syntactic and Semantic Alignment. Technical Report 327/03, Technical University of Kaiserslautern, Germany, 2003.

10. ITU-T: Recommendation Z.100 (11/99) Specification and Description Language (SDL). International Telecommunication Union, Geneva.
11. J. Ousterhout: TCL and the Tk Toolkit. Addison-Wesley, 2002.
12. R. Reed: Methodology for Real Time Systems. Computer Networks and ISDN Systems, Special Issue on SDL and MSC, 28 (1996), pp. 1685-1701.
13. F. Rößler, B. Geppert, P. Schaible: Re-Engineering of the Internet Stream Protocol ST2+ with Formalized Design Patterns. Proceedings of the 5th International Conference on Software Reuse (ICSR5), Victoria, Canada, 1998.
14. F. Rößler: Collaboration-Based Design of Communicating Systems with SDL. Ph.D. Thesis, Computer Science Department, Technical University of Kaiserslautern, Germany, 2001.
15. P. Schaible: Reuse-based Development of Communication Systems. Ph.D. Thesis, Computer Science Department, Technical University of Kaiserslautern, Germany, 2004 (in german).
16. Telelogic AB: Tau 4.4 SDL Suite, 2002.
17. Telelogic AB: Tau 3.4 SDT Methodology Guidelines – Part 1: The SOMT Method, 1998.

Comparing UML 2.0 Interactions and MSC-2000

Øystein Haugen

Department of Informatics, University of Oslo, Norway
oysteinh@ifi.uio.no

Abstract. This paper is a brief comparison between the Interactions of UML 2.0 as defined by the Final Adopted Specification (OMG ptc/03-07-06) and MSC-2000 as defined by Z.120 (ITU 1999). The comparison investigates whether UML 2.0 has serious shortcomings relative to MSC-2000. The paper also discusses whether MSC-2000 is still needed in the future or should be retired.

1 Introduction

Message Sequence Charts emerged from the SDL (ITU-T Specification and Description Language) community leading to its first ITU-T recommendation in 1992 [9]. Later there have been revisions of MSC in 1996 [10], in 2000 [11], and more recently in 2004 [12].

UML 1.0 appeared in 1999 [20] and it did have some simple sequence diagrams similar to those found in MSC-92. UML went through small revisions leading to UML 1.5 in 2003. Still over the last three to four years a major revision of UML has taken place leading to UML 2.0 [21] which will become an available technology from OMG (Object Management Group) in 2004. In UML 2.0 also sequence diagrams (or Interactions) have been thoroughly revisited and revised.

Having led the work towards MSC-2000 as ITU-T Rapporteur, and towards UML 2.0 Interactions as the editor of that chapter, we think it may be of interest to give a comparison between the two. For obvious reasons many of the same requirements have affected the direction of the developments, but the differences in standardization style between ITU-T and OMG have also had influence [4, 7]. The first version of this paper has been input to the ITU SG17 discussions, but we thought the comparison could also be useful for a wider audience.

To read this paper it is helpful to have good knowledge of either MSC or UML sequence diagrams. This paper is not a tutorial for any of these languages.

The paper is organized as follows. First we give a comparison table that will give the readers a quick summary of the differences between MSC and UML Sequence Diagrams, and present the terms used. Then we present the diagrams and show examples of similarities and differences. We go in some detail into the important fragment concepts. Details of messages are commented before the areas of data and time are considered at greater length. Finally there is a summary and conclusion.

D. Amyot and A.W. Williams (Eds.): SAM 2004, LNCS 3319, pp. 65–79, 2005.

Table 1. Comparison of central concepts

MSC-2000	UML 2.0	Comments
MSC (Message Sequence Chart)	Interaction (Sequence Diagram; Communication Diagram; Timing Diagram; Interaction Overview Diagram)	The individual scenarios. MSC and UML have different approaches to language.
Event	EventOccurrence	
MSC Document	Class (or Collaboration)	The context of the scenarios.
Instance	Lifeline	Notice that a lifeline refers to a property (part) of a composite structure, while the instance is a part of a structure.
Message	Message	Both distinguish between asynchronous and synchronizing message.
Method call	Operation call	
Method (area)	ExecutionOccurrence	
Action	ExecutionOccurrence	
Suspension (area)	No direct counterpart	
Gate	Gate	In UML we have only message gates, while in MSC there are also general ordering gates.
No direct counterpart	Interaction fragment	See section 3.1.
Inline expression	Combined Fragment	UML 2.0 has introduced more operators.
Coregion	Coregion	In MSC this is a basic concept from 1992, but in UML 2.0 this is only presented as a shorthand for the par-operator. No semantic difference.
MSC reference	Interaction Occurrence	The ability to refer to another interaction. See also section 3.4.
Decomposition	PartDecomposition	How the aggregate hierarchy of the structure is reflected in interactions/MSCs.
General Ordering	General Ordering	UML does not have general ordering gates.
Condition (global state)	Continuation	This concept is basically a label being a syntactic way to combine pieces of the specification that are distributed.
Condition (predicate)	Interaction Constraint	
Relative time	Duration	
Absolute time	Time	
Time measurement	TimeObservationAction, DurationObservationAction	
Timer	No counterpart	

2   Comparison Table

The comparison in Table 1 is intended to give overview of the different central concepts in the field of Interactions / MSC such that those only familiar with one of the languages can see what terms have been used in the other language.

3   Diagrams and Concepts

MSC, in the tradition of the ITU languages, considers the graphical syntax tightly coupled to the concepts. In UML, however, one has tried (not always successfully) to distinguish between the concept and the presentation forms. The latter approach resembles what was done for SDL, where there was an abstract syntax on which the semantics was explained. In UML the abstract syntax is defined by what is called a metamodel. The metamodel is described in a subset of UML itself called MOF (Meta Object Facility).

MSC has two graphic forms, simple message sequence charts (Fig. 1) and high-level message sequence charts (Fig. 4). MSC also has a supposedly equivalent textual form.

In UML the concept referred in this paper is called *Interaction*. UML Interactions come in several graphic forms with different foci. The most expressive form is the *sequence diagram* (Fig. 2) and every concept of Interactions can be expressed in sequence diagrams.

The Fig. 1 shows an MSC-2000 diagram which is a piece of the specification of an access control system. We see initial global condition, a reference, messages,

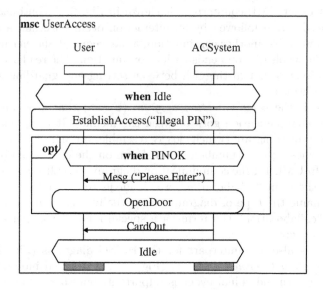

Fig. 1. Simple MSC-2000 diagram

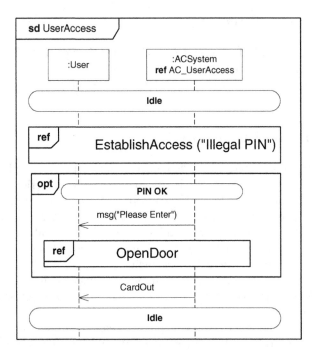

Fig. 2. Simple UML 2.0 sequence diagram

an optional inline expression including yet another initial condition, a message and a reference. The diagram ends with a setting condition.

An almost exact UML counterpart is shown in Fig. 2. A continuation is at the top of the diagram followed by an interaction occurrence and a combined fragment that includes another continuation, a message and another interaction occurrence. The whole diagram ends with a continuation. The reader may notice that continuations do not distinguish between setting and guarding as is done with MSC conditions.

Then there is the *communication diagram* (Fig. 3) that gives an overview of how simple communication goes between the lifelines. It is overloaded on a composite structure diagram (which closely resembles an SDL-96 block diagram [8]) where the messages are numbered and shown on the connectors (communication lines). In UML 1.x the communication diagram was called a collaboration diagram, but the term "collaboration" was inadequately overloaded and it was decided to rename the type of diagram that actually described an interaction. In UML 2.0 "collaboration" is a term for a special kind of classifier - a kind of generic class concept.

UML 2.0 has also a counterpart for the HMSC diagrams (Fig. 4), and it is called *Interaction Overview Diagram* (Fig. 5). For detailed interactions, the specification of each individual event is important, but there is often a larger picture where the general control flow is the most significant. For this purpose

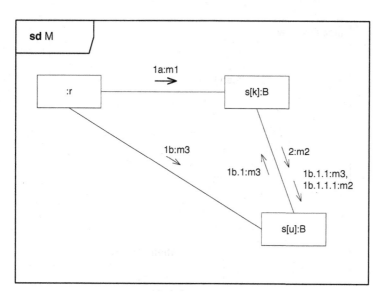

Fig. 3. UML 2.0 communication diagram

HMSC is a graphical form of MSCs that can be referred from simple MSCs and can themselves refer simple MSCs.

The HMSC in Fig. 4 has the same semantics as the plain MSC in Fig. 1 We notice that the conditions serve as nodes in the flowgraph. Other nodes are MSC references and the start and end symbols (triangles). In addition there is a circle that only serves as a join for graphical lines.

HMSC and Interaction Overview Diagrams are quite similar. The UML 2.0 variant can also have inline interaction diagrams (of any kind) as nodes. This is slightly more general than MSC.

We see this in Fig. 5 where continuations come in place of MSC conditions, and interaction occurrences or inline sequence diagrams replace the MSC references. Since the UML Interaction Overview diagrams follow the UML activity diagram syntax there are other supplementary symbols to describe branching, start and end.

In UML 1.x there was already activity diagrams that on a very rough abstraction level served the same purpose as HMSC. Therefore it was natural to try and reuse notation from activity diagrams when designing the UML 2.0 Interactions counterpart of HMSC (Fig. 5).

Still UML 2.0 Interaction Overview Diagrams are understood as Interactions rather than activities. This is important since activities are understood through Petri-net-like semantics while Interactions are understood through trace semantics.

Finally UML 2.0 has the timing diagram included for the purpose of focusing on timing issues. It is an interaction diagram even though the timing concepts have been made applicable not only for interactions.

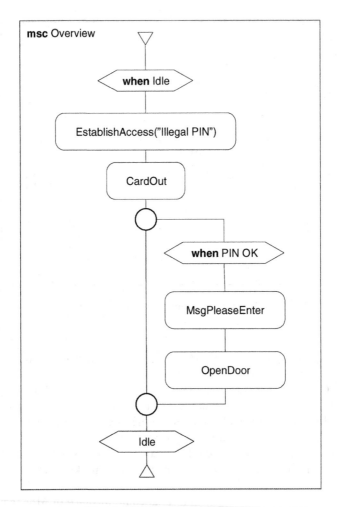

Fig. 4. HMSC - High Level MSC

In UML concepts may even exist without syntax, which means that it is up to the tool how to present the concept to the user - and this will often result in values given in a dialogue box. In MSC on the other hand, every concept has concrete syntax.

In UML 2.0 unlike in UML 1.x, the diagrams have a frame and a name like in MSC. UML has a textual form (XMI) which is the standardized format for model exchange.

3.1   Interaction Fragment

The UML concept Interaction fragment is only implicitly present in MSC. The more specific concept of MSC Inline Expression corresponds to UML 2.0 Combined Fragment.

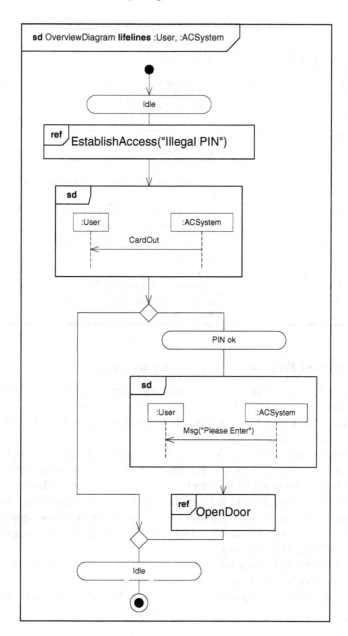

Fig. 5. UML 2.0 interaction overview diagram

This is a minor point, but introducing "interaction fragment" makes it a little easier to explain the semantics in a compositional way. The interaction fragment is the central recursive concept.

Table 2. Operators of combined fragments

MSC-2000	UML 2.0	Comments
Loop	Loop	Iteration construct.
Opt	Opt	Optional behavior.
Seq	Seq	Weak sequencing.
Par	Par	Parallel merge.
Alt	Alt	Alternatives.
Exc	Break	Exception as a special case of alternative. There is no semantic difference between MSC and UML here.
	Strict	For traces where the order is given by vertical coordinates also between lifelines.
	Neg	Negative traces. Introduces a more complex semantics.
	Critical	Critical region.
	Ignore/consider	Filtering of message types.
	Assert	A way to define what has to happen in a given situation.

3.2 Combined Fragments / Inline Expressions

Table 2 is a summary of operators of combined fragments. The reader will have to look up the detailed definition of an operator in the standards.

Furthermore in UML 2.0 it is possible to combine operators directly in the operator area as shorthand for nesting.

The operators are as the table above shows almost identical, but UML 2.0 has added a few. Neg and assert are introduced to make sequence diagrams more suitable to express requirements that are more absolute. The neg operator defines those traces that should not occur, and the assert defines the traces that should (mandatory) occur at a given point in the scenario. These operators are intended to bring the essence of Live Sequence Charts [2] into the compositional semantics of UML 2.0 interactions.

In the future we will probably see even more operators. One suggestion has been to distinguish between specifying potential alternatives and mandatory alternatives [6]. Others want to make interactions able to describe Java exceptions properly.

3.3 Conditions / Continuations

Already in MSC-92 we had the concept of "conditions". The term indicated that we were talking about predicates that had to be true for some behavior to take place. This turned out to be a slightly incorrect intuition and in MSC-2000 the condition concept came in two variants: the MSC-92 variant, which is really a label, and the guarding condition (predicate).

UML did already in its version UML 1.x have constraints and guards. The constraints could be put anywhere in the model, and guards could be put on messages to indicate when the executions could follow that message.

In UML 2.0 we have in the spirit of MSC-2000 included both the labeling variant of conditions called "continuations" and the predicate, guarding variant called "interaction constraints".

Disregarding the difference in terms, the concepts are comparable. The UML 2.0 concept "continuation" is deliberately made more narrow than the MSC-2000 concept "global state condition", but in practice they will serve the same purpose, namely to combine parts of the specification that are distributed for other reasons. Typically such combination is needed when the branching of control occurs within one diagram, and this branching should be continued in another diagram without having to check again for the same condition

3.4   Referring Another Interaction / MSC Diagram

To refer to another interaction from within a diagram is one of the most important structuring mechanisms, and the first to be asked for by the users.

The concept of MSC reference of Z.120 and Interaction Occurrence of UML 2.0 are almost identical. In its basic form they can both be understood by substituting the referred diagram into where the reference was.

MSC also features "reference expressions" where the text of the MSC reference can designate an expression like an inline expression. This may be understood as textual shorthand for more voluminous graphics. UML does not have a direct counterpart of this feature.

4   Context of the Scenarios

MSC defines a concept of its own "MSC Document" to define the context of an MSC (the individual scenarios). This context defines a composite structure of the instances playing in the MSC. The MSCs of the MSC Document are divided in *defining* and *utilities*. The defining MSCs are those intended to define the semantics of the MSC Document while the utilities are merely used directly or indirectly by the defining ones.

This is very similar to UML where the context may be a class or a collaboration. The latter is for more generic interactions. A class or a collaboration have a composite structure restricting the possible lifelines of the interactions. The composite structure of classifiers in UML is an innovation from version 2.0 inspired by SDL block diagrams and ROOM [22] structures. Composite structures may have ports on the edges and they may also be represented by lifelines in interactions [5]. To tie Interactions closely to the composite structure was a significant simplification step relative to earlier versions of UML where the participants of Interactions had lived their own life relatively unaffected by those specified in other parts of UML.

In UML there is no distinction between defining and utility behaviors, but a class may define a "classifier behavior" which is that designated behavior of an object of that class. This would be similar to a defining MSC. A classifier behavior in UML may be any behavior, which means it can be a state machine or an activity.

In UML, the class (collaboration) has a number of other purposes than serving as the context for interactions, and as such defines the bridge between the interaction part of the language and other parts like state machines and activities. With MSC, it is necessary to assume a mapping between concepts in MSC and corresponding ones in SDL. This mapping is, however, mostly trivial.

4.1   Decomposing the Structure

In MSC, the MSC Documents represent an aggregate hierarchy of structure, and in UML 2.0 classes and collaborations may have composite structures which also represent an aggregate structure.

The natural question is what happens to a scenario specified for a high aggregate level when the constituents are decomposed.

The concept in MSC and that of UML are designed to be as similar as possible since the UML concept was modeled according to the MSC counterpart.

As a graphical option, in UML 2.0 lower aggregate levels can be shown directly inline under a Lifeline representing a higher aggregate level. Thus a sequence diagram may contain lifelines on different aggregate levels, which is impossible in MSC.

4.2   Messages

UML 2.0 and MSC do not have exactly the same tradition with respect to what kind of scenarios they have been used to describe. While UML has a tradition of using interactions to describe the control flow of a sequential program, MSC considers a set of entirely concurrent instances where the method calls are considered remote procedure calls.

This difference in tradition does make some difference in requirements, but neither language should have any restriction limiting their usage in this respect.

Technically MSC considers method calls and replies a concept area of its own, UML 2.0 considers operation calls as just one kind of message. However, in both cases the semantics is given by the traces of the events leading from the initiation of the operation call (MSC: method call) to the reception of the reply.

The difference in tradition is also highlighted by UML usage of interactions where also passive objects are depicted as lifelines. In MSC passive objects would always be modeled as variables of the active instances.

Therefore what UML users sometimes describe using messaging, MSC users would only consider as operations on variables. In the UML community we have therefore experienced a very strong need to have data guards for alternatives that cover more than one lifeline since it is in practice possible to determine that the covered lifelines are never concurrently executing.

4.3   Suspension Area

The suspension area is a part of the lifeline where no events should appear (with certain strict restrictions). This is given explicitly and is not always the case when there are method calls. This is because method calls can appear from different sub-lifelines if the lifeline represents a composite structure. That would mean that even when there is a method call the whole object will not have to wait for the reply.

In UML 2.0, the suspension region concept was considered, but removed at a late stage of the process.

4.4   Data Concepts

The approaches to data in MSC and in UML are both similar and different.

In both languages it is considered desirable that the users can choose to apply the data manipulation language of his preference rather than a standard data-manipulation sub-language of the modeling language. This is contrary to SDL (Z.100), which does have a data language of its own.

Data in MSC-2000. The data concepts of MSC-2000 is characterized by a rather elaborate scheme designed to give the user the necessary freedom of expression without sacrificing precision and formality.

In order to let the users write the data portions without being hampered by all kinds of escape notation, there is a way to define parts of the syntax of the preferred data language within MSC-2000. Through declarations it is possible to define characters for parentheses etc. It is recognized that most data languages have a nested structure where parenthesizing is important. It is possible to declare syntax for nestable as well as non-nestable parentheses. Through these "meta" declarations of syntax, it is possible for the user to write data expressions in his favorite data language without any extra wrapping syntax, and still the MSC analyzer can extract the appropriate data strings in a general way.

For the MSC analyzer to "kick down" to analyzing the extracted data strings, a number of interface functions are defined. Some of these functions controls the static requirements of the data language such that the MSC analyzer can apply these functions which must be defined for the data language used.

Finally there are a few functions that are required to define the dynamic semantics of the combined MSC and Data language. These functions represent a way to parameterize the semantics of the MSC language modulo different data languages.

The ITU has standardized such a binding between SDL data language and MSC in Recommendation Z.121 [14]. This formally combines the data aspects of SDL and MSC tightly together.

Data in UML 2.0. Data is in principle an integrated part of the UML modeling language, but there is little UML-specific rules for concrete syntax. Most of this must be found through examining the chapters on Actions (and Activities) in UML 2.0.

There is no UML concrete syntax for actions, and there is no counterpart to the language specific way in which the syntax can be defined within the language as one can find in MSC.

There has been talk about defining concrete syntax for an action language, but nothing concrete has come out of this yet.

Data Summary. MSC has a reasonably well founded formalization of how different action/data languages can be combined with core MSC, but this is a relatively elaborate scheme not easily conceived by the users. Furthermore the MSC approach to data is not directly aligned with SDL (representing the more imperative style of modeling within the same tradition). The connection to SDL is taken care of through defining the necessary interface functions for SDL as required by MSC described above. This task is done but still not implemented in any publicly available tool.

Formally associating data with the lifelines of the interaction is necessary to produce any formal analysis or model transformation for practical purposes. In practice both MSC and UML 2.0 tools are adapting programming languages (such as Java or C) as their action language. The connection with the rest of the standard language is done ad hoc and not necessarily following the principles of the standards.

5   Time Concepts

MSC-2000 defines time concepts and mechanisms to define constraints on absolute and relative time related to events. This is also the case in UML, but in UML time constraints are found not in the section on Interactions, but in the section on Common Behavior intended to hold for all of UML, not only for the Interactions.

For the user MSC-2000 and UML 2.0 will appear as close to identical when it comes to specifying timing constraints.

Some users of UML will want to use a more elaborate time model than the simple one included with UML 2.0 proper. There is a profile (i.e., extension) of UML 1.4 called "UML Profile for schedulability, performance and time specification" that comprises a more comprehensive understanding of time. One important point is that the simple time model is close to assuming one global time. There will be an update of that profile to match UML 2.0.

Timers are not included in UML 2.0, but they exist in MSC. In UML 2.0 the user is recommended to use separate lifelines within Interactions to model timers. This does work reasonably well for Interactions, but there is definitely the argument that timer is such a common concept that it deserves to become a concept of the language. This has resulted in that, for instance, the UML Testing Profile [19] augments UML 2.0 by timers and time zones.

6   Generics

MSC-2000 has the possibility to parameterize the charts with data, instances, message types and timers. In UML 2.0 the Interactions are also general Behaviors that may have normal value parameters corresponding to data parameters of MSC-2000.

Message types as well as instance parameters must be dealt with in UML 2.0 through the mechanism of template parameters. Lifelines as parameters are not discussed in UML 2.0.

Timers are not included as separate concepts of the UML language.

7   Formal Semantics

It has been customary to argue that UML has no (formal) semantics. And from MSC people it has been commonplace to note that MSC does have a formal semantics. Both of these statements are dubious. The practical difference between UML and MSC regarding formality is not as big as the SDL/MSC community likes to pretend. The determining interpretations come in both languages from reading the informal specification and adjusting it to the situation where it is going to be applied. It is still the case that MSCs / Interactions are used more for illustration and discussion than formal requirements specification and verification [3].

Historically, in the mid-1990ies there was a lot of exploratory academic work on MSC [1, 15, 16, 17, 18], while recently academics in general are turning more towards UML for the same opportunistic reasons as does the industry. We will probably see contributions in the UML community that corresponds well with results in the SDL/MSC community in the previous century [6].

Even though the semantics of MSC may be slightly more formally defined through the early work on MSC-96 [13] and the precision of the Z.120 standard, than the UML 2.0, the average user will not notice.

8   Discussion

The purpose of this paper was to examine whether there is a need for both MSC and UML 2.0 Interactions. Should the ITU retire MSC, or should MSC become a profile of UML 2.0?

The question is clearly not only to be settled on technical grounds. We have seen no tools yet, neither for the full MSC-2000 nor UML 2.0 Interactions. MSC-2000 has been around for about 4 years, why should there suddenly be a renewed interest from the tool vendors? Possibly the reason lies in the challenge from UML 2.0?

Technically the following statements summarize the main issues:

1. MSC-2000 is a language in its own right. This is an advantage and a disadvantage since MSC on its own is seldom enough.
2. UML 2.0 Interactions are dependent upon other parts of UML 2.0. This means in principle that if you choose UML 2.0 Interactions over MSC, you

will need to take the whole UML 2.0 to go with it. This would in practice mean also substituting SDL with UML 2.0 in your development process.

3. Assuming that tools existed for both MSC-2000 and UML 2.0, there are few technical reasons for choosing one before the other provided scenarios are your only interest.

4. There may be need for UML profiles that focus on extending Interactions and also making specific choices for the semantic variation points. We have already the forthcoming UML Testing Profile [19]. A specific MSC profile of UML 2.0 could add the innovative data mechanism which possibly could make it easier to handle Interactions formally.

9   Conclusion

MSC-2000 and UML 2.0 Interactions are very similar, which is exactly what was expected and intended.

Proper tool support and how those tools integrate with SDL and UML 2.0 respectively, will determine which language will survive. There is also the possibility that the languages will co-exist and cross-pollinate as we have seen SDL and UML do over the last years.

From a pure market view it seems probable that the next couple of years will choose a winner. If the UML community can reach real code generation and machine-supported verification, their market position will make them the winners. On the other hand if UML users are unable to reach the level of automatic support that is commonplace in the SDL community, UML will vanish. Whether new products and languages will take their place or SDL/MSC will again be fashionable, remains to be seen.

References

1. Baeten, J.C.M. and S. Mauw: Delayed choice: an operator for joining Message Sequence Charts. FORTE'94, Bern, Switzerland.
2. Damm, W. and D. Harel: LSCs: Breathing Life into Message Sequence Charts. Third International Conference on Formal Methods for Open Object-Based Distributed Systems (FMOODS), 1999.
3. Haugen, Ø. Using MSC-92 Effectively in SDL'95 with MSC in CASE. Seventh SDL Forum, North-Holland, Elsevier, 1995.
4. Haugen, Ø: Converging MSC and UML Sequence Diagrams. Beyond the Standard UML'99 – The Unified Modeling Language. Fort Collins, USA, 1999.
5. Haugen, Ø., B. Møller-Pedersen, and T. Weigert: Structural Modeling with UML 2.0. L. Lavagno, G. Martin, and B. Selic (Eds.) UML for Real. Kluwer Academic Publishers, 2003.
6. Haugen, Ø. and K. Stølen: STAIRS - Steps To Analyze Interactions with Refinement Semantics. P. Stevens, J. Whittle, G. Booch (Eds) UML'2003 – Modeling Languages and Applications. Volume 2863 of Lecture Notes in Computer Science, Springer, 2003, 388–402.

7. Haugen, Ø: From MSC-2000 to UML 2.0 - The Future of Sequence Diagrams. R. Reed, J. Reed (Eds) SDL Forum 2001. Volume 2078 of Lecture Notes in Computer Science, Springer, 2001, 38–51.

8. ITU-T: Z.100 Addendum 1 (10/96). Corrections to Recommendation Z.100, CCITT Specification and Description Language (SDL), 1996, International Telecommunication Union, Geneva.

9. ITU-T: Recommendation Z.120 (03/93), Message Sequence Charts (MSC). E. Rudolph (Ed.), 1993, International Telecommunication Union, Geneva. 36 pages.

10. ITU-T: Recommendation Z.120 (10/96), Message Sequence Charts (MSC). E. Rudolph (Ed.), 1996, International Telecommunication Union, Geneva. 78 pages.

11. ITU-T: Recommendation Z.120 (11/99), Message Sequence Charts (MSC). Ø. Haugen (Ed.), 1999, International Telecommunication Union, Geneva. 126 pages.

12. ITU-T: Recommendation Z.120 (04/04), Message Sequence Charts (MSC). C. Jervis (Ed.), 2004, International Telecommunication Union, Geneva.

13. ITU-T: Recommendation Z.120 Annex B (04/98), Formal semantics of message sequence charts. S. Mauw, et al. (Eds), 1998, International Telecommunication Union, Geneva. 76 pages.

14. ITU-T: Recommendation Z.121 (02/03), Specification and Description Language (SDL) data binding to Message Sequence Charts (MSC). 2003, International Telecommunication Union, Geneva.

15. Mauw, S.: The formalization of Message Sequence Charts. Computer Networks & ISDN, June 1996, 1643-1659.

16. Mauw, S. and E.A. van der Meulen: Generating tools for Message Sequence Charts. E.U.o.T. Philips (Ed). Technical Report TD60, ITU-TS SG10 Interims Meeting, Geneva, Switzerland, 1994.

17. Mauw, S. and M.A. Reniers: An algebraic semantics of Basic Message Sequence Charts. The Computer Journal, 1994, 37(4).

18. Mauw, S. and M.A. Reniers: Operational Semantics for MSC'96. A. Cavalli and D. Vincent (Eds) Tutorials of the Eighth SDL Forum (SDL'97), 1997, 135-152.

19. OMG: UML Testing Profile. I. Schieferdecker (Ed.), 2003, Object Management Group.

20. OMG: Unified Modeling Language 1.4. 2000. Object Management Group.

21. OMG: Unified Modeling Language: Superstructure 2.0. 2003. Object Management Group.

22. Selic, B., G. Gullekson, and P.T. Ward: Real-Time Object-Oriented Modeling. Wiley, 1994.

Data Encoding for SDL in ITU-T Rec. Z.104

Rick Reed

Telecommunications Software Engineering Limited,
The Laurels Victoria Road Windermere,
Cumbria LA23 2DL United Kingdom
`rickreed@tseng.co.uk`

Abstract. When SDL is used for the implementation, different parts of the system may be implemented by different tools. Data communicated between different parts needs to be encoded and decoded in the same way by each part if the information encoded by one part is to be seen as the same value by another part. The ITU-T Recommendation Z.104 'Encoding of SDL Data' that is currently being refined for approval, allows the data encoding to be specified for communication paths or for specific encoding and decoding expressions. This paper presents the Recommendation in a less formal way than the ITU-T document. The presentation adds examples illustrating uses. The use of the ASN.1 encoding and text encoding is shown. One principle of Z.104 is to introduce an implicit data type that represents all the signals that can be received on a path. The paper further extends SDL to introduce ways to use implicit data types associated with interfaces.

Keywords: SDL, Data, Encoding, ASN.1, Text encoding.

1 Introduction

This paper is about the Z.104 [6] Recommendation, which commenced the ITU-T approval process in July 2004. The SAM 2004 workshop therefore came at an opportune time to comment on the then current draft, which was being edited by the author. Feedback from the paper review process and the SAM workshop itself was valuable in shaping the version submitted to the approval process. This is therefore a revised version of the paper presented that reflects the feedback and the submitted Recommendation.

2 The Need for Data Encoding

When SDL [4] is used to implement a system that handles a protocol, there normally needs be a precise description of how the messages sent and received should be encoded, so that the bits actually sent in the message are interpreted as meaning the same abstract value at the sender and the receiver. Without such a description it is possible that the encoding at one end will be incorrectly

D. Amyot and A.W. Williams (Eds.): SAM 2004, LNCS 3319, pp. 80–95, 2005.

decoded at the other end unless both sender and receiver software are generated using the same tool and implemented on the same kind of platform. Even under these circumstances the actual encoding may change between versions of the tool, or variations in the platform.

Of course, it is precisely to overcome these variations that ASN.1 [2] is usually used, so that the abstract data values can be sent and received using encoding defined by encoding rules [3]. Alternative mechanisms exist, such as passing information as text streams, or the use of XML [7] but these still rely on both sides agreeing the encoding - for example for text it would be safest to stick to the internationally defined characters with defined encoding as in the International Reference Alphabet [1]. Whichever choice is taken, at some point encoding has to be defined. The software will have to make sure the internal representation of values is transformed to this encoding when information is output and from this encoding to the internal values when the information is input.

When the encoded data is being passed through a lower layer protocol, the information is passed to the lower layer rather than a peer entity at the same level in the hierarchy. In general such a lower layer does not know what the structure of the information of the higher layer is, so that the data is usually encoded before it is passed down and the lower layer sees some ubiquitous data item as a bit or octet or character string. This encoding is (of course) reversed when the information is passed from the lower layer to a higher layer. If the higher layer is written in SDL, the encoding needs to be associated with sending of the message containing the information, and similarly decoding needs to be associated with receipt of the message at the higher layer. However, there is no language defined for such encoding and decoding mechanisms in either the SDL standard [4] or the standard for the use of ASN.1 with SDL [5].

If the lower layer is not implemented in SDL, from an SDL point of view these peer entities may appear to communicate directly, and no further encoding or decoding would be needed within the SDL. How communication with the non-SDL lower layer is effected will have an impact on where in the SDL encoding and decoding needs to be invoked. If the lower layer is called by a function or procedure call, the data needs to be encoded/decoded as part of the call. If the lower layer is called by a signal interface, the encoding/decoding needs to be part of the OUTPUT and INPUT (respectively). In this case, the two entities could be shown as in the same SDL system or in separate SDL systems (for example, in "half call" modelling). If they are shown in the same system, then this is equivalent to a model where there is no lower layer and two peer entities communicate directly but there is a requirement that a particular encoding is used. For example, the channel connecting the two SDL entities could represent a physical connection on which there is a normative requirement for the encoding of the protocol data.

Typically ASN.1 is used to specify protocol data units, and the use of SDL with ASN.1 has become a mature approach for this use both in industry for system development as well as within ITU-T and ETSI. This is supported in SDL-2000 by the combination of ITU-T Recommendations Z.100 [4] and Z.105 [5].

When an interface or protocol is designed which carries data using ASN.1, there can be ASN.1 encoding rules [3] that determine exactly how the information is encoded. However ASN.1 does not have to be used when SDL is used, and there are no established standard encoding rules for SDL data.

3   Purpose and Scope of Z.104

The purpose of the ITU-T Recommendation Z.104 [6] with the title 'Encoding of SDL data' is to determine the encoding of data used in SDL descriptions, so that data values can be communicated between separately implemented pieces of SDL in an implementation independent way. To achieve this objective, data can be encoded in a text format or (if and only if the data on the interface is defined by an ASN.1 CHOICE data type) according to encoding rules defined in the ITU-T Rec. X.690 series [3]. If the encoding rule is one defined by the X.690 series the result is either a BIT STRING or OCTET STRING.

The restriction to an ASN.1 CHOICE data type for ASN.1 encodings is because Z.104 is essentially intended for encoding protocol data units. For this reason, there is a further restriction that the names of the choices shall correspond to the set of signal names for the signals on a given path and the data items for the choice be the same as the corresponding signal parameter. When an ASN.1 CHOICE type is used from an ASN.1 module, this can also be used as an implicit definition of an **interface** that contains the necessary signals therefore removing the need for the user to define the signals explicitly.

ASN.1 data types are restricted to sets of values, which in SDL-2000 would be expressed as a **value type** definition. There is no mechanism in ASN.1 for expressing Pid values to reference agents, nor is there a mechanism to express SDL objects types, that is references to values.

3.1   Object Data Types

Object data types were introduced to SDL in SDL-2000, and are defined by an **object type** definition. A definition:

> **object type** Obj3D { **struct** x, y, z Integer; }

defines the Obj3D data type that references structure values with x, y and z Integer fields in the referenced values. A variable of type Obj3D does not contain the structure, but only references it. The main benefit of such types is that the structure data (which often is larger and more complex than the example) does not have to be copied from once place to another when an assignment is made, instead the reference can be assigned to another Obj3D variable which then references the same data.

However, object data also leads to some complications keeping track of how many references there are to the data, and creation and deletion of the referenced data items. SDL-2000 is designed so that references can only be exchanged between two agents if both agents are processes and are both contained within a common process (which may be one of the two processes). In this case the processes never run concurrently and it is safe to share data between the processes. Otherwise an object data type as a signal parameter, causes the referenced data to be sent in the signal and a new data object is created to hold the data when the signal is received.

Because communication of encoded data is only likely to be between agents that can be concurrent, there is no need for Z.104 to support object data. In any case, as far as the author is aware, no commercial tools currently support object data as it is defined in SDL-2000. Moreover, in most SDL models the legacy **newtype** syntax is still used to define data types rather than the SDL-2000 **value type** syntax, and this does not permit object data types to be defined. For these reasons encoding of object data is not supported by Z.104. In rest of this paper legacy syntax is used.

3.2   Encoding on Paths

Z.104 focuses on the data communicated by signals. Although it was in the original study terms of reference to consider the encoding of any data item, a conclusion of the study was that there is no real need to define the encoding of data internal to the state machines of agents. Moreover, it is not every signal that needs its encoding defined: encoding is needed only for signals on communication paths that are normative, or between parts of a SDL model that are likely to be implemented separately. The normative paths are most likely to be connected to the environment of the SDL system, but may also be between parts of the SDL system. In the latter case, the normative paths would normally be the only way of passing information between the two parts of the SDL system. Z.104 therefore defines encoding as a property of communication paths: that is, encoding is defined for channels and gates.

One objective of encoding is to ensure that messages received on a communication path can be uniquely decoded. Therefore all the signals carried by the path have to be encoded. This means that it is a requirement that all the data types used for parameters of signals on the path are encodable: none of the parameters should have object data types.

When there is layer to layer communication, the data units received by a higher layer are often conveyed without change as a data item of the protocol data units of the lower layer. If the handler for each layer at one end of the protocol is modelled by a separate SDL agent, the data unit of the higher layer is usually passed to the lower layer in a signal. In this case, the data unit can be encoded in the higher layer and passed to the lower layer as a string. This string can then be passed by the lower layer to the lower layer handler at the other end of the protocol without change (except possibly encoding and decoding on the actual connection path). At the receiving end the string is passed back to the higher layer where it is decoded. To support the use of encoding and decoding in this way, two built-in functions are provided to encode a data unit and decode a data unit. Like encoding and decoding for communication paths, these functions are defined only for data types corresponding to a set of signals attached to a communication path.

4   The Extensions to SDL

The proposed standard does not change anything defined by the SDL-2000 standard, but instead adds to the grammar (syntax and semantics) of SDL. Names for encoding rules are introduced as the elements of an enumerated data type (see 4.1), communication paths are extended to denote the encoding required (see 4.2), and the semantics of input and output of signals is extended to include the encoding (see 4.3). A textual encoding is provided (see 4.4) as well as encoding based on ASN.1 (see 4.5). The language is extended to allow an encoded signal to be received as an encoded value (see 4.6), and encoded data to be output as the corresponding signal (see 4.7). Expressions are provided for explicit encoding or decoding (see 4.9).

4.1   Encoding Rules Data Type

To be able to refer to encoding rules, a data type is added to the Predefined data package of SDL. The names for language recognised encoding rules are defined as:

> **newtype** Encoding
>   **literals** text,
>   BER, CER, DER,
>   APER, UPER, CAPER, CUPER,
>   BXER, CXER, EXER;
> **endnewtype** Encoding;

where the set of values denote

text: text encoding rule (see 4.4) and produces a Charstring;
BER: Basic Encoding Rules of ASN.1 and produces an Octetstring;
CER: Canonical Encoding Rules of ASN.1 and produces an Octetstring;
DER: Distinguished Encoding Rules of ASN.1 and produces an Octetstring;
        and for each variant of the Packed Encoding Rules of ASN.1 (PER)[1]
APER: basic Aligned variant of PER and produces an Octetstring;
UPER: basic Unaligned variant of PER and produces an Bitstring;
CAPER: Canonical Aligned variant of PER and produces an Octetstring;
CUPER: Canonical Unaligned variant of PER and produces an Bitstring;

The most common PER variant is assumed to be APER, and for that reason a synonym is defined in the Predefined data package as follows:

> **synonym** PER Encoding = APER;

4.2   Communication Paths with Encoding

If a channel or gate is to have an encoding rule applied, this is specified after the gate or channel name as the keyword **encode** followed by the encoding

---

[1] The name(s) for PER were changed compared to earlier drafts - see section 5.

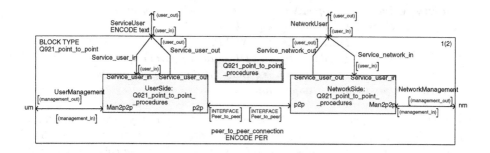

Fig. 1. Specifying encoding on paths

rule identifier. In the example based on ITU-T Rec. Q.921 in fig. 1, the gate *ServiceUser* has the *text* encoding rule and the channel *peer_to_peer_connection* has the *PER* encoding rule[2].

When a channel is connected to a gate, if they both have encoding rules these rules must be the same. If only one of them has an encoding rule, this rule applies to the communication path. The encoding for a communication can be specified on any channel or gate of the path. Typically encoding will be given for channels.

If a communication path is bi-directional the same encoding applies in each direction. To specify different encoding in each direction two paths have to be specified.

The Q.921 signals for service communication can be defined by:

> **signallist** user_in = DL_establish_req, DL_release_req,
> DL_data_req, DL_unit_data_req;
> **signal**   DL_establish_req, DL_release_req,
> DL_data_req(L3PDU), DL_unit_data_req(L3PDU);
> **signallist** user_out = DL_establish_ind, DL_establish_conf,
> DL_release_ind, DL_release_conf,
> DL_data_ind, DL_unit_data_ind;
> **signal**   DL_establish_ind, DL_establish_conf,
> DL_release_ind, DL_release_conf,
> DL_data_ind(L3PDU), DL_unit_data_ind(L3PDU);

Because encoding is invoked on the gate *ServiceUser*, there is an implicit **choice** data type definition for each direction that corresponds to the signals defined for the path. For the inward path of *ServiceUser* using the signals defined by *user_in*, the implicit data type is (italic used to emphasise it is *implied* and not written by the user):

---

[2] ITU-T Rec. Q.921 does not use either ASN.1 or PER encoding. Instead encoding is specified less formally by text and tables.

newtype *Implicit_Unique_Name /*not known by the user*/*
          choice *DL_establish_req NULL;*
                 DL_release_req   NULL;
                 DL_data_req   DL_data_req_paramtype;
                 DL_unit_data_req DL_unit_data_req_paramtype;
endnewtype *Implicit_Unique_Name;*

where *DL_data_req_paramtype* and *DL_unit_data_req_paramtype* are implicit data types with anonymous names defined for the parameters of the corresponding signals. Such a data type is always a **struct** even (as in these cases) the signal has only one parameter. The field names for selecting parameters are 1, 2, 3 etc.. For the *user_in* example, the implicit data types are (italic used to emphasise they are *implied* and not written by the user):

newtype *DL_data_req_paramtype /*not known by the user*/*
          struct *1 L3PDU* **optional***;*
endnewtype *DL_data_req_paramtype;*
newtype *DL_unit_data_req_paramtype /*not known by the user*/*
          struct *1 L3PDU* **optional***;*
endnewtype *DL_unit_data_req_paramtype;*

In the example, the two signals with parameters happen to carry the same information, but of course this would not normally be the case. All the structure fields are optional, because it is allowed (though not generally advisable) in SDL to omit some or all of the the actual parameters of a signal.

The implicit **choice** introduced above is used in conjunction with encoding and decoding expressions (see 4.9 below). These implicit types are described in this part of the paper for two reasons:

1. They are implied whenever **encode** is specified on a communication path, even though (as shown below) a user may not need to know they exist;
2. To keep the illustration of the implied definitions near to the associated definitions for *user_in* that would be given by a user.

4.3   Input and Output Using Encoding

If the intention is merely to ensure that the specified encoding is used on the communication, the implicit data types are not used, because the encoding and decoding takes place as part of the input and output of the signals. For example, the handling of signals on the gate *ServiceUser* within the **block type** *Q921_point_point_procedures* is illustrated in fig.2.

In the **block** *UserSide* the information received on gate *ServiceUser* is to be decoded from text. The relevant **choice** data type is given above and it can be assumed that a text stream received on the gate is a series of encoded choice values. If the encoding matches the choice for the signal *DL_establish_req*, this signal is decoded and if the process *point_to_point_procedures* is in the state *1_TEI_unassigned* the transition shown to *3_establish_awaiting_TEI* will be taken.

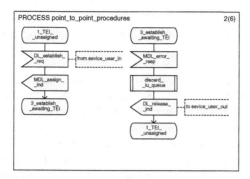

Fig. 2. Input and Output using encoding specified

In the state *3_establish_awaiting_TEI* of process *point_to_point_procedures* in **block** *UserSide*, when the signal *MDL_error_resp* is received the transition shown is taken and signal *DL_release_ind* is output. The signal is encoded as text and is conveyed to the destination connected to the gate *ServiceUser*.

Note that coding is not specified for the corresponding input and output in the **block** *Networkside*. This is because (like the channel from which inputs are received or to which outputs are sent) the encoding rule is dependent on the context in which a type is used (here **block type** *Q921_point_point_procedures*).

4.4   Text Encoding

The text encoding scheme specified is based on a scheme implemented in the Telelogic Tau tool. A single signal is encoded as a *Charstring* enclosed in { and } braces. The value encoded within these braces corresponds to a choice value for the implicit data type associated with the communication path. For example, for the incoming signals on gate *ServiceUser* the **choice** data type is defined above. If the intention is to convey the data as text to another component that is implemented using the text encoding scheme and the same definition of the interface between the components, there is no need for the user to know about the implied data type or the **choice** data type.

The text encoding rule is defined for *Boolean, Character, Charstring* (including equivalent ASN.1 data types such as *IA5String*), *Integer* (including *Natural* because it is a **syntype** based in *Integer*), *Real, Duration, Time, Bit, Bitstring* (denoted BIT STRING in ASN.1) and *Octet* because it is a **syntype** based on *Bitstring*), Octet and Octetstring (denoted OCTET STRING in ASN.1). The *Null* value of the data type *NULL* is a special case and is simply encoded as a 0 (zero) character.

The text encoding given for *Pid* allows six options: *ApplicationDefined, Integer, Octetstring, Bitstring, Charstring* and a composite {**struct** *identity Charstring; instance Natural*} option. SDL-2000 also has pid sorts that are subtypes of *Pid* and therefore use the same encoding. However, the encoding is not fully defined for *Pid*, so it is quite likely that encodings from one tool (or version of a tool) may be incompatible with those from a different tool. It would also be impractical to pass such values between separately generated systems or across normative interfaces. For these reasons the use of encoding for pid values should be avoided.

As well as these basic types defined in the SDL standard, text encoding is defined for the composite data types *String* (plus ASN.1 SEQUENCE OF data types because these map to *String*), *Array*, *Vector*, *Powerset* and *Bag* (plus ASN.1 SET OF data types because these map to *Bag*).

Finally text encoding is defined for the data type constructors **struct** (plus ASN.1 SEQUENCE and SET which both map to **struct**), **choice** (plus ASN.1 CHOICE which maps to **choice**), and enumerated types defined with **literals** (plus ASN.1 ENUMERATED which maps to the SDL enumerated types).

Rather than give all the encodings in this paper, an example is given. Assume that:

syntype L3PDU = Octetstring **endsyntype** L3PDU;

The encoding of the message for the input primitive *DL_data_req*('12ADCDEF'H) would be the character string:

{2,{'12ADCDEF'}}

where the whole signal is enclosed in braces. Commas are used to separate values. White space is ignored. The initial 2 denotes the value belongs to the third choice (first choice is zero) of the implicit **choice** data type: that is, in this case the choice *DL_data_req* of the type *Implicit_Unique_Name* above. The remainder of the signal gives actual signal structure value enclosed in another pair of braces after the comma. In this case there is only one element in the structure, an *Octetstring* which is simply encoded as a Character String representing the Octet string. If the structure has more fields, the values would be separated by commas. There will always be a pair of braces around signal parameters. If an actual signal parameter is omitted nothing is encoded. For example:

{2,{}}

represents a *DL_data_req* primitive with no actual parameter.

A special case is when the signal has no formal parameter. In this case the data type is *NULL*, which has only one value: *Null*. It therefore makes no difference if the value is included or not and it is simplest to omit it. For example, the text encoding below represents a sequence of three *DL_release_req* signals:

{1}
{1,}
{1,0}

4.5   Interfaces and Encoding Based on ASN.1

Encoding using ASN.1 defined encoding rules such as PER (packed encoding rules) can only be used if the set of signals carried by the communication path that invokes the encoding rule corresponds to an ASN.1 `CHOICE` definition. To correspond, the signal names have to be the same as the `CHOICE` selectors and data type of the selected choice for a name has to correspond to the signal parameters for the signal with that name. However, this can be easily achieved by importing the ASN.1 data type as an **interface**. In this case an **interface** of the same name with the signals equivalent to the `CHOICE` alternatives is implied.

For example, the package use area

USE Q921ASN1/INTERFACE Peer_to_peer;

attached to the diagram for the system or the **block type** *Q921_point_to_point*, implies the **interface** *Peer_to_peer*. If the Q921ASN module is defined as:

```
Q921ASN1
         DEFINITIONS AUTOMATIC TAGS ::=
BEGIN
        Peer-to-peer ::= CHOICE {
                i       Information,
                rr      ReceiveReady,
                rnr     ReceiveNotReady,
                rej     Reject,
                sabme   SetAsynchronousBalancedMode,
                dm      DisconnectedMode,
                ui      UnnumberedInfo,
                disc    Disconnect,
                ua      UnnumberedAck,
                frmr    FrameReject,
                xid     ExchangeIdCode}
- - the data types mentioned above such as Information
- - and ReceiveReady are defined here.
END
```

the implied SDL **interface** is (in italic as the user does write this):

interface *Peer_to_peer* {
    signal *i (Information) ,*
          rr (ReceiveReady) ,
          rnr (ReceiveNotReady) ,
          rej (Reject) ,
          sabme (SetAsynchronousBalancedMode) ,
          dm (DisconnectedMode) ,
          ui (UnnumberedInfo) ,
          disc (Disconnect) ,
          ua (UnnumberedAck) ,
          frmr (FrameReject) ,
          xid (ExchangeIdCode); }

A package use clause that imports an ASN.1 `CHOICE` data type therefore enables the ASN.1 to be used for signal definitions without writing any further SDL.

The ASN.1 CHOICE definition name can then be used as an **interface** identifier on a channel to define the set of signals conveyed by the channel in one direction. In fig.1 *Peer_to_peer* is used in both directions on channel *peer_to_peer_connection* and the *PER* encoding rule is associated with the channel.

4.6   Input of an Encoded Message Without Decoding

Instead of automatically decoding messages from communication paths with encoding, data can be received or stored in a format as if it had been encoded for a path with encoding. It is allowed to receive the message in a variable corresponding to the encoding data type: for example, *Charstring* if the encoding rule identifier is *text*, an *Octetstring* if the identifier is *BER*, and *Bitstring* if the identifier is *UPER*.

This form is specified by giving in an input the keyword **encode** then the name of a variable with the matching sort of data followed by the keyword **as** then the communication path the identity of the communication path with encoding. For example, a variable to hold the *Peer_to_peer* messages in encoded form would be a *Octetstring* such as:

dcl messagebits Octetstring;

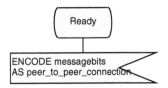

This input handles all the signals that can be received from the specified path, therefore it is not allowed to mention any of these signals in another save or input for the same state. The meaning of this construct is defined as first receiving the signal with decoding and assigning any signal parameters to implicit variables, then assigning the value of the received variables to the variable given (in this case *messagebits*). The definition is given this way so that no extension of the SDL semantic model was needed. However, it is expected that an implementation will skip the decoding and use of the intermediate implicit variables and assign the message directly to the variable with the path based data type. For example, if the actual message received was *i (ivalue)* where *ivalue* is a valid value expression of type *Information*, the result would be the same as

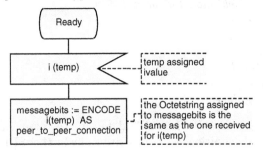

The meaning of the **encode** expression is explain in 4.9 below, which also explains the **decode** expression, that can be used to extract the signal information from the string (in this case the *Bitstring* in *messagebits*).

4.7   Output of an Encoded Message Without Encoding

One real benefit of not decoding received signals is that they can be output again without re-encoding[3]. This is the inverse of the corresponding input except an expression can be used instead of a variable. The expression has to be of the appropriate type for the encoding on the communication path: for example *Charstring* for *text*, *Octetstring* for *BER*, and *Bitstring* for *UPER*. There is a further constraint that the string if decoded must match one of the valid signals for output on the path, otherwise an *OutOfRange* exception is raised. The path is specified by a **via** path in the output. For example, to retransmit the message stored in *messagebits* the following construct is used

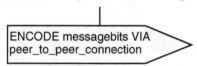

In a similar way to the corresponding input, output with encoding is defined in terms of first decoding the expression, and then outputting the appropriate signal. The following declaration and fragment illustrates this using the **decode** expression (described in 4.9 below).

dcl peermessage **as** peer_to_peer_connection;

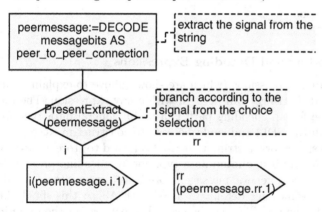

Note the *peermessage* declaration has the data type **as** *peer_to_peer_connection*. This refers to the implicit **choice** data type for the path (see 2 above). The **decode** expression produces a value of this type. Because *peermessage* is a **choice** type, it can store any message format. The *PresentExtract*(*peermessage*)

---

[3] For received signals to be re-output without re-encoding the signal list and encoding for the input and output channel must be the same, otherwise the encodings are (of necessity) different and re-encoding is essential.

expression returns a value that can be used in a decision or a comparison with the names of the choices: that is, *i, rr, rnr, rej, sabme, dm, ui, disc, ua, frmr* and *xid* in the example. It is therefore possible to selectively branch to different transition paths. In the above decision fragment, the decision is incomplete and should have alternatives to output each of the possible signals. In the output of signal i, the actual parameter value is field 1 of the **struct** for the choice *i* of the *peermessage* value. The signal is then re-encoded as it is output.

However, it should be emphasised that the above is only an illustration. In practice the requirement is not to actually decode and re-encode the string, but will output the string as is after checking that the string is a valid encoding of a signal for the path.

4.8   Output from a Choice Type

As an alternative to output of a message that is already encoded as a string, it is also allowed to use an expression that has the implicit choice data type corresponding to the signals that can be sent on the path. If the path is bi-directional the data type includes choices for signals for both directions, but a signal carried both directions has only one choice. Of course, for peer-to-peer protocols the same signals are usually carried in either direction. In this case the expression of the choice data type is simply given as the body of the ouput, for example if *peermessage* has been assigned a value for a signal, this can be output by:

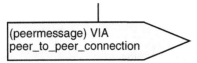

4.9   Explicit Encoding and Decoding Expressions

The **encode** and **decode** expressions (which are shown above to explain input and output using encoded strings) can be used within any expression. The implicit **choice** data type for an encoding path is a useful general data type for storing messages within the SDL, and could be used to construct messages.

The **decode** expression allows a string that has been used to store a message to be converted into the implicit **choice** data type for an encoding path. It is therefore possible to receive a generic message, store it as a string, then decode the string to examine the message details. Coupled with ASN.1 this should be a major improvement in the way SDL can be used. The pattern for the **decode** expression is:

> **decode** matching_string_expression **as** path_id;

The result of a **decode** expression is a value of the implicit **choice** data type for the path.

Similarly the **encode** expression allows the string value for an encoded message to generated at any point in the SDL. This can be stored and then an output with **encode** invoked to send whatever message had been previously stored. The pattern for the **encode** expression using a signal identity is:

encode signal_id(parameters) as path_id;

Alternatively the pattern for for the **encode** expression using an expression that corresponds to the implclit choice type is:

encode choice_expr as path_id;

where *choice_expr* is an expression matching the implicit **choice** data type for the path. Note that this avoids the need for decision branches to convert the choice values into encode strings. The result of a **encode** expression is a value of the encoding string data type for the path.

When using the **encode** and **decode** expressions, it is possible that no signals are actually sent on the path that has encoding specified. For example, this path might represent peer to peer communication at layer 3, whereas the messages are actually encoded and encapsulated in layer 2 messages. This does not appear to be a problem for the language, but might cause some warnings from tools that no signals are being sent on the path.

4.10   User Defined Encoding Rules

The set of encoding rules can be extended by defining a new data type *Encoding* that **inherits** from the Predefined data type *Encoding* **adding** a literal for each user defined encoding rule. The added literal name defines an encoding rule and can be used in the same way as the names such as *text* and *BER*.

However, in this case two procedures have to be supplied for each set of signals for which the encoding is used: one for encoding and the other for decoding. If the name of the added literal is *myrules* for use on the path *thegate* the procedure signatures correspond to:

encodemyrules(**as** thegate) -> Astring;
decodemyrules(Astring) -> **as** thegate;

where *Astring* is *Charstring*, *Octetstring* or *Bitstring*
and **as** thegate is used to denote the implicit choice type.

The actual procedures can be provided as application or tool specific built-in procedures, **external** procedures or procedures defined in SDL.

The procedures are called whenever encoding or decoding is required, such as from an **encode** or **decode** expression, or when an input or output takes place suing a path with the encoding rule.

5   Review Comments and Future Extensions

One objective of this paper for the SAM work shop was to obtain comment and feedback before the Z.104 is consented for approval. The author thanks the reviewers of the paper for their comments, many of which have been included. For example, it was noted there are four variants of PER (`basic` or `canonical` that are `aligned` or `unaligned`) and neither the original paper nor the contemporary draft of Z.104 stated which variant should be used. The actual names and most common variant are now agreed and are consistent with ASN.1 names.

A related issue to the PER variants is whether padding bits are part of the *Bitstring* for the encoding. When the result of encoding is an outermost value, it is required the number of bits in the outermost value is rounded up to a multiple of eight by adding bits set to zero if necessary. These padding bits are only needed for an outermost value, and for unaligned PER variants as far as the SDL *Bitstring* value is concerned these bits can be ignored and the length excludes the end padding. The padding bits can be simply added when needed.

One reviewer noted that the SDL Task Force has proposed a similar mechanism for the encoding of variables and a tool available supporting this mechanism. While there is no specific relationship between these developments, as Z.104 has been slowly evolving since 2000, it is encouraging that this group has reached a similar conclusion.

There were a number of comments that the list of encoding rule names should be extensible. After discussion the scheme outlined above in 4.10 was agreed and has been included in the standard for approval.

It was pointed out at the SAM-2004 workshop that there needs to be a mechanism for handling a failure to decode a message. Although at the workshop this was noted as an item needing attention, in fact this was already included in the January 2004 version though it had not been mentioned in the paper: a decode failure raises an *InvalidReference* exception which can be handled by the normal SDL exception handling mechanism.

Another issue raised was the use of a number to indicate a choice in the text encoding rules, rather than the identifier for the choice alternative. The use of an identifier is certainly a possibility, though usually there is some requirement for an encoding to be concise and in general a number will be shorter. In SDL there can be only one definition of the choice type, so the numbers must be unique. The main purpose of *text* encoding is to provide a textual form for easier handling by systems, rather than specifically to make the encoding readable. The use of a number or an identifier needs to be debated further before Z.104 is finalised.

It may be a common occurrence that input with **encode** is used so that the string can then be decoded and assigned to a variable of the implicit **choice** data type for an encoding path. This would probably be useful even if no encoding is specified for the path. A further extension would be to allow the input **encode** variable to have the **choice** data type and automatically do the conversion.

6   Conclusion

The process of presenting this paper at SAM-2004 was effective both in improving the quality of the paper and (more important) the standard itself.

The Recommendation consented for approval included only features of data encoding that had been clearly agreed at standards meetings. Additional language features that may be considered essential for effective use of the standard should be communicated to the author (as Z.104 editor) or to ITU-T Question N/17 (tsg17qn@itu). However the approval process has already started and it is expected that the standard will be fully approved by the time this paper is published.

SDL is already a large language, and it would be undesirable to add features to the language for which there is no real need. Obviously it would have been easier to justify the standard if there had been existing tool support from at least one (preferably more) tool vendor before starting the approval process. The current situation is that the standard is not supported by any tool. However, a repesentative of one tool vendor expressed intent to support the standard, so perhaps tool support will exist in a reasonable amount of time.

References

1. ITU-T: Recommendation T.50 (09/02), International Reference Alphabet (IRA) (Formerly International Alphabet No. 5 or IA5) - Information technology - 7-bit coded character set for information interchange. International Telecommunication Union, Geneva.
2. ITU-T: Recommendations X.680-683, Abstract Syntax Notation One (ASN.1). International Telecommunication Union, Geneva.[4]
3. ITU-T: Recommendations X.690-694, ASN.1 encoding rules. International Telecommunication Union, Geneva.[4]
4. ITU-T: Recommendation Z.100 (08/02), Specification and Description Language (SDL). International Telecommunication Union, Geneva.[4]
5. ITU-T: Z.105 (07/03), SDL combined with ASN.1 modules (SDL/ASN.1). International Telecommunication Union, Geneva.[4]
6. Reed, R.: Encoding of SDL Data. ITU-T Study Group 17 Study Period 2001-2004, Contribution COM17-C86-E, January 2004. Revised as Delayed Contribution COM17-D151-E July 2004, and further revised as TD3259 July 2004.
7. http://xml.coverpages.org/xml.html

---

[4] see http://www.itu.int/ITU-T/studygroups/com17/languages/ for ITU-T language Recommendations in PDF format.

SDL in a Changing World

Edel Sherratt

Department of Computer Science,
University of Wales Aberystwyth,
Penglais, Aberystwyth, Ceredigion SY23 3DB, Wales UK
eds@aber.ac.uk
http://users.aber.ac.uk/eds/

Abstract. SDL has provided robust and adaptable modelling capabilities through many developments in the world of telecommunications. In recent years, however, that world has undergone deeper and more frequent paradigm shifts than hitherto. This paper briefly summarises the emergence of grid computing, pervasive computing and mobile and ad-hoc communications. It explores developments in modelling, as reflected by the emergence of SDL-2000 as an ITU standard, and the subsequent publication of UML 2.0. It considers the relationship between SDL and UML, including establishment of SDL as a UML profile, work by the MODA-TEL project and the formation of the ETSI specialist task force 250. It concludes with suggestions for specific tasks in the development of the next revision of SDL. This does not represent any new development for SDL, nor does it present any new applications of SDL. Rather it focuses on the forces affecting the evolution of SDL, and the opportunities to be grasped and challenges to be faced.

1 Introduction

The Specification and Description Language (SDL), together with Message Sequence Charts (MSC) and the related ITU-T notations and languages have provided a robust and adaptable modelling formalism particularly well suited to specification, design and simulation in the telecommunications domain over many years. In recent years, however, the development of new forms of telecommunications and networking, and the convergence of software engineering with telecommunications have presented new challenges.

The following sections briefly review some recent trends in communications and networking, and explore parallel developments in SDL and the related ITU-T languages, and in UML, specifically focusing on the emergence of SDL 2000 [12] and UML 2.0 [16].

Following a discussion of directions that SDL might follow, the paper concludes with some suggestions for specific tasks to be addressed in the development of the next release of SDL.

D. Amyot and A.W. Williams (Eds.): SAM 2004, LNCS 3319, pp. 96–105, 2005.

2   Recent Trends in Communications and Networking

Recent trends in communications and networking are giving rise to serious challenges to our capacity to specify and describe the systems we wish to develop. This section gives a brief overview of three of the most active areas in this domain: Grid Computing, Ubiquitous and Pervasive Computing, and Ad-hoc networking. It draws together common themes that arise from these kinds of communications, and that place specific requirements on specification and modelling formalisms.

2.1   Grid Computing

A computing grid is essentially a pool of resources that can be used as required by different applications. Grid computing is a highly active area and has led to the draft specification of an open grid services infrastructure [23], as well as to numerous activities, including the Welsh e-science centre [24], with its focus on distributed service oriented computing to support the sciences.

One of the more recent definitions of a grid is given in the form of a checklist [8]:

> *A Grid is a system that*
> 1. *coordinates resources that are not subject to centralized control,*
> 2. *using standard, open, general-purpose protocols and interfaces,*
> 3. *to deliver nontrivial qualities of service.*

This constitutes a remarkably succinct definition of what telecommunications has been working towards since the foundation of the CCITT in 1865!

The demand for shared access to resources that are not subject to centralized control is a key requirement in modelling grid computing. Grid resources are essentially active elements, which can be accessed as required, and whose usage is monitored and managed according to a variety of mutually independent policies.

2.2   Ubiquitous and Pervasive Computing

From an early vision [1], ubiquitous and pervasive computing have now become an everyday reality. We have personal digital assistants, mobile telephones, smart vehicles, and even devices that respond directly to biosignals [21].

Ubiquitous computing has implications for both cultural [2] and physical environments. This area is developing rapidly, with an emerging technical emphasis on Java-based solutions [22, 14].

The modelling and specification requirements for ubiquitous computing include a need to describe an enormous variety of different kinds of signal, the possibility to define interworking communities of different kinds of active entity, and a host of natural-artificial modes of interaction. The ongoing drive towards greater interworking of disparate devices also means that pervasive computing entails networking and communications.

2.3   Ad-Hoc Networks

Ad-hoc networks allow mobile hosts to communicate with each other whenever they are close enough to do so. The hosts are assumed to have similar transmission power and computation capacities [11], and can communicate directly, or through multihop routing.

Modelling demands implied by ad-hoc networks include the need to be able to simulate and compare different routing strategies. For example, appropriate simulation can help compare strategies based on a virtual backbone with those based on a predefined backbone, and strategies that make use of specialized nodes whose purpose is to maintain a database of node locations with strategies where the task of maintaining up-to-date routing tables for portions of the ad-hoc network is distributed across all nodes.

2.4   Common Demands

Bringing together the concepts of grid computing, ad-hoc networks and pervasive computing leads to communications where

- nodes are not subject to centralized control, and can form networks on an ad-hoc basis,
- use of standard, open, general-purpose protocols and interfaces is expected,
- many kinds of devices and interaction are to be found, and
- nontrivial qualities of service are required.

Systems like this place specific demands on modelling formalisms. For example, in addition to the usual need to model at various levels of abstraction, and according to various views or aspects, it must also be possible to

- model active entities,
- model exchange of signals and data where the communications infrastructure is itself subject to dynamic reconstruction.

As the next section discusses, the ITU-T languages, including SDL, address these issues, and they have also been very effectively tackled by the UML.

3   Specification and Description Languages

3.1   The ITU-T Languages

The ITU-T Z-series recommendations cover a range of languages and software issues for communication systems. As well as the specification and description language, SDL (recommendation Z.100), the series includes Message Sequence Charts, MSC (Z.120), the ITU object definition language (Z.130), Testing and Test Control Notation version 3, TTCN-3 (Z.140, 141, 142), User Requirements Notation, URN (Z.150), and many others.

Between them, these specifications address current and emerging modelling needs identified via the ITU working groups.

SDL has evolved from its first version, released in 1976, through a series of revisions, of which the most recent major revision is SDL 2000 [4, 17], the ITU-T standard Z.100 [12].

The fundamental concepts of SDL 96 [5] are 'system', 'block' and 'process'. An SDL specification is a structured as a hierarchy of blocks and processes. At the lowest level, processes are described as communicating state machines, which can send and receive signals and whose behaviour in response to external signals is formally defined. Processes are combined into blocks, blocks into higher level blocks, and at the top level, the whole is combined as a system. The hierarchy is quite strict – it is not possible to include a process and a block within the same diagram.

In SDL 2000 [4], the concept of 'agent' is introduced, where an agent can be a system, or a block or a process. An agent may contain variables, procedures, a state machine and other agents. A block agent can contain process or block agents [17], while a process agent can only contain process agents. The active elements (agents and state machine) within a block agent execute concurrently and asynchronously [17], while active elements in a process are interleaved with atomicity at the transition level [4].

The capacity to model active elements in this way represents an important advantage to anyone wishing to model the kinds of network and communications that are emerging today. SDL 96 has already proved equal to the challenges of modelling mobile protocols [3], reactive systems [15], and pervasive heterogeneous environments [18], and were suitable tool support available, there would be further benefits to be derived from the facilities of SDL 2000. These would provide enhanced capacities for describing and specifying independent interacting entities.

SDL 2000 also provides facilities for structuring and abstraction. These include the concept of type and interface. Types can form inheritance hierarchies. For example, agent type has subtypes system type, block type and process type. Types can be abstract, so that they have no instances, but only subtypes. Interfaces are used to group signals, remote procedures and variables, and also exceptions – in fact, any of the information that can be exchanged between agents [4].

Further features include packages, which form nested libraries of elements that can be (re)used, and gates, which appear in block type specifications and model the connectivity required by block instances. This last is highly suitable for modelling plug-and-play, a fundamental requirement for dynamic networking environments.

3.2   The UML 2.0 Family of Languages

The Unified Modelling Language (UML) provides a rich array of modelling notations and formalisms for describing object oriented systems. UML is defined in several layers, with each level providing rules for defining the next more concrete level. The most recent set of specifications, define UML 2.0 [16] using a four-layer metamodel hierarchy.

The most concrete level, M0, contains run-time instances of the model elements used by an engineer to specify and describe a system being designed.

Level M1 defines the classes or types of model elements used in a model. For example, level M1 might contain class definitions that act as templates for level M0 run-time instances. These definitions are defined by an engineer in order to specify a system under design. They define how their instances will be created and destroyed, and how their instances will behave, and it is in this sense that level M1 acts as a metamodel for level M0.

Level M2 includes the rules for creating models using the UML 2 constructs. Level M2 provides the rules for creating the different kinds of diagrams used to define level M1 classes or types, and so acts as a metamodel for M1.

Level M3 provides rules for level M2 rules. It can be thought of as a meta-model for a metamodel – that is, a meta-metamodel. The Meta Object Facility of UML (MOF) is an example of a level M3 meta-metamodel.

The primary purpose of this layering is to allow the creation of families of languages that can be used together. For example, the Object Constraint Language (OCL) has now been removed from the UML core, and has been redefined as a 'cousin' of UML that can be used with UML specifications.

3.3   Dynamic Modelling with UML 2.0

The engineer using UML is primarily concerned with the kinds of diagrams that need to be drawn to specify a system, and the ways that diagrams are organised into views, each providing a different abstraction of the system under design. There are many different kinds of diagram in UML, of which the most widely used are use-case diagrams and static diagrams illustrating the relationships between interfaces and classes. However, in the current context, the facilities provided by UML 2.0 for real-time modelling are of most interest.

These include activity diagrams, which have been redeveloped in UML 2.0 to model dynamic behaviour using a semantics based on Petri Nets. Active classes and objects can also be modelled, and behavioural state machines and protocol state machines respectively provide the means to model the complex life cycle of an object and the environment in which the active entity resides together with the interfaces to that environment.

The facilities for dynamic modelling in UML 2.0 are derived from ROOM [20] (Real-Time Object Oriented Modelling) and are also heavily influenced by Harel state charts, which came to UML via Rumbaugh's Object Management Technique (OMT) and, more recently, by SDL.

3.4   SDL and UML

Recent years have seen the convergence of SDL and UML. In particular, the ITU-T recommendation Z.109 [13] provides a profile that maps UML 1.5 directly to SDL, and enables the integrated use of UML and SDL.

A further real-time profile, compatible with the OMG Profile for Performance Scheduling and Real-time, was also developed by the IST project OMEGA, and adapted to SDL [10].

The Moda-Tel Project (IST-2001-37785) [9], has also reviewed a broad set of ITU-T languages in the light of the OMG Model Driven Architecture (MDA).

A UML 2.0 profile for communication systems is also currently under development by the ETSI Specialist Task Force 250 [7]. The intention is that this profile will be based on, but not limited to SDL, and will be of interest to users of SDL, MSC and UML.

The release of UML 2.0 has implications for the positioning of SDL with respect to UML. In particular, because UML is no longer specified in terms of UML, but in terms of the more abstract MOF, it is now possible to extend the UML either by using stereotypes [1], which can be collected into a profile, or by creating a new instance of the MOF [6].

Extending UML by means of the profiles mechanism provides a clear route from the newly defined stereotypes back to the underlying metamodel. It is a relatively lightweight approach to extension that facilitates development of variants of UML.

Extending by means of the MOF results in a first class extension – a new member of the UML family of languages. This allows the developers of the modelling language to focus more clearly on issues of concern in that language. For example, OCL is clearly focused on constraints, and is not sidetracked into other modelling issues addressed by UML.

The decision to remain with the profiling approach, updating it to reflect changes in UML, or to move to a full blown MOF extension is not obvious in the case of SDL and the other ITU-T languages. Because there is a clear overlap between the issues addressed by the ITU-T languages and those addressed by UML, profiling represents a convenient way to specialize UML for use by developers who want or need to use SDL and its related ITU-T languages.

However, that same overlap means that one could legitimately ask why the specialization is needed in the first place. One form of the argument centers on the desirability of conformance with the OMG recommendation that models intended for use in conjunction with the model driven architecture should conform to the UML core, as opposed to the desirability of conformance with ITU-T standards for languages.

Although this argument would not be resolved by development of a first class MOF extension for the ITU-T languages, such an extension would certainly make the ITU-T languages more visible to the UML user community, and would clarify the advantages of the ITU-T standardisation processes.

4   Specifying and Modelling New Kinds of Communications

However, the real strengths of the SDL family will become most apparent when the advantages of these languages for tackling current challenges in telecom-

---

[1] A stereotype extends an existing element of UML. For example, the UML metamodel can be extended by extending a metaclass to produce a more specialized metaclass.

munications become apparent. In particular, their benefits for modelling loose collaborations of active elements that form ad-hoc networks in a pervasive way must be brought forward.

Both SDL 2000 and UML 2.0 provide facilities for specifying active entities, but both, at least implicitly, assume a static physical implementation environment.

This can be overcome by modelling the environment itself as an active entity, although that is arguably counterintuitive, and certainly goes against the implied philosophy of the UML 2.0 deployment diagrams.

However, SDL 2000 and the other ITU-T languages, have two major advantages when it comes to modelling new kinds of communications:

− they are primarily designed for the communications domain, and
− they are directly influenced by work of the ITU study groups.

5   Directions for SDL

SDL is currently due for a major revision, and it is important that this revision takes account of external developments as well as of the more introspective desire to perfect SDL as a modelling language.

External factors to be taken into account include:

− the emergence and growth of new kinds of communications devices and networks,
− the release of UML 2.0, and the position of SDL in the UML family of languages.

Regarding new kinds of communications, the work of the ITU study groups must be taken into account. Particular attention needs to be given to the work of study groups 11 (protocols) and 13 (multi-protocol and IP), the special study group (SSG) whose area of concern is International Mobile Telecommunications (IMT) and, of course group 17, the study group that deals with the ITU-T family of languages.

Regarding UML 2.0, the implications of the emerging profile [7] for SDL should be taken into account. It will also be important to consider and debate the desirability or otherwise of creating a first-class instance of the MOF to define SDL and its related languages as a fully distinct set of modelling formalisms related to UML.

Internal factors affecting the directions for SDL include:

− economical disincentives and technical challenges that discouraged tool developers from providing full support for SDL 2000,
− current work on identifying the simplest useful subset of SDL [19].

Following the release of SDL 2000, it became clear that this was a challenging language to support. This led to the formation of the SDL Task Force, whose chief aim was to identify the simplest useful subset of SDL. One question we should ask is whether or not this subset should form an SDL core, whose extensions constitute full SDL. This is not a trivial issue, since it is not clear at present whether or not the constructs in the proposed subset will in fact have a semantic definition compatible with full SDL.

This technical challenge was exacerbated by developments in the tool vendors market, which effectively removed the incentives to develop support for SDL 2000.

UML 2.0 is also a large and complex family of notations, and it is possible that the technical challenge of developing tools to support UML 2.0 will likewise prove too great. However the syntactic definitions required for tool interoperability have been put in place, and this should facilitate the development of tools.

Moreover, UML has a high visibility, and a very large community, which will tend to encourage efforts to overcome any challenges posed by the notations.

6   Conclusion

Overall, SDL has proved equal to meeting the challenges posed by developments in telecommunications and other areas involving networks and distribution over many years, and it possesses great strengths derived from the structured way in which its evolution is agreed amongst interested parties.

Nonetheless, complacency is not appropriate, as UML now has sufficient formality to present a real challenge in the world of modelling and specification, and it also has a large and diverse user base.

Various forces are affecting the whole area of specification and modelling, and should be taken into account during the coming revision of SDL. Some suggestions for specific activities in this work are indicated below.

1. Develop exemplars involving grid computing, pervasive computing and ad-hoc networking for use in evaluating new SDL revisions.
2. Review the output ITU study groups, with particular attention to groups leading work in protocols, mobility and other emerging areas.
3. Evaluate the relative merits of representing SDL and the related ITU-T languages as a UML profile as opposed to deriving a new MOF instance to represent them. This is a substantial and important undertaking.
4. Look into the possibility of defining a kernel SDL, analogous to the UML core, which comprises the smallest useful subset of SDL, together with analogous subsets of the other ITU languages.
5. Conduct a serious market study between potential tool users and tool vendors to develop feasible proposals for real tools to support the next version of SDL.

These represent a formidable and challenging set of tasks, but they also represent a fine opportunity to retain the position of SDL, MSC and the related ITU-T languages as the premier specification, description, modelling and simulation formalisms for many years to come.

References

1. Abowd, G. D., Mynatt, E. D.: Charting Past, Present and Future Research in Ubiquitous Computing. ACM Transactions on Computer-Human Interaction, vol. 7, no. 1, March 2000, 29–58.
2. Benford, S., Davies, N., Gaver, B.: Art, Design, and Entertainment in Pervasive Environments. Guest Editors' Introduction, Pervasive Computing, IEEE (2004).
3. Colás, J., Pérez, J. M., Poncela, J., Entrembasaguas, J. T.: Implementation of UMTS Protocol Layers for the Radio Access Interface. Edel Sherratt (Ed.) Telecommunications and Beyond: The Broader Applicability of SDL and MSC. Volume 2599 of Lecture Notes in Computer Science, Springer (2003), 74–89.
4. Doldi, L.: SDL Illustrated: Visually design executable models. Laurent Doldi 2001, ISBN 2-9516600-0-6, available through the SDL forum society or directly from the author.
5. Ellsberger, J., Hogrefe, D., Sarma, A.: SDL: Formal Object-oriented Language for Communicating Systems. Prentice Hall (1997).
6. Eriksson, H.-E., Penker, M., Lyons, B., Fado, D.: UML 2 Toolkit. Wiley Publishing Inc., Indianapolis, Indiana, OMG Press (2004).
7. ETSI Specialist Task Force 250: Methods for Testing and Specification (MTS); UML 2.0 profile for communication systems. Technical Report DTR/MTS-00085 to appear at http://portal.etsi.org/stfs/mts/STF250.asp
8. Foster, I.: What is the Grid? A three point checklist. GRIDToday, July 20, 2002, available at http://www.globus.org/research/papers.html
9. Gavras, A. (Ed.): Considerations on telecom modelling languages. MODA-TEL project IST-2001-37785, Deliverable D3.add2, Moda-Tel consortium (2003).
10. Graf, S., Ober, I.: A Real-Time Profile for UML and How to Adapt It to SDL, R. Reed, J. Reed (Eds.) SDL 2003: System Design, Volume 2708 of Lecture Notes in Computer Science, Springer (2003) 55–76.
11. Haas, Z. J., Liang, B.: Ad Hoc Mobility Management with Uniform Quorum Systems, IEEE/ACM Transactions on Networking, vol. 7, no. 2, April 1999.
12. ITU-T: Recommendation Z.100 (08/02), Specification and Description Language (SDL), International Telecommunication Union, Geneva (2002).
13. ITU-T: Recommendation Z.109 (11/99), SDL combined with UML. International Telecommunication Union, Geneva (1999).
14. JSLEE and the Jain Initiative Web pages. http://java.sun.com/products/jain
15. Metzger, A., Queins, S.: Model-based Generation of SDL Specifications for the Early Prototyping of Reactive Systems. Edel Sherratt (Ed.) Telecommunications and Beyond: The Broader Applicability of SDL and MSC. Volume 2599 of Lecture Notes in Computer Science, Springer (2003), 158–169.
16. OMG: UML 2 working documents (2004), available from http://www.omg.org/technology/documents/modeling_spec_catalog.htm#UML
17. Reed, R.: SDL 2000 for New Millenium Systems. Free for download at http://www.itu.int/itudoc/itu-t/com17/tutorial/78255.html
18. Schaible, P., Gotzhein, R.: Development of Distributed Systems with SDL by Means of Formalized APIs. R. Reed, J. Reed (Eds.) SDL 2003: System Design, Volume 2708 of Lecture Notes in Computer Science, Springer (2003) 317-334.
19. SDL Task Force: SDL'03 Task Force Enhanced Subset of SDL (draft). http://www.sdl-task-force.org/library.htm
20. Selic, B., Gullekson, G., Ward, P.: Real-Time Object-Oriented Modelling. Wiley and Sons, New York USA (1994).

21. Stanford, V.: Biosignals Offer Potential for Direct Interfaces and Health Monitoring. Editor's Introduction, Pervasive Computing: Applications, IEEE, January-March 2004.
22. Tsuei, T.-G., Sung, C.-T.: Ubiquitous Information Services with JAIN Platform. Mobile Networks and Applications, 8, 655-662, Kluwer (2003).
23. Tuecke, S., Czajkowski, K., Foster, I., Frey, J., Graham, S., Kesselman, C., Maguire, T., Sandholm, T., Vanderbilt, P., Snelling, D. (Eds.): Open Grid Services Infrastructure (OGSI) Version 1.0. Global Grid Forum Draft Recommendation, 6/27/2003.
24. Welsh e-Science Centre/Canolfan e-Wyddoniaeth Cymru: http://www.wesc.ac.uk/

Early Validation of Deployment and Scheduling Constraints for MSC Specifications

Ferhat Khendek, Christophe Lohr, Li Xin Wang, Xiao Jun Zhang, and
Tong Zheng

ECE Department - Concordia University,
1455, de Maisonneuve W., Montreal (QC), Canada H3G 1M8
{khendek, lohr, lxwang, xjzhang, zhengt}@ece.concordia.ca

Abstract. Message Sequence Charts are widely used for the specification of functional requirements, including timing requirements. These requirements can be validated and used as input for the design stage, and subsequent phases. Deployment constraints are generally taken into account at the implementation stage only. These constraints may conflict and invalidate some of the functional/behavioral requirements already validated at a high level of abstraction in the requirement phase. In this paper, we propose to take into account some deployment constraints at the very early stage of development and check if the system functional requirements will not be impossible to meet at later stages when constraints like communication channel delays, process assignment to CPUs, and scheduling policies are taken into account.

1   Introduction

Messages Sequence Charts (MSC) [11] are widely used for the specification of functional/behavioral requirements in terms of scenarios. The MSC specification of a target system is usually used as input to design, which can be automatically generated from the MSCs or validated against the MSCs. The design specification generally given in SDL [12] or other design languages is used as input for generating the target system code, either manually or using commercial code generators. The deployment constraints of the target system are usually taken into account at a very late stage of the development process, i.e., low level design or implementation. These constraints may invalidate and conflicts with functional requirements, such as timing requirements. In this paper, we look at the problem of validating functional requirements while taking into account very early certain deployment constraints, such as communication channel delays and scheduling policies. The work presented in this paper builds on previous contributions [22] and tackles the issue of deployment constraints. In other words, our goal is to validate the MSC while taking into account more constraints than the usual functional/timing requirements.

For a quick illustration purpose, let us consider, for instance, the example in Fig.1. Part (a) of the figure describes functional requirements, while part

D. Amyot and A.W. Williams (Eds.): SAM 2004, LNCS 3319, pp. 106–121, 2005.

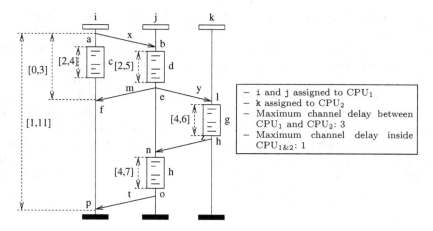

Fig. 1. (a) Functional requirements and (b) Sample deployment constraints

(b) states certain deployment constraints. One may notice the extension to the action box with time constraints, which intuitively mean a time duration for the action box. This can also be interpreted as a delay between the first action and the last action in the box. This extension is not the main purpose of this work and will be discussed briefly later on. Functional requirements specified by the MSC in Fig.1a can be checked for consistency using the approach introduced in [22] for instance. This MSC is (logically) consistent. The next question that can be asked is: Can these functional requirements still be satisfied by a system in the context of the deployment constraints given in Fig.1b?

As we can see, one deployment constraint assigns instances i and j to the same CPU. Therefore, action box c (with time constraint $[2, 4]$) and action box d (with time constraint $[2, 5]$) have to be executed in a sequence. The first action box requires a minimum of 2 units of time; the other one also requires a minimum of 2. Assuming we cannot interrupt action box execution, a minimum of 4 units of time is needed for the execution of both action boxes in sequence. However, the constraint $[0, 3]$ in the instance i between the sending of message x and reception of message m requires that both action boxes are executed within a maximum of 3 units of time. The MSC is not anymore consistent when these deployment constraints are taken into account. We also say the functional requirements cannot be met under the stated deployment constraints.

Our goal in this paper is to answer the aforementioned question. We proceed in a stepwise manner. For a given MSC specification, we first check the (logical) consistency of time constraints in the MSC as introduced in [22]. This is a high level validation assuming processes will have all the resources they need for their execution, communication channels are instantaneous, etc. In the second step, for a (logically) consistent MSC, we take into account the communication channel delays and check the consistency of the functional requirements in light of these delays. In the third step of the approach, we assign processes instances to CPUs for execution and check for the feasibility of such an assignment with respect to the functional requirements. For a given number of process instances assigned to a CPU, the previous step gives, whenever feasible, a schedule. This schedule does not take into account any scheduling policy, which we integrate in the last phase of our approach where an explicit scheduling algorithm is taken into account.

The paper is organized as follows. Our approach for checking the consistency of timed MSCs is briefly reviewed in Section 2. Section 3 discusses the handling of communication channel delays. Section 4 presents an algorithm for finding, whenever possible, a schedule when two or more processes are assigned to the same CPU, without following any specific scheduling algorithm. Section 5 presents early results for finding, whenever possible, a schedule for a predefined scheduling policy. Section 6 discusses briefly related work. We conclude our work in the last section.

2   Consistency of Timed MSCs

Zheng, in his thesis [22], addresses the validation of timed MSC specifications with absolute and relative time constraints for the description of quantified timing requirements. The validation is necessary to ensure that an MSC specification does not contain semantic errors, such as timing conflicts and inconsistencies caused by time constraints. Intuitively, an MSC is consistent if all its events could be executed with the satisfaction of their time constraints and causal orders. Algorithms have been designed for checking the consistency.

2.1   MSC Action Box with Time Constraints

MSC defines *action boxes*. Action boxes are drawn as rectangles along instances (see Fig.2). Action boxes may contain formal or informal actions. Our extension allows for expressing durations of action boxes. An action box has a *starting* event and an *ending* event. A time constraint between these two events expresses a duration of the action box. It can also be seen as relative time constraint between the starting event and the ending one. This second interpretation will allow for reusing the algorithms in [22] without modifications.

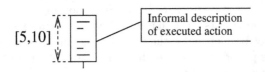

Fig. 2. Action box with a time constraint

We still assume reception or sending events are instantaneous, i.e., do not consume time. In this paper, we also assume that action boxes cannot be preempted, i.e., every action box is executed from the starting event to the ending event without any interruption.

2.2   Checking Time Consistency

Here we briefly review the algorithm for checking time consistency [22] of a basic MSC (bMSC).

Event Order Table. Partial orders described by an MSC may be represented as an *event order table*. Such a table is indexed by the events of the MSC and contains the information about event precedence. For instance if event a precedes event b, the cell indexed by a and b will be set to *True* (T). Of course when this specific cell is set to T, the cell indexed by b and a will be set to *False* (F).

First the table is filled with the explicit precedences such as precedence between sending and a reception of a message, and for events along an instance as shown in Fig.3b. Then, the transitive closure is determined as shown in Fig.3c. Because an MSC defines a partial order, some entries remain with no value. Notice that the transitive closure will detect inconsistencies. MSC depicted in Fig.3d for instance is inconsistent.

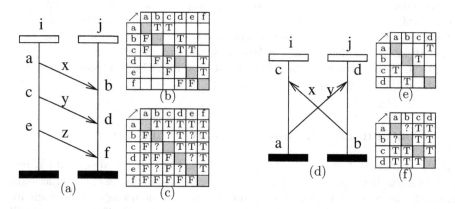

Fig. 3. Event order table and transitive closure

Distance Graph and Reduced Absolute Time Constraint. Deciding if an MSC is time consistent is equivalent to solving the simple temporal problem in *distance graph* [8]. A bMSC can be seen as a *distance graph*, where events are represented by nodes and causal orders between events are represented by directed edges labeled by relative time constraints between events. If a precedes b there exists an edge $a \rightarrow b$ labeled by the upper bound of the time constraint between a and b, and another one is $b \rightarrow a$ labeled by the negative of the lower bound of the time constraint. A special event (node) e_0 is added to the graph; it occurs causally before all other events, and it occurs at time zero. So absolute time constraints can be translated as relative time constraints between events and e_0.

An MSC and its corresponding distance graph are shown in Fig.4.

The simple temporal problem is to decide if each node can be assigned to a value such that the time constraints between nodes are all satisfied. If such

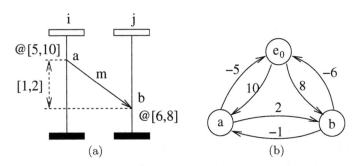

Fig. 4. An MSC and its corresponding distance graph

assignments exist, the associated MSC is consistent. As discussed in [8], the consistency can be decided by using the Floyd-Warshall algorithm to compute all pairs of shortest paths in a corresponding distance graph. If there are no cycles with a negative cost in the distance graph, then the MSC is consistent. If an MSC is consistent, a unique interval for each node e can be obtained, in which each value can be an assignment to e such that the graph is consistent. Such an interval is defined as a *reduced absolute time constraint*.

For instance, events of example in Fig.4 have for reduced absolute time constraint: $a@[5,7]$, $b@[6,8]$.

3   Communication Channel Delay Constraints

At the deployment stage, the low level design has to be mapped into a real architecture. Communicating instances, assigned to CPUs, exchange messages through physical communication channels. These communications channels introduce delays. Therefore, it is important to know very early if those delays will not invalidate the functional properties already checked.

A communication channel delay is generally given as an interval, with a minimum and a maximum delay. The minimum being always smaller than the maximum delay, therefore we only have to worry about the later in our approach. Therefore, a communication channel is always characterized by its maximum delay in the rest of this paper.

As mentioned earlier, at this stage we assume we checked the functional requirements as discussed in Sec.2. The distance graph produced in Sec.2 contains shortest paths, and therefore gives relative time values $[m, M]$ on edges from *send(i,j,x)* to *receive(i,j,x)* events, for all instances i and j and for all messages x. Therefore, we only have to check if a channel delay D related to instances i and j is lower or equal to M. If not, then the MSC cannot be deployed with such a communication delay because functional requirements will not be satisfied.

For instance, the MSC in Fig.5 states that relative constraint between the sending of message m and its reception is $[1, 2]$ units of time, which means that message m should be delivered to instance j within $[1, 2]$ unit of time

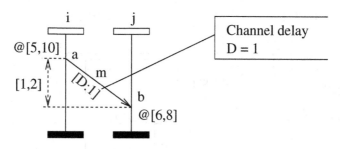

Fig. 5. Channel delay constraint

after its sending. Consistency of this MSC has been checked previously, and corresponding distance graph is given in Fig.4b. Assume the communication channel between instances i and j may take a maximum of 1 unit of time to convey the message. In this case, the functional requirements are still satisfied. However, if the communication channel can take up to 3 units of time, the functional requirements are not satisfied anymore.

The algorithm 1, given below, checks again the functional requirements taking into account the communication channel delays. It proceeds as follows: relative time constraints between sending and receiving events of each message are the shortest paths in the distance graph as computed in Sec.2. The upper bound is then compared to the corresponding communication channel delay.

Algorithm 1.

Let $\mathcal{E}$ be the set of directed constraint graph edges.
For each edge $\{send(i,j,x), receive(i,j,x), [m,M]\} \in \mathcal{E}$ loop
  If $D > M$ then
    Abort("System not deployable!")
  End if
End loop

4   Processes Distribution

At deployment stage, processes (or instances) of a bMSC are assigned to CPUs. Also, instances located on one given CPU have to share the CPU resources, and are not anymore running in true concurrency. This may have an impact on the functional requirements. Some functional time constraints may be violated, depending on the order chosen to run instances/events by the CPU. To check this, we have to try all possible serializations of events/actions/instances running on the same CPU. Serializing events means adding new order between unordered events of a bMSC (just a part of a bMSC) that respects specified orders. Once all events running on a CPU are totally ordered (e.g., serialized), we have again to check the time consistency of this order using the algorithm presented in Sec.2.2. For one CPU (and a set of instances assigned to this CPU), we have to explore

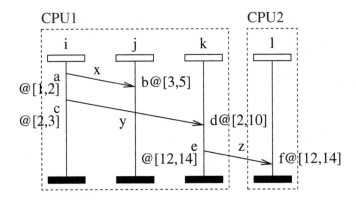

Fig. 6. Instances distribution and events serialization

all the possible serializations. If there exists at least one consistent serialization, we say the set of instances assigned to this CPU is schedulable in this CPU and we have a schedule of their events/actions. If we have the same for all the CPUs, then we say the functional requirements can still be satisfied in the given CPU assignment.

Let us consider the example in Fig.6, where instances i, j and k are assigned to *CPU1* and instance l assigned to *CPU2*. *CPU1* has to execute $\{a, b, c, d, e\}$ events one after another. Following the existing order, event b can run before or after c, and event b can run before or after d. According to time constraints, event b should run after c. To give a formal answer, we have to build every possible serialization of events and check its consistency.

In this section we propose an algorithm to build possible serializations of events. The idea of this algorithm is to try to fill "undetermined" entries in the event order table, i.e., replace '?' symbols by *True* or *False* (and replace their symmetrical entries by *False* or *True*). Events are totally ordered when corresponding rows and columns do not contain any "undetermined" entry. Intuitively, Algorithm 2 given below, works as follows:

1. First, find from the beginning to the end of the table each undetermined ordered pair of events belonging to the CPU under consideration, and replace it with *"True/False"* and *"False/True"*.
2. Then, calculate the partial order transitive closure to create a new event order table according to the changed condition.
3. Last, if the new event order table has no undetermined orders, then the new event order table is transferred into distance graph, and the Floyd-Warshall algorithm is used to check time consistency; or else, recursively call itself until there is no any undecided ordered event.

Developers have to decide for the CPU assignment. One might also specify communication channel delays inside and between CPUs. The information may be provided as follows:

- Let $\mathcal{P}$ be the set of available CPUs.
- Let $\mathcal{I}$ be the set of bMSC instances (or processes).
- Let $\Phi : \mathcal{I} \to \mathcal{P}$ be the instance distribution function that associate a CPU for each instance.
- Let D be the time domain.
- Let $\Delta : \mathcal{P} \times \mathcal{P} \to D$ be the function that gives maximum channel delays between each pair of CPUs.
- Let $\delta : \mathcal{P} \to D$ be the function that gives maximum channel delays inside each CPU.

Algorithm 2.
Let N be the maximum event number.
Let $A[N][N]$ be the event order table.
Let C be the considered CPU.
Procedure *TFReplacement(A, N, C)* is
  For all $i \in \{0 \ldots N\}$ loop
    For all $j \in \{0 \ldots N\}$ loop
      If $A[i][j] =='?'$ and $\Phi(i) == C$ and $\Phi(j) == C$ then
        Let $B = A$ /* a copy of the event order table */
        $A[i][j] = 'T'$ /* Let's try a first replacement */
        $A[j][i] = 'F'$
        If *TransitiveClosureSucced(A, N)* then
          If *TotalyOrdered(A, N, C)* then
            CheckMSCConsistence(A, N)
          Else
            recall *TFReplacement(A, N, C)*
        Else   /* Let's try the second replacement */
          $B[i][j] = 'F'$
          $A[j][i] = 'T'$
          If *TransitiveClosureSucced(B, N)* then
            If *TotalyOrdered(B, N, C)* then
              CheckMSCConsistence(B, N)
            Else
              recall *TFReplacement(B, N, C)*
          Else
            Exit   /* Terminate recursion */
          End if
        End if
      End if
    End loop
  End loop
End procedure

This algorithm exhibits all consistent serializations of events running on a given CPU. A serialization takes the form of a lists of events with theirs reduced absolute time constraints as described in Sec.2.2. If no serialization exists, then MSC is *not deployable* with the given constraints.

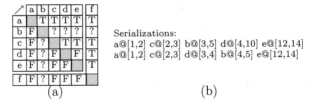

Fig. 7. Serialization example

For an illustration purpose, Fig.7a shows the event order table corresponding to the MSC in Fig.6. After 4 iterations the algorithm exhibits 2 consistent serializations in Fig.7b.

Complexity Estimation. Serializing partial orders of MSCs may lead into a combinatorial explosion. These issues has been investigated and discussed in [1, 2, 15] for instance, for model-checking MSCs. Except for some specific cases like *weak "realizability"* defined in [3], this problem has a non-polynomial complexity.

In the best case, all pairs are ordered. To traverse all the cells, we have n^2 steps. Therefore, the lower bound is $O(n^2)$.

In the worst case, when the n events are unordered, there are $\frac{n^2}{2}$ pairs of unordered events. (Because $O(n^2)$ is bigger than $O(n)$, we omit n in the $n^2 - n$ corresponding to withdrawn matrix diagonal.) The true/false replacement algorithm stated above tries two values for each pair of unordered events. In the worst case there are $2^{\frac{n^2}{2}}$ combinations. Therefore, the upper bound of the worst case is $O(2^{n^2})$.

Because $\log(n^n) = n\log(n)$, then $\log 2^{\frac{n^2}{2}} = \frac{n^2}{2}\log 2$. Moreover, $n\log(n) < \frac{n^2}{2}\log 2$ when $n \geqslant 1$. Therefore, $n^n < 2^{\frac{n^2}{2}}$. And finally, $O(n^n) < O(2^{n^2})$.

So, the algorithm has a non-polynomial complexity. However, in the average case, transitive closure operation (which is done in $O(n^2)$) drastically divides the number of remaining unordered events pairs to be checked. This number is the exponential factor in the above formula (2^{n^2}) and it impacts the most on the algorithm efficiency. This is why in practice Algorithm 2 is rather efficient.

5   Scheduling Policy

In the previous section we have seen how we can come out with a schedule, whenever possible, of the events when the instances are assigned to CPUs. This schedule does not take into account any pre-defined scheduling policy. This is what we are proposing to take into account in this section. A scheduling policy defines the rules for sharing the CPUs between the competing instances. This could be a simple Round-Robin scheduling policy, or scheduling with priorities, preemptive or non-preemptive, etc. [10].

For instance, let us consider the MSC in Fig.6, and events running on CPU1. The consistency of this MSC was checked and we obtained the event reduced

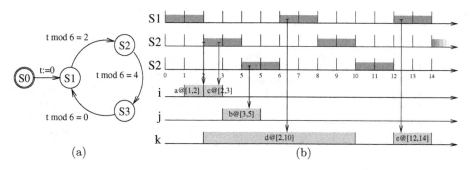

Fig. 8. Scheduling events with a scheduling policy

absolute time constraints. Instance i has events $\{a@[1,2], c@[2,3]\}$, $j : \{b@[3,5]\}$, and instance $k : \{d@[2,10], e@[12,14]\}$. We would like, for instance, to check if these events could be run by the simple scheduler given in Fig.8a: a non-preemptive Round-Robin scheduling algorithm. The scheduler has three states (in general it has as many states as competing instances, where every state would correspond to the execution of one instance), with the same priority, and it has a time slot of 2 units of time. Whenever the time progresses by two units, the scheduler moves from one state to the next. This is a Finite State Machine representation of a scheduling policy. The question can be rephrased as follows: Can we find a one to one mapping between the scheduler states and the competing instances? For the specific MSC in Fig.6, a solution can be found as given in Fig.8b.

5.1   Associating a Scheduler State to Each MSC Instance

In this section, we will assume that a scheduling policy can be described by a Finite State Machine. The scheduling problem in this case can be stated as follows: Find a way to associate a scheduler state to each competing instance in order to run each event within its time constraints. To find such a solution, we proceed as follows:

1. First, for each event, according to its reduced absolute time constraint, we list time slots during which the event can be executed. For each time slot, we mark the corresponding scheduler state. So that we have the list of scheduler states where we can execute this event. For instance, event $a@[1,2]$ can run at time slot $ts1=[0,2)$ or at time slot $ts2=[2,4)$, e.g., by scheduler state $S1$ or $S2$ (see Fig.9a).
2. Once we get the list of scheduler states for each event along an MSC instance, we take the intersection of these lists. This intersection list contains the scheduler states able to run this instance with its events. Also instance j for example can be associated to scheduler state list $\{S2,S3\}$. If the list is empty, then the functional requirements cannot be satisfied with scheduling policy.

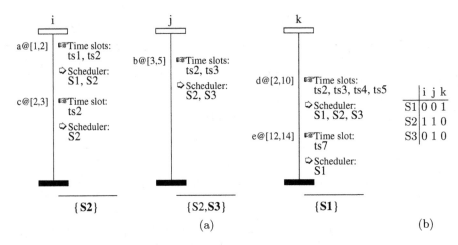

Fig. 9. Mapping between scheduler states and instances

3. We repeat point 2 for each instance. If a scheduler state is not listed anywhere then the system cannot be scheduled with the policy. Otherwise, we may obtain many possibilities for associating one (and only one) scheduler state to an MSC instance. We also build the list of possibilities. (Algorithm 3 proposed bellow lists such possibilities.) In our example, the list contains only one possibility to associate a scheduler state to an MSC instance: { (i,S2), (j,S3), (k,S1)}.

4. Once the mapping between scheduler states and instances is done, we have to make sure that the order is preserved between the sending and the reception of each message. Also, for each message exchange inside the considered CPU, we check that time slot number attributed for sending message is lower than time slot number attributed for receiving message. For instance, let us consider message y for c@[2,3] to d@[2,10] of our example. Let us assume the possibility we found previously for associating a scheduler state to an MSC instance. Also, we plan to run event c at time slot *ts2 (S2)* and event d at time slot *ts4 (S1)*. For this case, order is preserved form sending to receiving message. Otherwise, we would have had to withdraw the possibility we assumed from the list.

5. Moreover, for each message exchange between instances in different CPUs, we check that time slot dates attributed for sending message is lower than time slot dates attributed for receiving message. In the same way, event e@[12,14] of our example run at time slot *ts7:[12,14]*, according to the possibility we retained. When CPU2 schedulability will be checked, we will have to check if dates of time slot for running f do not precede dates for e : [12,14). If this order is not preserved, we have to eliminate this solution.

As described in the aforementioned algorithm, once we get the list of scheduler states able to run the events for each instance (point 2), we have to build the list of possibilities to associate one (and only one) scheduler state to each instance (point 3). We can proceed as follows:

Let the matrix M record scheduler states able to run instances as computed in the aforementioned point 2: $M[x, y] = 1$ means that instance number x may be associated to scheduler state number y (See Fig.9b). Matrix M has for dimension the number of instances (columns) and the number of scheduler states (rows).

Let vector V, of dimension the number of scheduler states, records the instance number associated to each scheduler states. Vector V represents one association possibility. Vector V is initialized with zeros. Following algorithm builds as many V as possible.

Algorithm 3.

For each instance number $\#x$ (column), loop
  For each scheduler state $\#y$ (row), loop
    If $V[x] == 0$ and $M[x, y] == 1$ then
      $V[x] = y$
    End if
  End loop
  Print V
End loop

Complexity Estimation. Here we will be briefly sketch a proof for the complexity of this algorithm. There are several aspects to check. However each aspect has a polynomial complexity. Let n be the number of events, p the instances (and scheduler states) number ($p \leqslant n$), h the maximum events number along one instance ($h \leqslant n$), and m the messages number ($m \leqslant n$).

1. Listing relevant time slots and scheduler states for each event is linear. It has $O(n)$ complexity.
2. Computing conjunctions of such lists along each instance is $O(h.p^2)$.
3. Computing possibilities to associate instances and scheduler states is $O(p^2)$. Let q be the possibilities number ($q \leqslant n^2$).
4. Checking such possibilities according to send/receive message order is $O(q.m)$.

So a pessimistic upper bound complexity is of $O(n^3)$, which is better than the serialization of events proposed in Sec.4, which has a non-polynomial complexity. This is due to the fact that serialization is a special and a weak constrained scheduling policy that allows every permutation. In fact, an aspect is not listed above: the way a given scheduling policy distributes time slots to processes along the time line. For some scheduling policies (e.g., serialization), this operation can have a non-polynomial complexity.

5.2   Modeling Scheduling Policies

In this section we have been able to check if the MSC functional requirements can still be satisfied following a given scheduling policy. In the previous example we have been able to associate a scheduler state to each MSC instance in order to run each of its events within the specified functional time constraints. The role of a scheduling policy is to distribute time slots along the time line. Therefore we need a way to predict time slots and their corresponding scheduler state. In our case study we choose a Round-Robin scheduler. For this scheduling policy, predicting time slots is easy. It is more complex for most of the other scheduling policy used in practice. Also our approach relies on the modeling of the scheduling policy.

Paper [7] lists different ways to handle scheduling problems. Scheduling policy may be modeled using Timed Petri Nets extensions: Stochastic Timed Petri Nets [16, 17, 18], or dedicated Scheduling Extended Timed Petri Nets [13, 19, 20]. With such models it is possible to generate a state graph, which represents all possible traces including the fact that deadlines are respected or not.

We decided to handle scheduling problems using timed automata. Real-time systems, e.g., tasks and scheduler, may be modeled using a dedicated timed automata extension [6, 14]. Moreover, a scheduling problem can be transformed into a reachability analysis problem for these timed automata, and thus it is decidable [10]. In this approach, tasks are modeled as durations. At the opposite, we have atomic events that occur at absolute time. So we cannot exploit directly this work.

6   Related Works

System development processes use to postpone the performance issues to the last stages. As a result, performance requirements have to be met at a stage where the system development is well advanced. Selected solutions may be contradicting the required performance and the system development has to backtrack to early phases to come out with other solutions.

The authors in [9, 21] discussed the risks of separating performance evaluations from software development process. To help in solving this problem, the authors propose a model integrating performance and functional specifications. They proposed annotations to the MSC-96 language, called Performance Message Sequence Charts (PMSC). These annotations allow for the specification of performance requirements, resource constraints as well as the specification of the available resources. PMSC is supported by the DO-IT toolbox, which provides the early evaluation of the performance of SDL systems and an optimized scheduling policy of tasks at compilation time. The toolbox analyzes the cost of components using information provided in PMSC specification, proposes code optimization strategies and generates an efficient code from SDL specifications.

The approach proposed in [4, 5] considers integrating appropriate scheduling paradigms at the (SDL) specification level of the development process. Aim of this work is to handle scheduling constraints at the early stage of SDL validation. The authors use Rate-Monotonic Analysis (RTA) techniques that provide quantitative methods to analyze and predict the timed behavior of real-time systems. RTA helps to organize processes and resources during the design phase. In this approach, SDL has been extended in order to take into account real-time constraints. Preemptive scheduling with fixed priorities is used. The overall procedure is to get an SDL-like formalism that fits the real-time modeling requirements up to specific details in the architecture.

Our approach shares this point of view: deployment issues (performance requirements, available resources constraints, scheduling policy, etc.) should be taken into account at a very early stage. However, we strongly feel that using a single language for expressing functional requirements, performance requirements, scheduling constraints, etc. will certainly lead to a very complex and not intuitive language.

In the previous section we have mentioned the approach proposed in [6, 10, 14]. It is supported by the tool TIMES. It handles the schedulability analysis problem of real-time systems using timed automata and a model-checking technique. The main idea in this approach is to associate each location of an automaton with a task (an executable program characterized by its worst execution time and its relative deadline). An automaton may perform two types of transitions. Delay transitions correspond to the execution of running tasks and idling for the other waiting tasks. Discrete transitions correspond to the arrival of new task instances. Whenever a task is triggered, it is put into the *scheduling queue* for execution by the processor. Tasks are executed according to a given scheduling strategy and removed from the queue, and other idling tasks decrease their deadline delay of the executed task duration. In practice, a scheduling strategy is a function that sorts the task queue according to task parameters whenever a new task arrives. Such a sequence of tasks is schedulable if all the tasks can be executed within their deadlines. Following these principles, schedulability can be seen as a reachability analysis problem and proved using a model-checking technique.

This work reports strong results for schedulability analysis and is certainly a good candidate to evaluate in our future work. However, there is a big gap between TIMES and the work reported in this paper. TIMES tasks are characterized by their duration and their deadline relative to their starting point. On the other hand, MSC events are atomic, with no duration, and their deadline cannot be relative to their starting point. Deadlines for MSC events are expressed as absolute time constraints or relative time constraints.

7   Conclusion

In this paper we have introduced an approach to handle certain deployment constraints at the very early stage of system specification. We are interested in checking if the functional requirements can be satisfied when more and more concrete deployment constraints are taken into account. This will avoid backtracking from very late stages in the development to the specification and analysis stage when the system cannot be deployed.

We have considered only few deployment constraints; other constraints and resources can be taken into account in the same manner. Our plan is to take into account more constraints and resources. The main issue, as we have seen it in Sec.5, will be probably the modeling. With the exception of the Sec.2 and Sec.3, the work presented here is applicable to bMSCs only. The work presented in Sec.4 and Sec.5 has to be extended to high-level MSCs.

The other interesting question is to consider this problem the other way around and solve the following question: given a consistent MSC, is it possible to find all the possible scheduling policies (or other constraints) with which the functional requirements can be satisfied?

Acknowledgement

This work has been partially supported by the Natural Sciences and Engineering Research Council (NSERC) of Canada.

References

1. Alur, R., Holzmann, G., Peled, D.: An analyzer for message sequence charts. Tools and Algorithms for Construction and Analysis of Systems. Volume 1055 of Lecture Notes in Computer Science, Springer-Verlag (1996) 35–48
2. Alur, R., Yannakakis, M.: Model checking of message sequence charts. 10th Conference on Concurrency Theory. Volume 1664 of Lecture Notes in Computer Science, Springer-Verlag (1999) 114–129
3. Alur, R., Etessami, K., Yannakakis, M.: Realizability and verification of MSC graphs. 28th International Colloquium on Automata, Languages and Programming. Volume 2076 of Lecture Notes in Computer Science, Springer-Verlag (2001) 797–808
4. Alvarez, J., Diaz, M., Llopis, L., Pimentel, E., Troya, J.: Integrating schedulability analysis and SDL in an object-oriented methodology for embedded real-time systems. 9th SDL Forum, Montréal, Canada, Elsevier Science (1999) 241–256
5. Alvarez, J., Diaz, M., Llopis, L., Pimentel, E., Troya, J.: Schedulability analysis in real-time embedded systems specified in SDL. Workshop on Real-Time Programming, Palma de Mallorca, Spain, Elsevier Science (2000) 125–131
6. Amnell, T., Fersman, E., Mokrushin, L., Pettersson, P., Yi, W.: TIMES: a tool for schedulability analysis and code generation of real-time systems. Formal Modeling and Analysis of Timed Systems. Volume 2761 of Lecture Notes in Computer Science, Springer-Verlag (2003)
7. Braberman, V.: On integrating scheduling theory into formal models for hard real time systems. In: WorkShop on Formal Methods for the Design of Real-Time Systems, Villa Olmo, Como, Italy (1997)
8. Dechter, R., Meiri, I., Pearl, J.: Temporal constraint networks. Artificial Intelligence **49** (1991) 61–95
9. Faltin, N., Lambert, L., Mitshele-Thiel, A., Slomka, F.: An annotational extension of message sequence charts to support performance engineering. 8th SDL Forum, Every, France, Elsevier Science (1997) 307–322
10. Fersman, E., Pettersson, P., Yi, W.: Timed automata with asynchronous processes: Schedulability and decidability. Tools and Algorithms for the Construction and Analysis of Systems. Volume 2280 of Lecture Notes in Computer Science, Springer-Verlag (2002) 67–82
11. ITU-T: Recommendation Z.120 (11/99), Message Sequence Charts (MSC). International Telecommunication Union, Geneva.
12. ITU-T: Recommendation Z.100 (08/02), Specification and Description Language (SDL). International Telecommunication Union, Geneva.

13. Lime, D., Roux, O.: Expressiveness and analysis of scheduling extended time Petri nets. 5th IFAC International Conference on Fieldbus Systems and their Applications, (FET'03), Aveiro, Portugal, Elsevier Science (2003)
14. Norström, C., Wall, A., Yi, W.: Timed automata as task models for event-driven systems. Real-Time Computing Systems and Applications, Hong Kong, China, IEEE Press (1999)
15. Peled, G.: Specification and verification using message sequence charts. Electronic Notes in Theoretical Computer Science. Volume 65, Elsevier Science (2002)
16. Robert, P., Juanol, G.: Modélisation et vérification de politiques d'ordonnancement de tâches temps-réel. 8ème Colloque Francophone sur l'Ingénierie des Protocoles (CFIP'2000), Toulouse, France, Hermes Science (2000) 167–182
17. Robert, P., Juanol, G.: Modélisation et évaluation de performances d'une architecture d'ordonnancement hétérogène. Application à un système vidéo à qualité de service garantie. 9th Conference on Real-time and Embedded Systems (RTS'2001), Paris, France (2001) 27–42
18. Robert, P.: Contributions à un système vidéo à qualité de service garantie appliqué à une fonction de guidage (phase finale d'atterrissage) par acquisition de l'environnement. PhD thesis, Université Paul Sabatier, Toulouse, France (2001)
19. Roux, O., Déplanche, A.: Extension des réseaux de Petri T-temporels pour la modélisation de l'ordonnancement de taches temps-réel. 3e congrès Modélisation des Systèmes Réactifs (MSR'2001), Toulouse, France, Hermes Science (2001) 327–342
20. Roux, O., Déplanche, A.: A T-time Petri net extension for real time-task scheduling modeling. European Journal of Automation (JESA) **36** (2002)
21. Slomka, F., Zant, J., Lambert, L.: Schedulability analysis of heterogeneous systems for performance message sequence chart. Workshop on Hardware/software codesign, Seattle, Washington, United States, IEEE Computer Society Press (1998) 91–95
22. Zheng, T.: Validation and Refinement of Timed MSC Specifications. PhD thesis, Concordia University, Montreal, Canada (2004)

Scenario Synthesis from Imprecise Requirements

Bill Mitchell[1], Robert Thomson[2], and Paul Bristow[2]

[1] Department of Computing, University of Surrey,
Guilford, Surrey GU2 7XH, UK
w.mitchell@surrey.ac.uk
[2] Motorola UK Research Lab, RG22 4PD, UK
{brt007, paul.bristow}@motorola.com

Abstract. Discovering faults in requirements specifications for distributed reactive systems is a challenging problem since many issues that need to be uncovered are a result of subtle component interactions that are implied by the requirements, but not explicitly described by them. A further difficulty is caused by the imprecise nature of industrial requirements specifications. This makes it difficult to construct valid models of the possible compositions between the requirements, which would be a valuable aid in uncovering such interactions. The paper defines a formal semantics that characterizes a particular type of imprecise compositional semantics derived from industrial case studies, and a process algebra that describes the valid requirements compositions for that formal semantics.

1 Introduction

Telecommunications protocol requirements specifications often consist almost solely of normative MSC scenarios, together with English text. Requirement specification MSC scenarios tend not to provide a comprehensive set of examples, and contain implicit behaviour that can easily be missed, or misinterpreted by software developers. Studies have shown that approximately a third of all serious defects are a result of poor requirements [13]. It is therefore important to derive a comprehensive set of scenarios describing implicit compositions between the requirements for use in uncovering potential defects in the specifications and as test purposes for the development process. However, in various case studies at Motorola it has been shown that although MSC scenarios are precise about message definitions and exchanges, industrial requirements specifications are often imprecise about their compositional semantics. That makes it difficult to construct a valid model of the requirements compositions. The MSC scenarios in the case studies were annotated with global state like information, which should make composition straightforward. However, these states were often used imprecisely across different requirements scenarios. Therefore not all the compositions that result from treating the states as if they are precisely defined will be valid. We will refer to these state like constructs as phases. Intuitively a phase represents a set of global concurrent states with imprecise compositional semantics.

D. Amyot and A.W. Williams (Eds.): SAM 2004, LNCS 3319, pp. 122–137, 2005.
© Springer-Verlag Berlin Heidelberg 2005

Where the same phase occurs in two MSC scenarios it is not immediate that it represents the same global states in both scenarios. They can only safely be assumed to be the same states if the phase is reached in a consistent manner in both scenarios.

The paper defines a formal phase semantics for MSC scenarios, which was formulated from an industrial case study involving around three hundred MSC scenarios. This formalizes when two occurrences of a phase are consistently reached and define the same global concurrent states. This leads to a technique for synthesising *phase composition processes* from a collection of requirements scenarios. These characterise the 'valid' compositions of requirements specifications that have imprecise compositional semantics. The compositions are a subset of those given by regarding the phases as precisely defined concurrent global states. Note we use the term 'valid' within the context of the industrial case studies.

Related Work

Preliminary results were first reported in [9], [10]. The current paper differs in that it allows phases to be simultaneously active, describes how to combine processes rather than traces and permits a temporal context that controls when features can be concurrent.

There appears to no work in the literature that attempts to define a formal semantics for composition of informal MSC scenarios. There are however several papers concerned with model synthesis of formal MSC scenarios. In [2] they describe how to generate some implied scenarios from basic MSCs. In [12], [11] they address the problem of synthesising statecharts from MSC scenarios. In [12] they compose synchronous MSC-s into statecharts by using global state names incorporated in the MSC scenarios. Phases are closely related to global states, but they are not the same. They have state like semantics when certain behavioural constraints hold. This state like semantics is dynamically determined by the concurrent behaviour described by the requirements. In [3], [4] they define scenario and program synthesis from live message sequence charts (LSCs). They do not use global state annotation, however the phase semantics here incorporates some of the ideas of mandatory behaviour from LSCs that permits the state like semantics to be determined dynamically.

2   MSC Phase Transition Scenarios

In this paper we assume MSCs are defined in accordance with the MSC 2000 standard [8]. An MSC scenario describes message exchanges between processes that achieve a transition between major operational phases of the system. Consider figure 4, which describes how a 'Browser' process downloads a Java application iteratively from the 'Air Interface' process until it receives the 'EOF' message, or it detects that the file is corrupted. The shortened hexagonals are MSC condition symbols that describe which operational phase is active at any time. To emphasize this point we will refer to them as phase symbols from now on. Phase symbol labels will be identified with propositional boolean formulae in the paper. In figure 4 'Browser' starts the scenario in phase 'Inactive', that is the proposition 'Inactive' is given value true and all other phases are made false for that process. Then phases 'Active' and 'Load File' become active simultaneously, hence are given value true and 'Inactive' is given value false. The point at which a phase symbol is introduced into a scenario is defined as a phase transition. This interpretation of MSC condition symbols is an extension of the MSC 2000 standard where condition symbols have no formal semantics. Common engineering practise treats MSC condition symbols as global states, but unfortunately in an imprecise fashion that forces the phase semantics that are discussed in this paper.

3   Phase Composition Semantics

Each process behaviour described by an MSC scenario can be defined as a process algebra term that characterises this behaviour up to strong bisimulation equivalence [6]. From now on we will identify an MSC with the set of process algebra terms it defines. For a process P we can extract from each MSC scenario M_i a process algebra term Q_i that defines the behaviour of P in M_i. In section 4 we will define a process algebra that permits us to join together these different Q_i into a process that describes the implicit phase transitions of the requirements scenarios. In this section we will motivate the formal semantics with an informal definition.

For a set of requirements specification scenarios let $\mathcal{P}$ be the set of possible phases that can occur and E be the set of events that can occur. We regard $\mathcal{P}$ as a set of boolean propositions.

Definition 1. *A phase trace is a sequence of triples* (S_i, e_i, S_{i+1}), *for* $0 \leq i \leq n-1$, *where each* $e_i \in E$ *and* $S_i, S_{i+1} \subseteq \mathcal{P}$. S_i *denotes the set of phases that are active before event* e, *and* S_{i+1} *denotes the phases that are active immediately after* e.

In practise S_i and S_{i+1} are usually the same as they represent the major operational phases of the protocols defined by the requirements, which do not change after every single event. A triple (S_i, e_i, S_{i+1}) is referred to as an annotated event. When a phase trace ends in an annotated event (S, e, S') where $S \neq S'$ we say t is a phase transition trace and (S, e, S') is a phase transition.

Figure 1 describes a requirements scenario where the mobile handset has a dedicated key that causes a menu of Java applications that are available for download to be presented to the user. Once the user selects one of these applications from the menu the 'Phone' process delegates the task of downloading the application to the (WAP) 'Browser' process. Within this scenario it is not specified how this downloading occurs, it is abstracted away by the action box 'Download File'.

In figure 1 each process generates a single phase trace. For example the phase trace t_0 for the 'Browser' process is:

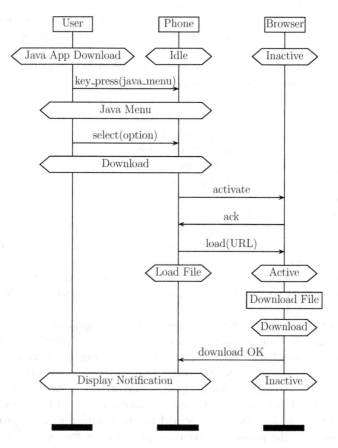

Fig. 1. Java application download

({Inactive},   ?activate,   {Inactive})
({Inactive},   !ack,   {Inactive})
({Inactive},   ?load(URL),   {Active})
({Active},   Download File, {Download})
({Download},   !download OK,   {Inactive})

3.1   Informal Phase Composition Semantics

Informally we can give requirements scenarios the following semantics, which will allow us to construct phase composition processes from them. Suppose we have a scenario M that defines message exchanges between processes, including the process Q.

Consider two phase transition traces t_1 and t_2, where t_2 is a suffix of t_1 and terminates with a phase transition (S_0, e, S_1). I.e., $t_1 = t_3 \cdot t_2$ for some t_3. In this case we say t_1 and t_2 match and that S_1 is reached consistently. Hence we can suppose each occurrence of S_1 defines the same set of concurrent global states.

This leads us to the idea of phase transition simulation between processes based on the idea of one process simulating another once a common phase is shown to be consistently reached.

A process P simulates the phase transitions of Q when the following holds. If we observe a trace of annotated events of P that leads to a phase transition, with some suffix equal to a phase trace of Q, then P must be able to *simulate* the behaviour of Q from then on. Hence, if there are traces t_1 and t_2 as above such that $P \xrightarrow{t_1} P_1$, and $Q \xrightarrow{t_2} Q_2$ then P_1 must be able to simulate Q_2 (in the conventional sense). Given a number of specification processes Q_i it is possible to define a canonical process that simulates the phase transitions of them all as will be defined in section 4. That canonical process captures the legitimate compositions of the scenarios within an imprecise setting.

Note the above semantics is true if we can assume a phase symbol is a global state name for some statechart, and is in fact a weakening of such state semantics. The phase semantics above allows a phase to act as a global state once there is a match between the behaviour of two different scenarios. By using such an overlap between scenarios to define when phase symbols can act in a state like way, we ensure that they can only be used to compose scenarios where they are consistently applied.

Consider the examples of figures 1 and 2. Figure 2 describes how the 'Browser' process downloads a file iteratively once it receives the ?load(URL) message in the 'Inactive' phase. Recall that figure 1 abstracted out the details of how the Java application is downloaded. We can suppose these two scenarios are defined by different feature teams, quite likely at different times. Perhaps figure 2 is a legacy requirement specification. Given the informal semantics we can see how the two 'Browser' processes can be joined together within a single process that represents some of the phase transitions implied by the two scenarios.

Suppose we observe the initial trace of annotated events for t_0 from figure 1 consisting of

$$t_1 = (\ \{\text{Inactive}\}, \ ?\text{activate}, \quad \{\text{Inactive}\})$$
$$(\ \{\text{Inactive}\}, \ !\text{ack}, \qquad \{\text{Inactive}\})$$
$$(\ \{\text{Inactive}\}, \ ?\text{load(URL)}, \ \{\text{Active}\})$$

In figure 2 the initial annotated event of process 'Browser' is
$$t_2 = (\ \{\text{Inactive}\}, \ ?\text{load(URL)}, \ \{\text{Load File}\})$$
This causes a phase transition from 'Inactive' to 'Load File'. Let us assume within the context of receiving load(URL) that whenever 'Active' is an active phase then so is 'Load File'. Hence the end of t_1 matches t_2. That means after the first two annotated events have occurred t_1 matches t_2 in that they contain the same events and are consistently annotated.

Therefore whenever process 'Browser' initially follows the scenario given by figure 1 up to the first phase transition, it must be able to simulate the subsequent scenario given by figure 2. That means we can combine the two scenarios into that described by figure 4. Note that although figure 1 gave no account of what might happen if the file being downloaded was corrupted the new scenario describes this case. This would make a valuable test purpose.

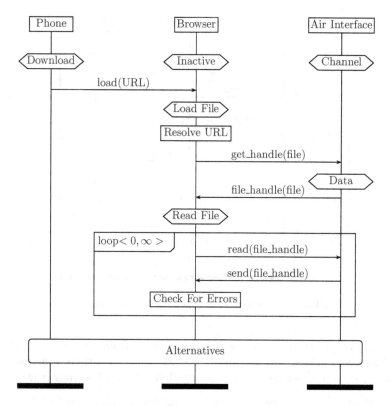

Fig. 2. Download file with browser process

3.2   Formal Semantics of Phase Compositions

We will use a Hennessy Milner style of temporal logic [7] to permit phases to act as a type of temporal guard. A temporal model M consists of a directed graph G, with vertex labelling $\nu : G_V \longrightarrow 2^{\mathcal{P}}$, edge labelling $\varepsilon : G_E \longrightarrow E$, and some vertex i that represents the initial moment. We can think of M as representing a model of the system global states and execution traces.

Temporal formulae are defined as usual:

- $M, v \vDash \langle e \rangle \phi$ iff there is an edge $(v, w) \in G_E$ such that $\varepsilon(v, w) = e$, and $M, w \vDash \phi$. I.e., there is some execution trace from v starting with e where ϕ holds.
- $M, v \vDash [e]\phi$ iff for every edge $(v, w) \in G_E$ where $\varepsilon(v, w) = e$, $M, w \vDash \phi$. I.e., for every execution trace from v starting with e, ϕ holds.
- $M, v \vDash \Box\phi$ iff $M, v \vDash \phi$ and $M, w \vDash \Box\phi$ for every edge $(v, w) \in G_E$. I.e., for all execution traces from v, ϕ holds.
- $M, v \vDash \Diamond\phi$ iff there is some vertex w reachable from v such that $M, w \vDash \phi$. I.e., for some execution trace from v, ϕ holds.

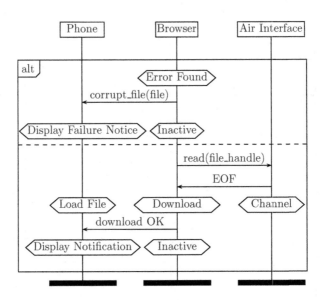

Fig. 3. Alternatives reference for figures 2 and 4

- $M, v \vDash \psi \, \mathcal{U} \, \phi$ iff there is some vertex w reachable from v such that $M, w \vDash \phi$, and for every vertex u on that path to w $M, u \vDash \psi$. I.e., there is an execution trace from v where ψ holds until we reach w when ϕ becomes true.

The satisfiability of ordinary boolean formulae is defined as usual. Formula ϕ is satisfied in M when $M, i \vDash \phi$. ϕ is valid when it is satisfied in every model, when we write $\vdash \phi$. For formulae ψ and ϕ we write $\psi \vdash \phi$ to denote that $\vdash \psi \Rightarrow \phi$.

Definition 2. *For a set $S \subseteq \mathcal{P}$, define $\bigwedge S = \bigwedge_{x \in S} x$. For a phase trace $t = (S, e, S') \cdot t'$, define its temporal semantics as*

$$\|t\| = \bigwedge S \wedge \langle e \rangle (\bigwedge S' \wedge \|t'\|)$$

This formula represents that somewhere within the model M there should be at least one execution trace with states and events that match those of t. A context $\mathcal{X}$ is any temporal formulae over $\mathcal{P}$ and E. It controls how phases are related across the requirements scenarios. For the example above, where we assumed that whenever a load(URL) message is received then Active implies 'Load File' until Inactive, the context would be

$$\Box([\mathsf{load(URL)}](\mathsf{Active} \Rightarrow (\text{'Load File'} \; \mathcal{U} \; \mathsf{Inactive})))$$

The temporal context also permits phases defined by different development teams to be given a consistent meaning across all the scenarios.

Definition 3. *For context $\mathcal{X}$ we define phase trace t to match phase trace t' when*

$$\mathcal{X} \vdash (\|t\| \Rightarrow \Diamond \|t'\|)$$

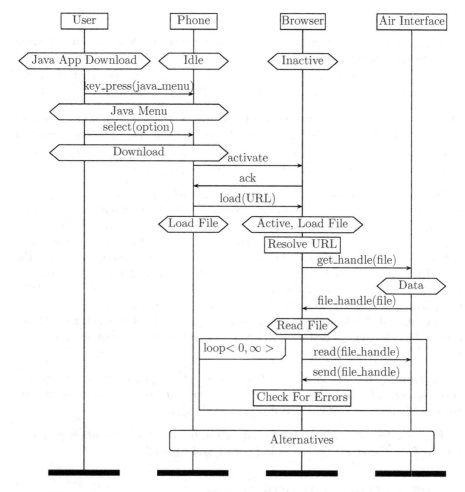

Fig. 4. Synthesized scenario of error checking with Java app download

The matching formula is true when some suffix of the sequence t contains exactly the same event trace as the whole of t', and the phase annotations of the corresponding events are logically consistent within the context defined by $\mathcal{X}$. Note t_1 matches t_2 in the informal semantics example since

$$\Box([\text{load}(URL)](\text{Active} \Rightarrow (\text{'Load File'} \; \mathcal{U} \; \text{Inactive}))) \vdash (\|t_1\| \Rightarrow \Diamond\|t_2\|)$$

Given processes whose actions are annotated events we define first simulation, and then phase transition simulation. For annotated events $a = (S, e, S')$ and $b = (U, g, U')$ define $a \Leftarrow_\mathcal{X} b$ when $e = g$, $\mathcal{X} \vdash \bigwedge U \Rightarrow \bigwedge S$ and $\mathcal{X} \vdash \bigwedge U' \Rightarrow \bigwedge S'$.

Definition 4. *Define P to simulate process Q within context $\mathcal{X}$, written as $P \sqsupseteq_\mathcal{X} Q$, if $\forall a$ such that $Q \xrightarrow{a} Q'$ there is some a' where $P \xrightarrow{a'} P'$ such that $a' \Leftarrow_\mathcal{X} a$ and*

$$P' \sqsupset_{\mathcal{X}} Q'$$

This simulation relation forces phases to be compatible as well as ensuring the events are simulated correctly.

For a phase trace $t = a_0 \cdot a_1 \cdots a_{n-1}$, let $P \xrightarrow{t} P'$ denote that there are processes P_i, for $0 \leq i \leq n$, such that $P_i \xrightarrow{a_i} P_{i+1}$, $P_0 = P$ and $P_n = P'$.

Definition 5. *Define P to simulate the phase transitions of process Q within context $\mathcal{X}$, written as $P \trianglerighteq_{\mathcal{X}} Q$, when the following holds. For all phase transition traces t such that $Q \xrightarrow{t} Q'$, and for all phase traces τ that match t, whenever there is a process P' such that $P \xrightarrow{\tau} P'$ then $P' \sqsupset_{\mathcal{X}} Q'$.*

In other words, if after being active for some arbitrary time, P subsequently generates a trace of annotated events that match a phase transition trace of Q, then P must be able to simulate Q from that time onwards. This implies that a phase transition trace of Q acts as a kind of temporal guard. If ever the guard is triggered, in the sense that P can match the phase transition trace, then the rest of the behavior of Q is then simulated. Note this is a strict weakening of the global state semantics as in [12], [11] where the phase symbols of the MSC scenarios are identified with global state names in UML statecharts.

Let $\{M_i \mid 0 \leq i \leq n\}$ be a set of scenarios, let Q_i be a process from M_i for each i. That is each Q_i defines exactly the observed behaviour of one process in scenario M_i.

Definition 6. *We define process P to represent the phase transitions of processes Q_i when $P \trianglerighteq_{\mathcal{X}} Q_i$ for each i. The overlaps of P are those phase transition traces of P that are not contained in any of the Q_i.*

Figure 4 describes one of the overlaps given by the phase transition representation of the 'Browser' processes in figure 1 and figure 2.

4   Phase Composition Processes

Let $\mathcal{A}$ be the set of annotated events. Let $+$ be the usual choice operator over process terms. Let $\cdot$ be the usual composition operator of atomic actions and process terms. Let $\rho(\mathcal{X}) : \mathcal{A} \longrightarrow \mathbb{B}$ be a boolean valued function that defines when an annotated event is a phase transition. That is $\rho(\mathcal{X})(S, e, S') = \mathsf{t}$ when $\mathcal{X} \nvdash (\bigwedge S \Rightarrow \bigwedge S')$. Note when $\mathcal{X}$ is a tautology, then $\rho(\mathcal{X})(S, e, S')$ denotes that S and S' are disjoint. For annotated events $a = (S, e, S')$ and $b = (U, e, U')$ define $a + b = (S \cup U, e, S' \cup U')$. For a set of processes Q consisting of processes Q_i, for $1 \leq i \leq n$ let πQ denote $Q_0 \parallel Q_1 \parallel \cdots \parallel Q_n$.

In figure 5 we briefly describe a process algebra that defines how to synthesise a phase transition representation from a set of processes described by the requirements scenarios. For this algebra we further define $\mid$ to be commutative and $(P\langle\Rightarrow\rangle Q) = (Q\langle\Leftarrow\rangle P)$ and the process 0 to act as a multiplicative zero element for these two operators, so that $(0\langle\Leftarrow\rangle Q) = 0$, and $0 \mid Q = 0$. Notice that $a + b$ is equivalent to $b + a$, hence in the penultimate axiom

$$P \parallel Q \quad = (P\langle\Leftarrow\rangle Q) + (P\langle\Rightarrow\rangle Q)$$
$$a \cdot P\langle\Leftarrow\rangle b \cdot Q = a \cdot P\langle\Leftleftarrows\rangle b \cdot Q \quad \text{when} \quad a \Leftarrow_{\mathcal{X}} b$$
$$a \cdot P\langle\Leftarrow\rangle b \cdot Q = a \cdot (P\langle\Leftarrow\rangle b \cdot Q) \quad \text{when} \quad a \not\Leftarrow_{\mathcal{X}} b$$
$$a \cdot P\langle\Leftleftarrows\rangle b \cdot Q = (a + b) \cdot (P\langle\Leftleftarrows\rangle Q) \quad \text{when} \quad a \Leftarrow_{\mathcal{X}} b \text{ and } \neg\rho(\mathcal{X})(a)$$
$$a \cdot P\langle\Leftleftarrows\rangle b \cdot Q = (a + b) \cdot (P \mid Q) \quad \text{when} \quad a \Leftarrow_{\mathcal{X}} b \text{ and } \rho(\mathcal{X})(a)$$
$$a \cdot P\langle\Leftleftarrows\rangle b \cdot Q = a \cdot P + b \cdot Q \quad \text{when} \quad a \not\Leftarrow_{\mathcal{X}} b \text{ and } \rho(\mathcal{X})(a)$$
$$a \cdot P\langle\Leftleftarrows\rangle b \cdot Q = a \cdot P \quad \text{when} \quad a \not\Leftarrow_{\mathcal{X}} b \text{ and } \neg\rho(\mathcal{X})(a)$$
$$a \cdot P \mid b \cdot Q = (a + b) \cdot (P \mid Q) \quad \text{when} \quad a \Leftarrow_{\mathcal{X}} b$$
$$a \cdot P \mid b \cdot Q = a \cdot P + b \cdot Q \quad \text{when} \quad a \not\Leftarrow_{\mathcal{X}} b \text{ and } b \not\Leftarrow_{\mathcal{X}} a$$

Fig. 5. Phase composition process algebra

$$a \cdot P \mid b \cdot Q = (a + b) \cdot (P \mid Q)$$

when $a \Leftarrow_{\mathcal{X}} b$ or when $b \Leftarrow_{\mathcal{X}} a$. Finally we assume all the defined compositional operators in the algebra distribute over summation of processes. The algebra essentially defines an algorithm for the construction of a minimal phase transition representation as explained in theorem 8.

The process $P \parallel Q$ will consist of P and Q glued together along traces from each process that match. The process $P\langle\Leftarrow\rangle Q$ defines joins between the processes where a trace from P matches a trace from Q. Process $P\langle\Leftarrow\rangle Q$ acts like P until it reaches an action that Q is able to perform (if there is such a place). It then changes to the process $P\langle\Leftleftarrows\rangle Q$. This process now allows P and Q to unfold in lock step. If this continues until there is a phase transition, then we have a match between a trace in P and Q. The process $P\langle\Leftleftarrows\rangle Q$ will now become $P \mid Q$. If there is no such match then essentially Q is discarded. Process $P \mid Q$ allows P and Q to unfold in lock step until they diverge, at which point it splits into the summation of the two processes.

Lemma 7

- There are two traces $P \xrightarrow{t_1} P'$ and $Q \xrightarrow{t_2} Q'$ where t_1 matches t_2, if and only if there is a trace

$$P \parallel Q \xrightarrow{t_1} P' \mid Q'$$

- If there are no matches between any traces of P and Q then $P \parallel Q$ degenerates into $P + Q$.

- If there is a trace t such that $P \xrightarrow{t} P'$ and $Q \xrightarrow{t} Q'$ for some P' and Q' then

$$P \mid Q \xrightarrow{t} P' \mid Q'$$

- If there are no common actions for P and Q, that is there is no action a such that both $P \xrightarrow{a} P'$ and $Q \xrightarrow{a} Q'$ for some P' and Q' then $P \mid Q$ is bisimulation equivalent to $P + Q$.

- Because it is possible for a process to have a non-degenerate match between two of it's own traces, it is not the case that $P \parallel P$ is necessarily equivalent to P.

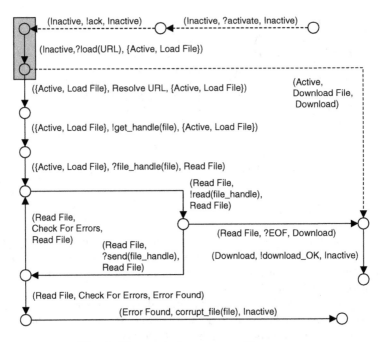

Fig. 6. 'Browser' phase composition process

Theorem 8. *Given a set Q of processes Q_i from requirements scenarios M_i for $0 \leq i \leq n$, then*

$$P = \pi Q$$

is a phase transition representation of Q.

Process P is canonical upto simulation equivalence. That is if P' is another phase transition representation of Q, then $P' \sqsupseteq_\chi P$. Define P to be the phase composition process for Q.

In general the phase composition process P is built by joining together specification scenario processes wherever there is a match between phase transition traces. Suppose there are two specification processes Q_0 and Q_1, where there is a phase transition trace t_0 within the body of Q_0 that matches some phase transition trace t_1 at the start of Q_1. Then P will contain a copy of Q_0 joined to Q_1 along the end of t_1 that corresponds to t_0. By exhaustively joining all such matches together in a single process we construct P. The process algebra of figure 5 captures this idea formally.

To see how this works consider the two 'Browser' processes defined in figures 1 and 2. Figure 6 is the phase composition process of these two 'Browser' processes. The dotted arrows represent the part of the process behaviour that is exclusive to figure 1. The solid arrows are the behaviour that is defined by figure 2. The grey box denotes where phase trace t_1 matches t_2. This match defines where the two 'Browser' processes are joined together. The process is depicted as a

$$
\begin{aligned}
I &= \text{Inactive} & a &= activate \\
A &= \text{Active} & ack &= ack \\
L &= \text{Load File} & l &= load(URL) \\
D &= \text{Download} & rs &= \text{Resolve URL} \\
R &= \text{Read File} & gh &= get\_handle(file) \\
E &= \text{Error Found} & fh &= file\_handle(file) \\
& & df &= \text{Download File} \\
& & r &= read(file\_handle) \\
& & s &= send(file\_handle) \\
& & c &= \text{Check For Errors} \\
& & e &= EOF \\
& & d &= \text{download\_OK} \\
& & cr &= \text{corrupt\_file}
\end{aligned}
$$

Fig. 7. Abbreviations for scenario identifiers

finite state automaton, where the edges are labelled with annotated events. The temporal context here causes **Active** and **Load File** to be simultaneously valid, hence both phases are included in the relevant annotated events. Where a set of phases in an annotated event only contains a single phase we leave out the surrounding braces for that set and just write the phase on its own.

We will now consider in a little more detail how this composition works. In order to keep the calculation compact we will abbreviate the identifiers in the scenarios as shown in figure 7. The first column shows phase abbreviations, and the second shows event abbreviations. From figure 1 using these abbreviations we can write the 'Browser' process for that scenario as

$$
B_1 = (I, ?a, I) \cdot (I, !ack, I) \cdot (I, ?l, A) \cdot (A, df, D) \cdot (D, !d, I) \cdot 0
$$

The 'Browser' process of figure 2 is recursive and can be written as the following process algebra term B_2, where we have used the context to replace phase L with the set of phases $\{A, L\}$. This makes it much simpler to apply the rules for the process algebra when considering $B_1 \parallel B_2$. When simplified, $B_1 \parallel B_2$ reduces to the automaton in figure 6.

$$
\begin{aligned}
B_2 &= (I, ?l, \{A, L\}) \cdot (\{A, L\}, rs, \{A, L\}) \\
&\quad \cdot (\{A, L\}, !gh, \{A, L\}) \cdot (\{A, L\}, ?fh, R) \cdot B_3 \\
B_3 &= (R, !r, R) \cdot B_4 \\
B_4 &= (R, ?e, D) \cdot (D, !d, I) \cdot 0 + (R, ?s, R) \cdot B_5 \\
B_5 &= (R, c, R) \cdot B_3 + (R, c, E) \cdot (E, !cr, I) \cdot 0
\end{aligned}
$$

This algebra term is also depicted by figure 8. Here B_2 is shown as a state automaton, and we label the relevant states with the B_i processes that they represent. Conveniently there is only one match between traces of B_1 and B_2. This is the match between the phase traces t_1 and t_2 introduced in section 3.1. In the abbreviated notation we are using in this section we can write these traces as:

$$
\begin{aligned}
t_1 &= (I, ?a, I) \cdot (I, !ack, I) \cdot (I, ?l, A) \\
t_2 &= (I, ?l, \{A, L\})
\end{aligned}
$$

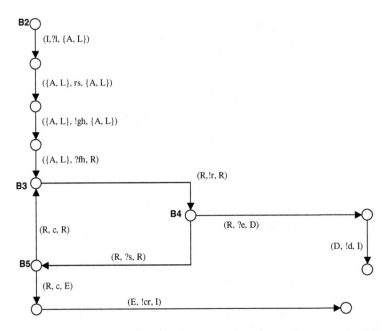

Fig. 8. 'Browser' process from figure 2

Since there will be no traces of B_2 that match a trace of B_1, $B_1\langle\Rightarrow\rangle B_2$ will be the zero process. Hence $B_1 \parallel B_2$ reduces immediately to $B_1\langle\Leftarrow\rangle B_2$ via the first axiom in the process algebra. This process will act like B_1 until it reaches a point where both B_1 and B_2 can perform a common action. Hence we can write $B_1\langle\Leftarrow\rangle B_2$ as

$$(I, ?a, I) \cdot (\{A, L\}, rs, \{A, L\}) \cdot \Big(((I, ?l, A) \cdot (A, df, D) \cdot (D, !d, I) \cdot 0)\langle\Leftarrow\rangle B_2 \Big)$$

The annotated event $(I, ?l, A)$ is a phase transition, so that $\rho(\mathcal{X})(I, ?l, A)$ is true. From the local context we have

$$(I, ?l, A) \Leftarrow_\mathcal{X} (I, ?l, \{A, L\})$$

and $(I, ?l, A) + (I, ?l, \{A, L\}) = (I, ?l, \{A, L\})$. Let B_2' be the process that B_2 becomes after action $(I, ?l, \{A, L\})$. Hence

$$((I, ?l, A) \cdot (A, df, D) \cdot (D, !d, I) \cdot 0)\langle\Leftarrow\rangle B_2$$

simplifies to

$$(I, ?l, \{A, L\}) \cdot \Big(((A, df, D) \cdot (D, !d, I) \cdot 0) \mid B_2' \Big)$$

In this simplification we used the second and forth of the axioms for the process algebra. The only action B_2' can perform is $(\{A, L\}, rs, \{A, L\})$. For this annotated event:

$$(\{A, L\}, rs, \{A, L\}) \not\approx_\chi (A, df, D) \text{ and}$$
$$(A, df, D) \qquad\qquad \not\approx_\chi (\{A, L\}, rs, \{A, L\})$$

This trivially holds since the underlying events df and rs are different. Therefore we can apply the last axiom of the algebra to show that $((A, df, D) \cdot (D, !d, I) \cdot 0) \mid B_2'$ simplifies to

$$((A, df, D) \cdot (D, !d, I) \cdot 0) + B_2'$$

These simplifications have reduced $B_1 \parallel B_2$ to the automaton of figure 6. As a process algebra term we have shown that $B_1 \parallel B_2$ reduces to

$$(I, ?a, I) \cdot (I, !ack, I) \cdot (I, ?l, \{A, L\}) \cdot \left(B_2' \cdot +((A, df, D) \cdot (D, !d, I) \cdot 0) \right)$$

The $\parallel$ composition of regular process algebra terms is always regular, and MSC processes derived from individual instances are always regular. Note it is not the case that a process that describes the combined behaviour of a group of instances has to be regular [1], hence the following result is valid for processes that correspond to instances in an MSC.

Theorem 9. *The phase composition process of theorem 8 is regular. That is it can always be represented by a finite state automaton.*

If in fact phase symbols truly are global state names, then the phase composition process will always be simulated by the resultant statechart. Hence traces of the phase composition process are also traces of any future refinements of the scenarios that transform phase symbols to global states.

Motorola Pilot

The process algebra in figure 5 can be implemented in an efficient manner to provide an automated mechanism for generating phase transition representations of requirements scenarios. A prototype version of this has been implemented by Motorola UK Research Labs [9] as an extension of their test generation tool set [5]. Their current prototype does not allow iterative processes, and has not implemented temporal contexts. The prototype has been used on various existing 3G requirements scenarios and is currently being used as part of a pilot study during the development of new products.

Phase Composition Test Purposes

It is possible to automatically generate test purposes from the phase composition process. The phase composition process can be used to generate new MSC scenarios that describe implicit phase transitions within the requirements. Figure 4 is derived in this way from figure 6. Such new MSC scenarios can be used to generate test suites via tools such as *ptk* [5]. *ptk* can derive TTCN2, TTCN3 or SDL test cases directly from MSC requirements using a number of algorithms to choose which MSC traces to generate the tests from.

5   Conclusion

Around a third of significant defects can be traced to requirements specifications. Hence it is important to be able to construct a model of possible compositions of the requirements as an analytic tool to facilitate the detection of such defects. Such a model is also useful in ensuring sufficient coverage of test cases for feature interactions implied by the requirements, which are often caused by composition between requirements for different features.

Unfortunately MSC requirements scenarios usually have imprecise compositional semantics that makes it hard to synthesise an analytical model of their possible compositions. The difficulty arises where different requirements specifications use global state like constructs (phases), which are not consistently used across a large repository of scenarios. We have identified a particular formal semantics that allows us to identify when such state like constructs should be allowed to have state like compositional semantics.

We have codified the semantics in the form of a process algebra that defines how such imprecise scenarios can be composed. The semantics for this process algebra are based on an extensive eighteen month case study conducted by Motorola Research Labs. The resulting process algebra accurately captures the valid compositions from that case study. The algebra allows phase symbols to have global state like semantics when there is a suitable overlap of concurrent behaviour between scenarios. This ensures composition occurs only where phase symbols have consistent state like definitions.

References

1. Alur, R., Yannakakis, M.: Model checking of message sequence charts. Proceedings of the Tenth International Conference on Concurrency Theory, Springer Verlag, 1999.
2. Alur, R., Etessami, K., Yannakakis, M.: Inference of Message Sequence Charts. Proceedings 22nd International Conference on Software Engineering, 2000, 304–313.
3. Bontemps, Y., Schobbens, P.-Y.: Synthesis of Open Reactive Systems from Scenario-Based Specifications. Third International Conference on Application of Concurrency to System Design (ACSD'03), 2003.
4. Bontemps, Y., Heymens, P.: Turning high-level live sequence charts into automata. Proc. of Scenarios and State Machines: Models Algorithms and Tools, 24th International Conf. on Software Engineering, May 2002.
5. Baker, P., Bristow, P., Jervis, C., King, D., Mitchell, B.: Automatic Generation of Conformance Tests From Message Sequence Charts. E. Sherratt (Ed.), SAM 2002: Telecommunications and Beyond, Volume 2599 of Lecture Notes in Computer Science, Springer, 170–198.
6. Gehrke, T., Hilhn, M., Wehrkeim, H.: An Algebraic Semantics for Message Sequence Chart Documents. Formal Description Techniques (FORTE), Chapman Hall, 1998.
7. Hennessy, M., Milner, R.: Algebraic Laws for Nondeterminism and Concurrency. Journal of the ACM, 32: 137-161, 1985.

8. ITU-T: Recommendation Z.120 (11/99) Message Sequence Chart (MSC). International Telecommunication Union, Geneva.

9. Mitchell, B., Thomson, R., Jervis, C., Phase Automaton for Requirements Scenarios. D. Amyot, L. Logrippo (Eds.), Feature Interactions in Telecommunications and Software Systems VII, IOS Press, 2003, 77–84.

10. Mitchell, B., Thomson, R., Bristow, P.: Imprecise Synthesis. Proc. of Scenarios and State Machines: Models Algorithms and Tools, 24th International Conf. on Software Engineering, May 2002. To appear IEE publications, 2004.

11. Schumann, J., Whittle, J.: Generating Statechart Designs From Scenarios. Proceedings 22nd International Conference on Software Engineering, 2000.

12. Uchitel, S., Kramer, J., Magee, J.: Synthesis of Behavioral Models from Scenarios. IEEE Transactions on Software Engineering, vol. 29, no. 2, February 2003.

13. Wong, E., Horgan, J. R., Zage, W., Zage, D., Syring, M.: Applying Design Metrics to a Large-Scale Software System (Motorola), Proceedings of the 9th International Symposium on Software Engineering Reliability (ISSRE '98), Paderborn, Germany, November 4-7, 1998.

Applying Reduction Techniques to Software Functional Requirement Specifications

Jameleddine Hassine[1], Rachida Dssouli[2], and Juergen Rilling[1]

[1] Department of Computer Science, Concordia University, Montreal, Canada
{j_hassin, rilling}@cs.concordia.ca
[2] Concordia Institute for Information Systems Engineering, Montreal, Canada
dssouli@ece.concordia.ca

Abstract. *Requirement Specification* is gaining increasingly attention as a critical phase of software systems development. As requirement descriptions evolve, they quickly become error-prone and difficult to understand. Therefore, the development of techniques and tools to support requirement specification development, understanding, testing, maintenance and reuse becomes an important issue. This paper extends the well-known technique of program slicing to *Functional Requirement Specification* based on the Use Case Map notation. This new application of slicing, called *UCM Requirement Slicing* is useful to aid requirement comprehension and maintenance. In contrast to traditional program slicing, requirement slicing is designed to operate on the requirement specification of a system, rather than the source code of a program. The resulting requirement slice provides knowledge about high-level structure of a system, rather than its low-level implementation details. In order to compute a UCM Requirement slice, we provide a three steps slicing algorithm.

Keywords: Functional requirement specification, program slicing, Use Case Maps, comprehension, maintenance.

1 Introduction

Over the last several years, requirements specification and engineering is gaining in importance, as part of the ongoing trend towards improving the software development and maintenance process. Requirement analysis is the first step in the development process, capturing the functionalities of systems, often in the form of scenarios and use cases.

In the early stages of common development processes, system's functionalities are captured in terms of scenarios and use cases. Scenario-driven approaches are widely accepted based on their intuitive syntax and semantics (Amyot and Eberlein [1] provide an extensive survey of scenario notations). Use Case Maps (UCMs), can be applied to capture and integrate functional requirements in terms of causal scenarios representing behavioral aspects at a higher level of abstraction, to provide the stakeholders with guidance and reasoning about the

D. Amyot and A.W. Williams (Eds.): SAM 2004, LNCS 3319, pp. 138–153, 2005.

system-wide functionalities and behavior. Use Case Maps are part of a proposal to ITU−T for a *User Requirements Notation (URN)* [9]. However, a suitable description notation syntax and semantics alone cannot overcome the problems caused by inherent system complexity. There is a need for techniques and tools to simplify requirement specifications in order to support their comprehension, testing, maintenance and reuse.

In our research we address these issues by introducing a new approach to reduce the complexity of the requirement specifications. Our new approach is based on *slicing techniques* to guide requirement engineers, designers and programmers during the comprehension process of requirement specifications. Program slicing was originally introduced as a technique to simplify programs to provide support during debugging and program comprehension [18, 19] and has been applied to a wide variety of problems including: program understanding, maintenance [5], debugging, differencing, integration, testing [18] and model checking [13]. Program slicing, a program reduction technique, allows one to reduce the size of the source code of interest by identifying only those parts of the original program that are relevant to the computation of a particular function/output of interest [19]. It is crucial that slicing preserves the semantics of the original program with respect to the slicing criterion [19].

Our paper introduces a new form of slicing, referred to as *UCM (Use Case Maps) Requirement Slicing*, to aid UCM comprehension and maintenance.

The organization of the paper is as follow: in the next section, we briefly describe the traditional approaches to program slicing. Section 3 introduces the Use Case Maps notation and presents an UCM example. In section 4, the UCM slicing approach is presented and an example is given followed by a discussion on the application of UCM slicing in section 5. Section 6 discusses the UCM data flow and presents the limitations of the proposed approach. Section 7 presents related work. Finally the paper concludes with section 8.

2   Traditional Program Slicing

The notion of program slicing originated in the seminal paper by Weiser [19]. Weiser defined a slice S as a reduced, executable program P' obtained from a program P by removing statements such that S replicates parts of the behavior of the program. Informally, a static program slice consists of those parts of a program that potentially could affect the value of a variable V at a point of interest. Korel and Laski introduced in [10] the notion of dynamic slicing that can be seen as a refinement of the static approach. The dynamic slice preserves the program behavior for a specific input, in contrast to the static approach, which preserves the program behavior for the set of all inputs for which a program terminates. Furthermore, different slicing techniques and criteria are required because various applications require different properties of slices. In recent years, the application of slicing has been extended to other software artifacts [16] including: software architecture [20], requirement models [7, 11] and formal specification [2, 13, 14]. A detailed survey of different slicing techniques and their applications can be found in [4, 18].

3   Describing Requirements Using Use Case Maps Notation

3.1   Use Case Maps

A UCM [8] describes a system in terms of causal relationships between responsibilities (e.g., operation, action, task, function, etc.) along paths allocated to a set of components. The relationships, representing the UCM control flow, are said to be causal because they involve concurrency, partial ordering of activities and they link causes (e.g., preconditions and triggering events) to effects (e.g., postconditions and resulting events). A responsibility can potentially be associated or allocated to a component. In UCMs, a component is generic and abstract enough to represent software entities (e.g., object, agent, process, etc.) as well as non software entities (e.g., actors or hardware). With the UCM notation, scenarios are abstracted above the message exchange level, and therefore are to some extend independent from the underlying implementation level. Path details can be hidden in sub-diagrams called plug-ins, contained in stubs (containers) on a path. A stub can be either static (represented as plain diamond) which contains only one plug-in, or dynamic (represented as dashed diamonds) which may contain several plug-ins whose selection can be determined at run time according to a selection policy. The main UCM constructs are: OR-Fork (alternative scenarios), OR-Join (merging scenarios), AND-Fork (concurrent scenarios), AND-Join (synchronizing scenarios). More details on the UCM semantics can be found in [8].

3.2   Case Study –A Simple Telephony System

Figure 1 shows a UCM model that was originally introduced in [12], describing the connection request phase in an agent based telephony system with user-subscribed features.

It contains four components (originating/terminating users and their agents) and two static stubs. Upon the request of an originating user (req), the originating agent will select the appropriate user feature (in stub Sorig) that could result in some feedback. This may also cause the terminating agent to select another feature (in stub Sterm) which in turn can cause a number of results in the originating and terminating users. Stub *Sorig* contains the originating plug-in whereas stub *Sterm* contains the Terminating plugin. These sub-UCMs have their own stubs, whose plug-ins are user-subscribed features.

1. Stub *Sscreen*:
   - OCS (Originating Call Screening): blocks calls to people on the OCS filtering list.
   - Default: used when not subscribed to any other originating feature.

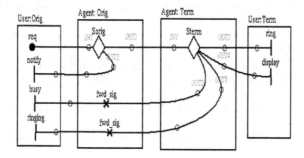

Fig. 1. UCM model (Root Map)

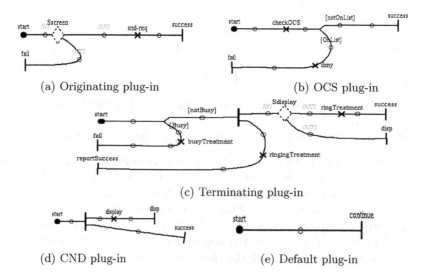

(a) Originating plug-in   (b) OCS plug-in

(c) Terminating plug-in

(d) CND plug-in   (e) Default plug-in

Fig. 2. Plug-ins

2. Stub *Sdisplay*:
   - CND (Call Name Delivery): displays the caller's number on the callee's device (display) concurrently with the rest of the scenario (ringing).
   - Default: used when not subscribed to any other terminating feature.

The set of global variables for the UCM map are: Busy (the callee is busy), OnOCSList (the callee on OCS list), subCND (the callee is subscribed to CND), subOCS (the caller is subscribed to OCS).

Each plug-in (Fig. 2) is bound to its parent stub, i.e., stub input/output segments (IN1, OUT1, etc.) are connected to the plug-ins start/end points, as follow:

1. Sorig Stub : Originating UCM. Condition: *true*.
   Binding:((IN1, start), (OUT1, success), (OUT2, fail))
   - Sscreen Stub

- OCS UCM. Condition: subOCS. Binding: ((IN1, start), (OUT1, success), (OUT2, fail))
- Default UCM. Condition: ¬ subOCS. Binding: ((IN1, start), (OUT1, continue))

2. Sterm Stub : Terminating UCM. Condition: True. Binding: ((IN1, start), (OUT1, success), (OUT2, fail), (OUT3, reportSuccess), (OUT2, disp))
   - Sdisplay Stub
      - CND UCM. Condition: subCND. Binding: ((IN1, start), (OUT1, success), (OUT2, disp))
      - Default UCM. Condition: ¬ subCND. Binding:((IN1, start), (OUT1, continue))

4   Use Case Map Slicing

Intuitively, a UCM slice may be viewed as a subset of the behavior of a global UCM. While a traditional slice intends to isolate the behavior of a specified set of program variables, a UCM slice intends to isolate a set of scenarios that lead to a specific behavior. When a UCM slicer is invoked, it takes as input:

1. A complete system requirement specification based on the UCM notation
2. A slicing criterion.
   Note: The choice of slicing criteria will be discussed in detail in section 4.2.

Depending on the user's interest, the UCM slicer computes a backward slice with respect to the selected slicing criterion. While performing the backward traversal, the slicer collects all the logical predicates, defined on UCM global variables, leading to the execution of the targeted criterion and produces what we refer to as *reachability expression*. The reachability expression is solved by finding the initial variable values and/or the sequence of inputs that the environment has to provide to be able to reach the slicing criterion.

4.1   Definitions

In order to focus on the key ideas of UCM slicing, we give the following definitions:

Definition 1 (Use Case Maps). *We assume that a UCM Requirement specification RS is denoted by (D, C, V, G, λ, Bc, S, Bs) where:*

- *D is the UCM domain, composed of sets of typed elements. D= SP ∪ EP ∪ R ∪ AF ∪ AJ ∪ OF ∪ OJ ∪ Tm ∪ ST ∪ Ab. Where SP is the set of Start Points, EP is the set of End Points, R is the set of Responsibilities, AF is the set of AND-Fork, AJ is the set of AND-Join, OF is the set of OR-Fork, OJ is the set of OR-Join, Tm is the set of Timers, Ab is the set of Aborts and ST is the set of Stubs.*
- *C is the set of components in RS (C = ∅ for unbound UCM)*
- *G is the set of guard expressions over V, where V is the set of global variables in RS*

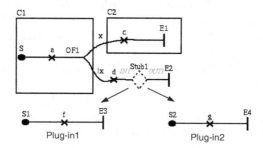

Fig. 3. A UCM example

- λ *is a transition relation defined as:* $\lambda = D \times D \times G$
- *Bc is a component binding relation defined as Bc* $= D \times C$. *Bc specifies which element of D is associated with which component of C.*
- *S is a plug-in binding relation defined as* $S = ST \times RS \times G$.
- *Bs is a stub binding relation and is defined as Bs* $= ST \times RS \times \{IN/OUT\} \times SP/EP$. *Bs specifies how the start and end points of the plug-in map would be connected to the path segments going into or out of the stub.*

Note: This definition represents our interpretation of Use Case Maps to provide the basis setting for our UCM slicing approach.

The UCM of Figure 3 is described as follows:

- D={S}∪{E1, E2}∪{a, c, d}∪{OF1}∪{Stub1}, where OF1 is the OR-Fork.
- C={C1, C2}; V={x, y}; G={x, ¬x, y, ¬y }
- λ={(S, a, true),(a, OF1, true),(OF1, c, x),(OF1, d, ¬x),(d, Stub1, true), (Stub1, E2, true)}
- Bc={(S, C1),(a, C1),(OF1, C1),(c, C2),(E1, C2)}
- S={(Stub1, Plug-in1, y), (Stub1, Plug-in2, ¬y)}
- Bs = {(Stub1, Plug-in1,IN1, S1),(Stub1, Plug-in1,OUT1, E3),(Stub1, Plug-in2, IN1, S2),(Stub1, Plug-in2, OUT1, E4)}

Where Plug-in1 is defined as: D={S1, f, E3}; λ= {(S1, f, true),(f, E3, true)}; C=V=G=Bc=S=Bs=∅
And Plug-in2 is defined as: D={S2, g, E4}; λ= {(S2, g, true),(g, E4, true)}; C=V=G=Bc=S=Bs=∅

In order to define a *UCM slice*, we introduce the concept of: reduced domain, reduced stub, reduced component, reduced guard set, reduced transition relation and reduced binding relations.

Definition 2 (Reduced UCM elements).
   Let RS = (D, C, V, G, λ, Bc, S, Bs) be an UCM Requirement Specification.
- *A reduced domain is a set D′ that is derived from D by removing zero, or more elements (i.e., D′ ⊆ D).*
- *Since a plug-in is also a stand alone UCM, a reduced plug-in can be defined in the same way as a reduced UCM(see definition 3).*

- *A reduced stub is a stub that contains reduced plug-ins and may have fewer plug-ins than the original stub.*
- *A reduced component c′ is a component that has less functionalities than the original component.*
- *A reduced guard set G′ is a set $G' \subseteq G$ that is derived from G by removing zero, or more expressions.*
- *A reduced transition relation λ′ is a relation derived from λ by removing zero or more tuples (i.e., $(d_1,d_2,e) \in \lambda$ and $(d_1,d_2,e) \notin \lambda'$).*
- *A reduced component binding relation Bc′ is a relation derived from Bc by removing zero or more couples (i.e., $(d,c) \in Bc$ and $(d,c) \notin Bc'$).*
- *A reduced plug-in binding relation S′ is a relation derived from S by removing zero or more tuples.*
- *A reduced stub binding relation Bs′ is a relation derived from Bs by removing zero or more tuples.*

Given a UCM, our goal is to compute a UCM slice which corresponds to a subset of the original UCM that preserves the semantics of the UCM with respect to chosen slicing criterion.

Note: We can have as a result a set of flat scenarios (i.e., sequential traces where no concurrency nor choices are involved). However the original UCM semantics will not be preserved.

Definition 3 (Reduced UCM). *Let $RS = (D, C, V, G, \lambda, Bc, S, Bs)$ and $RS' = (D', C', V', G', \lambda', Bc', S', Bs')$ be two UCMs. RS′ is a reduced UCM of RS if:*

- *D′ is a reduced set of D*
- *$C' = c'1, c'2,..., c'n$ is a subset of C such that for k=1, 2,...,n. c′k is a reduced component of ck*
- *V′ is a reduced set of V and G′ is a reduced set of G*
- *λ′ is a reduced transition relation of λ*
- *Bc′ is a reduced component binding relation of Bc*
- *S′ is a reduced plug-in binding relation of S*
- *Bs′ is a reduced stub binding relation of Bs*

4.2   Use Case Map Slicing Criteria

The selection of a slicing criterion depends on the particular analysis task. The focus is frequently on the examining of the requirement with respect to particular functionality, e.g a particular system feature or a particular behavior.

Definition 4 (UCM Slicing Criteria). *Let RS be a Requirement Specification. A slicing criterion (SC) for RS may be:*

- *A responsibility*
  or
- *Start/end point*

The slicing criterion may eventually include a UCM component. Based on the task and the degree of system understanding a user may choose between specifying only a responsibility or a start/end point as a slicing criterion (Ignoring where the responsibility takes place) or a responsibility and a specific component (to focus the analysis on one specific component).

For the scope of this paper, we limit ourselves to *unbound UCMs* since the *reduced architecture* (set of reduced components) can be easily added (from the original UCM) once we obtain an unbound UCM slice.

4.3   Slicing UCM Constructs

Figures 4 and 5 show different UCM constructs and their potential reduced versions after applying program slicing. E is a generic end point which is added after the SC to form a valid reduced UCM. In the reduced OR-Fork (Figure 4 (aa)), only one path is included in the reduced UCM.In the reduced OR-Join (Figure 4 (bb)), the non-determinism is preserved. In the reduced AND-Fork (Figure 5 (cc)), the interleaving semantics is preserved, since concurrent responsibilities SC and d may occur in different order($SC;d$ or $d;SC$).

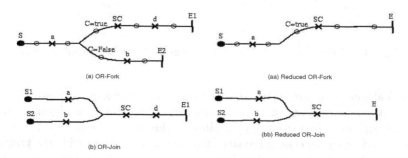

Fig. 4. UCM constructs and its reduced form(1) (SC is the slicing criterion)

Figure 5(gg) shows the slice obtained for a UCM with a dynamic stub. The selection policy between plug-in1 and plug-in 2 is based on the value of global variable C:(1) C=*true*→ Plug-in 1 (connects IN1 to OUT1)(2) C=*false* → Plug-in 2 (connects IN1 to OUT2). Plug-in 1 is sliced out because its end point is bound to end point E2. The resulting stub is a reduced stub with only one exit point *E1* containing plug-in 2. In this case, the *reachability expression* is reduced to the plug-in selection condition: *C=false*.

4.4   UCM Slicing Algorithm

In what follows, we present our UCM slicing algorithm, which is based on a backward traversal of the UCM specification. Figure 6 describes the high level schema of the UCM Slicing algorithm.

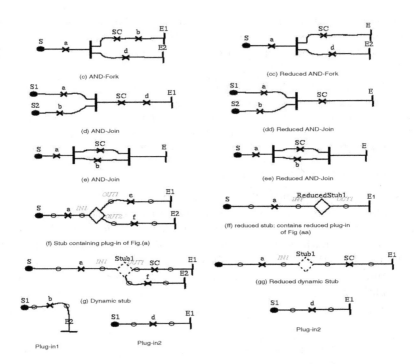

Fig. 5. UCM constructs and its reduced form(2) (SC is the slicing criterion)

Logical conditions are collected as the traversal progresses. Each stub defines a level of abstraction and is treated separately. Therefore, we obtain reduced stubs at different abstraction levels. Since a plug-in can be installed in many stubs according to the chosen scenario, the user is asked to provide the targeted stub to which the SC belongs. This information is essential because of the 'many-to-many' association between plug-ins and stubs.

It should be noted that the presented algorithm is not necessarily the most time and space efficient approach to compute UCM slices. The algorithm will terminate due to the backward traversal step and the fact that there is a finite number of responsibilities in the UCM.

4.5   Solving the Reachability Expression

The Boolean Satisfiability Problem (SAT). The resulting slice is considered to be correct if and only if the set of computed conditions are satisfied. Given a reachability expression the question is: *Exist there any true/false assignments that will change the entire expression to true?*. Since UCM deals only with boolean variables, the reachability problem can be reduced to an instance of the boolean Satisfiability Problem (SAT) [3]. SAT is the first known NP-complete problem, as proved by *Stephen Cook* [3] in 1971. There are many approaches for solving instances of SAT in practice. Just to name few: Davis-Putnam, GRASP,

```
Input:UCM + slicing criterion SC(Responsibility or start/end point)
Output: Reduced UCM, Reachability Expression
Step1:(*Searching SC*)


Traversal of the all UCM maps using a depth first algorithm
IF (SC not found) THEN notify the user;exit
ELSE IF (SC part of the root map) THEN Go to step 2
     ELSE Read(targetStub) (*User is asked to provide the targeted stub*)
          IF (plug in is part of Dynamic stub) THEN
               globalReachability := selectionCond (*Selection policy for dynamic stubs*) ENDIF
     Point to TargetedStub and start at SC
     Go to step 2 ENDIF
ENDIF
```

Step2:(*UCM Backward Traversal: executed for every single path (recursively); Read Previous element, collect conditions, etc. use access functions defined over the different sets of the UCM definition*)

```
WHILE (not(startPoint)) DO Read_previous(element)
rootStack := rootStack + ((element) or (stub to which the SC belongs))
IF (OR-Fork) THEN reachabilityExpression:=reachabilityExpression AND (OR-Fork condition)ENDIF
IF (OR-JOIN) THEN  FOR (each alternative path i) create new stack (Stack_i)
                    to handle the alternative path and repeat step2 (recursive traversal)ENDIF
If (AND-Join) THEN FOR (each concurrent path) create new stack (stack_j)
                    to handle the concurrent path and repeat step2 (recursive traversal)ENDIF
IF (AND-Fork) THEN FOR (each concurrent path) create new stack (stack_k)
    perform a forward traversal and save elements in the stack til reaching the end points ENDIF
IF (Static Stub) THEN rootStack := rootStack + StubName ENDIF
IF (Dynamic Stub) THEN select only plugins bound to the exit point
                    from which the backward traversal entered the stub ENDIFENDWHILE
```

Step3:(*Construct the UCM slice: Convert stacks into sequences*)

```
UCMSlice:= (generic end point, SC) // Initialize Slice
FOR (each stack) DO
     stack.pop(element)
     UCMSlice := UCMSlice + (element.construct)
     IF (stack of dynamic plug-in) THEN
        Add for each plug-in a new alternative to the reachability expression
        global_ReachExp := globalReachExp OR (selection condition)
     ENDIF
ENDFOR
```

Fig. 6. Slicing algorithm for unbound UCMs

WALKSAT, GSAT, CHAFF and SATO. Finding a solution to the reachability expression is outside the scope of this paper. For a detailed coverage of this problem refer to [6].

Conflicting Conditions and Non-Determinism. We may obtain unsatisfiable reachability expressions in the following situations:

1. Conflicting conditions: unsatisfiable set of conditions in successive alternatives found in OR-Forks (For example: C1 and ¬C1), in selection policies of nested dynamic stubs, etc.
2. Non-determinism

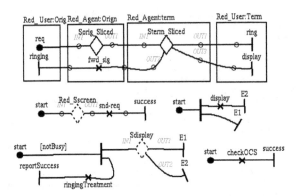

Fig. 7. Simple telephony system slice with respect to SC:*display*

UCMs may contain some non-deterministic behavior due to overlapping conditions (For example: in an OR-Fork, conditions *Cond1:(C1=true)* and *Cond2:(C1=true and C2=true)* overlap when *C2=true*. This will result in a non-deterministic execution. Hence, the resulting initial condition does not guarantee the execution of the computed slice.

Note: Parnas tables can be applied at specification time to determine, if a collection of conditions is deterministic and complete [15].

5   Discussion on the Application of UCM Slices

UCM slices help analyse to what extent the behavior and/or architecture of the system might be affected by a specific maintenance task. For each slice, a maintainer can identify the part of the particular scenario that contributes to the slicing criterion (on both architectural and behavioral parts).

5.1   Applying UCM Slicing for the Simple Telephone System

In what follows, we apply the slicing algorithm for the Simple Telephone System presented in Section 3.2. Suppose that we want to perform an upgrade to the CND feature. The upgrade will involve the display not only of the Caller's name but also his/her service provider. This maintenance task cannot take place until the maintainer understands how the particular feature works and how it interacts with other system features. Knowing all the details of the requirement specification is almost never necessary; an experienced maintainer will try to extract only just enough information to perform the task at hand. The goal is to extract the scenarios leading to the display function (responsibility). Hence, the slicing criterion is the responsibility *display*.

Figure 7 describes the resulting UCM obtained from the original UCM of figure 1 with respect to the slicing criteria *display*. Figure 8 shows the corre-

$$((subCND = true) \text{ AND } (Busy = false) \text{ AND } (subOCS = false)) \ (1)$$
$$OR$$
$$((subCND=true) \text{ AND } (Busy=false) \text{ AND } (subOCS=true) \text{ AND }$$
$$(OnOCSList=false)) \ (2)$$

Fig. 8. Reachability equation for responsibility *display*

sponding *Reachability Expression.*The first part of the reachability expression ((1) in Fig 8) illustrates the fact that the default plug-in is selected *(subOCS = false)* and the second part of the expression ((2) in Fig 8) expresses the fact that the OCS plug-in was selected.

In our example the Reachability Expression itself provides the initial values of global variables leading to the slicing criterion and no further computation is needed.

6 UCM Data Flow

6.1 Variable Assignment

So far, global boolean variables were assigned values only at initialization time. However, UCM responsibilities and end points may affect the content of value identifiers ("$\longleftarrow$" denotes the assignment operator). As a result, the reachability expression may not hold and the correctness of the computed slice is affected.

Case1: Suppose that in the UCM of figure 9, responsibility a:$C\longleftarrow \neg C$. Consequently, the new definition of variable C should be considered in the reachability expression : $C = true$, $C \longleftarrow \neg C$.

Case2: Suppose that in the UCM of figure 9, responsibility b:$C\longleftarrow \neg C$. The update happened after a path has been taken. The reachability expression should not be affected and should remain: $C=true$.

This mixture of predicates and assignment statements should be eliminated before applying a satisfiability algorithm [6]. In order to obtain a reachability expression containing only predicates, we substitute the affected variable of the assignment statement in the logical prediactes(also called *unification*). For example: $C = true$, $C\longleftarrow \neg C \Longrightarrow true=\neg C$. This problem is formalised and solved by the two following rules:

Rule 1. *If a variable has been assigned a new value before participating in a choice condition, then the variables of the choice are are substituted with the new variable assignment.*

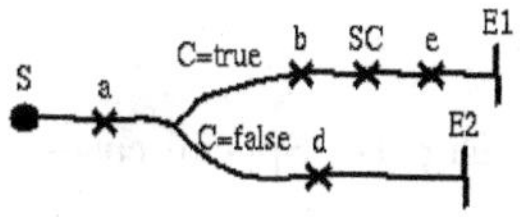

Fig. 9. Responsibilities updating boolean variables

$$v \longleftarrow f(x_1,\ldots,x_n), \; g(y_1,\ldots,y_n,v) \Longrightarrow g(y_1,\ldots,y_n,f(x_1,\ldots,x_n))$$

where v is a boolean variable, f and g are logical expressions.

Rule 2. *If a variable has been assigned a new value after participating in a choice condition, the predicate condition is retained in the reachability expression and the assignment is ignored.*

$$g(y_1,\ldots,y_n,v), v \longleftarrow f(x_1,\ldots,x_n) \Longrightarrow g(y_1,\ldots,y_n,v)$$

where v is a boolean variable, f and g are logical expressions.

6.2   Limitations

While the underlined rules are easy to apply and help reducing the reachability expression, they are not applicable in the following circumstances:

Loops. When a UCM contains loops, the number of times a loop is visited is known only at run time. Such information, which depends on the variable's initial values and guard's evaluation, is needed in order to compute the slice and to solve the reachability expression. For example, in the simple UCM of Figure 10(a), the number of times the loop is entered (zero or one time) is not available when the backward traversal is performed.

In a more complex situation, where instead of having only a responsibility like R2 of Figure 10(a) we have a dynamic stub where the selection of plug-ins depends on the values of the variables at run-time. Hence, non executable plug-ins may be part of the resulting slice whereas they should be left out.

Non-Determinism. Figure 10(b) shows a UCM with two interleaving responsibilities R1 and R2. SC is reached only when R2 is executed after R1. One possible option is to investigate all possible alternatives (i.e., execution paths). Each alternative will be evaluated separately and considered in the resulting slice if it is a consistent one. Therefore, the resulting slice will be the union of all consistent executions. Another option is to keep the non-determinism. Then the user can analyze the resulting slice and make the appropriate decision.

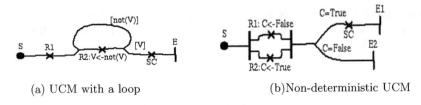

(a) UCM with a loop   (b)Non-deterministic UCM

Fig. 10. Special cases

7   Related Work

Our work on UCM slicing builds on from prior work in the following two primary areas: functional requirement slicing and architectural slicing.

7.1   Slicing of Hierarchical State Machines

Heimdahl *et al.* [7] apply slicing to the requirement specification language RSML (Requirement State Machine Language). Their proposed method consists on reducing the requirement specification based on a specific scenario of interest. The reduced specification contains only the behaviors that are possible when the operating conditions defining the reduction scenario are satisfied. Such a reduced specification is called the *interpretation* of the specification under this scenario. Next, the produced interpretation is sliced based on different entities in the model to highlight the portions of the specification affecting an output variable or a specific transition. This is achieved through a data and control flow information analysis. The slices can be arbitrarily combined using standard set of operations to construct a combined slice containing the information of interests.

7.2   Slicing of State Based Models

Korel *et al.* [11] presented an approach of slicing EFSM (Extended Finite State Machines) models. Their approach produces an EFSM slice based on EFSM dependence analysis. The resulting slice may further be reduced by merging states and transitions to construct a non-deterministic EFSM. This is called non-deterministic slicing.

RSML and EFSM slicing emphasizes only the behavioral part of the requirement specification. The architectural part is left aside. Use Case Maps scenarios combine both aspects (i.e., behavioral and architectural) in a single representation. Our proposed technique took advantage of this dual representation.

7.3   Architectural Slicing

Zhao [20] introduced a new form of slicing called *the Architectural slicing* to aid architectural understanding and reuse. He applied slicing to an architectural specification of a software system written in WRIGHT, which is an Architectural Description Language (ADL). A Wright architectural specification of a system is defined by a set of component and connector type definitions, a set of instantiations of specific objects of these types, and a set of attachments. Attachments specify which components are linked to which connectors. Each component has an interface defined by a set of ports and each connector has an interface defined by a set of roles. In order to compute an architectural slice, an Architecture information flow graph is constructed then a traversal algorithm is applied. The reduced architectural description contains only the lines of ADL code that could be associated with a particular slicing criterion. In [17, 20] the slicing criterion is either a set of ports of a component or a set of roles of a connector. Stafford *et al.* [17] presented a closely related method to Zhao's work. They introduced a software architecture dependency technique called chaining. Their work consists on extracting a chain of dependences (called links) between the specification's elements based on a set of ports of a component (slicing criterion).

8   Conclusion

In summary, our approach for slicing Use Case Maps allows an analyst to reduce a requirement specification based on a selected slicing criterion. Our approach is *two tiered*. First, we allow an analyst to reduce a UCM specification according to a slicing criterion. Second, a reachability expression is attached to the slice, which provides insight on the feasibility of the selected scenarios. We illustrated potential uses of UCM slicing in testing and requirement comprehension of complex specification, by reducing the complexity of the given specification. Furthermore, we see potential application domains for UCM slicing in feature extraction, impact analysis, and reuse of requirements. In fact, while reuse of code is important, more significant improvements in productivity and quality can be expected from reuse of software designs and requirement patterns. By slicing a UCM requirement, a system designer can extract reusable parts from it, and reuse them into new system designs for which they are appropriate. As part of our future work, we will investigate the use of dynamic slicing that may significantly reduce the size of a UCM slice. Providing inputs helps reducing the domain of the UCM and only the parts that comply with the input values are kept in the final slice. Consequently, the reachability expression is also reduced. We are currently investigating those research directions.

Finally the approach outlined in this paper is not limited to Use Case Maps specifications. The approach is general enough to be applied to all languages with guarded transitions such as activity diagrams part of UML.

References

1. Amyot, D., Eberlein, A.: An Evaluation of Scenario Notations and Construction Approaches for Telecommunication Systems Development. Telecommunications Systems Journal, 24:1, 61–94, September 2003.
2. Chang, J., Richardson, D.G.: Static and dynamic specification slicing. Proceedings of the Fourth Irvine Software Symposium, April 1994.
3. Cook, S.: The complexity of theorem proving procedures. Proc. 3rd ACM Symp. On Theory of Computing (1971) 151–158.
4. De Lucia, A.: Program slicing: Methods and applications. 1st IEEE International Workshop on Source Code Analysis and Manipulation (Florence, Italy, 2001), IEEE Computer Society Press, Los Alamitos, California, USA, pp. 142–149.
5. Gallagher, K.B., Lyle, J.R.: Using program slicing in software maintenance. IEEE Transactions on Software Engineering, SE-17(8): 751-761, August 1991.

6. Gu, J., Purdom, P.W., Franco, J., Wah, B.W.: Algorithms for satisfiability (SAT) problem: A survey. DIMACS Volume Series on Discrete Mathematics and Theoretical Computer Science, 1996.

7. Heimdahl, M.P.E., Whalen, M.W.: Reduction and Slicing of Hierarchical State Machines. Proceedings of the 6th European conference held jointly with the 5th ACM SIGSOFT international symposium on Foundations of software engineering, Zurich, Switzerland, 1997, pp. 450–467.

8. ITU-T, URN Focus Group (2002): Draft Rec. Z.152 - UCM: Use Case Map Notation (UCM). Geneva. http://www.UseCaseMaps.org/urn/

9. ITU-T: Recommendation Z.150 (02/03), User Requirements Notation (URN) - Language Requirements and Framework. International Telecommunication Union, Geneva.

10. Korel, B., Laski, J.: Dynamic program slicing. Process. Letters, 29(3), Oct. 1988, pp. 155–163.

11. Korel, B., Singh, I., Tahat, L., Vaysburg, B.: Slicing of State-Based Models. Proceedings of the International Conference on Software Maintenance 2003. IEEE Computer Society, Washington, USA.

12. Miga, A., Amyot, D., Bordeleau, F., Cameron, C., Woodside, M.: Deriving Message Sequence Charts from Use Case Maps Scenario Specifications. Reed, R., Reed, J. (Eds) 10th SDL Forum (SDL'01), Copenhagen, 2001. Volume 2078 of Lecture Notes in Computer Science, 268–287.

13. Millett, L., Teitelbaum, T.: Slicing Promela and its applications to model checking. Proceedings of the 4th International SPIN Workshop, 1998.

14. Oda, T., Araki, K.: Specification slicing in formal methods of software engineering. Proceedings of the Seventeenth International Computer Software and Application Conference, November 1993.

15. Parnas, D.L., Madly, J., Iglewski, M.: Precise Documentations of Well-Structured Programs. IEEE Transactions on Software Engineering, Volume 20, Number 12 (December 1994), 948–976.

16. Sloane, A.M., Holdsworth, J.: Beyond traditional program slicing. Zeil, S.J. (Ed) Proceedings of the 1996 International Symposium on Software Testing and Analysis, 180–186, New York, January 1996. ACM Press.

17. Stafford, J.A., Wolf, A.L.: Architecture-Level Dependence Analysis in Support of Software Maintenance. Proceedings of the Third International Workshop on Software Architecture, November 1998, pp. 129–132.

18. Tip, T.: A survey of program slicing techniques. Journal of programming languages, 3:121–189, 1995.

19. Weiser, M.: Program slicing. IEEE Transactions on software Engineering, SE-10(4):352–357, July 1984.

20. Zhao, J.: Applying slicing techniques to software architectures. 4th IEEE Int. Conf on Engineering of Complex Computer Systems, 1998, Monterey, California, and 5th European Conf. on Software Maintenance and Reengineering (CSMR01).

Proving a Soundness Property for the Joint Design of ASN.1 and the Basic Encoding Rules

Christian Rinderknecht

Groupe Léonard de Vinci, École Supérieure d'Ingénieurs Léonard de Vinci
D.E.R. Génie Informatique, F-92916 Paris La Défense Cedex (France)
Christian.Rinderknecht@devinci.fr

Abstract. The Abstract Syntax Notation One (ASN.1) can be used to model types of values carried by signals in SDL or MSC but is also directly used by network protocol implementors. In the last few years, the press has reported several alleged vulnerabilities of ASN.1 and the Basic Encoding Rules (BER) related to network protocols like SNMP and, more recently, OpenSSL. In reality it has been shown that the security issues (theoretically denial of service attacks) were due to low-quality and poorly-tested compiler implementations. We use some formal methods to go further. We review formally the design of the BER themselves and prove that, under some assumptions, it is flawless whatever the network protocol is and whatever the values to be transmitted are. More precisely, we start with a formal modeling of the BER which abstracts away low-level details but captures the design principles. Then we define a soundness property stating that the composition of encoding and decoding yields a value which is equivalent to the original. Finally we prove that this property holds for all values specified with ASN.1.

Keywords: Abstract Syntax Notation One, ASN.1, Basic Encoding Rules, BER, protocol, specification, vulnerabilities, formal methods.

1   Introduction

The wide variety of software and hardware architectures in distributed systems and telecommunications makes it valuable to use a common high-level data notation in protocol specifications. To fulfill this need, the ISO organization and the International Telecommunication Union (ITU) defined the Abstract Syntax Notation One (ASN.1) series of standards. ASN.1 [1,2,3,4,5] is a language for data types allowing the protocol designer to capture numerous networking concepts, such as protocol data units, without worrying about the possible environment and implementation heterogeneity of the peers. The peers share a set of ASN.1 modules and agree upon a set of *encoding rules*, such as [6,7], which is a method for encoding values produced at run-time by the communicating applications, into series of bits. ASN.1 has been adopted for a wide range of applications, such as network management, secure e-mail, mobile telephony, air traffic control etc.

D. Amyot and A.W. Williams (Eds.): SAM 2004, LNCS 3319, pp. 154–170, 2005.

In the last few years, the press has reported several alleged vulnerabilities of ASN.1 and the Basic Encoding Rules (BER) related to network protocols like SNMP and, more recently, OpenSSL. Each time, an accurate description of the problem has been finally published, showing that the weakness lay in *implementations* poorly written and insufficiently tested. The real vulnerabilities were almost all related to improper decoding of ill-formed BER encodings (or *codes*) causing buffer overflows, unspecified (non-deterministic) behaviours, stack corruptions and, in the end, a possible denial of service.

From now on, it is important to understand and remember that ASN.1 and the BER, intrinsically, have nothing to do with security or cryptographic protocols. Both are used for modeling and handling the data part of protocols, not the control. As a consequence, the soundness property we aim at in this article must not be considered as a security property about *control* but as mere correctness of composition of encoding and decoding with the BER of *values* specified by means of ASN.1. For instance, there are no attackers, no nonces etc. here. Nevertheless, the difficulty is not lesser.

More precisely, in this work we want to prove that the design of the BER themselves is flawless, whatever the network protocol is and whatever the values to be transmitted are. To achieve this goal we need the support of formal methods. We start by a formal modeling of the BER which abstracts away low-level details but captures the design principles. Then we define a soundness property representing the security warranty we require and finally we prove that this property holds for all values that can be specified with ASN.1.

2   Modeling

An ASN.1 compiler accepts a set of ASN.1 modules representing the *Protocol Data Unit* (PDU) and, according to a given set of encoding rules and a peer-specific target programming language, produces a set of data type definitions in that programming language, together with a codec (encoder/decoder) for the values to be exchanged. Then these pieces of source code are compiled and linked separately against the communicating application. Let us make some remarks and assumptions.

- The peers share a set of ASN.1 modules and the assumption that the encoding rules are the BER. Without loss of generality, we can reduce the common knowledge to one module and even a unique ASN.1 type.
- In order to be independent from the application programming languages, we shall assume that both peers express directly their values in ASN.1 (in reality they are produced in memory at run-time).
- At this stage, it is important not to be drawn into too much details due to encoding and decoding series of bits. Instead, we chose to represent codes with a more abstract syntax than bits, which will allow us to easily reason by induction. That way we can convince ourselves that the underlying principles of the BER are sound. In a second stage we can study separately the encoding and decoding between our abstract codes and the transmitted bits.

- The standard document specifying the BER [6] says nothing about the decoding procedure except "It is implicit in the specification of these encoding rules that they are also used for decoding." We shall then explicitly propose a decoding from our abstract codes to ASN.1 (accordingly with the two previous assumptions).
- *The BER encodings may not be unique for a given value.* Indeed the BER allow the sender to choose independently from the receiver different encodings for a class of types. For instance, the encoding of the boolean value TRUE can be any non-zero octet [6, §8.2.2] and the encoding of a SET value imposes no order on the component encodings [6, NOTE in §8.11.3]. Mathematically, the BER define an application, not a function. (The restricted form of the BER, called the Canonical Encoding Rules (CER) and the Distinguished Encoding Rules (DER), are functions.) This leads us to require an *equivalence relationship between codes* which would be enough discriminative but would nevertheless make equivalent all the encodings of a value.

Proposition 1. *All the BER encodings of a given value, according to a given type, are equivalent.*

Network. We assume that the network transfer does not alter the codes, despite the publicised vulnerabilities mentioned in the introduction being due to possibly forged BER codes. We ignore this point precisely because it has been shown that these vulnerabilities were due to non-robust decoders, and our aim here is to prove that the BER *themselves* are not flawed.

Well-Formedness. The front-ends of the ASN.1 compilers must check that the type T and the value v are well-formed. These properties are intrinsic to ASN.1 and include, for the types, the uniqueness of names and tags of component types. For instance T ::= CHOICE {a INTEGER, a REAL} and U ::= CHOICE {a INTEGER, b INTEGER} are not well-formed. Indeed, the encoding of t T ::= a : 0 would be ambiguous (i.e. non-deterministic) since 0 can denote either an INTEGER or a REAL value and u U ::= a : 0 would make the decoding non-deterministic because the tags of fields a and b are identical (INTEGER's tag). In both examples, there would be no way for the encoder or the decoder to solve the ambiguity.

Value Equivalence and Soundness. As we mentioned previously, the standard says little about the receiver's behaviour, but, since the BER embed all the tags in the codes, the uniqueness of tags is clearly intended to make the decoding a function, i.e. it returns always the same value on the same code. This is not stated explicitly in the standard and it is imaginable that the decoder sorts some decoded parts before passing the whole input to the application, but the standard seems to favour an asymmetric model in which the sender may spend some time reorganising the encoded data (i.e. not following strictly the order of the ASN.1 specification) and the receiver fastly decodes them as they arrive, without any subsequent processing. With the same asymmetrical focus, we believe that the receiver is the peer who is mostly concerned with security: the soundness property we propose consists in defining an *equivalence relation-*

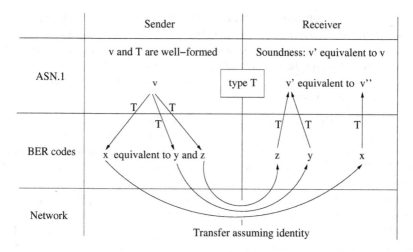

Fig. 1. Soundness property with equivalence entailment

ship between ASN.1 values (therefore independent from the BER) and in stating that the decoded value is equivalent to the (unknown) one the sender emitted.

Theorem 1 (Soundness). *Let v be a well-formed value of the well-formed type T. Then the BER decoding of any BER encoding of v is equivalent to v.*

Code Equivalence. The figure 1 shows the model we described so far. We understand better now why it is important for the equivalence on codes to be enough discriminative: otherwise many codes would be equivalent despite their ASN.1 values not being related. As we said, the BER embed all the tags (collected from the type of the value) in the codes, so, if the type is well-formed, the codes would capture enough structure (from the type) to allow a rather natural and discriminative equivalence relationship to be defined. Moreover, the equivalence will not need the knowledge of the type to be decided (tags in the codes suffice). We already identified the need for an equivalence relation on ASN.1 values in order to express a soundness property, and since, according to our method, we define separately an equivalence relation on codes, we need the following property to be satisfied.

Proposition 2 (Equivalence entailment). *Let c_1 and c_2 be two equivalent codes. Then the decoding of c_1 is equivalent to the decoding of c_2 assuming the same type.*

This way, we can maintain the soundness property despite the encoding procedure is not a function. In particular we suggest that the decoding is a non-injective function (decoding of two different codes can lead to the same value, e.g. TRUE).

Typing. In figure 1 we annotate the arrows between the "ASN.1" and the "BER codes" layers with T to mean that a value is encoded following the type T or a code is decoded assuming the type T. The encoding and decoding of a value assumes that this value is of a given type. This does not imply that we need to formalise the typing relation independently, it actually means that part of the typing is embedded in the encoding and decoding relations. In other words, the encoding only does the type-checking needed to allow the decoding with the same typing assumption.

Subtyping. The BER do not take into account the subtyping constraints. Since these constraints restrict the set of values of a given type, the set of values considered by the BER is greater than the specified PDU. The Packed Encoding Rules [7] (PER) consider the subtyping constraints and define a notion of *PER-visibility* upon them. This also amounts to making an approximation of the exact set of values. These behaviours are not a design flaw. Indeed, when the encoder receives a value from its application, it should first check whether this value fits the PDU and, if so, it would be encoded after. The decoder, on the other hand, when receiving a code, decodes it first, then checks whether the value fits the PDU and, if so, passes it to its application. Keep in mind also that the encoding rules try to minimise the length of the codes according to different strategies (contrast BER and PER), so they *must* approximate the data in order to find some regularities — as a cloud of points can be compactly approximated by its convex hull.

It is up to the ASN.1 compiler, not to the encoding rules themselves, to generate the code checking whether a value fits the PDU. The great expressiveness of the ASN.1 subtyping paradigm makes it very difficult to calculate the exact set of values of a subtype, even in particular to detect and reject empty PDUs [8]. However, the attacks mentioned earlier were based on forged BER codes which were not out of the PDU but merely ill-formed or took advantage of recursive types in order to overflow the receiver's stack. In any case, the decoders (generated by ASN.1 compilers) must be robust and the limits we just mentioned about determining the exact set of values of the PDU has more to do with ASN.1 modules validation rather than soundness of data transmission — at least until now. Thereupon, the BER can take into account the structural subtyping constraints (requiring a component to be ABSENT, PRESENT or to remain OPTIONAL).

Core ASN.1 Next, we note that *the BER only apply to a subset of ITU-T Rec. X.680* [2] (X.680 does not contain information objects, non-subtyping constraints and parameterization). For instance, the BER standard does neither consider COMPONENTS OF clauses in ASN.1 types nor selection types as well. The tagging policy (EXPLICIT, IMPLICIT or AUTOMATIC) is not considered either. Another example is BIT STRING values which are supposed not to be specified with named bits. All this suggests that the whole ASN.1 can be reduced to an inner subset which has the same expressivity, i.e. a sub-language which can express all what can be expressed with the whole language and nothing more. For the sake of brevity, in this paper we shall cope with X.680 and show that a simpler sub-language exists by giving a series of rewriting rules which preserves the set of values of a given type. In fact, it is even useful to reduce further our sub-

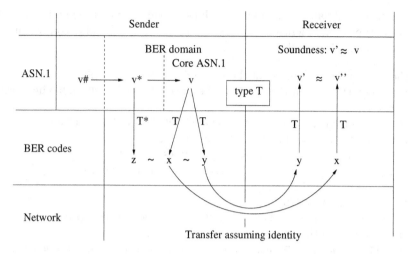

Fig. 2. Core ASN.1 and soundness property

ASN.1 (we call it *BER domain* in figure 2) into a smaller one that we call *core ASN.1.* The purpose is to get rid of some more syntactic constructs which are not fundamental, but are mere facilities, and thus to ease the formalisation and ensure some properties. One technical side effect is that the equivalence on values does not require the knowledge of their type, because *the values in core ASN.1 are not syntactically ambiguous* (e.g. 0 is a value for both REAL and INTEGER types in full ASN.1, but in core ASN.1 it is only of INTEGER type — in the other case it is rewritten 0.0). Another very interesting property is the following.

Theorem 2 (BER termination). *The encoding of core ASN.1 values with the BER always terminates.*

The reason is that we detect and reject as illegal the infinite values, i.e. the recursive values, during the reduction phase. If we want to convince ourselves that the design of the BER is sound, we need to understand well ASN.1 and how to reduce it to a manageable kernel.

Figure 2 gives the final model we arrived at. We note now $v^\#$ and $T^\#$ the values and types in X.680, v^* and T^* the values and types in the BER domain, and simply v and T when they are in core ASN.1. Let us note $v' \approx v$ the proposition "Value v' is equivalent to value v." Let us note $c' \sim c$ the proposition "Code c' is equivalent to code c." The figure 2 makes it clear that we need to guarantee that *all the encodings of v^* are equivalent to all the encodings of v.*

3 Core ASN.1

ASN.1 syntax is involved because it aims at allowing the specification of as many networking concepts as possible. For instance types, values and subtyping constraints may depend on each other: a type may contain constraints (on components) and values (e.g. default values), a value has a type and constraints rely upon types (e.g. inclusion constraint) and values (e.g. value constraint). We define core ASN.1 such that

- the default tagging mode of the module is EXPLICIT TAGS;
- tags obey the standard rules, like alternative types in CHOICE having distinct tags etc.;
- the built-in types are explicitly tagged IMPLICIT and UNIVERSAL;
- tags are explicitly either IMPLICIT or EXPLICIT;
- IMPLICIT tags apply only to untagged types;
- tag values are numeric INTEGER values (not value references);
- there are no DEFAULT component types;
- there is no COMPONENTS OF clause;
- there are no ABSENT, PRESENT or OPTIONAL component constraints;
- there is no selection type, e.g. no T ::= i < U;
- the BIT STRING and INTEGER type do not define constants, e.g. no INTEGER {c(1)} or BIT STRING {a(x)};
- the only BIT STRING values are series of bits, e.g. '1110'B;
- ENUMERATED types define constants with explicit numeric integers;
- REAL values are not legal tokens for INTEGER values and conversely (e.g. 0 is *only* of type INTEGER);
- REAL values do not use the *(mantissa, base, exponent)* form;
- there are no references in values (thus no recursive values).

We relax the first assumption we made in section 2 and assume now that we have one ASN.1 module, syntactically correct with respect to X.680. It is reduced to core ASN.1 by applying the following series of rewritings which do not commute in general. For we lack of room to give the formal rewriting rules, we only illustrate the process on short examples.

1. We remove the selection types, taking care of tags:

$$
\left\{
\begin{array}{l}
\text{A ::= [0] i < [1] B} \\
\text{B ::= [2] C} \\
\text{C ::= [3] CHOICE\{i [4]D\}} \\
\text{D ::= [5] INTEGER}
\end{array}
\right.
\longrightarrow
\left\{
\begin{array}{l}
\text{A ::= [0][4][5] INTEGER} \\
\text{B ::= [2] C} \\
\text{C ::= [3] CHOICE\{i [4]D\}} \\
\text{D ::= [5] INTEGER}
\end{array}
\right.
$$

Note that the selection types that do not define a unique type lead to recursive type definitions whose pattern is X ::= X, as in

$$
\text{T ::= CHOICE \{a a < T\}}
$$
$$
\longrightarrow
\left\{
\begin{array}{l}
\text{T ::= CHOICE \{a A\}} \\
\text{A ::= a < T}
\end{array}
\right.
\longrightarrow
\left\{
\begin{array}{l}
\text{T ::= CHOICE \{a A\}} \\
\text{A ::= A}
\end{array}
\right.
$$

2. The top-level type references are unfolded, i.e. the type references at the declaration level are replaced by the type they reference, as in

$$
\left\{
\begin{array}{l}
\text{T ::= U (C)} \\
\text{U ::= REAL (D)}
\end{array}
\right.
\longrightarrow
\left\{
\begin{array}{l}
\text{T ::= REAL (D \^{} C)} \\
\text{U ::= REAL (D)}
\end{array}
\right.
$$

Beware of the case of constrained references to SET OF types:

$$\left\{ \begin{array}{l} \text{A ::= SET OF C} \\ \text{B ::= A (SIZE (7))} \end{array} \right. \longrightarrow \left\{ \begin{array}{l} \text{A ::= SET OF C} \\ \text{B ::= SET (SIZE (7)) OF C} \end{array} \right.$$

The result B ::= SET OF C (SIZE (7)) would be wrong!

This step is difficult because it removes all recursive types declarations that do not lead to a uniquely defined type, like T ::= T or T ::= CHOICE {a a < T} etc. (See step 1.)

3. The default values are expanded and the DEFAULT annotation is replaced by OPTIONAL, like in the following example

$$\left\{ \begin{array}{l} \text{v T ::= \{\}} \\ \text{T ::= SET \{a U DEFAULT w\}} \end{array} \right. \longrightarrow \left\{ \begin{array}{l} \text{v T ::= \{a w\}} \\ \text{T ::= SET \{a U OPTIONAL\}} \end{array} \right.$$

4. The COMPONENTS OF clauses are expanded:

$$\left\{ \begin{array}{l} \text{T ::= SET \{COMPONENTS OF [6] A\}} \\ \text{A ::= SET \{a REAL\}} \end{array} \right. \longrightarrow \left\{ \begin{array}{l} \text{T ::= SET \{a REAL\}} \\ \text{A ::= SET \{a REAL\}} \end{array} \right.$$

If the tagging mode is AUTOMATIC TAGS, we must *previously* compute the current component tags and then insert the components referred by COMPONENTS OF.

$$\left\{ \begin{array}{l} \text{PDU DEFINITIONS AUTOMATIC TAGS ::=} \\ \quad \text{A ::= SET \{a SET OF B, COMPONENTS OF B\}} \\ \quad \text{B ::= SET \{b [2] INTEGER\}} \\ \text{END} \end{array} \right.$$

$$\longrightarrow \left\{ \begin{array}{l} \text{PDU DEFINITIONS AUTOMATIC TAGS ::=} \\ \quad \text{A ::= SET \{a [0] SET OF B, b [1][2] INTEGER\}} \\ \quad \text{B ::= SET \{b [2] INTEGER\}} \\ \text{END} \end{array} \right.$$

5. INTEGER and BIT STRING constants are replaced by their definition and removed from their defining type:

$$\left\{ \begin{array}{l} \text{T ::= INTEGER \{c(x)\}} \\ \text{v T ::= c} \end{array} \right. \longrightarrow \left\{ \begin{array}{l} \text{T ::= INTEGER} \\ \text{v T ::= x} \end{array} \right.$$

This step may reveal some recursive values, as in

$$\left\{ \begin{array}{l} \text{T ::= INTEGER \{c(v)\}} \\ \text{v T ::= c} \end{array} \right. \longrightarrow \left\{ \begin{array}{l} \text{T ::= INTEGER} \\ \text{v T ::= v} \end{array} \right.$$

6. For BIT STRING values which are specified by means of a series of bit names, we unfold their associated references and replace the value by an equivalent string of bits:

$$\left\{ \begin{array}{l} \text{T ::= BIT STRING \{msb(x),lsb(y)\}} \\ \text{v T ::= \{msb,lsb\}} \end{array} \right. \longrightarrow \left\{ \begin{array}{l} \text{T ::= BIT STRING} \\ \text{v T ::= '10000001'B} \end{array} \right.$$

assuming the excerpt   x INTEGER ::= 7   y INTEGER ::= 0
Also, values in hexadecimal form are translated into binary form:

$$x\ U\ ::=\ 'A'H \longrightarrow x\ U\ ::=\ '1010'B$$

7. We unfold the value references, disallowing at the same time the recursive values, like v T ::= {v}

8. We unfold the ENUMERATED constants and add the missing integers:

$$\begin{cases} \text{T ::= ENUMERATED\{a(v),b\}} \\ \text{v INTEGER ::= 3} \end{cases} \rightarrow \begin{cases} \text{T ::= ENUMERATED\{a(3),b(4)\}} \\ \text{v INTEGER ::= 3} \end{cases}$$

9. We unfold the tag values (this always terminates because there are no more recursive values since step 7), checking that they are syntactically integers:

$$\begin{cases} \text{T ::= [APPLICATION v] IMPLICIT REAL} \\ \text{v INTEGER ::= 3} \end{cases}$$
$$\longrightarrow \begin{cases} \text{T ::= [APPLICATION 3] IMPLICIT REAL} \\ \text{v INTEGER ::= 3} \end{cases}$$

10. The tagging mode becomes EXPLICIT TAGS, like

$$\begin{cases} \text{PDU DEFINITIONS IMPLICIT TAGS ::=} \\ \quad \text{A ::= SET \{a [0] SET OF B\}} \\ \quad \text{B ::= [1] CHOICE \{b [2] REAL\}} \\ \text{END} \end{cases}$$
$$\longrightarrow \begin{cases} \text{PDU DEFINITIONS EXPLICIT TAGS ::=} \\ \quad \text{A ::= SET \{a [0] IMPLICIT SET OF B\}} \\ \quad \text{B ::= [1] EXPLICIT CHOICE \{b [2] IMPLICIT REAL\}} \\ \text{END} \end{cases}$$

11. We make explicit the tags of the built-in types:

$$\text{A ::= INTEGER} \longrightarrow \text{A ::= [UNIVERSAL 2] IMPLICIT INTEGER}$$

12. We reduce the IMPLICIT tags, as

$$\text{T ::= [0] IMPLICIT [1]EXPLICIT [UNIVERSAL 9]IMPLICIT REAL} \longrightarrow$$
$$\text{T ::= [0] IMPLICIT REAL}$$

13. We apply and reduce the structural subtyping constraints ABSENT, PRESENT and OPTIONAL, like

$$\text{T ::= CHOICE\{a REAL,b REAL\} (WITH COMPONENTS\{a(PRESENT)\}) } \rightarrow$$
$$\text{T ::= CHOICE \{a REAL\} (General case complex but tractable.)}$$

It is important to understand that in core ASN.1 it is still possible that

- types have only infinite values: T ::= SET {a T}
- values are ill-typed: v REAL ::= ""
- values do not conform to all additional X.680 requirements, like

$$\left\{ \begin{array}{l} \texttt{T ::= SEQUENCE \{a BOOLEAN, b INTEGER\}} \\ \texttt{t T ::= \{b 7, a TRUE\}   -- illegal} \end{array} \right.$$

- subtyping constraints are inconsistent: `T ::= REAL (SIZE(7))`
- subtypes are empty: `T ::= SET ((SIZE(1))^(SIZE(2))) OF REAL`
- subtypes have no value set: `T ::= REAL (ALL EXCEPT T)`

The reason why this is not a problem is that core ASN.1 has been defined with the BER modeling in mind, in particular we do not aim here at a full validation of ASN.1.

Abstract Grammar. We formally define the constructs of core ASN.1 by means of an *abstract grammar* implemented with the algebraic data types of the functional programming language Objective Caml (O'Caml, for short) [9], which is a full-fledged programming language, as well as, historically, a logic meta-language. The core ASN.1 parser output is a pair of a type environment and a value environment. The former is a mapping from type names to types, corresponding to the type declarations in the ASN.1 specification, and the latter is a mapping from value names to values, corresponding to the value declarations. The types and values are *abstract syntax trees*, complying with the abstract grammar. We except from the abstract grammar the `OBJECT IDENTIFIER` and `RELATIVE-OID` types and values for the sake of brevity. We also ignore the extension markers and the subtyping constraints because they play no role in the BER [6, §8.1.1.4] (however we considered some constraints at step 13).

Values. The abstract grammar for core ASN.1 values is defined as follows. Firstly, we assume that the parser removes the ambiguity between enumeration constants [2, §19] and value references [2, §11.4]. For instance, in `a T ::= b`, the token `b` can denote either an enumeration constant or a value reference, depending on the definition of type `T`. The ambiguity can always be removed just by looking at the type definition (this is easy in core ASN.1). The type *item* is used later in the enumerated constants and the type *label* denotes component names.

type *item* = *string* **and** *label* = *string*
type *core_value* = ['SetOf **of** *core_value list* | 'SeqOf **of** *core_value list* | 'Set **of** (*label* × *core_value*) *list* | 'Seq **of** (*label* × *core_value*) *list* | 'TRUE | 'FALSE | 'Enum **of** *item* | 'Int **of** *int* | 'Real **of** *float* | 'NULL | 'MINUS_INFINITY | 'Chosen **of** *label* × *core_value* | 'String **of** *string* | 'BitStr **of** *bool array* | 'PLUS_INFINITY]

where 'SetOf corresponds to values of `SET OF` and 'SeqOf to values of `SEQUENCE OF` types [2, §25, §27]; 'Set models values of the `SET` type and 'Seq models values of `SEQUENCE` types [2, §24, §26] (the argument is a mapping from labels to values); 'TRUE and 'FALSE are obvious; 'Enum models enumerated constants; 'Int and 'Real stand for `INTEGER` and `REAL` values (for simplicity, we assume they fit the built-in arithmetic of O'Caml); 'NULL models the special `NULL` value [2, §23]; 'PLUS_INFINITY and 'MINUS_INFINITY correspond to `PLUS-INFINITY` and `MINUS-INFINITY`; 'Chosen corresponds to `CHOICE` values [2, §28] (thus its argument is a pair of a label and a value); 'String concentrates all kinds of character strings;

'BitStr represents BIT STRING constants [2, §21] and OCTET STRING values [2, §22]. O'Caml values of type core_value will be noted v.

type *tagged_type* = *tag* *list* × *core_type*
and *tag* = (*tag_class* × *int*) × *tag_mode*
and *tag_class* = UNIVERSAL | PRIVATE | APPLICATION | Context
and *tag_mode* = EXPLICIT | IMPLICIT
and *core_type* = ['CHOICE **of** *label* → *tagged_type* | 'OCTET_STRING
| 'SET **of** *components* | 'SEQUENCE **of** *components* | 'BIT_STRING
| 'SET_OF **of** *tagged_type* | 'SEQUENCE_OF **of** *tagged_type* | 'NULL
| 'ENUMERATED **of** *item* → *int* | 'INTEGER | 'BOOLEAN | 'REAL
| 'String | 'TRef **of** *string*]
and *components* = (*label* × *tagged_type* × ['OPTIONAL] *option*) *list*

The type *tagged_type* models the tagged types of core ASN.1, in which a type (*core_type*) can be preceded by a list of tags. Constructor names of type *core_type* are almost self-explanatory, except 'TRef which denotes type references. The type *components* defines the components of SET and SEQUENCE core ASN.1 types: it is a triple made of a label, a tagged type and an optional OPTIONAL component's attribute. O'Caml values of type *core_type* are noted T and *tagged_type* values $\overline{T}$. The mapping of type *label* → *tagged_type*, which is the argument of 'CHOICE, is noted F. Values of type *components* are lists noted Φ of components noted φ, e.g. 'SET $(\varphi :: \Phi)$. An ASN.1 module is modeled by a type environment which is modeled by a function Γ from type names to tagged types, since there are no more value references in core ASN.1. Values of type *tag* are noted ψ and lists of tags Ψ.

4   Coding and Decoding

BER codes. The structure of a BER code is based on the triple (*tag, length, contents*). The *tag* field corresponds to the tag of the value type in ASN.1, the *length* is the length of the contents field and the *contents* field is either another code (in which case the code is said *constructed*) or the encoding of a primitive type (in which case the code is said *primitive*). A primitive type is an ASN.1 built-in type which is not defined in terms of other types, e.g. the INTEGER type. If the contents length is unknown at the encoding-time, it is possible for the coder to provide a special dummy length and then close the code with an *ending octet*, in which case the code is said to be in *indefinite form*, as opposed to *definite form*. Definite form requires that the sender computes the whole code before sending it (in order to be able to compute the contents length) and it allows the receiver to allocate a bounded amount of memory to store the incoming code. The indefinite form allows the sender to encode the value coming from the upper application as it comes throughout a buffer (i.e. faster encoding within a bounded space) but it requires the receiver to handle carefully the incoming stack size. Indeed, the BER codes have a recursive structure and one of the advertised vulnerabilities was due to a deeply embedded code in indefinite form which overflowed the receiver's stack because the *implementation* was mishandling the memory.

Abstract BER codes. A complete formalisation of the BER first requires a model of the codes *at the octet level*, by means of a context-free grammar for instance, and the proof of some relevant properties on it. For example, from a soundness point of view, it is important to prove that the grammar is not ambiguous, i.e. a given code cannot be described in more than one way (exactly one derivation tree); from the decoder's efficiency point of view, it is important to prove that the grammar can be recursively analysed without backtracking and with a small constant amount of look-ahead. Unfortunately, due to the limited room, we have to skip this interesting stage. We shall assume that we already deal with *abstract codes*, which correspond to the abstract syntax trees of the compilers: an abstract code does not model the octets, but rather the structure of the codes. As a consequence, the length field is not included in an abstract code since, conceptually, an abstract code is a tree, not a series as the original codes. Moreover, the concepts of definite and indefinite form are not relevant for abstract codes, since they apply to octet streams only. The abstract codes are thus modeled with an O'Caml type since these types correspond to trees with user-defined nodes and leaves.

type *primitive_code* = Pint | Preal | Pminus_inf | Pplus_inf| Pstring
                    | Pbit_str | Pbool **of** *int* | Pnull
type *code* = (*tag_class* × *int*) × *contents*
and *contents* = Primitive **of** *primitive_code* | Constructed **of** *code list*

The type *primitive_code* captures the codes of the values from types INTEGER, REAL, BIT STRING, OCTET STRING, BOOLEAN, NULL and the numerous character string types. The abstract primitive codes carry little discriminative information for a given type; for example, *all* the INTEGER values are encoded into the same abstract code Pint, but codes of REAL values are still different (Preal). This way we abstract away octet-level details which would otherwise bring us too far. We nevertheless keep the BOOLEAN standard encoding: value FALSE is encoded as (Pbool 0) and TRUE is encoded as (Pbool n) for any $n > 0$. *This allows to maintain the non-determinism of the BER in the modeling.* A code is a triple made of a *tag_class*, a tag number (*int*) and *contents*. The latter is either a primitive or a constructed code. A constructed code is a list of codes.

Inference Rules. We define the encoding with a *system of inference rules*. These are logical implications $P_1 \wedge P_2 \wedge \ldots \wedge P_n \Rightarrow C$ graphically represented as

$$\frac{P_1 \quad P_2 \quad \ldots \quad P_n}{C}$$

where the P_i are the *premises* and C is the *conclusion*. When there is no premise, C is an *axiom* and is simply noted C. An inference rule can be interpreted also from a computational point of view: in order to compute C, we need to compute the P_i first (order is not specified). The rules and axioms can contain unquantified variables (*free variables*). In this case they are implicitly universally quantified ($\forall$) at the beginning. For instance $\dfrac{P_1(x) \quad P_2(y)}{P(x,y)}$ PROP actually denotes the property PROP which is $\forall x, y . P_1(x) \wedge P_2(y) \Rightarrow P(x, y)$. A system of inference rules is a non-ordered set of rules. A theorem is a judgement, i.e. a formal statement. A demonstration is a proof tree whose root (the conclusion) is the theorem, the inner nodes are the conclusions of its subtrees and the leaves are axioms.

Abstract BER. Let us note $\Gamma \vdash v : (\Psi, \mathrm{T}) \to c$ the judgement "In the environment Γ, the value v is encoded into the code c, following the type T with the tags Ψ." The environment models the module and is mandatory because recursive types are allowed, thus type references do exist. Given a type name x, the referred type is $\Gamma(x)$. Using a system of inference rules to define the encoding relation means that the successful encoding of a value matches a proof tree made with the following rules:

$$\frac{n > 0}{\Gamma \vdash \text{'TRUE} : ([\tau, p], \text{'BOOLEAN}) \to (\tau, \text{Primitive}\,(\text{Pbool}\,n))} \text{ TRUE}$$

$$\text{REF} \qquad \qquad \pi \text{ is a permutation on } components$$

$$\frac{\Gamma \vdash v : \Gamma(x) \to c}{\Gamma \vdash v : ([\,], \text{'TRef}\,(x)) \to c} \qquad \frac{\Gamma \vdash v : (\Psi, \text{'SEQUENCE}\,(\pi(\Phi))) \to c}{\Gamma \vdash v : (\Psi, \text{'SET}\,\Phi) \to c} \text{ SET}$$

$$\frac{\Gamma \vdash v : (\Psi, \mathrm{T}) \to c}{\Gamma \vdash v : ((\tau, \text{EXPLICIT}) :: \Psi, \mathrm{T}) \to (\tau, \text{Constructed}\,[c])} \text{ TAGS}$$

$$\frac{\varphi = (l, \overline{\mathrm{T}}, \text{Some 'OPTIONAL})}{\Gamma \vdash \text{'Seq}\,M : ([\psi], \text{'SEQUENCE}\,\Phi) \to c}{\Gamma \vdash \text{'Seq}\,((l, v) :: M) : ([\psi], \text{'SEQUENCE}\,(\varphi :: \Phi)) \to c} \text{ SEQOPTOUT}$$

$$\frac{\varphi = (l, \overline{\mathrm{T}}, \text{Some 'OPTIONAL}) \qquad \Gamma \vdash v : \overline{\mathrm{T}} \to c}{\Gamma \vdash \text{'Seq}\,M : ([\psi], \text{'SEQUENCE}\,\Phi) \to (\tau, \text{Constructed}\,C)}{\overline{c} = (\tau, \text{Constructed}\,(c :: C))}{\Gamma \vdash \text{'Seq}\,((l, v) :: M) : ([\psi], \text{'SEQUENCE}\,(\varphi :: \Phi)) \to \overline{c}} \text{ SEQOPTIN}$$

Due to the lack of space, we only presented the more interesting rules, of which we shall comment the conclusions before the premises. Lists are noted between brackets and $a :: A$ is a list whose head is a and sub-list is A. A pair is either noted (a, b) or a, b. Rule TRUE illustrates a primitive encodings which is non-deterministic (variable n is free). Pattern $[\tau, n]$ matches a list of a single element which is a pair whose first projection is named τ and the second is named n. Since we operate on core ASN.1, this tag is compulsorily the predefined UNIVERSAL and IMPLICIT tag of INTEGER. Rule REF matches the encoding of a type reference $\text{'TRef}(x)$ with no tags: we encode the referenced type $\Gamma(x)$. Rule TAGS apply when an EXPLICIT tag occurs first. Note that Ψ cannot be empty, i.e. $[\,]$, since an IMPLICIT tag only apply to a core type. Rule SET models the non-determinism of the BER with respect to the SET type: any permutation of the sub-codes is allowed.

Rules SEQOPTOUT and SEQOPTIN model another non-deterministic behaviour: a component value whose type is OPTIONAL may not be encoded, as a sender's option. Hence these *two* rules have the same conclusion (it is the only case), contrary to rule SET in which non-determinism is modeled by a free variable (π). We did not model the encoding errors: at any time, given an environment Γ, a tagged type (Ψ, T) and a value v, if no conclusion $\Gamma \vdash v : (\Psi, T) \to \star$ matches then it is a run-time error (we can build no code c in place of $\star$) and the implementation must handle properly this situation in an unspecified way. If the typing is statically done by the ASN.1 compiler, this should not happen, but since we decided not to model the typing, the typing is partly included in the encoding (i.e. at run-time).

Abstract Decoding. As we said in section 2, the BER decoding process is not published, is up to the ASN.1 compiler implementors and can be modeled by a non-injective function. We propose the following equational definition we expect to be faithful. Let us note $\mathcal{D}(\Gamma, c, (\Psi, T))$ the decoding of c in the environment Γ according to type T tagged Ψ.

$$\mathcal{D}(\Gamma, (((\mathsf{UNIVERSAL}, 1), \mathsf{Primitive}(\mathsf{Pbool}\,0))), ([], {}^{'}\mathsf{BOOLEAN})) = {}^{'}\mathsf{FALSE}$$
$$\mathcal{D}(\Gamma, (((\mathsf{UNIVERSAL}, 1), \mathsf{Primitive}(\mathsf{Pbool}\,n))), ([], {}^{'}\mathsf{BOOLEAN})) = {}^{'}\mathsf{TRUE}$$
$$\text{for all } n > 0$$
$$\mathcal{D}(\Gamma, c, ([], {}^{'}\mathsf{TRef}\,(x))) = \mathcal{D}(\Gamma, c, \Gamma(x))$$
$$\mathcal{D}(\Gamma, (\tau, \mathsf{Constructed}\,[c]), ((\tau, \mathsf{EXPLICIT}) :: \Psi, T)) = \mathcal{D}(\Gamma, c, (\Psi, T))$$
$$\mathcal{D}(\Gamma, (\tau, \kappa), ([], {}^{'}\mathsf{CHOICE}\,F)) = \mathcal{D}(\Gamma, (\tau, \kappa), F(l))$$
$$\text{where } F(l) = ((\tau, m) :: \Psi, T)$$

We do not provide the full definition for we lack of space and do not wish to drown the reader into too much technical details anyway.

5   Equivalences and Soundness

Value Equivalence. It is possible to present a complete definition of the value equivalence because we shaped core ASN.1 with this goal in mind. We note $A @ B$ the catenation of lists A and B. We have

$$v \approx v \quad \text{REFLEXIVITY}$$

$$\frac{v_1 \approx v_2 \quad {}^{'}\mathsf{Seq}\,M_1 \approx {}^{'}\mathsf{Seq}\,M_2}{{}^{'}\mathsf{Seq}\,((l, v_1) :: M_1) \approx {}^{'}\mathsf{Seq}\,((l, v_2) :: M_2)} \; \text{SEQ}$$

$$\text{TRANSITIVITY}$$
$$\frac{v_1 \approx v_2 \quad v_2 \approx v_3}{v_1 \approx v_3}$$

$$\frac{\exists l, v_2, M_2', M_2.M = M_2' @ (l, v_2) :: M_2 \quad v_1 \approx v_2 \quad {}^{'}\mathsf{Set}\,M_1 \approx {}^{'}\mathsf{Set}\,M_2}{{}^{'}\mathsf{Set}((l, v_1) :: M_1) \approx {}^{'}\mathsf{Set}\,M} \; \text{SET}$$

$$\frac{v_1 \approx v_2}{v_2 \approx v_1} \; \text{Symmetry} \qquad \frac{v_1 \approx v_2}{\text{'Chosen}\,(l, v_1) \approx \text{'Chosen}\,(l, v_2)} \; \text{Choice}$$

$$\frac{v_1 \approx v_2 \qquad \text{'SeqOf } V_1 \approx \text{'SeqOf } V_2}{\text{'SeqOf }(v_1 :: V_1) \approx \text{'SeqOf }(v_2 :: V_2)} \; \text{SeqOf}$$

$$\frac{\exists v_2, V_2, V_2'.V = V_2' @ v_2 :: V_2 \qquad v_1 \approx v_2 \qquad \text{'SetOf } V_1 \approx \text{'SetOf }(V_2' @ V_2)}{\text{'SetOf }(v_1 :: V_1) \approx \text{'SetOf } V} \; \text{SetOf}$$

Our value equivalence amounts to a structural equality modulo permutations on sub-values of SET and SET OF types.

Code Equivalence. The BER embed a lot of the type information into the codes through the use of tags and a structure isomorphic to types. This makes possible to define an equivalence relationship between codes that relies on two codes only — no further context is needed.

$$\text{Reflexivity} \qquad \frac{\text{Symmetry}}{c_1 \sim c_2} \qquad \frac{\text{Transitivity}}{c_1 \sim c_2 \qquad c_2 \sim c_3}$$
$$c \sim c \qquad \frac{}{c_2 \sim c_1} \qquad \frac{}{c_1 \sim c_3}$$

$$\frac{m > 0 \qquad n > 0}{(\tau, \text{Primitive}\,(\text{Pbool}\,m)) \sim (\tau, \text{Primitive}\,(\text{Pbool}\,n))} \; \text{True}$$

$$\frac{\tau = (\text{UNIVERSAL}, 16) \qquad c_1 \sim c_2}{(\tau, \text{Constructed}\,C_1) \sim (\tau, \text{Constructed}\,C_2)}{(\tau, \text{Constructed}\,(c_1 :: C_1)) \sim (\tau, \text{Constructed}\,(c_2 :: C_2))} \; \text{Seq/SeqOf}$$

$$\frac{\tau = (\text{UNIVERSAL}, 16)}{(\tau, \text{Constructed}\,C_1) \sim (\tau, \text{Constructed}\,C_2)}{(\tau, \text{Constructed}\,(c_1 :: C_1)) \sim (\tau, \text{Constructed}\,C_2)} \; \text{SeqOptOut}$$

Contrary to value equivalence, there are too many cases and hence we cannot present them all. Rule TRUE defines the equivalence of two possibly different encodings of the value TRUE. Rule SEQ/SETOF specifies when (and how, in fact) codes from values of types SEQUENCE and SEQUENCE OF are equivalent. By the way, note that the tags of these two types are identical, hence, in theory, this rule makes equivalent the encodings of, say, values of types SEQUENCE {a INTEGER} and SEQUENCE OF INTEGER, as soon as the integer value is the same. Rule SEQOPTOUT is dual to the homonym rule of the abstract BER where an optional value component is not encoded. Here, it is allowed to skip a sub-code when decoding. *We do not specify when a sub-code has to be skipped or in which code.* We leave this to a more refined specification and/or algorithm.

Equivalence Properties. The properties we expect to hold in our BER model can now be restated in a formal way. First of all, proposition 1, which states that all the BER encodings of a given value, according to a given type, are equivalent, becomes through the use of formal notations:

Proposition 3. *If $\Gamma \vdash v : \overline{T} \rightarrow c_1$ and $\Gamma \vdash v : \overline{T} \rightarrow c_2$ then $c_1 \sim c_2$.*

Next, proposition 2 which states that the decoding of two equivalent codes lead to two equivalent values is now restated in the following way:

Proposition 4 (Equivalence entailment).
$$c_1 \sim c_2 \implies \mathcal{D}(\Gamma, c_1, \overline{T}) \approx \mathcal{D}(\Gamma, c_2, \overline{T})$$

Finally, the soundness theorem 1, which says that the encoding and decoding of a core ASN.1 value v, following a core ASN.1 tagged type $\overline{T}$, leads to a value which is equivalent to v, is now formally rephrased:

Theorem 3 (Soundness). *If $\Gamma \vdash v : \overline{T} \rightarrow c$ then $v \approx \mathcal{D}(\Gamma, c, \overline{T})$.*

We have no room to show the proofs of these properties because they contain a great number of cases. One tricky aspect is the correct handling of sub-code permutations when dealing with SET OF and SET values: for a given unknown permutation on the sender's side, we must explicitly construct the reverse permutation on the receiver's side.

6   Conclusion

We presented a formal review design of the BER. On purpose, we abstracted away many low-level details in our model in order to understand, capture and formalise what are, according to us, the main characteristics of the BER. Therefore the further step would be to refine our model, by explicitly providing the coding and decoding functions for the primitive types, by reckoning with the various string types etc. Also we did not present evidences that the rewriting from the BER domain to its core ASN.1 subset conserves code equivalence, as pointed out in figure 2: this was a matter of room. We nevertheless think that our work dispels clouds of suspicion — if any — about the soundness of ASN.1 and the BER. More precisely, we mean that the composition of encoding and decoding yields a value which is equivalent to the original. The aim of our formal review design is to raise user's confidence on a solid ground and we doubt whether twenty more pages of formulæ would have been a stronger argument for the casual reader. Indeed, making explicit as many as possible assumptions and checking their consistence is inherently reassuring. The mere fact that we had to understand the rationale of the BER and put it into mathematical formalæ really brought to the fore a new understanding. Also the interest in choosing a system of inference rules to define our relationships is that this formalism closes the gap between specifications and algorithms. Besides, the suggested use of O'Caml as an implementation language is motivated because, as a descendant of a logic meta-language, it is precisely suited to implement algorithms specified by means of inference rules. The way of deducing them consists mainly in providing a deterministic and constructive refinement which is sound and complete with respect to the initial specification. By constructive we mean for instance to replace existential quantifiers, the symmetry rule etc. by explicit procedures, and determinism means, in the context of this work, having no backtracking implied (e.g. no overlapping conclusions).

References

1. Dubuisson, O.: ASN.1 — Communication Between Heterogeneous Systems. Academic Press (2000) ISBN 0-12-6333361-0, `http://www.oss.com/asn1/dubuisson.html`.
2. ITU-T Rec. X.680 (2002) or ISO/IEC 8824-1:2002: Information technology — Abstract Syntax Notation One (ASN.1): Specification of basic notation. (2002) `http://www.itu.int/ITU-T/studygroups/com17/languages/X.680-0207.pdf`.
3. ITU-T Rec. X.681 (2002) or ISO/IEC 8824-2:2002: Information technology — Abstract Syntax Notation One (ASN.1): Information object specification. (2002) `http://www.itu.int/ITU-T/studygroups/com17/languages/X.681-0207.pdf`.
4. ITU-T Rec. X.682 (2002) or ISO/IEC 8824-3:2002: Information technology — Abstract Syntax Notation One (ASN.1): Constraint specification. (2002) `http://www.itu.int/ITU-T/studygroups/com17/languages/X.682-0207.pdf`.
5. ITU-T Rec. X.683 (2002) or ISO/IEC 8824-4:2002: Information technology — Abstract Syntax Notation One (ASN.1): Parameterization of ASN.1 specifications. (2002) `http://www.itu.int/ITU-T/studygroups/com17/languages/X.683-0207.pdf`.
6. ITU-T Rec. X.690 (2002) or ISO/IEC 8825-1:2002: Information technology — ASN.1 Encoding Rules: Specification of Basic Encoding Rules (BER), Canonical Encoding Rules (CER) and Distinguished Encoding Rules (DER). (2002) `http://www.itu.int/ITU-T/studygroups/com17/languages/X.690-0207.pdf`.
7. ITU-T Rec. X.691 (2002) or ISO/IEC 8825-2:2002: Information technology — ASN.1 Encoding Rules: Specification of Packed Encoding Rules (PER). (2002) `http://www.itu.int/ITU-T/studygroups/com17/languages/X.691-0207.pdf`.
8. Rinderknecht, C.: An Algorithm for Validating ASN.1 (X.680) Specifications using Set Constraints. The Computer Journal **46** (2003)
9. Chailloux, E., Manoury, P., Pagano, B.: Programmation d'applications avec Objective Caml. O'Reilly France (2000) 700 pp. *English version at* `http://caml.inria.fr/oreilly-book/`.

Checking Secrecy by Means of Partial Order Reduction

Cas J.F. Cremers and Sjouke Mauw

Eindhoven University of Technology,
Department of Mathematics and Computer Science,
P.O. Box 513, NL-5600 MB Eindhoven, The Netherlands
{ccremers, sjouke}@win.tue.nl

Abstract. We propose a partial order reduction for model checking security protocols for the secrecy property. Based on this reduction, we develop an automatic tool that can check security protocols for secrecy, given a finite execution scenario. We compare this tool to several other tools.

1   Introduction

The transformation of our society into an information society proceeds faster than many have ever expected. Current society already relies heavily on networked information systems with the associated security risks. Digital information is not any more processed within a physically shielded environment, since networked computers are susceptible to attacks and information has to be conveyed over possibly insecure communication channels.

Such communications may represent a value, which can be of a direct or indirect nature. Purchasing, for instance, a piece of music over the internet has a clear direct value, while the indirect value of establishing one's identity in an e-banking application may be even larger. This value of information is closely connected to the classical quality factors of information, which are *confidentiality, integrity* and *availability*. Viewed in a different way, these three factors are the possible *security goals* to be achieved by a security-aware application. The most studied security goals are *authentication* (which counts as a form of integrity) and *confidentiality* (or secrecy). In contrast to authentication, the notion of secrecy does not leave much room for different interpretations. However, there is still no definitive answer as to verify secrecy effectively.

Security protocols are communication protocols dedicated to achieving such security goals. They can play a role at application level (e.g., establishing a user's identity in an electronic auction), but also at lower network levels (such as IPSec, which is the internet protocol enhanced with security features for authentication and confidentiality). Experience shows that it is not hard to develop a security protocol that appears correct at first sight, but shows security breaches when assessed more thoroughly. The reason is that it is very hard to protect against all possible attacks of every possible intruder.

D. Amyot and A.W. Williams (Eds.): SAM 2004, LNCS 3319, pp. 171–188, 2005.

Several decades ago, it was recognized that formal analysis of security protocols is imperative to establish secure information systems. Although formal methods suffer from the well-known problem of scaling up to large systems, security protocols have the advantage of being rather small, at least in their abstract form. Many formal methods have been developed for or made applicable to the area of security protocols.

Although the relatively small size of a security protocol makes it amenable to formal analysis, the complexity of the verification problem makes computer support essential. Theorem provers and model checkers are the two major branches of tool support in this area. Theorem provers assist the user in constructing a formal correctness proof for the protocol. They often need human guidance during the verification process. Model checkers, on the other hand, process the provided input automatically. While theorem provers provide full evidence of the correctness of a protocol, model checkers often only increase the confidence in the protocol. A model checker searches through all possible behaviours (or rather, states) of the protocol and checks whether they all satisfy the required security property. In general this state space grows exponentially with the size of the input problem, or may even be infinite. Therefore, much research is performed on reducing the explored state space. A prominent approach is the so-called partial order reduction [11]. It makes use of the fact that when exchanging two events in a trace it sometimes will not influence the property checked for in this trace. These traces are equivalent with respect to the checked property and only one of these equivalent behaviours has to be explored by the model checker.

The goal of this paper is to study the development of a dedicated model checker based on partial order reduction for verifying security protocols with respect to confidentiality. This may seem a rather trivial research goal, and indeed there are many general purpose model checkers that have been successfully applied to verifying secrecy in security protocols. However, we conjecture that these general purpose model checkers cannot make full use of the structure underlying the problem and thus are not fully optimized for this specific task. Therefore, the underlying assumption which we want to validate here is that a model checker dedicated to verifying confidentiality of security protocols will outperform a general purpose model checker instantiated for the chosen setting. We expect that studying the specific security goal, the specific intruder model, the specific agent execution model, the specific agent communication model, etc. gives insight in how to considerably reduce the explored state space. As a side effect, developing a dedicated model checker also allows us to develop a dedicated input and output format. This makes it easier to support formats that are most suited for displaying security protocols (and attack traces), such as Message Sequence Charts (MSCs). In this paper we make use of MSCs to express security protocols, scenarios and attack traces. The first two are manually crafted, but the attack traces are generated in an MSC format by our model checker.

This paper is structured in the following way. First we will discuss the general setting of security protocols in Section 2. In Section 3 we will show an algorithm for model checking secrecy, and propose a new algorithm. In Section 4 we discuss

Scyther, a tool we developed on the basis of the new algorithm. Section 5 is reserved for discussing related work and some experiments. Finally, in Section 6 we indicate some future work and conclude.

Acknowledgments. We thank Erik de Vink for the discussions on security protocol semantics and Ingmar Schnitzler for programming a prototype implementation of our model checking algorithm. Lutger Kunst is acknowledged for his contribution on displaying attack traces as Message Sequence Charts.

2   Security Protocols

In this section we will review some security protocol terminology and present an example of a security protocol, the Bilateral Key Exchange Protocol (BKE, see [1]). The goal of BKE is that two parties agree upon a freshly generated secret key. Secrecy of this key is only one of the requirements of this protocol, but we will not discuss the other requirements.

Figure 1 shows this protocol in a Message Sequence Chart. The two vertical axes represent the two *roles* of the protocol, which are the initiator role I and the responder role R. We list the initial knowledge of each of the roles above the headers of the roles. Thus, the initiator has an asymmetric key pair (SKi, PKi) and knows the public key of the responder PKr. Likewise, the responder has asymmetric key pair (SKr, PKr) and knows the public key of the initiator. The way in which this initial knowledge was established is not made explicit. The initiator starts by creating a fresh nonce ni. This is a random, unpredictable value which is used to make the exchanged messages unique and thus helps to counter play-back attacks. The first message sent by the initiator consists of the pair ni, I which is encrypted with the public key of the intended responder, denoted by $\{ni, I\}_{PKr}$. Encryption is used to guarantee that only the intended recipient can unpack the message. Upon receipt of the message, the responder creates his own fresh nonce nr and a fresh symmetric key kir that he wants to share with the initiator. Goal of the protocol is to transfer this key to the initiator in a secret way. Therefore, the responder replies with the message $\{h(ni), nr, kir\}_{PKi}$. With this message he proves that he was able to unpack the previous message (by showing that he knows nonce ni, witnessed by sending a hash $h(ni)$ of this nonce). Furthermore, this message contains the key kir and a challenge nr. The complete message is encrypted with the public key of the initiator to ensure that only I can unpack the message. Finally, the initiator responds to R's message by sending a hash of nonce nr encrypted with key kir. Herewith he acknowledges receipt of the previous message. At the end of the two roles we have listed the security claims as a special kind of event. Both participants claim that whenever they reach the end of their protocol the value of kir is not known to the intruder. The meaning of such an event is that in every trace of the system in which this event occurs the value of kir is not in the knowledge set of the intruder.

A system executing this protocol consists of a number of agents, each of which may execute one or more instances of both roles (in parallel). When an agent

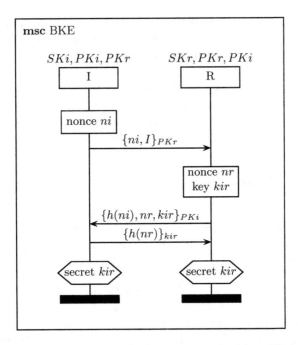

Fig. 1. The Bilateral Key Exchange protocol with public keys

executes a role from a protocol, we call this a run. Therefore, a system consists of a collection of runs exchanging messages to each other.

This simple model is not complete without describing the threats to which the system is exposed. Thereto, we assume the so-called Dolev-Yao intruder model (see [6]), which is considered the most general model of an adversary. This model implies that the intruder has complete control over the network and that he can derive new messages from his initial knowledge and messages received from honest agents. Hereby we assume that the intruder can only decrypt messages if he is in possession of the appropriate cryptographic key. Furthermore, we assume that a number of agents may conspire with the intruder and try to mislead the honest agents as to learn their secrets. Due to the capabilities of the intruder to intercept any sent message and to insert any message which can be constructed from his knowledge, we can model the existence of conspiring agents by assuming that their secret keys are in the initial knowledge of the intruder.

Now we come back to the Bilateral Key Exchange protocol. The specification from Figure 1 is correct if for any number of agents, executing any number of runs, in presence of a Dolev-Yao intruder, whenever an honest run enters a secrecy claim, the corresponding key kir is never exposed to the intruder.

We explain this in more detail using Figure 2. This Figure describes a sample scenario of the BKE protocol consisting of three runs, involving three agents a, b, and e, of which we assume that e conspires with the intruder. Thus we assume that the intruder has knowledge of the secret key SKe of agent e.

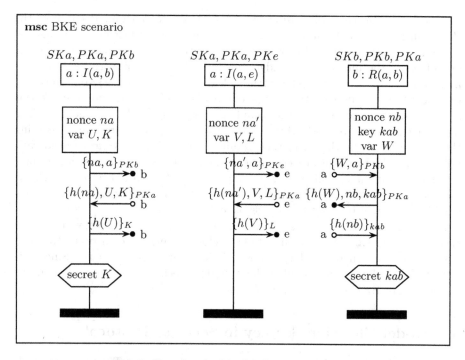

Fig. 2. Sample scenario for the BKE protocol

Each run is an instantiation of one of the two roles specified in Figure 1. The first run describes the behaviour of agent a performing the initiator role, expecting to be engaged in an execution of the BKE protocol with responder b. Notice that the incoming information (nonce nb and key kab) are stored in local variables (named U and K, respectively). The secrecy claim is therefore expressed with respect to the contents of variable K. The second run is also a run of agent a, performing the initiator role, but this time involved in a session with (conspiring) agent e. The third run is a run of agent b as a responder, involved with initiating agent a. In the second run, we did not include any secrecy claim. The reason for this is that if an agent starts a protocol session with an untrusted partner, his secrecy claim is bound to be violated and we will not consider this a protocol flaw. It is not required that within a scenario there is a matching responder role for every initiator role (or the other way around). The reason is that the intruder may abuse such non-matching runs to break secrecy of one of the involved keys.

Looking at the scenario, we see that there are three different types of events (ignoring the declaration of constants and variables). The first type is a send event. A send event may contain variables, but we require from the protocol that whenever a send is executed all its variables have already been assigned a value to. This does not hold for the second type of event, a read. Upon execution of a read event, its variables become bound to a concrete value. Finally, we have the secrecy claims, which, like a send event, have no uninstantiated variables upon execution.

The events on each run are executed from top to bottom. Because of the chosen intruder model sending a message has no direct effect on a message reception. Execution of a send merely means that the contents of the sent message are added to the intruder knowledge. For instance, if the first run executes its first event, this means that the intruder learns message $\{na, a\}_{PKb}$. Since the intruder does not possess the corresponding key SKb he cannot unpack this message, so he can only store the complete message in his knowledge base. The intruder can decide to route this message through to the third run. Executing the first event of the third run then results in assigning value na to local variable W and the protocol proceeds as expected. If the second run sends its first message, the intruder will be able to unpack it and learn nonce na', which he may be able to use to his advantage. Nevertheless, the secrecy claims of the first and third run will be valid in all possible execution orders.

In order to formally prove BKE correct for this scenario, we will have to check every possible interleaving of the included runs. And in order to prove BKE correct in general we have to do this for every finite scenario. Since this is rather complex we will explain how model checking can be used to prove correctness of BKE for a fixed set of runs.

3   Model Checking Secrecy in Security Protocols

We will develop our model checking algorithm in three steps. The first step yields a simple algorithm which naively searches through the complete state space. In the second step we transform this algorithm into an equivalent format that makes it possible to analyse which parts of the state space can be pruned. Finally, we present the reduced and efficient model checking algorithm.

In order to formulate our abstract algorithms we will need to formulate some of the notions from the informal explanation in the previous section a bit more precise.

Intruder Knowledge. The knowledge of the intruder is modeled as a set of closed terms. If he learns a term, he can unpack it and learn all its sub terms. The only restriction is that he can unpack encrypted terms only if he knows the corresponding key. Adding a term to the intruder's knowledge is denoted by the operator $\oplus$.

Enabled. Executing a scenario boils down to executing the events of the runs in a given order. For each run we keep track of which event is to be executed next. This is the set of *enabled* events, with the restriction that a read event is only enabled if the intruder can construct a matching term. Whenever enabled, a send event and a secrecy claim contain closed terms, but a read event may still contain variables. When executing a read event its contents will be bound to a closed term.

Match. The *match* function determines which closed terms match a given read event. When developing the algorithms below we had no specific match function in mind as long as it yields a finite number of matching closed terms for every open term. It is a parameter of the algorithm. A straightforward match function could require corresponding types of all sub-terms, but a more lenient match could, e.g., accept a nonce where a key would be expected and thus make the protocol susceptible to type flaw attacks. We will come back on type flaw attacks later.

After. After executing an event, the system comes into a new state. Variables may become bound and the run whose event executes proceeds one step. The after function used below models this transition.

3.1   Algorithm

Algorithm 1 describes a simple depth-first search of all system states. Provided that the input scenario is finite and that the match function always returns a finite number of matching messages, this algorithm checks whether the protocol guarantees secrecy on the input scenario.

The recursive procedure traverseFull has three parameters: runs (the input scenario), know (the intruder knowledge which is a set of closed terms, initialised with the initial intruder knowledge), secrets (the set of closed terms claimed to be secret up to now, initialised with the empty set). This procedure works as follows. If there is a claimed secret known by the intruder, the algorithm halts, signaling the violation. Otherwise, for every run, it is checked whether its first event is enabled or not. All these enabled events can be executed in turn and we recursively check whether the sub-tree resulting after such an execution still guarantees secrecy. Since there are three types of events we have to determine the effect of each of these types on the state of the system. If the selected event is a secrecy claim, we know that its argument is a closed term and we add this term to the set of claimed secrets. If the selected event is a send event, we also know that its argument is a closed term and we add this term to the intruder knowledge. Finally, if the selected event is a read event, it might still have uninstantiated variables. Executing such an event means that the intruder constructs a term from his knowledge, that matches the expected structure of the input term. Since we have to check correctness of the protocol for every possible behaviour of the intruder, we must recursively check every state resulting from every possible matching. This explains the for-loop in this case.

3.2   Transforming the Algorithm

In the next step, we transform Algorithm 1 into an equivalent Algorithm 2, which generates exactly the same traces. The transformation mainly consists of replacing the outer for-loop by tail recursion. For this purpose, we use a choose function, that picks any element from the set of enabled events. An element is chosen, handled as in Algorithm 1, and the remaining elements from the enabled set will be handled by the recursive call. To make this possible, a new parameter $except : \mathcal{P}(Event)$ is added to the function. This set represents the events that were already selected by the choose function at this point in the trace construction. In this way, we have split the subtree in two parts, one containing the traces starting with the chosen event, and one containing the traces where

---

Algorithm 1: traverseFull (runs,know,secrets)

---

if *any secret in* **know** then
   | exit ("attack")
else
   for *all ev* ∈ **enabled**(*runs*, *know*) do
      if *ev = secret(m)* then
         | traverseFull(**after**(runs, *ev*), know, secrets ∪ {*m*})
      end
      if *ev = send(m)* then
         | traverseFull(**after**(runs, *ev*), know ⊕ *m*, secrets)
      end
      if *ev = read(m)* then
         for *all m′* ∈ **match**(*know, m*) do
            | traverseFull(**after**(runs, *read(m′)*), know, secrets)
         end
      end
   end
end

---

this event is executed later. To facilitate this, we define a restricted enabled function that captures the remaining set of traces.

$$\text{enabled2}(\text{runs}, \text{know}, \text{except}) = \text{enabled}(\text{runs}, \text{know}) \setminus \text{except}$$

3.3   The Refined Algorithm

In the final step we reduce the number of traversed traces while retaining correctness of the algorithm. This results in Algorithm 3. The rationale for this reduction is that in many cases we can safely execute an event directly whenever it is enabled, while ignoring traces where this event occurs later.

The following lemma implies that whenever two closed events can be executed, it does not matter in which order they are executed. For send events this is trivial. For read events we use the fact that the intruder knowledge is non-decreasing, and for secrecy events we use the fact that the set of secrets is non-decreasing.

Lemma 1. *Suppose that in Algorithm 1 at a given state closed events e and f from different runs can be executed. Then, after executing event e, event f can still be executed. Likewise, after f, event e can still be executed. Moreover, the states reached after ef and fe are both equal.*

This does not imply that in a trace any two events may be exchanged. If the second event gets enabled due to execution of the first event (e.g., if the first event is a send and the second is the corresponding read) it is not possible to execute the second event first. In conclusion, any event may be shifted towards the beginning of the trace until the first moment when it was enabled. The above

---

Algorithm 2: traverseFull2 (runs,know,secrets,except)

---

if *any secret in* **know** then
   | exit ("attack")
else
   | if *enabled2(runs, know, except)* $\neq \emptyset$ then
   | | $ev =$ choose(enabled2(runs, know, except))
   | | if $ev = secret(m)$ then
   | | | traverseFull2(after(runs, ev), know, secrets $\cup \{m\}$, $\emptyset$)
* | | | traverseFull2(runs, know, secrets, except $\cup \{ev\}$)
   | | **end**
   | | if $ev = send(m)$ then
   | | | traverseFull2(after(runs, ev), know $\oplus m$, secrets, $\emptyset$)
* | | | traverseFull2(runs, know, secrets, except $\cup \{ev\}$)
   | | **end**
   | | if $ev = read(m)$ then
   | | | for *all $m' \in$ match(know, m)* do
   | | | | traverseFull2(after(runs, $read(m')$), know, secrets, $\emptyset$)
   | | | **end**
   | | | traverseFull2(runs, know, secrets, except $\cup \{ev\}$)
   | | **end**
   | **end**
end

---

lemma states that this can be done without changing the final state. Since the
intruder knowledge and the set of secrets is monotonously non-decreasing we can
simply discard the traces where this same event occurs later.

This motivates why we can simplify Algorithm 2 by omitting the recursive
calls at the lines marked with *. Whenever a secrecy claim (which is a closed
event) is enabled we can execute it and leave out the case where it is executed
at a later moment. Likewise for a (closed) send event. Treatment of a read
event is a bit more complex. Although it is safe to directly execute every closed
instance of a read event and discard later occurrences of this instantiation of
the read, it is erroneous to discard of every later occurrence of the read event.
The reason for this is that the set of matching terms depends upon the intruder
knowledge and that this knowledge may increase during the course of execution.
Since these future matches are not possible at the current moment, we must
allow the read to execute at a later moment too. However, we will then only
have to consider new matches. All matches that are already possible in the
current state must be avoided. To this end we introduce an extra parameter
forbidden : *Event* $\rightarrow$ *Knowledge* which assigns the current intruder knowledge
to the considered read event. We limit the possible future matching to the cases
which are not forbidden by this parameter. This is expressed in the following
narrowing of the **enabled** set:

enabled3(runs, know, forbidden) =

   $\{ev \in$ enabled(runs, know) $\mid ev = read(m) \Rightarrow \exists_{m' \in \mathtt{match}(know, m)} m' \notin$ forbidden$(ev)\}$

In the algorithm, we use forbidden[$ev \to know$] to denote the function that maps ev to $know$, and all events $e \neq ev$ to forbidden(e).

Algorithm 3: traverse (runs,know,secrets,forbidden)

---

if *any secret in know* then
  | exit ("attack")
else
  | if *enabled3(runs, know, forbidden)* $\neq \emptyset$ then
  | | ev = choose(enabled3(runs, know, forbidden))
  | | if $ev = secret(m)$ then
  | | | traverse(after(runs, ev), know, secrets $\cup \{m\}$, forbidden)
  | | end
  | | if $ev = send(m)$ then
  | | | traverse(after(runs, ev), know $\oplus$ m, secrets, forbidden)
  | | end
  | | if $ev = read(m)$ then
  | | | for *all* $m' \in match(know, m) \wedge m' \notin forbidden(read(m))$ do
  | | | | traverse(after(runs, $read(m')$), know, secrets, forbidden)
  | | | end
  | | | traverse(runs, know, secrets, forbidden[$ev \to know$])
  | | end
  | end
end

---

4 The Scyther Tool

Based on the proposed algorithm, we have developed a tool, called Scyther. Given a protocol and scenario description, this tool will construct a model and check it for the secrecy property.

The scenario consists of a number of runs. For each run, we define the protocol and role, and which agents are involved. The protocol and scenario descriptions are parsed by the Scyther tool and a model of the protocol with the scenario is constructed. This model is then checked for any violations of the secrecy property. Scyther enables the user to select various parameters such as the partial order reduction to be used, or any pruning behaviour when an attack is found.

When model checking an unknown protocol, choices have to be made for the scenario. With a small scenario, we will find a short attack quickly, but we can never be sure. On the other hand, a large scenario can take a long time to model check, even if there is a short attack. In many cases one would wish to have a breadth-first search, looking for short attacks first. Scyther's algorithm traverses the state space depth-first, to avoid any excessive memory requirements. To support some sort of breadth-first scan, Scyther allows for pruning the state space in the number of runs, or the maximum length of the traces. It can also automatically perform incremental state space searches, ranging over the number of runs or the maximum length of the traces.

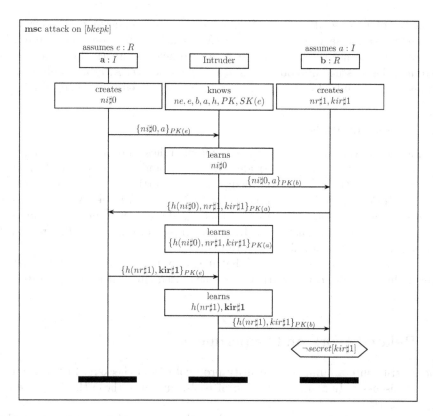

Fig. 3. Example output: an attack trace

4.1   Attack Output

If an attack is found in the model, the tool generates an attack trace which is output in either ASCII format, or optionally in LaTeX format. Using the MSC macro package (see [9]) this can be automatically translated into an attack diagram. An example of the output can be found in Figure 3.

The presented attack is an attack to a slightly modified version of the BKE protocol from Figure 1. We construct a flawed protocol by replacing the last message $\{h(nr)\}_{kir}$ by $\{h(nr), kir\}_{PKr}$. This may seem a futile modification, but it introduces the possibility of a so-called man-in-the-middle attack. This attack can be exploited using the scenario from Figure 2. There are only two runs needed for this attack (see Figure 3): a run of agent a executing the initiator role in a session with compromised agent e, and a run of agent b as a responder to initiator a. The runs are numbered $\sharp 0$ and $\sharp 1$. This numbering is visible in the naming of the local constants. So $kir\sharp 1$ means the (unique) key generated in run $\sharp 1$. The attack goes as follows. First, a sends an initialisation message to e. This message is intercepted by the intruder and because the intruder knows SKe he can unpack the message and learn $ni\sharp 0$ (as expressed at the axis representing the intruder). The intruder then constructs a new message, encrypted with the public key of b and sends it through to b, forging that the message comes from a. Then b sends a message encrypted with PKa, which the intruder cannot unpack. However, he can use the run of agent a as an oracle to unpack this message, so he routes the message unmodified to a, forging sender e. After a's reply to this message, the intruder learns key $kir\sharp1$, which is supposed to be secret for b.

4.2   Some Internals

The model checking algorithm of Scyther mainly relies on term set manipulation. Send events add terms to the intruder knowledge, and read events try to match their patterns to the intruder knowledge. A large portion of the model checking time therefore relies on operations on the intruder knowledge. Any non-empty intruder knowledge is an infinite set, as it is closed under encryption and tupling. However, because it is constructed from the empty set only by adding terms, it can be represented by a finite set of terms.

Scyther is set up in such a way that it is easy to implement various partial order reductions and compare them. We have used this feature to generate the various test results.

5   Related Work and Experiments

There exist quite a number of security protocol model checkers. In this section we will discuss only a small selection of tools, and only those that operate on finite scenarios.

We have chosen to compare our work to the closely-related Brutus tool, the Casper/FDR toolchain, and a fairly recent development based on Constraint Logic programming. We will first explain something about the differences between these tools and ours, before proceeding to some experimental results.

5.1   Brutus

A tool that is fairly comparable to ours is the Brutus tool [2]. As Scyther, it is based on partial order reductions, and also just explores a subset of all possible traces. However, instead of only checking for secrecy, Brutus can check for other properties as well.

Brutus reduces the set of traces on the basis of three observations:

- Internal events ordering.
- Send events ordering.
- Symmetry in the scenario.

The observations for the first two items can be explained as the fact that it is not relevant for the security property in which order some internal events occur. The same holds for send events: the order in which they occur can be neglected. In comparison to Brutus, Scyther uses a more powerful reduction. Scyther does not only consider the order of internal and send events, but that of all events.

For the third item, we have that in Brutus symmetry of the scenario is considered. Suppose in the scenario, there are two identical runs of the initiator role, with the same parameters. For checking secrecy it is not relevant which run executes its initial event first, as they are symmetrical. However, after the first event has occurred, the symmetry is broken. The gain of exploiting symmetry is considerably less than that of the other observations, as the authors of Brutus note in [2]. In fact, in the optimal case, the symmetry reduction used in Brutus decreases the number of states by a factor equal to the number of runs in the scenario. The current version of Scyther does not consider symmetry in the scenario.

Brutus uses a subset of ML as an input language for the protocol and the scenarios.

5.2   Casper/FDR

The toolchain Casper/FDR [7] is probably the most well-known tool in security protocol checking. It has been successfully applied to many protocols and has an extensive array of features. It can check for various security properties.

Casper is a compiler that will translate a security protocol into a CSP process algebra model. The requirements are translated into another CSP model. The model checker FDR is then used to make sure that the protocol model is a refinement of the requirements model. Any optimizations that FDR applies to the model checking process are in fact general CSP refinement optimizations. It is therefore difficult to exploit the specific structure of the problem.

The main problem of using this toolset is that it cannot handle larger protocols, because large amounts of memory are required to execute the refinement check algorithm. The other methods that are discussed here exploit depth-first search, which is very efficient in terms of memory usage.

On the positive side, many protocols have already been checked using this toolset, and there is currently no other tool that can handle the same range of security protocols or range of possible requirements as Casper/FDR.

Casper uses a custom input language specifically tailored for security protocol checking. It is convenient for specifying a protocol, but we found that defining a very specific scenario can be cumbersome.

The output of FDR consists of an attack trace of the model that was generated by Casper. This can be interpreted again by Casper, to yield an attack trace on the same level as the one at which the protocol was specified. For some attack types, Casper can do a superficial analysis of the attack and give some hints on its nature, e.g., reporting that "Alice thinks she is talking to Bob" when authentication is violated. However, in many cases we found it difficult to interpret the actual attack.

5.3   Constraint Logic Based Approaches

The current developments in approaches based on Constraint Logic [10, 3] are based on the idea that the instantiation of variables in the construction of a trace might be postponed. In our model, variables are instantiated when they first occur in a trace. This results in a large number of branches in the model, one branch for each possible value of the variable.

We can try to postpone this instantiation as long as possible, by defining a constraint for each variable. We define a simple constraint as a predicate $v : K$, expressing that a variable v can be instantiated with any value from a knowledge set K. The Constraint Logic algorithm postpones instantiation of a variable when a read event is executed, and introduces a constraint for the message instead. After a complete trace is constructed, it is checked whether the constraints can be satisfied.

The algorithm on complete traces was suggested by Millen and Shmatikov in [10], where they also proved that it terminates. The constraint logic algorithm was later refined by Corin and Etalle [3] to allow for on-the-fly checking, which reduces the number of states traversed significantly. It also allows for checking of attacks in which partial runs are involved.

A strong point of this method is that it performs equally well for detecting a class of so-called type flaw attacks as it does for non-type flaw attacks. A type flaw attack occurs when a run is expecting to receive, for instance, a nonce, but instead it gets sent an agent name, or a tuple (Key, Nonce). The constraint logic tools currently can detect the class of type errors with the restriction that tupling is taken to be non-associative. Scyther can only detect a small class of type flaw attacks, in which one basic type is mistaken for another basic type, e.g., when an agent name is mistaken for a nonce.

Both constraint logic tools use Prolog as input language for the protocol and the scenarios. The output of the tools is an uncommented attack trace. It gives almost no clues as to the nature of the attack, and it is up to the tester to try and reconstruct what has actually happened.

5.4   Experimental Results

Given that the various approaches have different underlying models, it is quite difficult to objectively compare them. Minor choices in the protocol or the scenario result in performance changes that can be quite different for each approach.

We note that in general, experimental results are more often than not very poorly documented, and not reproducible. To make sure our experiments are reproducible we have set up a web page with all the data we used for our experiments at [4], to make sure that these results may be verified. We are aware that to give a complete analysis, it would be necessary to test the tools with several types and sizes of protocols, and invoke each of these with several scenarios. Here we will only test a single protocol, with scenarios that differ only in the number of runs defined.

The experiments serve two purposes. The first purpose is to determine the effect that our proposed algorithm has on the number of states that are traversed in the system. This directly affects the performance of the tool. The second purpose is to give some kind of performance comparison between our tool and others. We will address these two issues in the next sections.

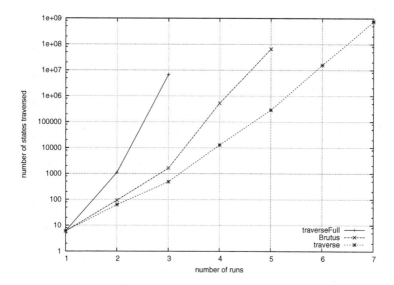

Fig. 4. State reduction

Partial Order Reduction Effectiveness. One important validation of our algorithm is the effectiveness of the partial order reduction. As we have mentioned already, other tools such as Brutus also use some kind of partial order reduction. We claim however that our reduction is more effective.

In order to test this, we have conducted experiments with three different algorithms implemented within the Scyther framework.

As an inefficient algorithm, we implemented *traverseFull* as in Algorithm 1. We also implemented an algorithm that is as close as possible to the optimizations used by the Brutus tool, except that we did not implement the symmetry reductions. Finally, we implemented our improved traverse as in Algorithm 3.

Using these three algorithms we tested the Bilateral Key Exchange protocol for secrecy. As this protocol is correct, no attacks are found, and the complete state space is traversed. At the end of each test, the algorithms report the number of states traversed.

In Figure 4 the state space sizes are shown for each algorithm on the vertical axis, using a logarithmic scale. On the horizontal axis we have shown the number of runs in the scenario. When the running time of a test exceeded 24 hours, we stopped the test.

These experiments clearly show that the partial order reduction is effective for reducing the state space. Without any reductions, we could not test more than three runs in a day. The new algorithm allowed us to check a scenario with seven runs.

Performance Comparison. The second type of experiment is meant to compare our tool with other tools, and is only measured in terms of computation time. Please refer to our web page [4] for the details of the machine used.

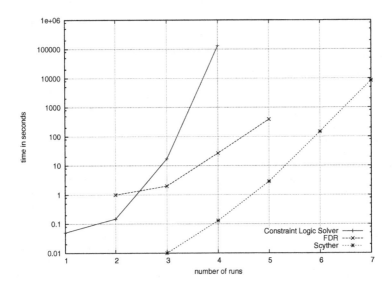

Fig. 5. Performance comparison

When model checking a scenario with a single run, or two runs, the algorithms are generally very fast. In some cases this caused the experiments to be immeasurable, reporting zero time usage. That is why we did not get sensible results for one run with Casper/FDR and with one or two runs with Scyther.

For Scyther and the Constraint Logic tool we aborted the test after running for 40 hours. In the case of Casper/FDR we did not reach this point, as the machine ran out of memory. This is inherent in the way the tools work. Scyther and the Constraint Logic tools use depth-first searches, and check each state for the secrecy property. This results in memory usage that is linear in the number of runs in the scenario, effectively making time the only limiting factor for checking large protocols. FDR on the other hand constructs two models, and tries to determine whether one model is a refinement of the other. This causes memory requirements for FDR to be exponential with respect to the number of runs.

The results are summarized in Figure 5. On the horizontal axis we again find the number of runs. The vertical axis is now the time taken by each test, on a logarithmic scale. We can see that Scyther outperforms the other two tools, and allows for checking larger models.

When we set up these experiments, we expected the constraint logic tools to outperform Casper/FDR. As it turns out, Casper/FDR gains significant performance at the cost of exponential memory usage.

6   Conclusions and Future Work

We have presented a new algorithm for model checking secrecy in security protocols, based on partial order reductions. The new algorithm significantly reduces the number of states that need to be traversed in model checking. As a results, it becomes feasible to check more intricate protocol scenarios as well as more extensive protocols.

The partial order reduction presented here was tailored specifically for the secrecy property in security protocol verification. For this property the reduction is sound and complete. However, there are many security properties, such as synchronisation [5] or agreement [8], for which this reduction is not complete. In the near future we will look into partial order reductions that are sound and complete for other security properties. We will investigate whether we can use these reductions to extend Scyther to be able to check a number of other security properties as well.

Furthermore, our proposed algorithm has a broader application than only for checking the secrecy property with a Dolev-Yao intruder. By varying over the match function, the contents of the system state and the security predicate, we are able to model check a wide range of security properties. We conjecture that correctness of our algorithm only requires the following two properties.

1. If closed events e and f can be executed, then after executing e event f can still be executed and the state reached after executing ef is equal to the state reached after executing fe.
2. The security predicate P is a monotonous predicate in the state of the system. By this we mean that if the system is in state σ and reaches state σ' after execution of any closed event, then $P(\sigma) \Rightarrow P(\sigma')$.

In this way we can, for example, strengthen the notion of secrecy as to require that trusted agents will also never learn the secret (unless they are explicitly allowed to). This generalization also makes it possible to vary over the intruder model. If we extend the state of the system with a buffer, containing sent messages and if we redefine the match predicate to take messages from this buffer rather than from the intruder knowledge, we have defined an intruder with just eavesdropping capabilities. Future work will examine the application scope of this algorithm.

In the scenarios checked, the constraint logic approach did not turn out to be very efficient in our tests. However, it has the advantage of being able to detect a class of type flaw attacks. We are currently investigating whether the constaint logic approach can be combined with the partial order reduction. This might result in a more efficient algorithm for checking secrecy with type flaw attacks.

References

1. Clark, J., Jacob, J.: A survey of authentication protocol literature. Technical Report 1.0 (1997)
2. Clarke, E., Jha, S., Marrero, W.: Partial order reductions for security protocol verification. Tools and Algorithms for the Construction and Analysis of Systems. Volume 1785 of Lecture Notes in Computer Science, Springer (2000) 503–518

3. Corin, R., Etalle, S.: An improved constraint-based system for the verification of security protocols. Hermenegildo, M.V., Puebla, G. (Eds.): 9th Int. Static Analysis Symp. (SAS). Madrid, Spain, Volume 2477 of Lecture Notes in Computer Science, Springer-Verlag (2002) 326–341 http://www.ub.utwente.nl/webdocs/ctit/1/00000096.pdf.
4. Cremers, C.: Scyther documentation (2004) http://www.win.tue.nl/~ccremers/scyther.
5. Cremers, C., Mauw, S., de Vink, E.: Defining authentication in a trace model. Dimitrakos, T., Martinelli, F. (Eds.): FAST 2003. Proceedings of the first international Workshop on Formal Aspects in Security and Trust, Pisa, IITT-CNR technical report (2003) 131–145
6. Dolev, D., Yao, A.: On the security of public key protocols. IEEE Transactions on Information Theory **IT-29** (1983) 198–208
7. Lowe, G.: Casper: A compiler for the analysis of security protocols. Proc. 10th Computer Security Foundations Workshop, IEEE (1997) 18–30
8. Lowe, G.: A hierarchy of authentication specifications. Proc. 10th Computer Security Foundations Workshop, IEEE (1997) 31–44
9. Mauw, S., Bos, V.: Drawing Message Sequence Charts with LaTeX. TUGBoat **22** (2001) 87–92
10. Millen, J., Shmatikov, V.: Constraint solving for bounded-process cryptographic protocol analysis. ACM Conference on Computer and Communications Security. (2001) 166–175
11. Peled, D.: Ten years of partial order reduction. Proceedings of the 10th International Conference on Computer Aided Verification, Springer-Verlag (1998) 17–28

Finding Covert Channels in Protocols with Message Sequence Charts: The Case of RMTP2

Loïc Hélouët

IRISA, Campus de Beaulieu, 35042 Rennes Cedex, France
loic.helouet@irisa.fr
http://www.irisa.fr/distribcom/Personal_Pages/helouet/LHengpage.html

Abstract. Covert channels are illegal information flows in systems. Recent research has shown how to detect covert channels in scenario descriptions. This paper recalls these results, and proposes a case study illustrating how scenarios can be used to detect illegal information flows from a scenario description of a protocol. Once a covert information flow is discovered, its bandwidth is computed using the $(max, +)$ algebra.

1 Introduction

The term *covert channel* has first been introduced by [11], and designates an illegal information flow inside a system. Covert channels (or CCs for short) are a threat for security: they allow information passing between parties that are not allowed to communicate, or for which communications are monitored. Very often, CCs use resources of a system in an obfuscated way to signal bits of information. The "disk full channel" is a typical example: a user (called the *sender*) fills a disk to pass bit 0, or leaves some free space to pass bit 1. Another user (the *receiver*) tries to write on this disk, and decodes the bit stored according to the occurrence of a disk full exception. Of course, this use of resources can result in an important penalty for other users, even if the system does not need to fulfill high security requirements or prevent information leaks.

CCs are often classified as storage channels (i.e., a resource is used to write data, that can then be read), or timing channels (the response time of a system can be modified in an observable way to pass bits of information). Clearly, almost everything in a system can be used to pass information, and closing all covert channels is considered as an impossible task [14], as it would necessitate to remove even internal clocks in computers!

CCs are not only characterized by this storage/timing channel classification. An important characteristics of a covert channel is its bandwidth, i.e., the number of bits per second that can be transferred using this channel. Usually, CCs are quite slow when compared to the parasited system. According to the type of system considered, and to the security level required, some bandwidths can be considered as acceptable. However, [17] considers that CCs with a bandwidth greater than 100 bits per second should be closed. Furthermore, the purpose of

D. Amyot and A.W. Williams (Eds.): SAM 2004, LNCS 3319, pp. 189–207, 2005.

covert channels is not performance, but rather secrecy, synchronization between several programs attacking a server, or billing systems bypassing.

The usual answer when a covert channel is found is to restrict the access to the resource used to transfer data. But as already mentioned, this is not always possible. Fortunately, closing a covert channel is not the only possibility to reduce its impact on a system. One can also add noise to reduce its bandwidth, or monitor a specific channel to ban corrupted users. Several security recommendations [4, 17] ask to perform a reproducible and systematic search for covert channels, compute their bandwidth, and then apply a solution (closing, noise insertion, monitoring) according to the system's security needs. In addition to this, [17] recommends to document all covert channels found with their scenarios of use. These recommendations naturally lead to formal modeling and analysis of systems.

Several model-based approaches to covert channel detection have been proposed. Bell and La Padula [3, 2] propose a definition of legal communications in a system: a security level is assigned to each object of the system, and there is a security violation if an object at a level can send information to another object at a lower level. Several approaches [1, 10] use this model to find unauthorized communications between systems users. A more recent approach [5] is based on the non interference relation, that says that A "interferes" with B if what A does has an influence on what B can observe. Usually, the approach proposed by non-interference is to partition a system in two levels, namely "high" and "low", and to deduce a non-interference property whenever a "low" process can get information from a "high" process, hence resulting in the possibility to encode a bit. Several approaches to non-interference have been proposed, through typing [21](a system contains interferences if it can not be correctly typed), or using process algebra [15]. These two approaches are based on an a priori definition of "who is allowed to communicate with whom", and communication between two unauthorized parties is immediately translated into a covert channel presence. However, covert information can also be passed over a legal communication, which is called "legitimate channels".

A reproach addressed to formal detection of covert channel is that models are sometimes too far from the implementation. Indeed, some assumptions and simplifications are made when a model is built. A formal analysis of a model can hence exhibit covert behaviors that are not realistic for the implemented system, or conversely miss some real covert channels. Note that CC search can not in general be exhaustive, and that model-based approaches only provide an additional help. As we are in general interested in finding upper bounds to CCs capacities, one should pay attention that the assumptions made during formal modeling do not minimize the bandwidth, hence giving an over optimistic view of a system's security. For a more complete bibliography on covert channels, interested readers are referred to [20].

This paper describes an new approach to covert channels detection based on Message Sequence Charts [8] and (max, +) algebra, and illustrates it with an example. This approach to CC detection is based on High-level Message Sequence

Charts, and was first proposed in [7]. It assumes that covert channel can also appear inside legal communications, and targets a specific covert communication mechanism in protocols. Roughly speaking, there is a covert channel between A and B if causal consequences of decisions of A can be observed infinitely often and decoded by B to build a message. When a covert scenario is discovered, its bandwidth is computed with the $(max, +)$ algebra as proposed by [12]. This approach is applied to a case study, the RMTP2 (Reliable Multicast Transport Protocol 2) protocol [16, 22]. A covert channel in the data retransmission part of RMTP2 is first identified, and the bandwidth of this channel is then computed for a large range of parameters.

This paper is organized as follows: Section 2 roughly defines the approach proposed in [7] to detect a potential covert channel, section 3 describes the part of the RMTP2 protocol where a covert channel has been detected. Section 4 explains how to compute a bandwidth from scenarios, and section 5 applies this method to the covert channel found in section 3. Section 6 concludes this work.

2   Covert Channels Detection

[7] has proposed an algorithm to characterize the presence of a covert channel in a scenario description. This approach uses a formal representation of Message Sequence Charts based on partial orders. Since [9], partial orders are an alternative representation to the algebraic semantics of MSCs [18, 19]. In fact, basic MSCs are almost lposets, and the translation is quite natural. Let us recall some basic notations and principles of this semantics. Basic Message Sequence Charts are considered as partial orders, and High-level Message Sequence Charts are seen as automata composing these orders.

Definition 1. *A basic Message Sequence Chart is a tuple* $M = (E, \leq, \alpha, \phi, A, I)$ *where E is a set of events, $\leq$ is a partial order (reflexive, transitive, antisymmetric) on these events, built from the order defined on instances and the causality between message emissions and receptions. A is a set of action names, I is a set of instances, and $\alpha : E \longrightarrow A$ associates an action name to each event, $\phi : E \longrightarrow I$ associates an instance to each event (ϕ is the location of an event).*

For a bMSC M, let us define by $Min(M)$ the set of minimal events for the causal order, i.e., the set of events in M that have no predecessor. The projection of a bMSC M on an instance $i \in I$ is noted $\pi_i(M)$, and is the restriction of M to events situated on i. The main basic operators for Message Sequence charts are alternative, loop, and sequential composition. Intuitively, sequential composition merges two basic Message Sequence Charts along their common instance axes. More formally, sequential composition can be defined as follows:

Definition 2. *The* sequential composition *of two bMSCs M_1 and M_2 is the bMSC*
$$M_1 \circ M_2 = (E_1 \uplus E_2, \leq_{1 \circ 2}, \alpha_1 \cup \alpha_2, \phi_1 \cup \phi_2, A_1 \cup A_2, I_1 \cup I_2), \text{ where}$$
$$\leq_{1 \circ 2} = \left(\leq_1 \uplus \leq_2 \uplus \{(e, e') \in E_1 \times E_2 | \phi_1(e_1) = \phi_2(e_2)\}\right)^*$$

Extending the definition of sequential composition, let us define M^n as the bMSC $M^n = M \circ M^{n-1}$ (with of course $M^1 = M$) for all $n > 1$. Sequential composition can also be defined for sets of bMSCs. Let $\mathcal{F}_a$ and $\mathcal{F}_b$ be two sets of bMSCs. $\mathcal{F}_a \circ \mathcal{F}_b$ is the set $\{f_a \circ f_b | f_a \in \mathcal{F}_a \wedge f_b \in \mathcal{F}_b\}$. MSC contain several operators such as alternative, iteration, etc. These operator can be expressed by means of inline expressions, or using High-level Message Sequence Charts, which can be roughly defined as bMSC automata.

Definition 3. *A High-level Message Sequence Chart (or HMSC for short) is a tuple $H = (N, \longrightarrow, n_0, F, \mathcal{M})$ where N is a set of nodes, $\longrightarrow \subseteq N \times \mathcal{M} \times N$ is a transition relation, $\mathcal{M}$ is a set of basic MSCs, F is a set of final nodes. For a peculiar transition $t = (n, M, n') \in \longrightarrow$, $l(t) = M$ will be called the label of t.*

A path in a HMSC is a sequence of transitions $p = t_1.t_2 \ldots t_k$ such that for all i, the goal of t_i is also the origin of t_{i+1}. A bMSC M_p can be associated to each finite path $p = t_1.t_2 \ldots t_k$ by sequential composition of labels, i.e., $M_p = l(t_1) \circ l(t_2 \ldots l(t_k))$.

A node n with several outgoing transitions is called a choice node. *A choice node is said to be* local *iff there exists an instance $i \in I$ such that for any path p leaving n, $\phi(min(M_p)) = \{i\}$. We will say that node n is controlled by i.*

The main idea proposed in [7] is to detect information flows from a scenario description. For the sake of completeness, the whole definition of covert channels is provided below. However, the readers may skip the rest of this section, and only keep in mind that a covert channel is characterized by as an information flow from a sender to a receiver. Several approaches based on non interference suppose that an unique occasion to share a single bit of information is sufficient to characterize a covert channel. However, [15] highlights that such covert channels' bandwidth tends towards zero, and that to be realistic, a covert channel should allow the transfer of an unbounded number of bits. This supposes the possibility to iterate a functionality of a protocol. Hence, in our scenario models, covert channels will be characterized by a set of cycles of HMSCs, that contain a common choice node controlled by the sender, and in which the receiver has several different behaviors.

Several assumptions are made to identify covert channels in scenarios. First, covert channels are used to transmit messages of arbitrary size. Hence, to transmit a message, a sender should repeat some behaviors, and the notion of covert channel is linked to cycles in the HMSC. The second idea for the kind of covert channel detected is to consider that a sending instance performs choices which causal consequences can be observed by the receiver. Hence, data encoding must use choices controlled by the sender, and scenarios for which the projection on receiving instance can be differentiated.

The last requirement is that the sending instance should keep control of the covert channel during information exchange. For this reason, message transmission should not be performed through decisions after which the sender may lose control of the protocol over an unbounded amount of time (either the protocol reaches a sink node, and the message transmission is definitely broken, or the protocol can stay in a cycle that is not controlled by the sender, and the transmission can be delayed for an unlimited amount of time). These considerations lead to the following definition:

Definition 4. *Let S, R be two instances. There is a* potential covert channel *from S to R at node n_c if:*

- *there is a set C of simple cycles from n_c to n_c such that $\forall p \in C, \pi_R(M_p) \neq \epsilon$ (where ϵ is an empty lposet),*
- $\exists c_1, c_2 \in C$ *such that* $\pi_R(M_{c_1}) \neq \pi_R(M_{c_2})$
- n_c *is controlled by S,*
- *all choice nodes that can enforce a path to leave C are either controlled by S or by R. Formally, for all $q = (n_1, M_1, n_2) \ldots (n_k, M_k, n_1) \in C$, if there is a node n_i, $i \in 1..k$, which is not controlled by S nor by R, then for any transition $(n_i, M, n_i') \in \longrightarrow$, the path $(n_1, M_1, n_2) \ldots (n_{i-1}, M_{i-1}, n_i).(n_i, M, n_i')$ is a prefix of some path of C.*

Note that C does not need to include *all* simple cycles from n_c to itself. Note also that a choice node n can be controlled by another instance than S or R as long as the decision taken does not prevent from eventually getting back to node n_c. The definition of potential covert channels in scenarios only says that there is a possibility of encoding information of unbounded size. However, this definition does not mean that this message can be decoded by the receiving instance. [7] propose a definition of an effective covert channel. A potential covert channel is effective if one can build a transducer (a formal model of decoding program) that takes as input an observation of the receiver (i.e., the labeling of a linearization of $(\pi_R(l(C))^*))$ and outputs the set of transitions that have generated this observation, and that this transducer is functional (i.e., there is no ambiguity for decoding the message read). However, this is out of the scope of this paper, and for the sequel, one can only remember that the existence of a covert channel is linked to the possibility of encoding information through decisions of a sending instance, and to the existence of a decoder.

3   A Case Study: RMTP2

Let us illustrate the approach of previous section on a case study, the RMTP2 protocol. RMTP2 [16, 22] is a reliable multicast transport protocol. It is organized as a tree. Data sent on the RMTP2 tree originates from a **source**, which is not a part of the tree. The root of the tree is called the **top node**, leaves of the tree are called **receivers**. The source multicasts information to the complete RMTP2 tree on a multicast channel. Receivers are the final recipients of the information transferred. They are usually grouped according to their geographical situation. The intermediate nodes are called **Control nodes**, and mainly forward packets. Some control nodes called **Designated Receivers** (or DR for short) also have a retransmission function. Figure 1 illustrates this architecture.

Let us give an overview of RMTP2 nodes functionalities (mainly data transport, tree integrity and congestion control) as detailed in [16]:

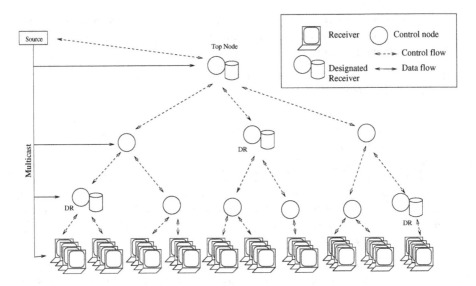

Fig. 1. The RMTP2 protocol: architecture of the network

Receiver Connection: Receivers have to contact a control node to be connected to a multicast channel. Upon successful connection, receivers are assigned an **identity**.

Data Emission: *Data* packets are assigned a sequence number by the sender node, and multicast on the data channel. When no data is available, for transmission, the sender node can send *Nulldata* packets in order to start acknowledgments collection, and maintain the data stream alive. In RMTP2, the data multicast from the source is not mandatorily sent using the same network as the control information. For example, data packets can be sent by a satellite while control and retransmission packets transit through a ground network. However, for the sake of simplicity, we will assume that the data and control network are identical.

Data Retransmission: When a node has missed several *Data* packets, it can ask a retransmission to its parent. Control nodes only forward retransmission demands to the upper level. To avoid a congestion of the whole network when losses occur, some designated receivers (DRs) keep a copy of *Data* packets, and retransmit them to their whole subnetwork. Retransmission uses two kind of packets. *Hack* packets from a node to its parent are used to send a bitmap representation of received/lost *Data* packets in a data window. When packets are declared lost, two cases can appear. If the parent node receiving hacks is a simple control node, it aggregates the losses declared by its children, and sends the result to the upper level in a new *Hack* packet. If the parent is a designated receiver, it retransmits the lost data to all its children using *Retransmission* packets. A receiver that has not received *Data* or *Nulldata* packets from its parent, may consider that the parent has failed, and try to connect to another branch of the tree. The RMTP2 specification says that data retransmissions have priority on new data transmissions.

Fault Detection and Congestion Control: RMTP2 control nodes are equipped with fault detection procedures that signal when a child node is not responding, or when it loosing too many *Data* packets. Faulty nodes, that may slow down the whole network, are ejected from the tree. To avoid congestion, limitations to retransmission demands are also imposed. First, a receiver that loses too many *Data* packets is banned from the RMTP2 tree. This prevents a whole region from suffering a performance penalty due to a single faulty node. In addition to this, retransmission demands do not concern a single packet, but a set of *Data* packets, encoded as a bitmap. Finally, packets acknowledgment are not systematic and are either guided by a turn-based policy (that will be described later) or by timeouts.

Of course, the description of RMTP2 given in this section is only a summary of RMTP2 architecture and functionalities. For more complete descriptions, interested readers should consult [16, 22]. This paper takes as example the behavior of a designated receiver with several leaves as sons, and shows that the retransmission mechanism in RMTP2 can be perverted to create a covert channel. RMTP2 has several important parameters that influence its behavior:

- B: the branching factor, is the maximal number of children allowed for a control node. This bound is also used to indicate the frequency of acknowledgments. In order to avoid systematic acknowledgment of *Data* packets, every receiver is allowed to send an *Hack* packet to its father node every B packet. In fact, to avoid situations where all receivers acknowledge packets at the same moment, each receiver is assigned an identity $id < B$, and sends an acknowledgment upon reception of *Data* packet with sequence number n such that $n \mod B = ID$.
- S: the size in bits of the bitmap. S determines the maximal size of the data window, i.e., the number of packets that can be sent by a source without receiving an acknowledgment.
- L: Loss rate. The loss rate is the allowed ratio of missed packets. This ratio is computed from the bitmap received in *Hack* packets. Faulty receivers that exceed the maximal loss rate are ejected from the RMTP2 tree.

Let us assume a loss rate of 25% and a bitmap size of 16 bits. Let us denote by $(n)_2$ the binary representation of a number n, and by $|P|_1$ the number of bits set to 1 in a binary word. Considering these parameters, the interactions between a peculiar receiver CR, its parent DR, and all other receivers can be depicted by the HMSC of Figure 2. This description contains several simplifications. First, all receivers except CR are gathered as a single instance "Other Receivers". Then, multicast messages, which do not exist within MSC are designed as pair of arrows going from the emitting instance (DR) to receivers (CR and Other receivers). A more general loop than what is currently proposed in MSC is also used: it allows for iteration on the elements of a set rather than on a discrete

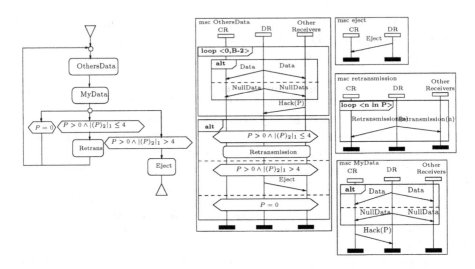

Fig. 2. HMSC for RMTP2 retransmission mechanism

interval, hence allowing the expression **loop p in P**. However, these new features can be considered reasonable and minor extension of existing MSCs (a proposal for multicast definition already appears in [6]).

Several hypotheses are made to model the RMTP2 retransmission mechanism. First, we consider that the multicast channel is the same as the control tree, hence all *Data* or *Nulldata* packets pass through a parent node before reaching a child. Then, we have considered that a copy of a requested packet was always available when needed. Our last hypothesis is that *Data/Nulldata* transmission by a control node is made after reception of an acknowledgment of previous packet by a child node. This assumption is discussed with regard to its influence on the upper bound for covert channels bandwidth in section 5.

The definition of covert channels only deals with HMSCs composing bMSCs without inline expressions. However, HMSC of Figure 2 can be transformed into HMSC of Figures 3 and 4 by instantiation of parameter P in all *Hack* messages and by unfolding of all inline expressions representing bounded loops. From now, $HackCR_i$ will denote the bMSC depicting an acknowledgment from the considered receiver CR with bitmap value i. Similarly, $HackO_i$ will denote the bMSC depicting an acknowledgment from another receiver with bitmap value i. $Retrans_i$ will denote the retransmissions performed by the designated receiver for a bitmap value i. Figure 4 shows several examples: $Retrans61440$ is the bMSC depicting the retransmission for a bitmap value 61440, which binary representation is 1111 0000 0000 0000 (the last 4 *Data* packets are declared lost).

Let us explain the HMSC of Figure 3. A Data/Acknowledgment phase is performed $B - 1$ times. This phase consists in an emission of *Data* or *Nulldata* packets, followed by an acknowledgment from one of the receivers. If the acknowledgment contains more than 4 bits set to 1, the receiver is ejected from the tree. This has no consequence for receiver CR. Otherwise, a retransmission

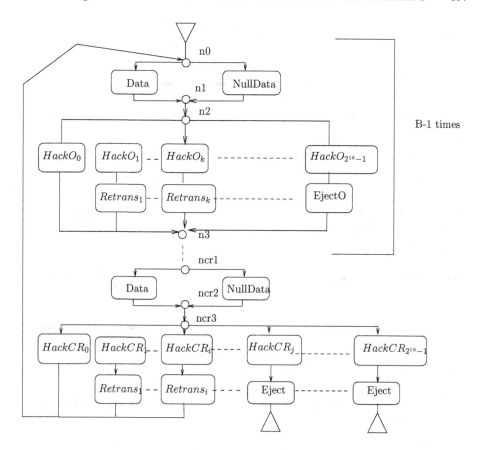

Fig. 3. Instantiation of parameter P

of missed packets is performed. The Bth retransmission starts at node $cr1$. The data/Nulldata phase is identical. When data is received, the receiver concerned (the Bth receiver in our case) sends a $Hack$ packet. If the bitmap contains more than 4 bits set to 1, then CR is ejected from the tree. This leads to an end node and CR can not receive the multicast stream any more and use it to maintain a covert channel. For example, $HackCR_{2^{16}}$ is an acknowledgment with bitmap 1111 1111 1111 1111, which leads to the ejection of CR.

The analysis of HMSC Figure 3 indicates the presence of a covert channel from CR to other receivers starting at choice node $ncr3$. Indeed, there is a set of cycles fulfilling our formal definition : each path starting with an $HackCR_p$ where p is a bitmap with at most 4 bits set to 1 eventually gets back to node $ncr3$. The covert channel contains all cycles leaving $ncr3$, i.e., the scenario for this covert channel is the HMSC of Figure 3 where all paths from $ncr3$ to an end node have been removed. The set of possible scenarios for the RMTP2 covert channel ($Covert$) can be defined as:

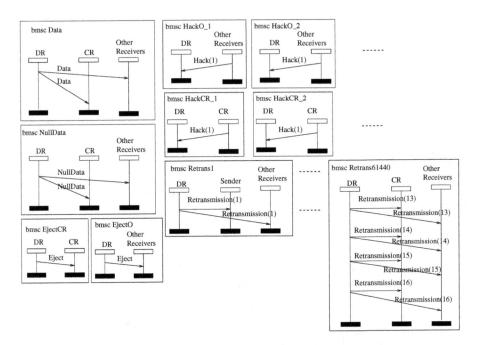

Fig. 4. bMSCs for Figure 3

$$\left(\bigcup_{1 < i < 2^{16}, |(i)_2|_1 \leq 4} HackCR_i \circ Retrans_i \right) \circ Others^{B-1} \circ \{Data, NullData\}$$

where

$$Others = \{Data, NullData\} \circ \left(\begin{array}{c} \bigcup_{1 < i < 2^{16}, |(i)_2|_1 \leq 4} HackO_i \circ Retrans_i \\ \cup \bigcup_{1 < i < 2^{16}, |(i)_2|_1 > 4} HackO_i \circ EjectO \\ \cup HackO_0 \end{array} \right)$$

The main principle behind this covert channel is to create ad hoc bitmaps to force retransmission of packets that are then observed and decoded by the receiving instance. Every time instance CR has to acknowledge the last 16 $Data$ packets, it can chose an ad hoc value for the bitmap that is carried by the $Hack$ packet. This value should not contain too many lost packets, as this would lead to CR's ejection. Following this decision, the receiver of the CC, which can be any of the other receivers, observes several retransmissions following a $Data$ packet. If the receiver knows the identity of CR in the tree (let us call it id_{CR}), it only has to observe retransmissions following $Data$ packets with sequence number n for which $n \mod id_{CR} = 0$. According to the number of packets retransmitted and to the position in the bitmap of each packet, the corrupted receiver deduces the value encoded by CR. If the position of CR is unknown, the receiver can observe in parallel $B - 1$ flows, and deduce from what happens which flow is the covert channel.

Note that the number of possible encoded values is not $|Covert|$, as the corrupted receiver does not control the reactions of other receivers and their losses. Hence, several observation performed by the receiver may be consequences of the same value encoded by the sender. Note also that the receiver can be any of the other receivers, as retransmissions are multicast to the complete subtree below DR. For RMTP2 parameters $B = 20$, $L = 25\%$, a corrupted sender is allowed to create a fake bitmap every 20 $Data$ packet. This bitmap is 16 bits long, but the losses should not exceed 25% of the data window represented by this bitmap (hence limiting the number of possible values encoded).

Maximal bandwidth evaluation has to consider pessimistic situations that maximize the number of bits per second transmitted. Each path chosen from $ncr3$ encodes the same number of bits, which is computed as the base 2 logarithm of the number of possible observations in the covert channel. Hence, in the RMTP2 covert channel, a similar number of bits can be sent when asking for up to 4 retransmissions. So, the emission time is not constant. Note also that the sending instance performs an initial choice, but that other instances may also impose retransmissions that will delay the next use of the channel. The bandwidth is maximal when honest receivers do not lose $Data$ packets, data retransmissions are only due to requests from corrupted receivers, and only concerns a single data packet. Hence, upon reception of each $Data$ packet, all honest receivers will answer with an $Hack$ packet containing the empty bitmap. Note that other receivers' losses slow down covert transmissions, but do not prevent them. In fact, they can be considered as noise addition to the covert channel (this issue is discussed in the conclusion).

4   Bandwidth Evaluation

A bandwidth of the RMTP2 covert channel can be computed from the scenarios identified in previous section. This is done with the $(\max,+)$ techniques for MSCs proposed in [12,13]. The main principles of this approach rely on computation of mean cycle times, and are briefly recalled below.

Definition 5. *Let M be a bMSC. One can associate to M two functions δ : $E \longrightarrow \mathbb{N}$ and $\tau : E \times E \longrightarrow \mathbb{N}$, that define respectively the duration of an event and the duration of a message transmission. Abusing our notation, we will consider that $\tau(e, e') = 0$ when e and e' are not the emission and reception of a message.*

When dealing with time, actions, messages and so on do not need to be considered. The only information of interest is the completion times of all events on an instance, of a complete scenario, and the constraints between execution times on instances. This can be expressed by a bipartite timed order, a kind of timed abstraction of MSC behaviors.

Definition 6. *A bipartite timed order (BTO for short) is a tuple $O = (I_0 \cup I_1, \leq, \Delta)$, where*

- I_0 and I_1 are copies of a set of instances I
- $\leq\,\subseteq I_0 \times I_1$
- $\Delta : I_0 \times I_1 \longrightarrow \mathbb{N} \cup -\infty$. $\Delta(x,y)$ indicates the time elapsed between an instant situated before the execution of the first event on instance x and the last event on instance y. If there is no causal relation from x to y, then $\Delta(x,y) = -\infty$.

Definition 7. A chain in a bMSC is a sequence of events $c = e_1 \ldots e_k$ such that $\forall i \in 1..k-1, e_i < e_{i+1}$. The duration of a chain c is the value $d(c) = \delta(e_1) + \tau(e_1, e_2) + \delta(e_2) + \ldots \tau(e_{k-1}, e_k) + \delta(e_k)$. Using this value, one can define the maximal duration $md(e, e')$ between a pair of events e and e' that are causally related as

$$md(e, e') = \max\{d(c) | c \text{ chain from } e \text{ to } e'\}$$

To obtain a BTO from a bMSC, one has to compute chains that begin on an instance and end on another. The timed order associated to a bMSC $M = (E, \leq, \alpha, \phi, A, I)$ with durations τ and δ is the order $O_M = (I_0 \uplus I_1, \leq_O, \Delta_M)$, where, I_0 and I_1 are disjoint copies of the set of instances I, $\leq_O = \{(x_0, y_1) | \exists e, e' \in\, \leq \wedge \phi(e) = x, \phi(e') = y\}$, and Δ_M is the function defined as follows: for each pair of instances, x and y, we define

$$\Delta_M(x, y) = \begin{cases} \max\limits_{e,e' \in \phi^{-1}(x) \times \phi^{-1}(y)} \{md(e, e')\} \text{ if } \exists e, e' \in \phi^{-1}(x) \times \phi^{-1}(y) \mid e \leq e' \\ -\infty \text{ otherwise} \end{cases}$$

Definition 8. The duration $D(M)$ of a bMSC $M = (E, \leq, \alpha, \phi, A, I)$ is the maximal duration for all pairs of instances in M, i.e., $D(M) = \max\limits_{x,y \in I^2}\{\Delta_M(x, y)\}$

Usually, bandwidth is not given by the durations of a single finite scenario, but rather by mean duration of infinite repetitions of a scenario. The asymptotic mean duration of an asymptotic behavior is defined by:

$$m(M^\omega) = \lim_{n \to +\infty} \frac{1}{n} D(M^n)$$

The asymptotic delay between two instances x and y is defined similarly, i.e.,

$$m_{x,y}(M^\omega) = \lim_{n \to +\infty} \frac{1}{n} \Delta_{M^n}(x, y)$$

The (max, +) algebra provides efficient means to compute these values. Note that the asymptotic mean duration can be lower than the duration of M as the systems described by MSCs are asynchronous. Hence, before starting a new iteration of a behavior M, an instance does not need to wait for the termination of M. Let us get back to our covert channels. Suppose that a MSC M can be used to transfer b bits of information from x to y. Then, the bandwidth of a covert channel that sends infinitely often a value encoded by M is:

$$Bw = \frac{b}{m_{x,y}(M^\omega)}$$

5   Application to RMTP2

Let us consider a RMTP2 tree with the following parameters: a bitmap size of 16 bits, and a maximal loss rate of 25%. The number of 16 bit bitmaps is 2^{16}, but all bitmaps can not be used to encode a value trough retransmissions, as declaring too many lost frames would result in ejecting the sender from the RMTP2 tree, which must be avoided. Usable bitmaps should contain at most 4 bit set to 1. Hence, the number of possible combinations is $\sum_{i=1}^{4} C_{16}^{i} = \sum_{i=1}^{4} \frac{16!}{i!(16-i)!} = 2516$. Hence, there are 2516 possible combinations of bits, and each one encodes $b = \log_2(2516) = 11.297$ bits of information. The bandwidth of our covert channel is maximal for an infinite repetition of the smallest scenario that can encode information. This smallest scenario is obtained when all receivers except CR send a $Hack$ with no losses ($Hack(0)$), and when the fake bitmap created by the corrupted receiver has only one bit set to 1. The shortest scenario to pass information requires only one retransmission, and is depicted in Figure 5.

To simplify the calculus, let us suppose that all events (message emissions, receptions, and actions) have the same duration D, and that message transmission takes T ms. With these parameters, one can compute symbolic values for the bipartite timed order associated to scenario of Figure 5. The result is given Figure 6. Let us comment the values labeling edges of this BTO. The edge from CR_0 to CR_1 is labeled by $(4B + 1).D + 2B.T$. This means that a corrupted receiver must wait $(4B + 1).D + 2B.T$ ms between two consecutive emissions of a fake bitmap. Note however that a similar computation can be performed when each event and each message transmission have a different duration (see [12] for details).

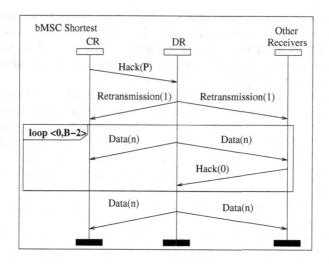

Fig. 5. Shortest scenarios

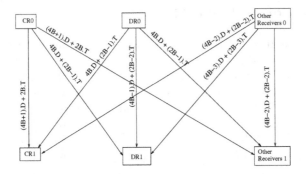

Fig. 6. Bipartite timed order for minimal scenario

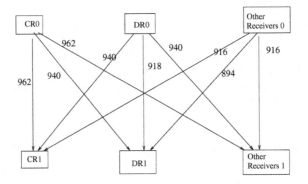

Fig. 7. Values for B=20, T=20, D=2

Let us assume that all messages are sent within $T = 20ms$, and that all internal events are performed in $D = 2ms$. For a branching factor $B = 20$, the bipartite timed order for the minimal scenario of Figure 5 is given in Figure 7. The average duration $md_{CR,O}(shortest^{\omega})$ is 962 ms. The bandwidth for these parameters is $Bw = \frac{11.29*1000}{962} = 11.74bits/sec$.

As one can see, the maximal duration of a scenario is $(4B+1).D+(2B).T$. The asymptotic mean duration of a transmission between a corrupted receiver and another anonymous receiver in the same subtree is also $(4B+1).D+(2B).T$. Note that that the mean cycle duration is not always equal to the maximal duration of the bipartite graph. In our case, as the last $Data$ message must be received before preparing a new fake bitmap, it creates a kind of acknowledgment. So, the fact that all instances are synchronized on the rhythm of the CC sender is not surprising. However, for specifications with more asynchronism, the mean asymptotic duration between two chosen instances can be much lower than the maximal duration in the bipartite graph, as transmissions do not need to be acknowledged and hence can be buffered in the system. Note that dividing B by 2 is equivalent to placing two corrupted receivers instead of one. Figure 8 below shows how the bandwidth evolves for various values of T and B when $D = 2$.

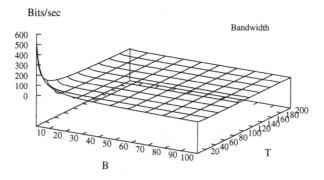

Fig. 8. Covert channel bandwidth for different values of B and T

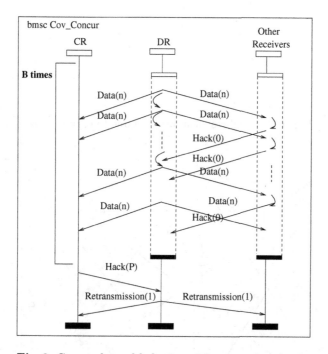

Fig. 9. Covert channel behavior without synchronization

So far, we have assumed that data was sent upon reception of an acknowledgment for previous packet. Usually, efficient protocols implement a sliding window principle, and send several *Data* packets before receiving acknowledgments. Now, let us assume that *Data* packets are not sent upon reception of an acknowledgment of previous packet, but rather that data is sent when possible, and as long as no retransmission request is received. [16] states that retransmissions have priority on data emission. With these considerations, the timed behavior of our covert channel would have the same timing properties as the bMSC *Cov_Concur* of Figure 9. This new model uses a general ordering im-

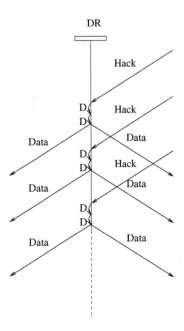

Fig. 10. Partial resynchronization due to data window

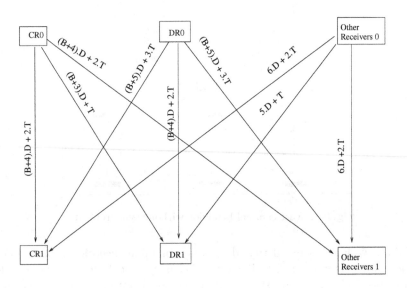

Fig. 11. BTO for the asynchronous case

posing an order between message emissions, between data reception and the corresponding acknowledgment.

For specification of Figure 10, the duration of a covert transmission decreases. Figure 11 gives the BTO for scenario of Figure 9. Even if the maximal duration

bits/sec

Bandwidth

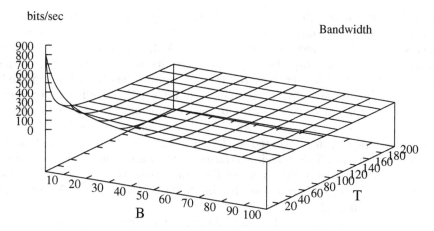

Fig. 12. Bandwidth for the asynchronous case

for the asynchronous scenario is $(B+5).D+3.T$, the asymptotic mean duration of a transmission between CR and O is $(B+4).D+2.T$. So the bandwidth for such scenario is $Bw' = \frac{b*1000}{(B+4).D+2.T}$.

However, scenario Cov_Concur depicts what happens in a single data window of size B. If $Data$ and $Hack$ packets are not synchronized any more, then $Data$ packets in the next B-sized data window can be sent before the reception of the retransmission demand $Hack(P)$ from CR. This means that the effective bandwidth of our covert channel could be higher than Bw', depending on how B-size data windows overlap. However, the RMTP2 specification says that new $Data$ packets can be created only when past packets are stable, i.e., they have been acknowledged by a sufficient number of recipients, and retransmission demands for these packets are not likely to occur. This produces a kind of resynchronization with $Hack$ packets inside a B-size data window, as depicted in Figure 10. Within this situation, the duration for the emission of B $Data$ packets increases. So, the exact bandwidth depends on the respective values of B, S, T and D, and Bw' must be considered as an vague approximation. However, this rough estimation of bandwidth shows that the duration of message transmissions has a lower influence than in the synchronized case. Figure 12 shows how Bw' evolves for different values of T and B. In the synchronous case, the bandwidth rapidly decreases, as in the asynchronous interpretation, for B=100 and T=200, the bandwidth is still 22.40 bits/sec.

6   Discussion and Conclusion

This paper has shown a scenario based formal approach for covert channel detection. This method was used to detect an illegal information flow in RMTP2 retransmission mechanism. This covert channel seems peculiarly dangerous, as the recipient of the covert message can be any of the receivers connected to the

DR node. The bandwidth of this channel rapidly decreases when the size of the network or the transmission times increase, but the backdoor remains usable when several synchronized receivers are placed ideally in the RMTP2 tree. Furthermore, this channel imposes a light time penalty to the system, making its detection at runtime harder. The detection algorithm has been implemented, but so far only supports HMSCs composing bMSCs without inline expressions. A desirable extension to this work is to deal with symbolic representations of parameters and loops. So far, covert channels are defined as the iteration of a set of behaviors, i.e., the corrupted sender always gets back to the same decision node that it controls. This encoding strategy is of course limited, and should be considered as a first step toward covert flows detection. We are currently investigating more elaborated strategies allowing to encode information from several decision nodes in a HMSC.

When a subset of the initial scenario description is identified as a covert channel, a $(max, +)$ analysis of this channel can be performed. So far, this analysis identifies a minimal scenario and computes an average asymptotic transmission time. It could be refined to take into account several scenarios and a probabilistic distribution to compute an average traffic. In the RMTP2 case, for example, one can assume that all values that can be encoded through retransmission demands have an identical probability, and define the average bandwidth as the expected value for the asymptotic mean duration. This average bandwidth can be much lower than the upper bound, as cycles used to encode data do not have the same durations. For the RMTP2 example, there are more values encoded with 4 bits set to 1 than with 3, and the retransmission is longer for 4 data packets than for 3. Hence, the average bandwidth can be influenced by the set of cycles used to encode values. Another open subject is to study how MSCs and $(max, +)$ analysis can be refined to deal with the sliding window effect depicted section 5, and give at least an upper bound for our bandwidth.

The RMTP2 covert channel identified in this paper only considered ideal cases, where retransmission packets were not lost, and where no messages could overtake, and so on. This situation defines a "perfect" covert channel, in the sense that the information received is exactly the information that was sent. If messages can overtake one another, or can be lost, or if some behaviors of the system are consequences of timer expirations, the messages observed by a receiver may comprise random parts. This can be considered as noise in our covert channel. The approach proposed in [7] and in this paper does not consider noisy channels. However, with an appropriate encoding, information can still be passed in a noisy environment. For such situations, the amount of information passed is probably better computed using tools such as information theory.

References

1. Andrews, G., Reitmans, R.: An axiomatic approach to information flows in programs. ACM transactions on Programming Languages and Systems **2** (1980) 56–76.
2. Bell, D., La Padula, J.: Secure computer systems: mathematical foundations. Mitre technical report 2547, MITRE (1973) Vol I.

3. Bell, D., La Padula, J.: Secure computer systems: a mathematical model. MITRE technical report 2547, MITRE (1973) Vol II.
4. Criteria, C.: Common criteria for information technology security evaluation part 3: Security assurance requirements. Technical Report CCIMB-99-033, CCIMB (1999).
5. Goguen, J., Meseguer, J.: Security policies and security models. Press, I.C.S. (Ed.) Proc. of IEEE Symposium on Security and Privacy (1982) 11–20.
6. Hélouët, L.: Distributed system requirements modeling with message sequence charts: the case of the rmtp2 protocol. Information and Software Technology **45** (2003) 701–714.
7. Hélouët, L., Zeitoun, M., Jard, C.: Covert channels detection in protocols using scenarios. Proc. of SPV'03 Security Protocols Verification (2003).
8. ITU-T: Recommendation Z.120 (11/99), Message Sequence Charts (MSC). International Telecommunication Union, Geneva.
9. Katoen, J.-P., Lambert, L.: Pomsets for message sequence charts. Proceedings of SAM98: 1st conference on SDL and MSC, Berlin (1998) 281–290.
10. Kemmerer, R.: Shared ressources matrix methodology: an approach to indentifying storage and timing channels. ACM Transactions on Computer Systems **1** (1983) 256–277.
11. Lampson, B.: A note on the confinement problem. Communication of the ACM **16** (1973) 613–615.
12. Le Maigat, P., Hélouët, L.: A (max,+) approach for time in message sequence charts. 5th Workshop on Discrete Event Systems (WODES 2000) (2000).
13. Le Maigat, P.: Techniques algébriques Max-Plus pour l'analyse des performances temporelles de systèmes concurrents. PhD thesis, Université de Rennes 1 (2002).
14. Lipner, S.: A comment on the confinement problem. Proceedings of the Fifth Symposium on Operating systems Principles (1975).
15. Lowe, G.: Quantifying information flow. Proceedings of the 7th European Symposium on Research in Computer Security(ESORICS) (2002).
16. Montgomery, T., Whetten, B., Basavaiah, M., Paul, S., Rastogi, N., Conlan, J., Yeh, T.: The RMTP2 protocol. IETF draft, Internet Engineering Task Force (1998).
17. NSA/NCSC: A guide to understanding covert channel analysis of trusted systems. Technical report, NSA/NCSC (1993).
18. Reniers, M.: Message Sequence Charts: Syntax and Semantics. PhD thesis, Eindhoven University of Technology (1998).
19. Reniers, M., Mauw, S.: High-level message sequence charts. Cavalli, A., Sarma, A. (Eds.) SDL97: Time for Testing - SDL, MSC and Trends. Proc. of the 8th SDL Forum, Evry, France (1997) 291–306.
20. Sabelfeld, A., Myers, A.: Language-based information-flow security. IEEE Journal on selected areas in communications **21** (2003).
21. Volpano, D., Smith, G.: Eliminating covert flows with minimum typings. Proc. 10th IEEE Computer Security Foundations Workshop (1997) 156–168.
22. Whetten, B., Paul, S., Taskale, G.: RMTP-II overview. Talarian white paper, Talarian Corporation (1999).

A Metamodel for SDL-2000 in the Context of Metamodelling ULF

Joachim Fischer, Michael Piefel, and Markus Scheidgen

Humboldt Universität zu Berlin, Institut für Informatik
Unter den Linden 6, 10099 Berlin, Germany
{fischer, piefel, scheidge}@informatik.hu-berlin.de

Abstract. Today the syntax of many languages is defined by using context-free grammars. These syntax definitions suffer from a major drawback: grammars do not allow the definition of abstract, reusable concept definitions. Especially in families of related languages, where multiple languages often share the same concepts, this limitation leads to unnecessary reproduction of concept definitions and a missing shared base for these related languages. Metamodels can contain inheritance hierarchies of concepts; thus multiple specifications can reuse and refine existing shared concept definitions. Therefore we propose a method to develop metamodels from existing syntax definitions. We explain our method by applying it to SDL-2000. The method starts with a mapping from BNF grammars into simple preliminary metamodels. Then, by supplying a relation between elements of these simple metamodels and abstract concepts, these metamodels are automatically transformed into metamodels that use existing descriptions of abstract concepts and thus allow a shared basis of common abstract concepts definitions.

1 Introduction

In the ongoing research on model driven software engineering the relations between different modelling languages are a key point. The approach in [2] uses model transformation between *eODL* [7] and *SDL-2000* [6] to drive software projects from design to implementation. Such a technology requires language alignment. To build such relations as transformation rules, between these languages, we needed unified specifications for both of the participating languages. The need of unifying the SDL-2000 grammar based syntax definition with the eODL metamodel started our research on developing a metamodel for the SDL-2000 syntax. But the metamodel of SDL-2000 only attacks the tip of a far more common problem.

ITU-T recommends a long series of formalized languages, such as MSC, ASN.1, TTCN and the already mentioned eODL and SDL. These languages were developed independently using different specification techniques. Unfortunately, this resulted in languages that are hard to relate to each other. But language alignment is crucial for model driven engineering. It is important to know where and how these languages can be used together, how to profit from an integrated

D. Amyot and A.W. Williams (Eds.): SAM 2004, LNCS 3319, pp. 208–223, 2005.
© Springer-Verlag Berlin Heidelberg 2005

use of these languages. Consequently, the ITU-T started the *Language Coordination Project* [11] with the goal to unify the mentioned languages, thus to form the *Unified Language Family (ULF)*. The *Language Coordination Project* considers two methodologies to achieve a coordinated syntax definition: a common syntax for BNF grammars (a common meta-metagrammar) and metamodelling.

We figured the metamodelling technology to be more appropriate to define the abstract syntax of a language, its concepts and its structure, than to use context free grammars. We give the reasons for this opinion in the following comparison of BNF grammars and metamodels:

Context free grammars, used in language specifications, are mostly in BNF. The BNF syntax was developed to specify concrete language syntax. It is a mathematicly exact method to determine which words are in the described language and which are not. To achieve this, grammars use rules; these rules specify a set of productions; these productions represent a set of words, words that form the language described by the grammar. However, what grammars do not provide are means for rule refinement or generalization, they do not allow modularization. It is not possible to refine rules to form generalization hierarchies or to build logical structures by using a namespace mechanism of some sort. Structure and abstraction hierarchies are always flat.

This is a severe grammar disadvantage. The following two profits, known from object-oriented languages, cannot be taken from a grammar based specification. First, generalization, and thus refinement and reuse, as well as logical structures, provided through mechanisms like namespaces and packages, are vital concepts for compact and easy to understand language specifications. With these features not only the words of a language can be specified, but the internal structure of the described language can be defined. This allows a natural evolution of language specifications and easy tool development. Second, in the context of language families, a package of shared abstract concepts, concepts that are refined in different languages, can directly align the concepts of different languages. This allows the notation of inter language relations at specification time, and thus allows unification of the participating languages.

These two points make clear that a modern language specification must offer more than a pure syntax definition, it must show the language's internal structure and make it accessible to other language specifications. This is to allow the notation of relations between different languages. Therefore we believe that a syntax specification technique must provide the following two important meta-meta-concepts. First, generalization; the building blocks of a syntax definition must be refinable. One must be able to define abstract concepts and one must be able to use them in multiple concrete refinements in the definition of the same and in the definition of different languages. Second, structural composition; to use the same concepts in different language definitions and to allow bigger language definitions, namespaces for structured specification must be provided.

Both concepts, generalization and structural composition, are provided by modern metamodelling architectures; Atkinson's work [1] gives a good introduction into the subject. As object-oriented modelling platforms, metamodelling architectures provide a generalization mechanism as well as a namespace mechanism. Metamodels are designed for abstract syntax, or better static concept definition. As a side-effect, the meta-language as well as the languages to be modelled are object oriented modelling languages. Due to that common nature, an expert in the specified language is often also well trained in the used specification technique.

After we were aware of the potential of metamodelling for language specification, we faced the problem of providing this metamodelling features to already existing, grammar based language specifications. Therefore we propose a method that allows to develop a metamodel from an existing grammar based syntax definition. The method fulfils two requirements: It is partially automated to avoid the error-prone task of manual grammar to metamodel transformation and the resulting metamodels use a set of abstract concept definitions. These abstract concepts are to be identified by a language expert and can be shared in the specification of different languages or in the specification of a hole family of languages.

To prove and explain our method, we applied it to a part of the abstract SDL-2000 [6] syntax. The developed metamodel covers all of SDL's structural concepts. The reason for modelling only structural concepts is that structural concepts are by far the best researched concepts, and various abstract concepts for many languages are already identified and modelled [9]. Thus, we can fully concentrate on the method and general metamodelling aspects. But of course the method is independent from what is modelled; therefore it also works for other parts of language specifications like the description of behaviour or data concepts.

We tried to stay as general as possible, to make the method applicable with most existing metamodelling architectures. But a few requirements had to be made. The metamodelling architecture has to consist of at least four layers [3]. The method is made for a strict [1] metamodelling environment; but that does not imply that it will not work for a loose metamodelling architecture as well. The used M_3 layer model must include a generalizable class concept, associations, namespaces and a package concept.

The mentioned properties are fulfilled by the most important metamodelling architectures: MOF 1.4 [10], UML 2.0 [9], OML [5], and even formal metamodelling techniques like VPM [13]. We used the meta-metamodel in [10] and implemented our method by using JMI [8], which is a MOF 1.4 based metamodelling standard [10].

In section 2 we give an overview over the developed method. The sections 3 and 4 cover the necessary steps of that method. The concluding section 5 compares the resulting SDL-2000 metamodel with the original grammar based syntax definition, it summarizes the paper, and it gives some further research perspectives.

2   A Method for Metamodelling Existing Languages

The steps involved in our method are presented in figure 1. The whole process is based on an already existing syntax and static semantics specification. This

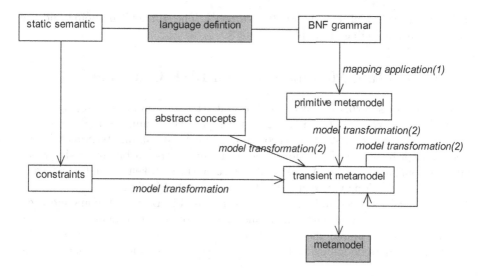

Fig. 1. The steps involved in the presented metamodel development

paper addresses only the grammar part of language definitions; it does not cover aspects of static semantics. A complete presentation of the method, including static semantics concerns, can be found in [12].

The development of a metamodel from a BNF grammar includes two steps. First a preliminary metamodel is generated from the existing BNF grammar. We required our method to do this step automatically, because a manual transformation from a grammar to a metamodel would be cause to many errors due to human failure. Metamodels are more expressive than grammars. Thus, it was easy to find a grammar to metamodel mapping. Section 3 describes this mapping.

Of course, implied by this automatic transformation, the resulting metamodel only uses meta-concepts already provided by BNF grammars. Therefore, neither generalization nor structural composition are used. All concept definitions reside in the same namespace and they form a flat hierarchy.

To use the more advanced concepts generalization and structural composition some human input is needed. Along our second method requirement two things have to be provided by a language expert. First, abstract concepts must be identified and modelled. Of course there are different levels of abstraction. Some concepts are very abstract and shared by many languages, like generalization, namespaces or a type system, others are more specific to the modelled language like SDL's instance sets. In section 4.3 we show the models of a package consisting of general abstract concepts and a package consisting of the abstract SDL concepts, that we could identify. The second kind of information that must be provided by a human expert is: Which concrete language concept is a refinement of which identified abstract concept? We call this information a semantic mapping. A model transformation engine can now use both inputs, abstract concept definitions and semantic mapping, to automatically convert the preliminary primitive metamodel into the final metamodel. The semantic mapping and the transformation engine are explained in 4.3.

3   Generating Metamodels from BNF Grammars

BNF grammars, primarily used in the definition of computer languages, are basically context free grammars. The rules of such grammars replace a non-terminal with a regular expression containing non-terminals and terminals. These regular expressions may use the composition, alternative, arbitrary, at-least-one and optional constructs. An example of such rules, taken from the abstract procedure definition syntax of SDL-2000, is presented in figure 2.

For a better understanding of the concepts used in BNF grammars and their relationships figure 3 presents a meta-metamodel for BNF grammars. Now we are modifying this grammar meta-metamodel until it becomes a meta-metamodel for common metamodelling architectures. Along the modifications made on the

Procedure_definition :: Procedure_name	1
Procedure_formal_parameter∗	2
[Result]	3
Procedure_graph;	4
	5
Procedure_name = Name;	6
	7
Procedure_formal_parameter = In_parameter	8
| Inout_parameter	9
| Out_parameter;	10

Fig. 2. SDL-2000 abstract syntax example

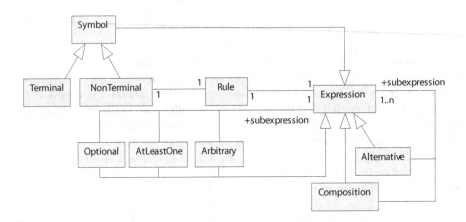

Fig. 3. BNF grammar meta-metamodel

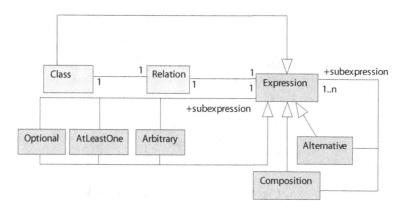

Fig. 4. Homomorphous modifications

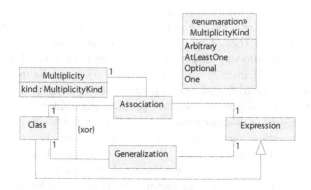

Fig. 5. Associations and generalizations for relations rather than compositions and alternativs as expressions

meta-meta-level, we show a mapping from BNF concepts to the concepts of metamodelling. Hence, we are creating transformation rules for the meta-level, which are used in the automatic grammar to metamodel conversion.

The first modification is to use concepts out of the concept space of object-oriented metamodelling, as long these concepts can replace the respective grammar concepts isomorphicly. Figure 4 shows a more general model than 3. It uses the metamodelling concepts class and relation for the grammar concepts symbol, terminal, non-terminal and rule. Unfortunately, the concept *Expression* and its specializations have no equivalent in metamodelling.

When you think about the semantics of *Composition* and *Alternative*, they turn out to be those of *Association* and *Generalization*. Associations allow the linear composition of classes, alias symbols, and specialized classes are alternative realizations of the general class, alias symbol. This leads to the idea of mapping compositions and alternatives to associations and generalizations. The expres-

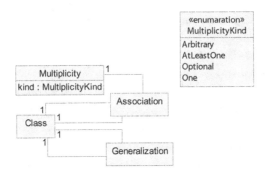

Fig. 6. A more usual meta-metamodel

sion kinds that describe multiplicities, can be compared to the multiplicity of association ends in object-oriented metamodelling. A modified meta-metamodel realizing this ideas is shown in figure 5.

Expressions allow the recursive composition of an unlimited depth of sub-expressions. To respect that, *Class* in figure 5 is modelled as a generalization to *Expression*, hence allowing *Expression* to relate with itself. But there is no reason not to completely identify *Class* with *Expression*, see figure 6.

Now it is easy to build transformation rules along the meta-metamodel evolution from figure 3 to figure 6. The only problematic things are the names for classes that represent sub-expressions. In BNF grammars sub-expressions are nameless and are only separated by the use of parentheses. But classes in meta-modelling are named model elements. We simply name the classes that represent sub-expression rather than symbols with unused new names.

The developed BNF grammar to metamodel transformation rules are:

1. Every symbol is represented through a class.
2. A rule with a single symbol on the right is represented through an association that associates the class representing the left hand symbol with the class representing the right hand symbol.
3. A rule with a composition on the right is represented through an association for every composed sub-expression.
4. A rule with an alternative on the right is represented through a generalization for every alternated sub-expression.
5. A sub-expression consisting only of a single symbol is represented through that symbol's class.
6. A sub-expression that is a composition or an alternative is represented through a new class, with a so-far unused name. The composition or alternative is transformed as in 2 or 3, but with the new class as the left hand representative.
7. A sub-expression of multiplicity kind, that is part of a composition, is transformed to an equivalent multiplicity kind of the proper association end.
8. An expression of multiplicity kind or a sub-expression of multiplicity kind, that is part of an alternative, is represented through a new class with a so far

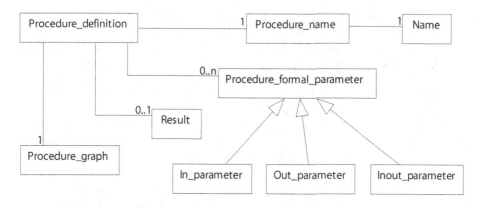

Fig. 7. The example grammar part mapped into a metamodel

unused name. An association is introduced between that new class and the class that represents the multiplied sub-expression, with proper multiplicity.

We implemented a simple tool, consisting of a BNF grammar parser, the implemented transformation rules, and a XML generator, producing the metamodel in XMI format. XMI is a standard format for metamodel exchange. This tool called *agramm* successfully transforms the abstract SDL-2000 grammar. Figure 7 shows a part of it. It shows that syntax part that is shown in the grammar example in figure 2 at the beginning of this section.

4   The Use of Abstract Concepts

4.1   Beyond the Grammar to Metamodel Mapping

The metamodels one gets by applying the described mapping from a BNF grammar can be called primitive at best. The reason is, of course, that those primitive metamodels can only be as expressive as the original grammar is. We identified three categories of problems in that the primitive metamodels must be improved.

First, those primitive metamodels suffer from the same drawback as the original grammars: They do not use and reuse abstract concept descriptions. One example are the structural type concepts in SDL-2000, namely *Agent type definitions* and *Composite-state type definitions*. These two concepts are generalizable, they can be instantiated, they are namespaces for a number of other SDL concepts, and so forth. But these abstract concepts are specified separately for both of that elements, instead of being defined once and then reused. Especially being a namespace is a property that even more SDL concepts like procedures and packages share. Furthermore, namespace is an abstract concept used by many other languages; take eODL for an example.

The second problem is that grammars are very limited in their meta-meta-concepts, and so there are many metamodelling features that are not used by the automatic generated metamodels. In the grammar example in figure 2, both

Procedure_definition and *Procedure_name* are described by a symbol. Therefore both concepts are modelled by a class in the generated metamodel. Of course, that is bad metamodelling technique. The name of a procedure should rather be modelled through a string attribute. The same problem lies in the modelling of associations. Metamodelling concepts like navigability, aggregation, etc. cannot be stated in grammars, and so they are not used in the generated metamodel, even if their usage would be appropriate.

The third problem is what can be called textual syntax rudiments. These are concepts like *identifier* and *qualifier*. In a text based language they are needed to identify objects. To do so they represent a logical relation between the object definition and its usage, like the definition of a variable and its usage in an expression. In a metamodel and its model instances these concepts are not necessary. These relations can be modelled by associations and their instances, called links. In other words these are concepts that already exist as meta-meta-concepts and have not to be redefined. Of course, *identifier* and *qualifier* are needed in concrete model notations to represent those relations, but they serve no purpose in an abstract language definition.

Of course the first problem category and its solution, that is the introduction of abstract concept definitions, is the most interesting. The usage of abstract concepts leads to better structured and reusable syntax definitions and thus presents the biggest advantage in comparison with a grammar based syntax definition.

In addition to that, it turned out that, in the case of SDL-2000, the most concepts that cause problems of the second and third category are potentially abstract concepts. Potential means that these are concrete concepts that should be replaced by abstract definitions. Thus, these faulty concrete realizations will vanish when abstract concepts are introduced. For example: The name feature in the procedure example causes a problem of category two; the concept name is realised through a class instead a string attribute. But it also is a potentially abstract feature. There are a lot of SDL concepts that have a name property. That is why it is most likely that after the introduction of an abstract named model element concept, the concrete concept *procedure definition* has lost its distinctive name property and inherits it from the abstract concept, instead. The same can be said about *identification* and *qualification*. They are often used by concepts that are potentially abstract, and thus they will not be used after well modelled abstract concepts have been introduced. In this paper we concentrate on the more interesting category one: The introduction of abstract concept definitions.

4.2   Abstract Concept Definitions

First we present the abstract concept definitions that we used for the SDL-2000 metamodel. There are different levels of abstractions. Some concepts are so general that they are used in virtually every object-oriented language, others are more specific and may only be reused among related languages or only within one language.

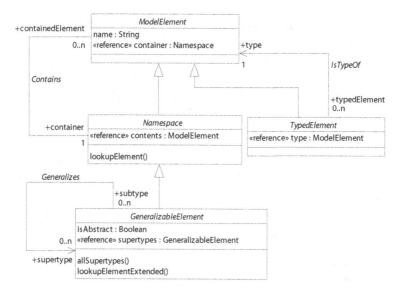

Fig. 8. Abstract concepts

Figure 8 shows the abstract structure concepts used by most object-oriented languages. A detailed explanation and documented development of that model can be found in [12]. The resemblance to the most known languages might strike the reader's eye. They are also used in the successful metamodels of UML and the meta-metamodel of MOF.

But even more abstract concepts could be obtained from SDL's syntax itself. Even if they may turn out to be more specific, perhaps distinctive to SDL, they still allow a more compact and therefore easier to understand and easier to use metamodel. Figure 9 presents the additional abstract concepts that we were able to identify in the SDL-2000 syntax. A few concrete concepts, those that are marked grey, are shown too. That is to ease the understanding and shorten the necessary explanations. A few remarks:

- Many SDL concepts reference a *body* of some sort. Procedures for example must contain a state automaton defining their behaviour. This state automaton is referred as a *body*. The same is true for process typed *Agents* or the bodies in *Composite-state types*. To respect the varying nature of bodies, they are modelled to be the most abstract concept: *ModelElement*.
- Parameters are used by a variety of SDL concepts. *Agent types, Procedures, Composite-state types* have parameters. Even if *Procedure* uses a special form of parameter, the parameter itself is a typed element in any case.
- In SDL-2000 two type concepts coexist. A type is something that describes a set of instances or values. In SDL a type can on the one hand be a data type, like a *Signal definition* or a primitive data type and on the other hand a type can be a structure type like *Agent type* or *Composite-state type*.

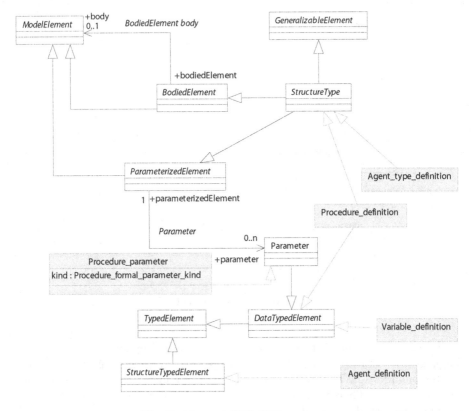

Fig. 9. Abstract SDL-2000 concepts

- Structure types are instanciable, generalizable, parameterized types. Therefore structure types are a combination of the generalizable concept, parameterized concept and the body possession concept.

As a reminder: one may criticize that the displayed model allows unwanted instances, that procedure for example may contain a non-procedure parameter, or a structure-typed element may reference a data type. Obviously some restrictions have to be added to the model. Actually these constraints are considered static semantics and are not covered by this paper, but [12] addresses that matter by using a predicate logic formalism to further limit the set of possible metamodel instances.

4.3 Combining Primitive Metamodels with Abstract Concept Definitions

Now we have sets of abstract metamodel elements and a generated primitive grammar-based metamodel. But how to combine these model elements to form a single metamodel? Two things must be realized: First, the concrete concepts must be marked as specializations of the introduced abstract concepts. And

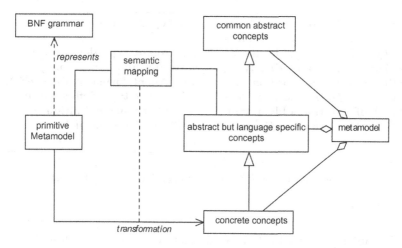

Fig. 10. Transforming the primitive metamodel

second, features and rudiments of concrete elements that are already defined or realized by the corresponding abstract model element must be removed. To accomplish this task, we use model transformation.

Figure 10 shows the basic idea of this transformation. We already have the grammar that is represented by the primitive metamodel, and we already have common as well as more language specific abstract model elements. To complete the metamodel, we have to transform the concrete concepts of the primitive metamodel to actually become specializations of the abstract model elements.

To do so some information from a language expert is needed. That is information about the nature of the concrete language concepts, something that can be given through a *semantic mapping* between the primitive metamodel elements and the abstract model elements. This mapping must say which concrete concept is a specialization of what abstract concept and how it refines the abstract concept. With this information the transformation itself can be done automatically.

How it works: The semantic mapping is a partial relation that assigns concrete metamodel elements to the most appropriate abstract model element. The mapping of model elements does not only involve a mapping between classes, but a mapping between relations as well.

As an example figure 11 presents a part of the semantic mapping used for the SDL-2000 metamodel. The first line assigns *Agent_type_definition* to be a specialization of the abstract concept class *StructureType*. The third line maps agent type definition's association with itself to be a specialization of the generalization association introduced by one of agent type definition's new super meta-classes: *GeneralizableElement*. Line four maps agent type definition's association with state machine definition to be a specialization of the body association introduced by another new super type of agent type definition: *BodiedElement*. Line five refines the inherited features of the abstract concept *ParameterizedElement*, the other lines refine the inherited features of the abstract concept *Namespace*.

```
agentTypeDefinition = new SdlStructureTypeAdaptor(          1
      "Agent_type_definition");                             2
agentTypeDefinition.addSupertypeType("Agent_type_defintion"); 3
agentTypeDefinition.addBodyType("State_machine_definition"); 4
agentTypeDefinition.addParameterType("Agent_formal_parameter"); 5
agentTypeDefinition.addContainedType("Agent_type_definition"); 6
agentTypeDefinition.addContainedType("Procedure_definition"); 7
agentTypeDefinition.addContainedType("Agent_definition");    8
      ...                                                    9
```

Fig. 11. An example taken from the semantic mapping used for the SDL-2000 meta-model

This mapping is actually Java code. That is because we realized the transformation using *JMI* [8] a Java based API for metadata management. For every abstract concept an adaptor class was written in Java. *SdlStructureTypeAdaptor* is such an adaptor. The inheritance hierarchy of the adaptors is aligned to the hierarchy form by the corresponding abstract concepts. Therefore, the super types of *SdlStructureTypeAdaptor* are *GeneralizableElementAdaptor*, *ParameterizedElementAdaptor*, *BodiedElementAdaptor*, *NamespaceAdator* and *ModelElementAdator*.

For every abstract concept class a adaptor class was written, for every concrete class a adaptor instance is created by the semantic mapping. The constructor that is used maps the concrete concept class to the abstract concept class. This means the constructor uses JMI to introduce a new generalization relation between the abstract concept class and the concrete concept class that is provided through the constructor's parameter.

For every abstract association or attribute a method was written. The method is owned by the adaptor class for the abstract concept class, that the association or attribute is originated in. For every concrete association a method call is used. This Java method call maps the concrete association to the corresponding abstract association. Therefore the Java method deletes the old concrete association, originally generated through the grammar to metamodel generator, and replaces it with a refinement of the abstract association. This refinement is done through the addition of a constraint. The concrete association is identified by taking the concrete class for one end and taking the class provided through the Java method's parameter for the other end.

For example, look at line three of the previous semantic mapping example 11. Originated in SDL's abstract grammar, a concrete association between *Agent_type_definition* and *Agent_type_definition* exists in the primitive metamodel. This association refers to the inheritance relationship between two agent types. Line three maps the abstract association *Generalizes* of *StructureType*'s and therefore *Agent_type_definition*'s meta- superclass *GeneralizableElement*. The invoked Java method removes the original concrete association and replaces it by a constraint that restricts the abstract inherited *Generalizes* association to allow only links between two instances of *Agent_type_definition*. The mapping of *StructureType* associations then continues for the abstract associations *Contains* and *Element-Body*.

This way the mapping works as a chain of commands that transforms the metamodel according to the semantics given by the mapping. After the whole mapping is applied, all concrete concepts are specializations of abstract ones, all concrete associations and rudiments have been removed and replaced by constraints that restrict abstract associations or attributes. The only things left are a few concrete concepts for which no appropriate abstract concepts could yet be identified. For these concepts some manual transformations have to be made.

In particular, the explained SDL-2000 metamodel lacks an abstract concept for the SDL communication concepts *channel* and *gate*, as well as the concrete agent-instance- set concept that uses minimum and maximum instance numbers. An abstract relation concept may be very useful, because relations occur in many languages as well as in the behaviour of SDL itself. Therefore it should be introduced when the metamodel family grows, and the abstract basis becomes larger. The second left-out concept on instance sets is, as far the authors know, unique to SDL, and therefore only a concrete description is needed.

5   Conclusions

We presented a method that allows the development of metamodels from existing syntax definitions. The presented method shows the following characteristics:

- It is partially automatic and thus less error-prone.
- The only human input that is needed is a model of abstract concepts; a mapping from concrete, grammar originated, model elements to abstract model elements; and a transformation rule for every abstract concept, that transforms generated concrete elements to become specializations of abstract elements.
- Modelled abstract elements and transformation rules are reusable and extendable and can be used in the development of multiple metamodels. That is an even bigger advantage in the modelling of language families.

We applied and tested our method on SDL-2000. The resulting metamodel shows the following characteristics and advantages, when compared to the original grammar based syntax definition.

- Due to the extensive usage of abstract model elements and refinement the resulting SDL metamodel is compact and easy to understand. Abstractions are already noted in the metamodel itself, they have not to be explained in additional text. The inheritance hierarchy of concepts can be directly and naturally used in the development of object-oriented SDL tools.
- The metamodel includes and is based on a reusable and refinable abstract basis. This basis can easily be reused in metamodels of languages that share the same concepts. A shared set of abstract concepts can be used in a unified

specification of language families and allows a direct alignment of languages that share the same abstract concepts.

- The concepts of the metamodel are well structured by the use of packages. Due to such structural concepts like namespaces and packages, metamodels can be easily combined and related to each other.

These advantages over grammars are mostly based on the metamodelling concepts generalizability and namespaces. Both are concepts that grammars can not support.

But even if we see many advantages of the metamodelling side, we have to admit that metamodels cannot replace grammars in the specification of concrete syntax. When it comes to the task of defining and parsing textual notation the formal foundations and exact semantics of grammars cannot be yet replaced. But in defining the concepts of a language in an abstract manner to derive semantics definitions, tool development and human understanding from it, the advantages of metamodels are superior.

We developed a series of tools to support the method application and metamodel development. A tool called *agramm* was created that allows automatic transformation from BNF grammar to MOF metamodels. The API *mmm*, based on *JMI* [8], is a framework for metamodel transformations that uses refinable transformation rules.

There are a few problems that should be addressed by further research. First, the metamodelling of behaviour concepts is not yet satisfactory. Abstract behaviour concepts must be identified and should be used for the completion of the SDL-2000 metamodel. Second, with the metamodel for SDL-2000 we started to build an abstract set of concepts. It should be used and extended in the metamodelling of other ULF languages. Third, the relations of abstract ULF concepts to the concepts used in UML should be researched for easier UML profiling or other language integration. And fourth and last, the most challenging problem is metamodelling of dynamics. The formal specification of SDL-2000 showed a way to specify a language's dynamic semantics, using *Abstract State Machines* [4]. Integration of that knowledge into metamodelling architectures could be result in a unified metamodelling technique for reusable syntax and semantics definition.

References

1. Atkinson, C.: Meta-Modeling for Distributed Object Environments. 1st International Enterprise Distributed Object Computing Conference (1997).
2. Böhme, H., Fischer, J.: eODL and SDL in Combination for Components. Amyot, D., Williams, A. (Eds.) Fourth SDL and MSC Workshop. Volume 3319 of Lecture Notes in Computer Science (2004) 19–34.
3. Crawley, S., Davis, S., Indulska, J., McBride, S., Raymond, K.: Meta-meta is better-better! IFIP WG 6.1 International Working Conference on Distributed Applications and Interoperable Systems(DAIS'97) (1997).
4. Gurevich, Y.: Evolving Algebras 1993: Lipari Guide. Börger, E. (Ed.) Specification and Validation Methods. Oxford University Press (1995) 9–36.

5. Handerson-Sellers, B., Firesmith, D., Graham, I., Page-Jones, M.: OPEN Modeling Language (OML) Meta-model Specification, Version 1.0. (1996).
6. ITU-T: Recommendation Z.100 (08/02), Specification and Description Language (SDL). International Telecommunication Union, Geneva (2002).
7. ITU-T: Recommendation Z.130 (07/03), Extended Object Definition Language (eODL). International Telecommunication Union, Geneva (2003).
8. JMI: The Java Metadata Interface(JMI) Specification(Final Release). Java Community Process (2002) JSR-000040.
9. OMG: UML 2.0 – Infrastructure Final Adopted Specification. Object Management Group (2003) ptc/2003-09-15.
10. OMG: MOF 1.4 – Meta Object Facility, Version 1.4. Object Management Group (2003) formal/2002-04-03.
11. Reed, R.: Language Coordination Project – Revised information – Workshop results, International Telecommunication Union (2003) TD 3145.
12. Scheidgen, M.: Metamodelle für Sprachen mit formaler Syntaxdefinition, am Beispiel von SDL-2000. Master thesis, Humboldt Universität zu Berlin, Germany (2004).
13. Varró, D., Pataricza, A.: VPM: Mathematics of Metamodeling is Metamodeling Mathematics. Journal of Software and Systems Modelling (2003) 1–24.

A Flexible Micro Protocol Framework*

Ingmar Fliege, Alexander Geraldy, Reinhard Gotzhein, and Philipp Schaible

Computer Science Department, Technical University of Kaiserslautern
Postfach 3049, D-67653 Kaiserslautern, Germany
{fliege, geraldy, gotzhein, schaible}@informatik.uni-kl.de

Abstract. Structuring and reuse are key approaches to the proper development and maintenance of software systems. System structuring is essential to controlling complexity, and is a prerequisite for the extraction of reuse artifacts. Reuse of solutions is crucial to controlling quality and productivity. In previous work, we have identified and applied the structuring unit *micro protocol*. We extend these results by defining a flexible micro protocol framework, and by applying it to the design of a functionally complete communication system, with SDL as design language.

1 Introduction

The development and maintenance of large distributed software systems is intrinsically difficult. Several key approaches to mastering these difficulties have been identified, including *structuring* and *reuse*. System structuring is essential to controlling complexity. Reuse of solutions is crucial to controlling quality and productivity.

Reuse has been thoroughly studied in software engineering, and has led to the distinction of three main reuse concepts: components, frameworks, and patterns. *Components* can be characterized as self-contained ready-to-use building blocks, which are selected from a component library, and composed. A *framework* is the skeleton of a system, to be adapted by the system developer. *Patterns* describe generic solutions for recurring problems, to be customized for a particular context.

To identify and extract reuse artifacts, i.e., components, frameworks, and patterns, the structuring of a software system plays a key role. Software systems may have a variety of structures, depending, for instance, on the type of system, the degree of abstraction, the development paradigm, and the developers view points. In general, we can distinguish between *architectural structuring* and the *structuring of behavior and data*. More specifically, structuring principles such as module structuring (e.g., agent modules, object modules, collaboration modules,

---

* This work has been supported by the Deutsche Forschungsgemeinschaft (DFG) as part of Sonderforschungsbereich (SFB) 501, *Development of Large Systems with Generic Methods*.

D. Amyot and A.W. Williams (Eds.): SAM 2004, LNCS 3319, pp. 224–236, 2005.

functional modules), hierarchical structuring (e.g., agent hierarchies, class hierarchies, state hierarchies), conceptual structuring (e.g., reference architectures), dynamic structuring (e.g., creation and termination of process modules, interaction relationships), operational structuring (e.g., system functions), temporal structuring (e.g., system phases or modes), and physical structuring (e.g., nodes, resources, topology) can be applied.

In previous work, we have identified and applied the structuring unit *micro protocol*, i.e., a communication protocol with a single (distributed) functionality and the required protocol collaboration [4, 5]. A *functionality* (e.g., flow control) is a single aspect of internal system behavior that may be distributed among a set of system agents, with causality relationships between single events. By *collaboration*, we refer to the interaction behavior of a distributed functionality. From a reuse viewpoint, micro protocols classify as components, they may be selected from a micro protocol library, and composed. However, it is not obvious how this composition can be accomplished. In this paper, we propose a flexible micro protocol framework for this purpose, and apply it to the design of a functionally complete communication system, with SDL [7] as design language.

The paper is structured as follows. In Sect. 2, we recall the notion of micro protocol, conceive a flexible micro protocol framework, and introduce a customized design process. In Sect. 3, these aspects are illustrated by means of a complete case study. Conclusions are drawn in Sect. 4.

2   Micro Protocol-Based Development

Micro protocols are structuring units of communication systems that encapsulate one single protocol functionality and the required protocol collaboration. Being ready-to-use building blocks, they can be combined into a component library, which then serves as a repository for a reuse-oriented communication system development. In this section, we present the main constituents of this development, namely micro protocols, a framework for the composition of micro protocols, and a customized design process.

2.1   Micro Protocols

Communication systems can be structured into smaller constituents in different ways. Generally speaking, a *communication component* is a self-contained, ready-to-use building block of a communication system. Various kinds of communication components can be distinguished, depending on the viewpoint of the communication systems engineer, e.g., protocol functionalities, protocol collaborations, protocol phases, protocol entities, and protocol layers.

In [4,5], we have introduced and applied a new type of communication component, called *micro protocol*, i.e., a communication protocol with a single (distributed) protocol functionality and the required protocol collaboration. Here, a *protocol functionality* is a single aspect of internal protocol entity behavior (*operational structuring*), e.g., flow control, loss control, corruption control. It is realized by a particular *protocol mechanism* (e.g., sliding-window, sequence numbering, checksum), and generally distributed among a set of protocol entities. A *protocol collaboration* is a self-contained subset of synchronization and causality relationships of a set of protocol entities. Because a protocol functionality covers only one single aspect of protocol behavior, a micro protocol is not decomposable into smaller protocol units. However, several micro protocols may be combined into a communication system, possibly in a hierarchical way, yielding *macro protocols*.

2.2   Micro Protocol Framework

Micro protocols can be composed to form protocols with more complex functionalities, called *macro protocols*. As we are dealing with components, no adaptation is necessary. However, different types of composition may be required to achieve a correct cooperation of protocol entities. For instance, micro protocol entities may be composed in sequence, yielding a signal processing pipeline. Also, protocol entities may be composed concurrently, if they do not cooperate directly, or in an interleaving manner by adding appropriate synchronization. To treat composition in a more systematical way, we now introduce a generic micro protocol framework [11, 2].

In a narrower sense, a framework is the skeleton of a system that is common to all systems of a given product family, i.e., a generic system architecture, possibly augmented with the behavior of certain system parts. In the context of communication systems, typical frameworks are defined as layered architectures (e.g., OSI Basic Reference Model, Internet architecture) that are completed by adding specific communication protocols, such as FTP (File Transfer Protocol), TCP (Transmission Control Protocol) and IP (Internet Protocol) in case of the Internet architecture.

This strict view of a framework is extremely useful, but tends to be rather inflexible as soon as different types of composition are to be combined. Therefore, we propose a more general characterization of the notion of framework in the micro protocol context: *a generic micro protocol framework is a set of general principles and rules for the composition of micro protocols*. This means that the system skeleton is not provided in advance, but is derived based on the knowledge of a given set of micro protocols and their intended composition. In other words, a generic micro protocol framework characterizes a *set of micro protocol architectures*, namely those architectures that are conforming to the set of general principles and composition rules. Thus, this notion of framework is compatible with the strict view, where one such architecture is determined.

In our case studies in the area of communication systems, we have identified the following types of composition:

- Generic composition:
  Often, the assembly of components can be reduced to a few basic operators. For micro protocols, e.g., concurrent composition, sequential composition, disruption, pipelining, and hierarchical composition are natural operators, which imply a precisely defined synchronization among components.

- Problem specific composition:
  Generic compositions such as mutual exclusion allow shared state components (e.g., a common signal input queue) to be used, but otherwise assume the functional independence of the composed micro protocols. If as, for instance, in case of composition of tightly coupled protocol phases this assumption is violated, a problem specific composition is required. This composition may build on a generic composition augmented by additional synchronization that refers to internal, problem specific protocol aspects.

2.3   Micro Protocol-Based Development Process

The micro protocol-based development process (see Figure 1) is part of an overall development process, and may be integrated in methodologies such as SOMT [12], SDL+ [10], or TIMe [1]. Starting point for the communication system design activity is a communication requirements specification, resulting from a thorough requirements analysis. These requirements are analyzed to identify the communication functionalities and their dependences, leading to an analysis model. To

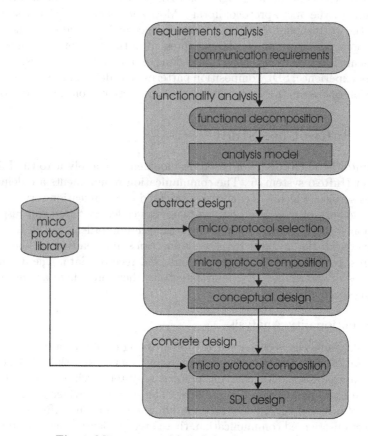

Fig. 1. Micro protocol-based development process

perform this analysis, thorough domain knowledge as well as analytical abilities is required.

For the subsequent design activities, the availability of a micro protocol library is assumed. This library can be understood as a repository of developer know-how, expressed in terms of communication components that can be selected and composed to form a particular communication system. The description of a micro protocol includes the abstract definition of the functionality as well as the concrete behavior, expressed in SDL, where each SDL micro protocol specification should be encapsulated into one SDL package. Furthermore, scenarios illustrate typical micro protocol behavior.

Based on the analysis model, micro protocols are selected from the micro protocol library and composed suitably, yielding a conceptual design. This design is still very abstract, and shows micro protocols as building blocks, and how they are assembled. For the composition, the rules and operators of the generic micro protocol framework are applied. The conceptual design captures all protocol functionalities and their dependences, and thus is a suitable starting point for producing a concrete design in SDL.

Based on the conceptual design, the SDL micro protocol specifications are extracted from the micro protocol library. More specifically, an SDL system that includes the corresponding SDL packages is specified. In addition, the dependences among the micro protocols, as expressed in the conceptual design, are to be represented in SDL. Currently, this is done on a case by case basis. However, with more experience, SDL composition patterns that define, for each conceptual composition operator, the corresponding SDL representation, may be provided.

3   The InRes Case Study

To illustrate the micro protocol-based development, we apply it to the Initiator Responder (InRes) system [6]. The communication requirements are defined by the InRes service, which is a connection-oriented communication service for the reliable exchange of messages between two users called *initiator* and *responder*. In addition to being reliable, it preserves the sending order. The InRes service is asymmetrical: the initiator requests connections and sends data, the responder accepts, refuses, and clears connections, and receives data. The destination of messages is determined by the architecture; therefore, there are no explicit addressing mechanisms.

3.1   Functionality Analysis

Functionality analysis is concerned with identifying communication functionalities that satisfy the set of communication requirements, and their dependences, yielding an analysis model. Starting point is a system architecture that shows the service users and the service provider. The service provider is then refined into a set of protocol entities and an underlying medium. The InRes service calls for connection-oriented communication, therefore, we identify the basic functionalities connection setup, connection release, and data transfer. Since the InRes service is asymmetrical, it suffices to support these functionalities in a unidirectional way. To map service data units to the underlying medium, encoding and decoding is needed. We assume that the underlying medium is order-preserving, connection-less, and may occasionally lose messages. Therefore, we add loss control to the set of communication functionalities. Finally, we decide to provide end-to-end flow control. Apart from identifying these functionalities, the analysis model also contains message scenarios for each functionality and their joint operation [2].

3.2   Micro Protocols

A micro protocol is specified operationally by defining protocol entity types that follow the protocol rules such that one protocol functionality and the required collaboration among protocol entity instances are covered. Methodologically, protocol functionalities and corresponding collaborations are isolated first, and then represented in SDL.

Conceptually, we model protocol entities by asynchronously communicating extended Mealy machines. Obviously, there are several ways to represent them in SDL, for instance, by specifying SDL block types, SDL process types, SDL service types[1], or SDL procedures. Which one to use depends on the composition of micro protocols, which in turn depends on the protocol that is to be configured.

Micro protocol definitions are organized using SDL packages. An SDL package is a collection of type definitions, and is used here to encapsulate SDL types belonging to the same micro protocol. This way, a micro protocol library can be expressed as a set of SDL packages, i.e., ready-to-use components. Also, common parts of a set of micro protocols may be extracted into a package that is imported by each micro protocol definition. Alternatively, several related micro protocols may be grouped into one package

In Figure 2, an excerpt of the SDL package ProtocolPhases containing the definitions of three micro protocols is shown. On the top level, the package ProtocolPhases contains the following type definitions:

- Process type ProtocolPhases:
  In SDL, processes are active objects. Process behavior is specified by an extended Mealy machine, which is either directly defined, or derived from the definition of submachines called SDL services.
- Signal (type) definitions ICONreq, DR, etc.:
  In SDL, active objects interact via signal exchange and shared variables. Signals are associated with gates and channels, and may carry parameters.
- Data type definition ISDUtype:
  Apart from built-in data types, problem specific data types can be defined and used, e.g., to declare context variables or signal parameters.

---

[1] In [5], we have proposed to use SDL composite states to specify micro protocols. However, because there is no tool support for composite states so far, we have decided to go back to SDL services.

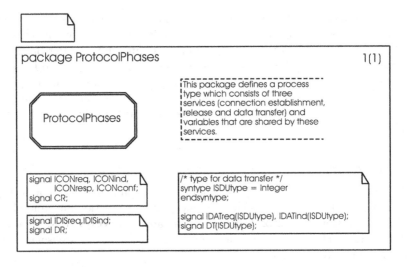

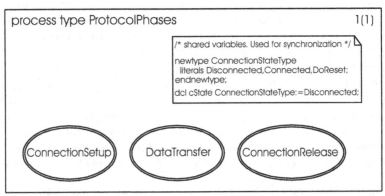

Fig. 2. SDL package ProtocolPhases (excerpt, part 1)

The InRes protocol phases are executed one protocol phase at a time. Therefore, the process type ProtocolPhases is refined into three SDL services, each encapsulating the functionality of a single protocol phase. These service types ConnectionSetup, ConnectionRelease, and DataTransfer are introduced in Figure 2.

Additionally, a shared variable cState, which is used for synchronization, is declared. To configure a protocol, SDL services are instantiated and composed by adding typed channels and connecting them appropriately.

In Figure 3, the complete definition of the micro protocol entity type Data-Transfer is shown, specified as the state diagram of an extended Mealy machine. Being in state idle, the automaton can accept signals IDATreq from the service user and DT from the underlying service, respectively. Depending on the existence of a connection (cState=connected), these signals are either forwarded to the recipient, or discarded. Similarly, micro protocol entity types for the remaining protocol phases are defined. A major difficulty here is to encapsulate protocol

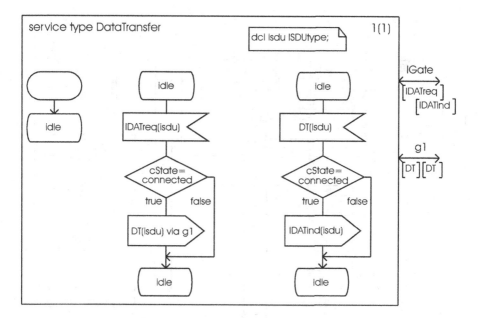

Fig. 3. SDL package ProtocolPhases (excerpt, part 2)

behavior in such a way that it can be composed afterwards, that the result of the composition is free of design errors (e.g., unspecified receptions, deadlocks), and that it provides a specified communication service.

The encapsulation of protocol phases into SDL services is just one way to represent micro protocols in SDL. We have found other solutions to express synchronization among protocol phases based on inheritance or usage of procedures, which will be discussed in Section 3.4.

3.3 Abstract Design

In Section 3.2, we have introduced three protocol functionalities that have been defined as micro protocols, namely connection setup, connection release, and data transfer. Conceptually, the data transfer phase is preceded by a connection setup and terminated by a connection release, which leads back to the connection setup phase. Furthermore, a connection setup may be disrupted by a connection release.

To complete the InRes protocol communication functionalities identified during functionality analysis, we add further micro protocols:

- leakyBucket realizes a specific flow control mechanism
- singleAck realizes a loss control mechanism, based on a timer and message repeats
- coDec realizes encoding and decoding of service data units

The conceptual composition of these micro protocol entities is represented in Figure 4. In the diagram, several generic composition operators are used:

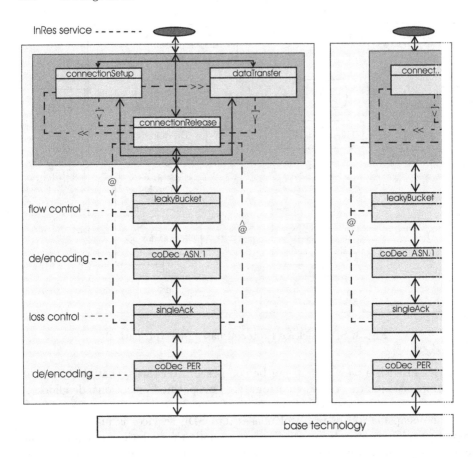

Fig. 4. InRes conceptual composition of micro protocol entities

- PE1 ∥ PE2: protocol entities PE1 and PE2 are executed concurrently, i.e., they both possess a thread of control. Concurrency can be reduced by explicit interaction, e.g., through shared variables or signal exchange. We assume that protocol entities are composed concurrently by default, unless otherwise stated. Therefore, we omit this operator, in order to avoid cluttering.
- PE1 ≫ PE2: PE1 enables PE2, passing the thread of control. Thus, PE1 turns inactive, while PE2 is activated and starts or continues operation. Note that PE1 is not terminated, but may be reactivated at a later point in time. When and how the enabling takes place is an internal decision of PE1.
- PE1 [> PE2: protocol entity PE2 disrupts PE1, taking the thread of control. Different from enabling, PE1 plays a passive role when the thread of control is moved. Again, PE1 is not terminated. When and how the disruption takes place is an internal decision of PE2.
- PE1 @> PE2: PE1 signals PE2, e.g., the occurrence of an event or an exception. Different from enabling, PE1 continues operation. This operator is a likely candidate for problem specific composition, if the type of event has

to be signaled to PE2, which can be expressed by adding parameters to the operator.

- PE1 $\rightarrow$ PE2: there is a data flow from PE1 to PE2, either through signal exchange or through shared variables. In particular, this includes pipelining of PDU data. If data flow is in both directions, we write PE1 $\leftrightarrow$ PE2. Again, operator parameters may be added to make the type of data flow explicit.

As shown in Figure 4, connectionSetup enables dataTransfer (operator $\gg$), which can be disrupted by connectionRelease (operator $[>$). Furthermore, there is bidirectional data flow between these micro protocol entities and the InRes service user. If message loss exceeds a given threshold, this is detected by singleAck and signaled to connectionRelease (operator @$>$). ConnectionRelease in turn cancels the established connection and signals to singleAck and leakyBucket (operator @$>$), thus triggering a reset.

3.4   SDL Design

Based on the conceptual design in Figure 4, a self-contained SDL design specification is to be derived. This concrete design specification is obtained by importing the corresponding micro protocols and by adding SDL representations of the composition operators (also called "glue code") such that the required synchronization is achieved. SDL offers several mechanisms that can be used to compose micro protocols. For instance, interleaving can be expressed by aggregation of SDL services (or composite states [5][8]), i.e., submachines of an automaton representing micro protocol entities. Pipelining is achieved by instantiating SDL processes and connecting them in sequence through SDL channels.

To express the conceptual composition of the InRes protocol phases in SDL, we have devised five different solutions:

- SDL services with shared context variables:
  In SDL, the behavior of a process can be decomposed into submachines (called SDL services) that may share one or more context variables, which are used to synchronize protocol phases (see Section 3.2).
- SDL services with distributed signal exchange:
  SDL services may interact via asynchronous signal exchange. In conjunction with priority signals, this gives rise to alternative solutions based on submachines. Synchronization functionality is integrated into each micro protocol, reducing the required glue. In this solution, each micro protocol is defined in one package.
- SDL services with central signal exchange:
  We have devised a solution that encapsulates all glue into one single managing SDL service realizing the synchronization. This solution is more generic in the sense that micro protocol specifications are less context-dependent.
- SDL process inheritance with shared states:
  In SDL, single inheritance among (block, process, service) types is provided, which is used here to establish a tight synchronization among protocol phases.

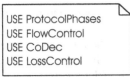

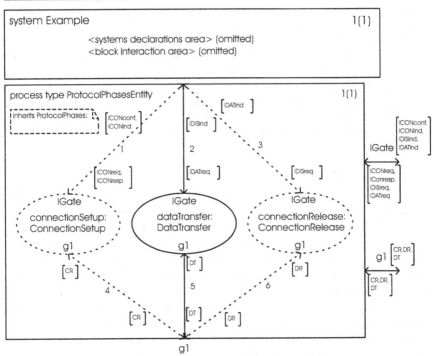

Fig. 5. InRes composition of micro protocols in SDL

- SDL procedures:
  SDL procedures are submachines of an SDL process that are executed under mutual exclusion. Synchronization is achieved by suitable sequencing.

In each of these solutions, a specific syntactical SDL specification of each micro protocol is required. For instance, if inheritance with shared major states is applied, each micro protocol is defined as an SDL process that inherits transitions from further micro protocols[2]. In general, micro protocols may be encapsulated into SDL block types, SDL process types, SDL procedures, or SDL service types. Which one to use depends on the composition of micro protocols, which in turn depends on the protocol to be configured. This drawback is remedied in SDL-2000 [8]. Here, micro protocols can be defined as composite state types,

---

[2] Please note that SDL does not support multiple inheritance, which would simplify this composition style.

which are then instantiated in SDL block types, process types, procedures and state aggregations as needed. In Figure 5, an excerpt of the solution that uses SDL services with shared context variables is shown. In this solution, the micro protocols are composed to yield the protocol entities of a system called Example in two steps. First, the protocol phases are composed into an SDL process type, resulting in macro protocol entity. Next, these phases are composed with flow control, coding, and loss control (not shown). All micro protocols are imported from the micro protocol library (USE clauses).

In Figure 5, the service types defined in ProtocolPhases are instantiated and composed, adding signal routes[3]. Please note that the process type ProtocolPhases including the shared context variable is inherited, supporting the required synchronization. In fact, Figure 5 represents two different macro protocols, namely a connection oriented solution (as shown), and a connectionless protocol that is obtained by removing all dotted symbols. This underlines the flexibility of the micro protocols defined in ProtocolPhases.

4   Conclusions

In this paper, we have defined a generic micro protocol framework, consisting of a set of general principles and rules for the composition of micro protocols. By instantiating this framework, a specific micro protocol architecture is obtained. Furthermore, we have introduced a micro protocol-based development process, which starts with a functionality analysis, followed by an abstract design, and completed by a concrete SDL design. The design activities are supported by a micro protocol library, from which micro protocols are selected and composed. All steps have been illustrated by the micro protocol-based development of the InRes protocol.

For the specification of the concrete design, SDL has been chosen, due to its suitability for communication systems, its broad dissemination, and the availability of tool support. Experience so far shows that SDL is sufficiently expressive to represent the composition operators used in the abstract design. There even exist several choices of how to represent a given operator, which adds some flexibility concerning composition styles, but also requires different representations of the same micro protocol. We expect that the latter disadvantage can be remedied with SDL-2000 and the use of composite state types, however, we did not exploit this option due to the lack of tool support. Currently, the dependences among

---

[3] A complication arises from the asynchronous nature of the signal exchange when protocol phases are composed. For instance, when a protocol entity releases a connection, the peer entity may still send data until realizing the release. This means that the entity initiating the connection release must be prepared to discard all incoming data indications, while being in the connection release phase or the subsequent connection setup phase. The solution adopted in Figure 4 is to keep all protocol phases activated, but to define a behavior that depends on the current phase (see Figure 3, decision cState=connected).

micro protocols, as expressed in the conceptual design, are represented in SDL on a case by case basis. With more experience, we plan to define, for each generic composition operator, an SDL design pattern that captures the corresponding SDL representation in a generic way.

In the InRes case study, we had to develop micro protocols from scratch. In the long run, a micro protocol library that contains a set of predefined, reusable micro protocols is to be built up. During communication system development, the protocol engineer can select micro protocols from this library, and compose them according to the micro protocol framework. Current work is directed towards building a library of routing and quality of service micro protocols.

Finally, it should be pointed out that micro protocols may pave the way to compositional testing. Here, communication systems are perceived as being built from components. Each of these components can be tested using well-proven techniques. However, when these components are put together, the resulting system is only tested for composition faults.

References

1. Bræk, R., Haugen, Ø.: Engineering Real Time Systems. Prentice Hall, 1993.
2. Fliege, I.: Definition and Application of an SDL Micro Protocol Library and a Micro Protocol Framework Exemplified by the InRes System. Diploma Thesis, Technical University of Kaiserslautern, Germany, 2003 (in German).
3. Fliege, I., Geraldy, A., Gotzhein, R., Schaible, P.: Design Reuse in Protocol Engineering – Components, Patterns, and Frameworks. SFB 501 Report Nr. 14/03, Technical University of Kaiserslautern, Germany, 2003.
4. Gotzhein, R., Khendek, F.: Conception avec Micro-Protocoles. Colloque Francophone sur l'Ingénierie des Protocoles, Montréal, Canada. Hermes Science, 2002.
5. Gotzhein, R., Khendek, F., Schaible, P.: Micro Protocol Design: The SNMP Case Study. E. Sherratt (Ed.) Telecommunications and beyond: The Broader Applicability of SDL and MSC. Volume 2599 of Lecture Notes in Computer Science, Springer, 2003, 61–73.
6. Hogrefe, D.: OSI Formal Specification Case Study: The InRes Protocol and Service, revised. Report No. IAM-91-012, University of Berne, May 1992.
7. ITU-T: Recommendation Z.100 (03/93, 10/96 addendum) Specification and Description Language (SDL). International Telecommunication Union, Geneva (1996).
8. ITU-T: Recommendation Z.100 (11/99) Specification and Description Language (SDL). International Telecommunication Union, Geneva (1999).
9. ITU-T: Recommendation Z.120 (11/99) Message Sequence Chart (MSC). International Telecommunication Union, Geneva (1999).
10. Reed, R.: Methodology for Real Time Systems. Computer Networks and ISDN Systems, Special Issue on SDL and MSC, 28 (1996), 1685–1701.
11. Schaible, P.: Reuse-based Development of Communication Systems. Ph.D. Thesis, Technical University of Kaiserslautern, Germany, 2004 (in German).
12. Telelogic AB: Tau 3.4 SDT Methodology Guidelines - Part 1: The SOMT Method, 1998.

ICT Convergence: Modeling Issues*

Rolv Bræk[1] and Jacqueline Floch[2]

[1] Department of Telematics,
Norwegian University of Science and Technology,
NO-7491 Trondheim, Norway
rolv.braek@item.ntnu.no
[2] SINTEF ICT, NO-7465 Trondheim, Norway
jacqueline.floch@sintef.no

Abstract. Even though ICT convergence is a well-established and a-dopted concept, there is no consensus about the underlying software engineering approach to convergent ICT systems. Telecom engineers and software engineers traditionally use different approaches when developing services and applications. A main question is whether or not the differences are justified and should be maintained in the context of convergence? In this paper, we seek to answer this question by analyzing the different nature of the telecom domain and the computing domain. We identify a few fundamental differences that must be bridged when making convergent systems and we investigate how UML can be used as an enabler to build such bridges.

1 Introduction

Since the introduction of software for the control of switching systems in the 1960s, telecommunication systems have increasingly depended on software. The separation between networks and services initiated by IN [12, 13] and continued with Parlay/OSA is a significant development in the telecommunication history. This separation, combined with general Internet access, has enabled services that integrate and combine traditional communication services with information services in innovative ways. It has also opened the network for third-party service providers (at least in principle). Such novel services encompass much more than connectivity. Users being exposed to computers and Internet have increasingly grown to expect more. As a result, service engineering is no longer limited to connectivity services, but will have to deal with a rich range of advanced application oriented services.

Beyond access to network resources through Parlay/OSA interfaces, there is no consensus in the telecommunication industry on what future service architectures will look like and which principles they should build upon. TINA [11]

---

* Both authors have contributed equally to this paper. Author names are listed in alphabetic order.

D. Amyot and A.W. Williams (Eds.): SAM 2004, LNCS 3319, pp. 237–256, 2005.

is a unique common trial to that end. Although TINA has not reached industrial strength, it provides concepts that will probably inspire the architects of the future services. A basic assumption behind TINA is that *no solutions to the challenge posed by the emergence of new information society will be found without putting together the best of telecommunications and information technologies.* Accordingly, TINA proposes software structuring principles using object-orientation and distributed computing techniques based on the OMG's object model [18] and CORBA [19]. Surprisingly, TINA neither discusses the ways concurrency is handled by objects, nor the nature of object behavior and interactions between objects. In these areas telecom and general software engineers use fundamentally different approaches for the development of services and applications. Both approaches have strengths and weaknesses and now that services are converging it is timely to ask which approach is best suited for the different classes of problems at hand? Is it possible to identify fundamental properties of services we may use to determine the right/best service architectures, delivery platforms and service engineering methods?

In the following we analyze the different nature of the problems solved by telecom and software engineers, and the differences between the development approaches and platforms they apply. We discuss bridges between the approaches and investigate how UML can be used as an enabler to build bridges. We will use the term "telecom domain" as a general term to designate the problems and technical solutions the engineers of telecom services typically deal with. We will focus on service issues and not address network or transport issues here. Using TINA parlance, we may say that we focus on the service architecture. We will use the term "computing domain" to designate the problems and technical solutions IT engineers typically deal with outside the traditional telecom domain. Note that our aim is to understand important differences in order to find ways of integrating convergent services. It is not our aim to provide an exact classification of systems.

2   The Shaping Forces

2.1   Different Domain Characteristics

If we step back and consider the origins of the telecom domain and the computing domain, the reasons why different approaches and traditions have developed in the two domains emerge. The original domains may be characterized as follows:

The Computing Domain:

- *Information processing by means of data and algorithms (or objects and methods).* Computing originally was, and still is, basically dealing with data structures and action sequences (algorithms). Encapsulating data in objects and introducing classes with inheritance does not fundamentally change this.
- *Communication by invocation.* The basic communication mechanism, apart from data sharing, is the procedure call or method call, which is tied to a

transfer of control from the calling entity to the called entity. The calling entity is blocked until control is returned from the called entity. This is sometimes referred to as synchronous communication[1]. This means that the actions of the caller and the called are performed as one thread of actions, and not as two separate behaviors.

- *Asymmetrical or client-server interactions.* Request-response types of communication dominate. This is an asymmetrical kind of communication in the sense that it imposes asymmetric roles on interacting objects; there is one initiating role and one responding role (or a client and a server).

- *Concurrency as add-on.* Although concurrency is essential to many application domains, it is often suppressed in the computing domain. Few programming languages support it directly [2], and there is a tendency to consider concurrency as a problem that should be hidden from application developers. Concurrency in the computing domain has been considered mainly as a mechanism to achieve performance and to support distribution (a necessary evil). Operating systems support the sharing of computing resources between applications, but few applications exhibit internal concurrency. The concept of multithreading (i.e., concurrent threads of control) is supported in a few programming languages (e.g., Java), but the concept is not well-understood by application programmers and often a source of error ("Thread programming can be tricky" [23]).

The Telecommunication Domain:

- *Active objects with concurrent behavior.* The domain is characterized by real objects, like users, that behave concurrently and need to interact and to be served concurrently. These are active objects executing their own behaviors and possibly taking initiatives independently of each other (without requiring invocation). Concurrency and communication among concurrent objects is at the heart of these applications.

- *Communication by signaling.* It follows from the nature of active objects with concurrent behavior that they cannot well communicate by control transfer (invocation). They need explicit communication mechanisms such as signal sending or messaging to interact. Active objects in the telecom domain are in general, loosely coupled and autonomous.

- *Symmetrical or peer-to-peer interactions.* Communication between two active objects may generally flow in both directions and concurrently. Initiatives may be taken independently and simultaneously and lead to conflicts that must be resolved. One cannot in general, assume that the objects take on asymmetrical roles, but must allow objects to communicate on an equal basis, with few restrictions. This can be achieved by asynchronous message

---

[1] Note that this is different from the notion of synchronous communication used in process algebras like LOTOS and CCS.

[2] CHILL and ADA are notable exceptions.

passing over a network (or other medium) connecting the objects. Asynchronous message passing may be used to implement any meaningful communication pattern, and is therefore the preferred approach in the telecom (and real-time) domain.

Note that the participants of a telecommunication service normally are distributed. Therefore, distribution, concurrency and peer-to-peer communication among users are inherent application domain properties, and not just implementation issues. Computing applications have, until recently, been primarily designed to deal with a single user. The main inter-user coordination is to ensure mutual exclusion so that only one user at the time may access the same data. Distribution and concurrency is introduced in order to support many users (multitasking), achieve better performance and to support physical distribution of resources.

The different nature of the domains described above, have resulted in different cultures and approaches to software system development. From time to time, this appears as a battle between cultures. The interesting question is whether this is just a matter of opinions and cultures or there are more objective and fundamental issues behind? *We contend that the need to support symmetrical and concurrent interactions among peers is a fundamental issue!* Synchronous communication by invocation is limited to client-server structures. Asynchronous communication by messaging may be used for both client-server and peer-to-peer structures and is necessary to support general peer-to-peer structures.

2.2   Different Modeling Approaches

Systems and service engineering is strongly biased by the concepts we use to model, understand, communicate and to reason about a problem domain and its design solutions. Therefore modeling concepts must be carefully chosen to reflect the domain they are intended for. Since the perspective and the concepts used in the models strongly influence the way we understand and deal with the topic domain, unsuitable modeling concepts may well lead to unsuitable system solutions.

Not surprisingly, the modeling concepts used in the computing and telecom domains differ both in formality and content (the kind of properties being modeled).

The Main Modeling Concepts in the Computing Domain Are:

- *Passive objects.* Passive objects represent information entities and their properties. The target objects being represented may, or may not, have real behavior, but this behavior is normally not reflected in the system. It is the information aspect that is represented.
- *Associations.* Associations play an important role because the relationships between objects are central in information models.
- *One-way interfaces and operations.* The description of object interfaces is limited to a static declaration of the operations provided over the interface

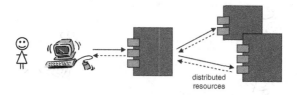

Fig. 1. Typical client-server structure

(operation signatures). Such interface descriptions may facilitate the construction of a system by providing a means for retrieving objects that may potentially offer a function or feature. They do not describe the interaction semantics, however, and therefore do not provide sufficient support for building a system that behaves correctly.

- *Client-server or asymmetrical interactions with one-way initiatives*. Relative to an interface, there is one active side taking all initiatives and one passive side that reacts and give responses.
- *Communication by invocation* is often assumed, but asynchronous communication by message passing may also be used.
- *Tree-like structure*. The overall structure of one service session is restricted by the nature of client-server interactions and synchronous communication to be tree-like, as illustrated in Figure1.

The Main Modeling Concepts in the Telecom Domain Are:

- *Active objects*. Active objects are usually modeled as autonomous entities that may execute their own behaviors without requiring method invocation. A common conceptual abstraction is communicating extended finite state machines, as found in SDL and UML.
- *Peer-to-peer or symmetrical interactions with multi-way initiatives*. Relative to a link between objects, both sides are active and may take initiatives independently. Hence it is possible that initiatives may be taken by both ends simultaneously and collide.
- *Two-way interfaces and protocols*. Normally signals/messages may flow both ways across an interface, and the ordering may be defined by a protocol. This means that interface definitions normally list the signals/messages going both ways and possibly also specify the protocol.
- *Asynchronous communication by message passing*. Communication is based on buffered signal/message passing which means that a sender is not blocked but may continue working (e.g., reply to some request) as soon as a message is sent. The degree of asynchrony may be determined by the size of intermediate queues.
- *Explicit states*. Interactions between objects may be complex and is often stateful. Therefore some form of state machine is useful to represent the object behaviors. Objects may be involved in several interactions (i.e., interact with multiple objects), possibly in a concurrent manner.

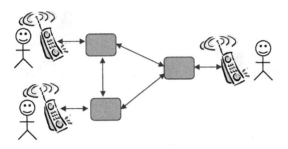

Fig. 2. Typical peer-to-peer structure

- *General network structure.* The overall system structure may form a network without structural limitations, as illustrated in Figure 2.

   Traditionally, the computing domain has favored informal/illustrative functionality models that are gradually elaborated and manually transformed into software realizations. In contrast, abstract and formal modeling has gained a stronger position in the telecom domain. Here formal models of application functionality that can be understood and analyzed independently from implementations and then automatically translated into efficient implementations have been developed. The two approaches have been termed the *elaboration approach* and the *translation approach* respectively in [2]. Many information processing applications may be modeled and understood quite well in terms closely related to the computing domain. Therefore, it has not been so necessary, or worth while, to develop conceptual abstractions that hide their computational nature. Information models are an exception, not surprisingly since their purpose is to focus on what information represents rather than how it is represented in the computing world. In the telecom domain, more has been to gain by developing conceptual abstractions that are closer to the nature of the domain. A conceptual abstraction that promotes human understanding and enables formal analysis of the correctness of complex behaviors has helped considerably to reduce the number of errors and hence, increase the quality of systems. The Model Driven Architecture, MDA [20], of OMG follows the elaboration approach and bears some promise that the two cultures may meet each other. But it will be extremely important that the fundamental nature of active entities and peer-to-peer communication is considered and properly supported if MDA is to succeed for convergent applications and services.

2.3   Two Notions of Services

In both the computing domain and telecom domain, a service is considered a partial functionality, but beyond that, there are important and fundamental differences. In the computing domain, it is common to consider a service as a computation or information processing operation (or set of operations) that is accessed through an interface using asymmetrical interactions. A service is provided by an object or a component. There may be many users accessing the service, more or less simultaneously, but initiatives come from one side only (normally from the users) and will not cross each other. Again we find asymmetry in the computer domain, and will use the term *client-server service* for this kind of service. In the telecom domain, services (or telecom services) result from collaboration between several active objects. Even though each service user may access the service through one interface, there may be several users and interfaces involved in a service, and several services may be accessed through the same interface. A telecommunication conference service is a typical case in point. It entails collaboration between the parties taking part in the conference, and cannot be understood simply as an interface. There is typically an n:m relationship between services and objects providing the services. We will use the term *peer-to-peer service* for this kind.

2.4   Two Application Architectures

There seem to be two main approaches to application system design. We will call them the *server oriented* and the *agent oriented*[3] architecture in the following. In the first approach, the system is decomposed according to the type of functionality it shall provide. This follows the tradition of functional decomposition often favored by computing professionals. The result is a set of singleton server classes with internal objects representing users and sessions. In the second approach, the system is decomposed according to the active environment it shall serve. This follows the tradition of environment modeling (mirroring) which is more common in the telecom domain.

The Server Oriented Architecture is Characterized by:

- Computation focus; servers and interfaces are addressed first and then users and other entities being served. Components are chosen to reflect the services to be provided.
- The responsibility of a component is to provide one or more services to many users.
- Users and sessions are represented by data inside a service providing component.
- Users may need to access different components to use different services.
- User data and profiles may be spread over different service providing components.

The Agent Oriented Architecture is Characterized by:

- Active-world focus, users and other entities being served are addressed first, and then services. Components (agents) are chosen to reflect the individuals

---

[3] Note that we use the term agent in a general sense here to mean an entity representing and acting on behalf of other entities, not as a particular construction such as an intelligent or mobile agent.

server oriented architecture   agent oriented architecture

Fig. 3. Two application architectures

(users and other entities) in the environment needing to be represented and
served.
- The responsibility of an agent is to represent a (single) user or other entity
  and perform services on its behalf. Agents may be used to represent virtual
  entities such as virtual classrooms, hospital rooms, or meeting places as well
  as physical entities like users and terminals.
- Services are performed by parts inside, or closely associated with an agent.
- Users may access all services in a service provider domain through one agent.
- User data may be integrated in one user agent.

Note that the server oriented architecture fits well with client-server-services,
while the agent oriented is best fit for peer-to-peer services. Agent oriented architectures will normally be based on asynchronous communication and therefore
be suitable for general peer-to-peer services as well as client-server services.

It should be noted here that it is possible to implement peer-to-peer services
in a server oriented architecture, if it is supported by asynchronous communication.

2.5   Computing Platforms

Following from the differences outlined above, the computing platforms developed for the computing domain have predominantly been client-server oriented
and based on communication by invocation, remote procedure calls (RPC).
CORBA, DCOM and Java-RMI are prominent examples of this. The distribution transparency they provide works fine as long as no errors or delays occur.
Concurrency is not an issue and is usually neither described at the application
level nor well-understood by programmers. The fact that problems invariably
pop up whenever one tries to shoehorn an application into a computing system
that does not fit, or even worse, if one tries to reshape the application problem
to fit the computing platform indicates that there are some fundamental problems. Computing platforms for the telecom domain (and in fact, most embedded
systems) have been peer-to-peer oriented and based on asynchronous communication by messaging. Note that asynchronous communication is always required

at the lower level of a distributed system. Communication by invocation in a distributed system needs to be layered on top of asynchronous communication by messaging. From a performance point of view, asynchronous communication by messaging will be the most efficient when it comes to networking. Asynchronous communication also provides better control for the developer when objects are distributed or when systems need to be reconfigured dynamically.

3   Foundations for Convergence

We see two important trends in convergence: telecommunication services being increasingly enhanced by possibilities coming from the computing domain, and computing applications becoming increasingly networked and distributed. Both trends have been clear for a long time, but a common understanding of what it takes in terms of modeling approaches and computing platforms remains to be developed. The telecom domain traditionally provides good tools for dealing with distribution and concurrency, but not for information modeling. Conversely the computing domain is pre-eminent when dealing with sequential programming and information processing, but less adequate when distribution and concurrency are concerned. A common foundation, therefore, should seek to combine the best from the two domains. The first question then is what should be the common core? The second is how to combine the best of both and provide interoperability? Given the considerations presented in the previous section, it is clear that the most general approach must be based on asynchronous communication by messaging in order to enable general peer-to-peer structures with active objects and agent oriented architectures. This is essentially the telecom approach, but it needs to be combined with and interoperate with solutions from the computing domain both to fit the widest possible range of applications and to bridge the cultures. A recent trend may prove important here: business applications are becoming more collaborative and communication oriented. In order to support this they need to shift from client-server towards peer-to-peer structures. Consequently, asynchronous communication by messaging is gradually being introduced into such applications as well.

3.1   Modeling Focus

We argue that modeling - not the computing platforms should be the preferred starting point when designing solutions to convergence. The concepts used in the models strongly influence the way we understand and deal with the topic domain. Therefore modeling tools are proposed as a means to solve convergence problems.

SDL [14] is widely used in the telecom industry and a number of successful experiences have been reported [4, 6, 7, 8, 9, 22]. However, SDL versions up to 1996 provide inadequate support for information modeling. In SDL-2000 there are better means provided by the new data formalism and the possibility to model data using UML class diagrams. Complex data types may be defined, but data are always encapsulated within active objects (SDL agents). By way of contrast UML [21] was initially developed for information modeling and general software engineering. It was recently extended with SDL-like concepts for active objects and part structures. Although the semantics of SDL is more completely and formally defined we assume here that UML is sufficiently well defined for our purposes. Earlier efforts related to the formalization of the language [5, 10] may contribute to the process of further formalizing UML (or parts of UML). It is therefore interesting to assess how the UML language may be used as an enabler for convergence. In addition to UML, MDA [20] may also help to build bridges towards convergence. MDA is proposed by the OMG as a means to solve integration problems. MDA encourages intensive use of modeling (with UML as the first language pillar) and the separation of application logic from implementations. It also envisions the automatic transformation of models at different abstraction levels. Such transformations may be exploited in order to generate glue between two worlds when needed. To our knowledge there is no tool among the numerous MDA CASE tools [10] that supports a mixed engineering approach and the modeling of both information processing and behavior providing services. Tools either focus on the computing domain (e.g., Objecteering [17] or the telecom domain (e.g., TAU Generation 2 [24]) depending of the domain where the tools were initially applied.

Further in subsequent sections, we discuss how the main divergences between the telecom domain and computing domain may be accommodated. We focus on modeling and also consider some realization issues.

3.2   Asynchronous Communication by Messaging

We contend that asynchronous communication by messaging should be supported at the core of a mixed engineering approach for three main reasons:

- It is the most general mechanism as it can support both peer-to-peer and client-server structures without restrictions.
- It is the basic mechanism for information transfer over networks.
- It supports distribution transparency in a natural way.

Synchronous communication by invocation cannot be discarded, though. It is a necessary programming level mechanism, and is extremely effective given a single address space and thread of computing. It is also very convenient seen from an application programmers point of view, and is supported by many mainstream middleware and distributed computing platforms. Many client-server applications and APIs are based on it. Consequently, a platform for convergent services will need to support both asynchronous communication and synchronous communication by invocation. A natural boundary goes between active objects and passive objects. Active objects have their own threads of behaviors and operate concurrently with each other, while passive objects are invoked by external threads of behavior. Active objects may well contain inner structures of passive objects being invoked. Structures of passive objects contained within active objects is therefore a solution which is supported directly by UML and SDL. This is not always enough, however. It may be necessary to support external invocation interfaces, typically:

- To interface with legacy systems and APIs.
- For convenience of application programming. Communication by procedure or method calls is especially convenient for value returning functions.
- When speed is critical. Local interactions within one address space may sometimes be faster than message passing, but remote interactions are bound to be slower.

The implication for the computing platform is that asynchronous message passing should be directly available to applications. Remote invocations should be available when needed. The implication for modeling is that asynchronous communication among active objects must be supported, which is the case for both SDL and UML. This will require that application developers learn to master asynchronous communication. Programmers in the computing domain are usually not familiar with this form of communication, so this will require some education. From our experience with students, we claim that the concepts of asynchronous communication are not difficult to master if properly supported in models and implementations.

3.3   Peer-to-Peer Structures Combined with Client-Server Structures

Peer-to-peer structures of active objects must be supported in a convergent engineering approach. The main reason being again, that this is the more general structure. A client-server structure can be realized as a special peer-to-peer structure, but the opposite is not the case. Client-server structures impose asymmetric roles on interacting objects, and fail to properly support symmetrical services (i.e., services resulting from collaborations between agents). It is quite common to find client-server sub-structures within peer-to-peer structures, however. Such sub-structures may well be modeled and realized using communication by invocation, given that certain restrictions are satisfied. Since the behavior of such sub-structures will be threaded into the behavior of the invoking active object, care must be taken to ensure that timing conditions are satisfied and undesirable interference with other active objects is avoided. Under what conditions asynchronous messaging at the modeling level (SDL) can be mapped to invocations at the realization level is explained in [3]. In SDL it is not possible to have passive objects outside active objects, and so there is no support for invocation of such objects outside active objects (i.e., Agents in SDL-2000), but the remote procedure call provides an invocation-like mechanism to use in application models. This is mapped to a protocol of implicit asynchronous messages in the semantics of SDL. UML is less restrictive by allowing passive objects to exist outside active objects and allowing invocation between objects in general. This gives freedom to mix communication forms as one sees fit, but also to introduce many of the classical errors associated with concurrency. It is therefore extremely important that the designer is aware of the concurrency and timing related problems and what conditions that must be satisfied when directly mixing communication forms. These issues are further discussed in Section 3.5.

3.4   Agent Oriented Architectures

We argue that agent oriented architectures should be possible in a convergent engineering approach. Agent oriented architectures enable better service integration; several services may be accessed through one agent. The agent oriented architecture also better supports personalization as agents are used to represent real world entities, for example users. Agent orientation contributes to the clarity of modeling stateful behaviors. (For truly stateless behavior server oriented architecture works just as well.) Server oriented architectures may be combined with agent oriented architectures when necessary, for example in the integration of web-server front-ends with database back-ends. UML has adopted the ideas introduced by architecture definition languages such as Darwin [16] and Koala [25] and provides means to describe component based architectures, among them agent oriented architectures. Agent structures can be described in terms of hierarchical component structures (components with inner parts), ports and connectors (communication channels) in a similar way as supported by SDL-2000 agents, gates and channels. Ports may have associated behavior, i.e., protocol roles. Finally UML also defines concepts for modeling agent collaborations.

3.5   Mixing the Communication Forms

As active and passive objects assume different communication forms, communication between active and passive objects require special attention. Asynchronous communication simplifies the modeling of concurrent behaviors, while synchronous invocation simplifies the modeling of simple data operations. Therefore we propose a transformation based approach where both communication forms can be combined.

The SDL Solution: Let us initially consider the SDL solution where active objects may communicate through remote procedure calls. Remote procedure calls are in SDL mapped to an exchange of implicitly defined signals. This means that invocation takes place between active objects by means of signal exchange. Figure 4 illustrates the transformation from remote procedure call to messages which is built into the language. Note that the transformation applies to models.

The big advantage of this approach is that invocation and messaging may be combined freely, and that invocation is no longer restricted to client-server structures. It illustrates well the advantage of having messaging as foundation, but falls short of providing the convenience of real invocation on passive objects. A main drawback of using remote procedure calls in this way is that a remote call needs to be handled in every state, and thus the benefit gained by using stateful behavior may be lost. It is therefore best suited for stateless, or rather single state, behaviors.

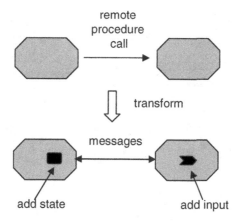

Fig. 4. Remote procedure calls in SDL

Invoking Passive Objects from Active Objects in UML: UML does not define any concept similar to the SDL remote procedure call, but active objects may provide both operation and message interfaces and it is possible to mix active and passive objects in the same diagrams. Let us first consider invocation of passive objects from active objects. Invoking a passive object from an active object is straightforward in UML using the synchronous call action, as illustrated in Figure 5a. The realization is also straightforward at the programming level since invocation of passive objects is directly supported by programming languages.

However the simplicity of modeling in UML and programming is misleading. The designer should be well aware of possible dangers when using direct invocations. In particular it is necessary to ensure mutual exclusion if several active objects may perform simultaneous invocations. It is possible to indicate in UML how this is to be achieved by specifying a CallConcurrencyKind {sequential, guarded, concurrent}. It is also necessary to ensure that the calling object never blocks too long while waiting for control to be returned. This blocking delay is increased when calls are guarded or objects are distributed. When several active objects are implemented in an alternating (run to completion) way, blocking the caller object will also block other objects. In order to avoid blocking of active objects, synchronous invocation may be transformed to asynchronous messaging as illustrated in Figure 5b. Edge objects (also called proxies) are then inserted that convert between messaging and invocation and the behavior of the active caller object is modified in a similar way as for remote procedure calls in SDL. Note that, in order to avoid blocking, the edge object should not run in the same thread of control as the modified active caller object. It is debatable whether or not such transformation of UML models should be hidden from the developer. But in order to decide on the best approach in each case, it is necessary to take concurrency and timing constraints into account as explained above. For this to be done automatically it is necessary to add information either to the original UML model, to a platform dependent model or to a deployment model.

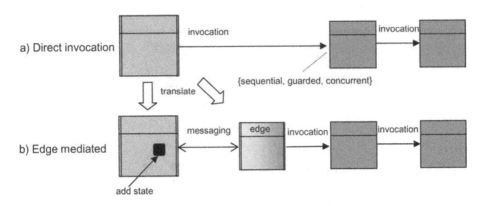

a) Direct invocation

b) Edge mediated

Fig. 5. Invoking passive from active objects

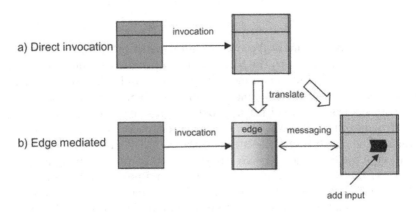

a) Direct invocation

b) Edge mediated

Fig. 6. Invoking active from passive objects

Invoking Active Objects from Passive in UML: Let us now consider communication from passive objects to active objects. Again there are two possibilities: direct invocation and edge mediated invocation as illustrated in Figure 6a and 6b.

If the passive and active objects run alternating in the same thread of behavior, there are few if any problems with direct invocation. In general we cannot assume they do, and therefore need to consider the well-known problems of mutual exclusion and blocking. Mutual exclusion may be ensured at the implementation level by careful scheduling or by using synchronized method calls. The latter may well increase the blocking delays, however. In order to avoid blocking and synchronization delays we may introduce edge objects that transform invocation to messaging, as illustrated in Figure 6b.

Note that the two cases illustrated in Figure 5 and 6 may well be combined to allow for interactions both ways between (sub-) systems using different communication forms, typically between peer-to-peer and client-server (sub-) systems.

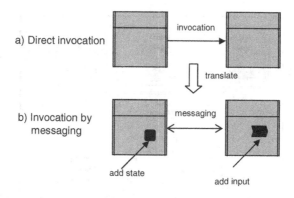

a) Direct invocation

invocation

translate

b) Invocation by
messaging

messaging

add state

add input

Fig. 7. Invocation by messaging in UML

Invocation Between Active Objects in UML: Invocation between active objects is the last case we need to consider. Since active objects may run concurrently, the mutual exclusion and blocking delay problems discussed above must be considered here as well. In special cases where scheduling and timing permits, direct invocation may be possible. A slightly more general solution is to ensure mutual exclusion by using synchronized method calls at the implementation level. One must then carefully consider the blocking delays this introduces and the deadlock possibilities that may be introduced by two active objects blocking to wait for each other. A more general option is to use an SDL like transformation approach whereby direct invocation in high level models is translated into messaging in more detailed models. This would provide the convenience of invocation in application models without sacrificing the generality and safeness of asynchronous messaging in the running system, see Figure 7.

Summary. The main issues determining which solution to use when mixing the communication forms are:

- Concurrency: are the parties concurrent or not?
- Initiative patterns: one-way or two-way?
- Communication structure: three-like or networked?
- Blocking delays: are they acceptable?
- Synchronization delays: are they acceptable?

4   A Convergent Service Example

In order to experiment with the proposed engineering approach we are developing a pilot application called AMIGOS [1]. Master students at NTNU have contributed to the development of AMIGOS and to the assessment of the platform technologies.

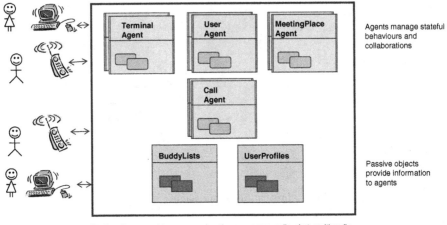

Meeting places provide presence, location awareness, calls, chat, multimedia
conferences, object sharing, ... for user groups like work-teams, classrooms, friends

Fig. 8. AMIGOS: a convergent teleservice using a mixed approach

AMIGOS is a meeting place service where different features can be plugged in dynamically, such as positioning and map information, buddy list support, presence, etc. The users may establish new meeting places and select the functionalities available in the meeting places. The service may be accessed from smart phones (e.g., Sony-Ericsson P-800), PDAs and PCs.

AMIGOS requires the capabilities of telecommunication services such as user co-ordination and call-control as well as the capabilities of information services such as user profile management, buddy list management, meeting place configurations. Profile and buddy list management involve setting of attribute preferences and are not necessarily time critical. As shown in Figure 8, some elements of the services may be modeled and realized as active objects, some as passive objects.

The following aspects have been modeled using UML:

- Collaboration structure, i.e., the agent roles involved in collaboration and the associations between roles.
- Collaboration sequences, i.e., the interactions between agent roles.
- Role state machine, i.e., the detailed Agent and Role behavior.
- The context and content constraints of Agent and Role types.
- Profiles and other passive objects.

A difficulty encountered during the development of AMIGOS is the lack of mature UML modeling tools. The lack of transformation tools is also a barrier. A flexible UML code generator has been developed at NTNU [15] and is currently being integrated with other tools to help support the student projects. Over and above tool support, good methodology support also needs to be developed.

The service core is implemented on EJBActorFrame, a service execution framework developed in the Avantel project [1] by Ericsson in Norway. EJBAc-

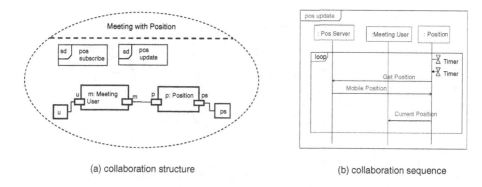

(a) collaboration structure   (b) collaboration sequence

Fig. 9. AMIGOS: modeling collaborations

torFrame combines the capabilities of a generic agent-oriented framework and those of an application server. EJBActorFrame is implemented on the JBOSS middleware that supports J2EE technologies. J2EE facilitates the integration of the service core with client applications through JMS, WAP, and Web services and with other application servers through interfaces such as Web Services and JMS. In addition there is an ActorFrame version that is not dependent on J2EE. It can run on terminals and small devices. This enables a homogeneous application environment all the way from terminals to application servers. Within the Avantel project, Telenor has provided a lab environment with access to live network resources over Parlay, Parlay-x and other interfaces. This means that the application framework (ActorFrame) need to interoperate both with messaging and invocation based interfaces. The principles outlined in the previous section are used to provide edge mediated adaptation (Figures 5b and 6b). The core concept of ActorFrame is the Actor, which is basically an active object according to UML2.0 with behavior defined by a state machine and with inner parts. This is illustrated in Figure 10.

Agents are special Actors that represent environment and domain entities. Agents may have service profiles and credentials. One big advantage of this environment is that it combines the power of application servers to handle persistent objects and transactions, with the power of collaborating state machines to provide complex peer-to-peer behaviors.

Using this environment, students have been able to develop and demonstrate convergent services within the timeframe of a semester. They have modeled using UML drawing tools rather informally, and implemented manually using the Java classes of ActorFrame. The biggest difficulties they have reported so far have been to make edges and to determine Agent functionalities. Detailed design and implementation has been relatively problem free. We are now taking measures to reduce their problems by providing standardized edges, by enabling ActorFrame to run on terminals and by providing design patterns.

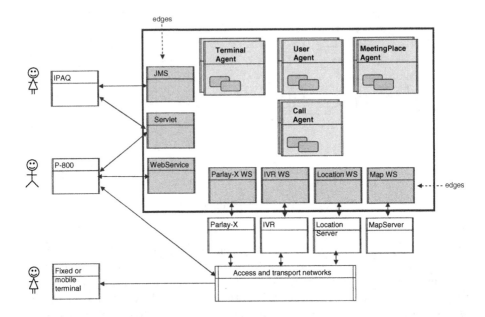

Fig. 10. ActorFrame illustrated with edges and AMIGOS Agents

5   Conclusions

Telecom and software engineers traditionally use different engineering approaches when developing services and applications. In this paper we have presented these differences in terms of domain properties, modeling concepts, services and architectures. The telecom approach and the computing approach have both strengths and weaknesses. A convergent approach should exploit these strong sides. We argue that the telecom concepts used to model and realize behaviors are more general and should be supported at the core of a convergent approach. Modeling is considered as an important foundation. Modeling will contribute to a unified concept framework and to a common understanding of systems. Since UML that was initially developed for information system modeling, was recently extended with concepts from the telecom domain, we have studied how UML may be used as a basis for convergence. By modeling and implementing a number of convergent service examples we have demonstrated that this is feasible, although not without considerable care. The fundamental nature of active objects and peer-to-peer communication must be considered and properly supported if an approach is to succeed for convergent applications and services. This may be achieved by employing a framework like the one we have presented here. We are currently elaborating a methodology for incremental development of convergent services, based on UML and the agent oriented framework outlined above. We seek to define guidelines that enable the developer to choose the appropriate architecture and communication concepts depending to the problem to be solved.

References

1. AMIGOS and the Avantel project. Information available at http://www.pats.no (accessed March 2004)

2. Bræk, R: On Methodology Using the ITU-T Languages and UML. Telektronikk, vol. 96, no. 4, pp. 96–106, 2000.

3. Bræk, R., Haugen, Ø: Engineering Real Time Systems. An Object Oriented Methodology using SDL. Hemel Hempstead, Prentice Hall, 1993.

4. Bræk, R., Sarma, A. (Eds.): Proceedings of the 1995 SDL Forum, North-Holland, 1995. ISBN 0-444-82269-0.

5. Bren, R., Hinkel, U., Hofmann, C., Klein,-C., Paech, B., Rumpe, B., Thurner, V.: Towards a formalization of the Unified Modeling Language. Proc. of ECOOP'97, 11th European Conference on Object-Oriented Programming, 1997, 344-366.

6. Cavalli, A., Sarma, A. (Eds.): Proceedings of the 1997 SDL Forum, Elvesier, 1997. ISBN 0-444-82816-8.

7. Dssouli, R., Bochmann, G.v., Lahav, Y. (Eds.) Proceedings of the 1999 SDL Forum, Elvesier, 1999. ISBN 0-444-50228-9.

8. Færgemand, O., Reed, R. (Eds.): Proceedings of the 1991 SDL Forum, North-Holland, 1991. ISBN 0-444-88976-0.

9. Færgemand, O., Sarma, A. (Eds.): Proceedings of the 1993 SDL Forum, North-Holland, 1993. ISBN 0-444-81486-8.

10. Fisher, C., Olderog, E.-P., Wehrheim, H.: A CSP View on UML-RT Structure Diagrams. Proc. of FASE 2001 - Fundamental Approaches to Software Engineering, 4th International Conference. Volume 2029 of Lecture Notes in Computer Science, Springer 2001, ISBN 3-540-41863-6.

11. Inoue, Y., Lapierre, M. and Mossoto, C. (Eds.): The TINA Book - A co-operative solution for a competitive world (1999) ISBN 0-13-095400-4.

12. ITU-T: Recommendation I.329/Q.1203 (09/97) Intelligent network - Global functional plane architecture. International Telecommunication Union, Geneva (1997).

13. ITU-T: Recommendation Q.1211 (03/93) Introduction to intelligent network capability set 1. International Telecommunication Union, Geneva (1993).

14. ITU-T: Recommendation Z.100 (11/99), Specification and Description Language (SDL). International Telecommunication Union, Geneva (1999).

15. Kræmer, F.: Rapid Service Development for ServiceFrame. M.Sc. thesis, NTNU, Norway, 2003.

16. Magee, J., Dulay, N., Eisenbach, S., and Kramer, J.: Specifying Distributed Software Architectures. Proc. of the Fifth European Software Engineering Conference, 1995.

17. Objecteering. Information available at http://www.objecteering.com (accessed March 2004).

18. OMG: Object Management Architecture Guide, Revision 2.0. Object Management Group, December 1993.

19. OMG: The Common Object Request Broker: Architecture and Specification, Revision 2.0. Object Management Group, July 1995.

20. OMG: Model Driven Architecture. Object Management Group, http://www.omg.org/mda (accessed March 2004).

21. OMG: UML 2.0 specifications. Available at http://www.omg.org/uml (accessed March 2004).

22. Reed, R., Reed, J. (Eds.): Proceedings of the 10th SDL Forum. Volume 2078 of Lecture Notes in Computer Science, Springer (2001). ISBN 3-540-42281-1.

23. Sun Microsystems: The Java tutorial. (accessed March 2004) `http://java.sun.com/docs/books/tutorial/essential/threads/`
24. Telelogic AB: TAU Generation 2. Information available at `http://www.telelogic.com` (accessed March 2004).
25. van Ommering, R., van der Linden, F., Kramer, J., Magee, J.: The Koala component model for consumer electronics software. IEEE Computer, Vol. 33, Nr. 3, March 2000, 78–85.

Dealing with Non-local Choice in IEEE 1073.2's Standard for Remote Control*

Arjan J. Mooij and Nicolae Goga

Technische Universiteit Eindhoven,
Department of Mathematics and Computer Science,
P.O. Box 513, 5600 MB Eindhoven, The Netherlands
{A.j.Mooij, N.Goga}@tue.nl

Abstract. Currently, communication protocols for medical devices are being developed for the IEEE 1073.2 standard. The protocol description in its draft remote control package consists of a collection of intended behaviors in terms of MSCs. We have contributed to actually constructing the protocol, ranging from determining an hMSC for these MSCs, via synthesizing process implementations, to integrating it with the basic underlying IEEE 1073.2 protocol. In this paper we report on the non-local choice problems we encountered. We present a practical solution (i.e., an implementation) which on the one hand is close to the behavior specified in the hMSC, and on the other hand meets correctness properties such as deadlock freedom. These properties have been checked using the Spin model checker. We also give some directions for generalizing and extending this work.

1   Introduction

At the moment of writing, the ISO/IEEE 1073 Standard for Medical Device Communications is being developed. The network protocols in this family of standards address the communication of patient-related data necessary for the treatment of patients or for the documentation of medical procedures. Although such a communication system in medical use must be extremely reliable under all circumstances, a formal analysis is no common part of their development.

The development of this standard is a long-term effort of a great number of parties, including manufacturers, each with a specific interest in this standard. We have actively participated[1] in the working group meetings and in ongoing discussions with the developers of the standard. The challenge is to successfully contribute to a yet incomplete standard which is subject to change.

In [14] we reported on our work on analyzing the base communication protocols of ISO/IEEE 1073.2 [11]: we analyzed and extended its draft state tables,

---

* This research is supported by the NWO under project 016.023.015: "Improving the Quality of Protocol Standards".
[1] As a recognition of the value of this work, we are in the ballot group and on the international coordination list.

D. Amyot and A.W. Williams (Eds.): SAM 2004, LNCS 3319, pp. 257–270, 2005.

and we proposed modifications to overcome the problems found. In the discussions about the results of this work, we were requested to become involved in the development of the optional remote control package [12].

The protocol in the current draft of the remote control package is specified by a collection of message sequence charts and accompanying textual descriptions. In this paper we describe the results of our attempts to extract and analyze the intended communication protocol. The resulting formal description of the protocol will be incorporated in the remote control standard.

In the literature, many algorithms have been proposed for synthesizing a protocol from a collection of message sequence charts. A well-known problem in the current protocol synthesis algorithms is dealing with non-local choice. In case of non-local choice, these algorithms usually introduce deadlocks, resulting in communication protocols with undesired behavior. We propose a new direction to solve this problem under some practical assumptions, and we apply it to the remote control package.

The remainder of this paper is organized as follows. Section 2 gives some theoretical background on the synthesis of protocols from MSCs and on the non-local choice phenomenon. Section 3 briefly presents the remote control package from the ISO/IEEE 1073.2 standard. Section 4 describes our attempts to apply the existing theory to the creation of the remote control protocol and shows the non-local choice situation for our case study. Section 5 explains why no existing algorithm could be fruitfully applied and it describes our solution. Section 6 presents the results of our verification of the remote control protocol. Section 7 outlines the conclusions and further work.

2   Related Work

This section contains a brief introduction to the techniques for extracting a protocol from a message sequence chart (MSC). A *basic* message sequence chart (bMSC) is used to describe a single scenario of system behavior. A collection of bMSCs can be structured using a *high-level* message sequence chart (hMSC) or a message sequence graph (MSG). The basic means to compose bMSCs are sequential (i.e., vertical) and alternative (i.e., choice) composition and sometimes parallel (i.e., horizontal) composition.

To increase the value of MSCs in designing a system, the MSCs should not only be used for describing some intended behaviors. For example, an (initial) implementation for the processes of the system might be synthesized. Thereto many algorithms (e.g., [6, 13]) have been proposed. Although they differ in the formalism that is used for the transformation (process algebra, automata theory, etc.) and the kind of output that is generated (Petri-net, state chart, etc.), they usually consist of the following three characteristic phases (see also [9]):

1. project the behavior of each bMSC on the individual processes;
2. compose the projected bMSCs per process as described by the hMSC;
3. minimize the process descriptions.

Composing the bMSC behaviors *per process* ignores some synchronization that seems to be imposed by the hMSC. Therefore sequential composition of bMSCs is usually interpreted as weak sequential composition, i.e., if two bMSCs are sequentially composed, processes that completed the first bMSC may start executing the second bMSC, while some other processes may still be executing the first bMSC. A consequence of using weak sequential composition is the danger of process divergence [5], in which some processes go on a potentially unbounded number of bMSCs ahead of other processes.

Another known source of problems are choice nodes in hMSCs, because all processes must make the same series of choices on these nodes. This problem is partly solved by interpreting choice in the hMSC as delayed choice [3], which is called the "wait-and-see" approach. Some synthesis algorithms obtain delayed choice semantics by first composing using ordinary choice and then applying some minimization. This is usually the main goal of minimization, but sometimes also an extra reduction of the size of the protocol description is achieved.

The main remaining problem is non-local choice [5, 8, 9] nodes, where the first action of the bMSCs that can be chosen is initiated by different processes. If the processes do not reach agreement on the choice, usual implementations can reach a deadlock state. In the literature there are three main views on non-local choice:

- *faulty hMSC*: non-local choice nodes are only part of erroneous hMSCs, so methods are needed that detect them (e.g., [9]);
- *implicit synchronization*: non-local choice nodes implicitly specify additional synchronization (e.g., a consensus protocol), so additional messages (and maybe even additional processes) must be explicitly introduced to obtain an implementation (e.g., [9, 13]);
- *implied behavior*: non-local choice nodes introduce behavior that must exist in any implementation that contains at least the intended behaviors, so these extra behaviors must be revealed and included (e.g., [1, 5, 15]).

For solving the general problem of non-local choice in implementing hMSCs, extra behavior must be introduced, like communicating extra messages [9] or accessing a global history variable [13]. In Section 5 we make some additional assumptions and propose a solution that can be classified as a combination of the last two views, viz. implicit synchronization and implied behavior.

3   Remote Control in ISO/IEEE 1073.2

After the previous introduction to protocol synthesis algorithms, in this section we give an overview of the ISO/IEEE 1073.2 standard and its remote control package. This standard deals with networks of medical devices and managerial computer systems. The patient-connected medical devices communicate patient-related physiological data to other devices and to computer systems. In this context, a manager/agent communication system is defined, in which the agent process usually incorporates a medical device that provides data, and in which the manager process receives data. The protocols are typically defined for one manager-agent pair, although a manager can possibly communicate with several agents.

The main concept that is used in these protocols is the containment tree. The containment tree, also called Medical Data Information Base (MDIB), is an abstract object-oriented model of the medical devices in the agent. The root of the containment tree is the Medical Device System (MDS) object, which is an abstraction of a device that provides medical information. Initially, the containment tree is accessible by the agent, and this standard's base protocols maintain a copy that is accessible by the manager.

Remote control functionality will be enclosed in ISO/IEEE 1073.2 to enable performing tasks on a medical device through a communication system. These tasks include obtaining medical information, and configuring, programming and operating the device. The base protocols of this standard support some kind of remote control called remote configuration, but it is considered to be too restrictive for full remote control.

In the case of remote configuration, the "Set" service of CMDISE (Common Medical Device Information Service Element) is used to change the values of *attributes* of the objects to be controlled. The limitations of this approach are the same as the ones that let to the inclusion of the encapsulation principle in object-orientation in general. The remote control package will rely on the "Action" service of CMDISE to perform *operations* on the objects to be controlled. A main requirement on the remote control package is that the extra functionality is provided as an extension of the existing containment tree.

3.1   Architecture

The remote control package considers an application running at the manager that must remotely control devices of the agent. Figure 1 shows such a manager application and four special components needed at the agent side: the context scanner, the operating scanner, the service and control objects, and the operation objects. The arrows indicate the directions of the main communication channels between those components.

The context scanner is inherited from the base standard in order to maintain the copy of the MDIB under device configuration changes. The newly-introduced operation objects represent remote controllable items of a medical device. The operating scanner is added to maintain the collection of operation objects, but the operation objects are only accessible for the manager application through the service and control object related to the operation object. Each service and control object (SCO) manages a group of (dependent) operation objects that are supported by a medical device, and it provides a locking mechanism for transaction processing.

3.2   Protocol

In this paper we only describe the remote control extensions of the base protocol (as described in [14]). After creation of the context scanner by the base

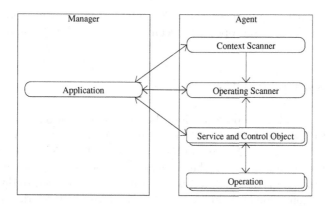

Fig. 1. Overview of the system

protocols, the initialization of the remote control system consists of the following consecutive phases:

- Object Duplication: The context scanner, right after its creation, copies the objects (including the SCOs, but excluding the operation objects) of the containment tree to the manager. Afterwards, the context scanner updates the active SCO list of the operating scanner.
- Operation Object Duplication: The manager enables the operating scanner of the agent. In turn, the operating scanner starts copying the available operations to the manager. Afterwards the operating scanner sends updates of the operation attributes to the manager.

After these start-up phases, the central Operation phase is reached. From this phase, four additional phases can be entered after which the components return to the Operation phase:

- Operation invocation: The manager sends an Operation Invoke message to the SCO, which in turn confirms the receipt of this message. The SCO deals with the actual execution of the operation, and with determining whether execution is allowed according to the locking mechanism. After successfully completing the execution of the operation, the SCO initiates the Reporting phase. If an error occurred during execution of the operation, or the execution was not allowed by the locking mechanism, the SCO sends an error report to the manager.
- Reporting: Upon completion of an operation or upon a device state change (possibly by a local user of the device), the Operating Scanner sends updates of the operation attributes to the manager.
- Refreshing: In case the manager detects an error situation that might have corrupted its copy of the MDIB, the manager can request the agent to refresh the set of available operations or their attributes. The agent, in turn, sends this information in a similar way as in the Operation Object Duplication start-up phase.

– Reconfiguration: Whenever the SCO detects that an operation has been deleted, it notifies the operating scanner. The operating scanner, in turn, notifies the manager.

4   Protocol Definition

The remote control draft package describes a communication protocol using a collection of typical intended behaviors in the form of MSCs and accompanying textual descriptions. Figure 2 contains some of the bMSCs, with an emphasis on the communication between the manager and the agent. However, the draft package contains no formal definition of the protocol. We tried to derive formal process implementations for this protocol in the form of state transition tables. In this section we describe the way we did this and the problems we encountered.

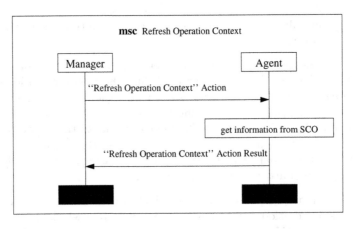

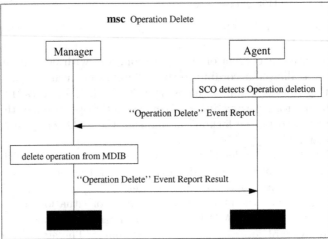

Fig. 2. Some of the remote-control bMSCs

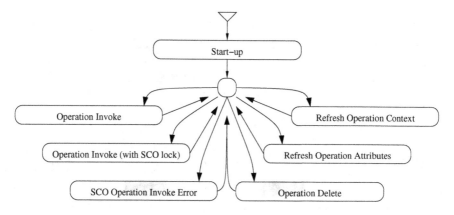

Fig. 3. Initial composed hMSC

We must first decide for which processes we must create an implementation in order to obtain an appropriate protocol description. For the remote control package there are roughly two possibilities:

– one combined manager process and one combined agent process;
– all individual processes mentioned in Figure 1.

The first alternative stresses the communication between the two combined processes, while the second one stresses the roles of the individual processes. The standard emphasizes the communication between the manager and the agent in order to leave more freedom for implementing the internal objects of the agent. Therefore our main interest is in the first alternative, but we also consider the second alternative.

We tried to apply standard synthesis algorithms to this draft standard, but we encountered the following problems:

– *missing hMSC*: the structure on the collection of bMSCs is only described verbally and not very explicitly;
– *missing bMSCs*: some intended behaviors are not explicitly mentioned, but they somewhat follow from the given bMSCs and the accompanying texts;
– *non-local choice*: the derived hMSC contains non-local choice nodes.

These three problems can easily be classified as omissions and errors in the draft standard. Nevertheless, we choose to see whether (and how) we can create a useful protocol that is close to the original intentions.

To overcome the first problem we use the textual descriptions in the standard to compose an hMSC, see Figure 3. In this way, we also noticed the second problem. An example of this problem are the operation invocation scenarios. There are two modes of the SCO's locking mechanism for invoking an operation, and there are two possible results (fail and success). However, only three out of these four combinations are described. We manually included the missing one. So these first two problems could easily be fixed.

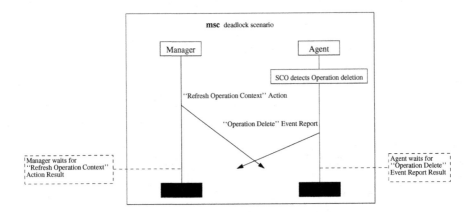

Fig. 4. Deadlock scenario

However, the last problem deserves more attention since non-local choice nodes cannot easily be eliminated without seriously modifying the protocol. In Figure 3 the most central node is a non-local choice node, since it can be followed by bMSCs that are initiated by different processes (see Figure 2). As discussed in Section 2, usual synthesized implementations of hMSCs with non-local choice nodes can reach a deadlock state, like the one depicted in Figure 4. In Section 5 we propose a way to deal with these non-local choice nodes.

5   A Non-local Choice Solution from Practice

From Section 2 we conclude that there is no standard solution for obtaining a proper implementation of an hMSC that contains non-local choice nodes. Nevertheless we want to obtain an implementation of the protocol described in this standard. In terms of the three views on non-local choice, it does not help to declare its hMSC to be faulty. Our composed hMSC is clearly the intended one, and any attempt to eliminate the non-local choice is likely to yield an unreasonably complicated hMSC containing parallelism and additional synchronization.

If the non-local choice should be viewed as implicit synchronization, extra mechanisms should be introduced that are not at all described in the standard. What remains is to declare it hidden implied behavior that should somehow be revealed. We will propose a solution to reveal this behavior based on some hidden synchronization.

After abstracting from the domain specific interpretation of the messages in the remote control package, it turns out that the non-local choice nodes have an interesting property. Actually, the initial message communications of the next bMSCs can be interpreted as the messages of an asymmetric synchronization protocol. Usual protocol synthesis algorithms do not take this into account, thereby generating implementations that can reach deadlocks states.

We propose to implement the processes such that these initial messages are part of a synchronization protocol. Then the behavior that previously led to a

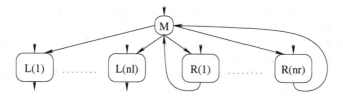

Fig. 5. Restricted non-local choice situation

deadlock remains to exist, but the deadlock itself is eliminated. Although these implementations deviate from the hMSC, their behavior is still close to it. Note that these synchronization messages also have an application specific meaning, so in fact they are combined messages. For each application of this technique, the validity of the additional behavior must be checked within the application domain. In the remote control case study, this additional behavior is valid.

In what follows, we abstract from the specifics of the remote control package to describe our approach in more general terms. Finally we discuss an example of its use in the remote control package.

5.1   Our Approach

Consider an hMSC as depicted in Figure 5 which contains a non-local choice node M. Suppose there are two processes called P and Q, and assume that bMSCs $L(1)...L(nl)$ start with an action of process P and bMSCs $R(1)...R(nr)$ start with an action of process Q. Whenever the system is in node M, usual synthesized implementations allow process P to initiate an L-bMSC and process Q to initiate an R-bMSC. Then both bMSCs have started, which is not allowed according to the hMSC, and it usually leads to a deadlock state.

To avoid this, we can impose an extra synchronization protocol that forces the bMSCs to be executed in some sequential order. Since after executing a bMSC R the same choices can be made as before, for non-local choice situations we introduce a "temporal" order such that the R bMSCs get priority over the L bMSCs. If process P wants to start execution of a bMSC L, it must send a 'request' message to process Q and wait for a 'confirmation' message of process Q that allows process P to start execution of the L bMSC. While process P is waiting for this confirmation, it must be able to execute an R bMSC (initiated by process Q). Process Q, having priority, does not need extra communications to start execution of a bMSC R. So process Q is a kind of arbiter that ensures that execution of the bMSCs conforms to the hMSC.

To avoid the introduction of additional message communications for this extra synchronization, the initial communication actions of the L bMSCs might be reused. Then we reuse the first action of the L bMSCs as the 'request' message from P to Q, and the second action as the 'confirmation' message from Q to P. Since these messages are also in the original MSCs, we must show that the bMSCs are independent in the sense that the first communication of each bMSC L may be delayed over executions of any bMSC R.

In general, such an independency is not guaranteed, but at least in the ISO/IEEE 1073.2 standard it was the case. Other applicable settings are two interconnected computers that report (and confirm) data to each other. Or a more asymmetric situation in which a sensor reports data to a monitor, and a monitor may send configuration messages to the sensor which are confirmed afterwards. It does not easily apply to standard examples that consider interaction between a human and a machine, because it is undesired to superimpose extra synchronization or communication on humans.

5.2   Formalization

Consider the situation of Figure 5, and let L denote the set of bMSCs $L(1)...L(nl)$, and let R denote the set of bMSCs $R(1)...R(nr)$. We consider two processes, viz. P and Q, which communicate via (non-fifo) buffers. The behavior of process P in each bMSC R starts with receiving a message from process Q, and the behavior of process P in each bMSC L starts with sending a 'request' message to process Q followed by receiving a 'confirmation' message from process Q. Finally we assume that these first two communications of the bMSCs L do not occur in any bMSC R.

Our formalizations are based on process algebra notation in ACP-style [4], like it is used by [6]. As formalization of node M in Figure 5 we obtain:

$$M \;=\; \left(\textstyle\sum_{m\in L} m\right) + \left(\textstyle\sum_{n\in R} n \cdot M\right)$$

Here operators $\sum$ and $+$ are used to denote delayed choice instead of ordinary choice. The corresponding standard implementations of processes P and Q are:

$$P \;=\; \Pi_P(M) \;=\; \left(\textstyle\sum_{m\in L} \Pi_P(m)\right) + \left(\textstyle\sum_{n\in R} \Pi_P(n) \cdot P\right)$$

$$Q \;=\; \Pi_Q(M) \;=\; \left(\textstyle\sum_{m\in L} \Pi_Q(m)\right) + \left(\textstyle\sum_{n\in R} \Pi_Q(n) \cdot Q\right)$$

Expression $\Pi_P(m)$ denotes the projection of an MSC m on a process P. As we explained before, this implementation may contain deadlocks. Our proposed implementation of the processes differs in process P, namely:

$$
\begin{aligned}
P \quad &= \quad \left(\textstyle\sum_{m\in L} hd(\Pi_P(m)) \cdot P'(m)\right) + \left(\textstyle\sum_{n\in R} \Pi_P(n) \cdot P\right) \\
P'(m) \quad &= \quad tl(\Pi_P(m)) \qquad\qquad\qquad\;\; + \left(\textstyle\sum_{n\in R} \Pi_P(n) \cdot P'(m)\right)
\end{aligned}
$$

$$Q \quad = \quad \left(\textstyle\sum_{m\in L} \Pi_Q(m)\right) \qquad\qquad + \left(\textstyle\sum_{n\in R} \Pi_Q(n) \cdot Q\right)$$

Expression $hd(m)$ denotes the first (communication) action in m, and $tl(m)$ denotes the remaining actions such that: $hd(\Pi_P(m)) \cdot tl(\Pi_P(m)) = \Pi_P(m)$.

This solution eliminates the deadlock state that is usually introduced when synthesizing a protocol from an hMSC that contains non-local choice nodes, while the amount of additional behavior is rather limited. It must be noted that the current asymmetric solution does allow infinite overtaking of any L bMSC by the R bMSCs. For further work we want to investigate more properties of this approach, and to see whether a similar approach can be applied to a more general situation, e.g., one with more than two processes.

In [7] another implementation is proposed for a situation like non-local choice. They also break the symmetry between the two processes, by calling them 'winner' and 'loser' respectively. When the processes detect interference between behaviors initiated by different processes, the synchronization between them is restored by discarding the behavior initiated by the loser. Their implementation also slightly deviates from the original specified behavior, but in a different way than our solution. In MSC applications like the remote control package, the implementation according to [7] is not acceptable. This shows again that the practical validity of such implementations must be checked per application.

5.3   Remote Control Application

Let us now reconsider the non-local choice node in the remote control package. From Figure 2 it follows that for our approach priority should be given to the agent process. Then the deadlock scenario of Figure 4 can be avoided by continuing the behavior as depicted in Figure 6. The developers of the remote control package have agreed with this solution.

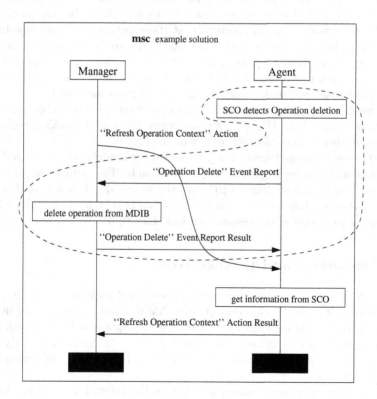

Fig. 6. Example solution

6   Analysis

In this section we address our analysis of the derived remote control protocols. Recall from Section 4 that we consider two protocols that differ in the collection of processes that are considered:

- one combined manager process and one combined agent process;
- all individual processes mentioned in Figure 1.

Also recall that the protocol considers only one manager and one agent. For systems with multiple managers or agents, or with devices that act as both a manager and an agent, simply multiple instances of the protocol are used. Hence, in our verification we also need to consider only one manager-agent pair.

Like in [14], we analyzed them manually and we performed an automated check for safety properties, viz. deadlocks and unreachable code. Since the required properties of the protocol are only the bMSCs, we did not verify any specific additional properties.

For the automated analysis we transform the state transition tables into a Promela model which we analyze using the Spin [10] model checker. After our first 'naive' application of a protocol synthesis algorithm to this standard, Spin made us aware of the resulting deadlock scenarios, like the one described in Figure 4. After introducing our special implementation of the non-local choice node, the Spin model checker confirms that there are no remaining deadlocks.

The Promela models of the state transition tables are basically rather straightforward. To ensure that they are manageable for verification, we applied some abstractions. As far as it does not influence the protocol, we abstracted from the contents of messages. Furthermore we abstracted from the details of the SCO's locking mechanism; thus invocations of the operations are non-deterministically accepted or rejected. In this way we can verify all possible locking regimes at once, and it also reduces the complexity of the model.

The before-mentioned safety properties of these models can be verified using the Spin model checker in just a couple of seconds. The number of states and transitions are both less than $7 \cdot 10^5$, and the search depth is less than $7 \cdot 10^4$. Also the corresponding memory usage is very acceptable, being less than 41 Mb and using state vector compression even less than 15 Mb.

7   Conclusions and Further Work

This paper describes our work on the remote control package of the ISO/IEEE 1073.2 standard. From a collection of seven bMSCs and accompanying descriptions we have derived an hMSC and a formal description of the protocol in the form of state transition tables. The state transition tables are currently being added to the remote control standard to serve as a kernel that incorporates its base functionalities.

This work is used as a basis for studying the integration of this protocol within the base communication protocols [11]. Since the remote control package is still a draft package, various extensions might be proposed. These extensions will be discussed on the basis of our formal description of the core protocol.

Upon trying to transform an hMSC in a formal protocol, we have encountered the problem of non-local choice nodes. Because no existing solution could be employed successfully, we have proposed an alternative approach that turns out to correspond to the intuition of the developers of the standard. Although this solution is inspired by the remote control case study, it can be applied in a more general setting.

In many theories in the literature, hMSCs with non-local choice nodes are classified as erroneous hMSCs. However, non-local choice nodes can easily (and almost unnoticed) be introduced in hMSCs. Since non-local choice cannot easily be eliminated, the attitude of declaring these hMSCs to be erroneous hinders the practical applicability of many of these theories.

At the moment of writing, we are also trying to extract a protocol from a collection of bMSCs for the HL7 medical standard [2]. Apart from some non-local choice problems, in this case study there are also other aspects that hinder the use of protocol synthesis algorithms. From these two case studies we conclude that practically modeling systems using MSCs and extracting protocols from them requires further attention.

We expect that the approach described in this paper is just a witness of a class of solutions, which needs to be further studied. Also the required assumptions for this approach needs further investigation, e.g., to generalize it to more than two processes. For this case study we showed that our approach is free of deadlocks using a model checker, but for maturing the approach general conditions are needed under which this property is guaranteed.

Acknowledgements

We thank Judi Romijn for the useful discussions and comments, and for her work on applying synthesis algorithm [6] to this case study.

References

1. Alur, R., Etessami, K., Yannakakis, M.: Inference of Message Sequence Charts. 22nd International Conference on Software Engineering (2000) 304–313.
2. American National Standard Institute: Health Level Seven HL7.
3. Baeten, J.C.M., Mauw, S.: Delayed choice: an operator for joining Message Sequence Charts. Formal Description Techniques (1995) 340–354.
4. Baeten, J.C.M., Weijland, W.P.: Process algebra. Cambridge Tracts in Theoretical Computer Science 18. Cambridge University Press (1990).
5. Ben-Abdallah, H., Leue, S.: Syntactic detection of process divergence and non-local choice in Message Sequence Charts. Tools and Algorithms for the Construction and Analysis of Systems. Volume 1217 of Lecture Notes in Computer Science, Springer Verlag (1997) 259–274.
6. Feijs, L.M.G.: Generating FSMs from interworkings. Distributed Computing **12** (1999) 31–40.

7. Gouda, M.G., Yu, Y.T.: Synthesis of communicating finite-state machines with guaranteed progress. IEEE Transactions on Communications **COM-32** (1984) 779–788.

8. Hélouët, L.: Some pathological message sequence charts and how to detect them. Reed, R., Reed, j. (Eds.) 10th SDL Forum. Volume 2078 of Lecture Notes in Computer Science (2001) 348–364.

9. Hélouët, L., Jard, C.: Conditions for synthesis of communicating automata from HMSCs. 5th International Workshop on Formal Methods for Industrial Critical Systems (2000) 203–224.

10. Holzmann, G.J.: The model checker Spin. IEEE Transactions on Software Engineering **23** (1997) 279–295.

11. Institute of Electrical and Electronics Engineers, Inc.: Health informatics - Point-of-care medical device communication - Application Profiles. ISO/IEEE 11073-20000.

12. Institute of Electrical and Electronics Engineers, Inc.: Health informatics - Point-of-care medical device communication - Application profile - Optional package, remote control. (2002) Draft Standard IEEE 1073.2.3.1.

13. Leue, S., Ladkin, P.B.: Implementing and verifying MSC specifications using Promela/XSpin. Grégoire, J.C., Holzmann, G., Peled, D. (Eds.) Proceedings of the DIMACS Workshop SPIN96. Volume 32 of DIMACS Series (1997).

14. Mooij, A.J., Goga, N., Wesselink, W., Bošnački, D.: An analysis of medical device communication standard IEEE 1073.2. Salvador, C.E.P. (Ed.) Communication Systems and Networks, IASTED, ACTA Press (2003) 74–79.

15. Uchitel, S., Kramer, J., Magee, J.: Detecting implied scenarios in message sequence chart specifications. Proceedings of the 8th European software engineering conference, ACM Press (2001) 74–82.

Guidelines for Using SDL in Product Development

Frank Weil and Thomas Weigert

Motorola Inc., 1303 East Algonquin Road,
Schaumburg, IL 60196 USA
{Frank.Weil, Thomas.Weigert}@motorola.com

Abstract. Over the course of several years working with many diverse projects using SDL for the design of commercial products, we have developed several practical guidelines related to creating SDL models for deployment. This paper discusses the SDL modeling guidelines, covering general recommendations, specific details about using SDL modeling features, performance considerations, platform interface considerations, and portability issues. These guidelines can be used by anyone who is creating design models that will be implemented, either through hand coding or automatic code generation.

1 Overview

The Software Design Automation Center, part of Motorola's Global Software Group, has been developing tools for model-based automatic code generation for more than 15 years. For the last seven years, our team has focused on automatically generating C code from SDL models. Over that time, the center has generated code from many hundreds of thousands of lines of SDL. The code produced is for telecommunications products that have been deployed in the field, encompassing many diverse platforms (from embedded components to infrastructure network elements) and product groups.

This experience has led to the development of several practical guidelines related to creating SDL models for deployment. These guidelines are the de facto standard for most SDL modeling projects within Motorola.

Because the ITU-T developed SDL [3] for use in all up-stream phases of the typical product development life cycle, not all of its features are appropriate for design models, especially if automatic code generation will be used. In most languages, there are many ways to represent the same functionality, and SDL is no exception. SDL often presents a bewildering array of choices. For example, functionality in SDL can be represented as processes, procedures, operators, remote procedure calls, external package components, macros, select definitions, etc., many of which can inherit properties from and specialize other components. While such flexibility is helpful for accommodating local conventions and preferences, unrestrained use of these features leads to a model that is at best difficult to read and at worst a nightmare of interleaved definitions and unused and irrelevant code.

D. Amyot and A.W. Williams (Eds.): SAM 2004, LNCS 3319, pp. 271–289, 2005.

For any discussion of modeling for product development, it is difficult to fully separate the modeling language from the tools that support it. While SDL2000 is the current standard, these guidelines reference the version of SDL supported by the most widely deployed tool: Telelogic TAU [5]. At times, for example with exception handling, SDL2000 provides a more elegant solution that unfortunately is not supported by most modeling tools. Where appropriate, we will point out what the SDL2000 construct would be, but we will discuss the practical solutions as required by tools supporting some mix of SDL'92 and SDL'96.

This paper provides a set of modeling guidelines that are useful in creating practical models. We begin by presenting general recommendations for design modeling and then discuss specific constructs in SDL. We then present discussions on performance considerations, interfacing with target platforms, and portability issues.

2   General Recommendations

There are a few guiding principles which we have found to be generally applicable to modeling activities. While these are by no means exclusive to SDL, we will discuss them in terms of SDL. We also present guidelines related to C or C++ as the implementation language since those are the most common cases. However, the guidelines are equally applicable to any implementation language.

2.1   Nondeterminism and Fairness

SDL has several nondeterministic features (e.g., spontaneous transitions). One of the guiding principles of good design is that nondeterminism should be avoided since nondeterminism does not imply fairness. This distinction is extremely important, but is one that is often misunderstood by modelers. Nondeterminism means that criteria *do not exist* for determining which choice will be made. A perfectly valid interpretation is that one choice is always made to the exclusion of the others. It will rarely, if ever, be the case that this is really the desired behavior.

2.2   Abstraction

One should start out creating a model of the system instead of immediately starting to design it. The key is abstraction. Make sure the model captures the concepts instead of irrelevant details. Two considerations will help guide model development in this direction: simplicity and efficiency.

To promote simplicity, review each model to look for opportunities to simplify cluttered graphics using techniques such as combining several sequential tasks into one, relegating commonly used patterns to procedures, compartmentalizing calculations into operators, and using textual algorithm forms to capture some common processing forms more succinctly (especially loops). There is a tool-related trade-off here, however, because symbol coverage analysis will not equate to path coverage when there are loops or branches in a text symbol.

Make some concessions to efficiency, but do not spend much initial effort on optimizations. It is extremely important to first capture the overall structure, decomposition, relationships, and data and control flows at the highest levels. The key is to make sure that the model captures the requirements in a clear manner. Only then should the developers address the design issues.

A good starting point when entering the design phase is to address the issue of limited resources in the target hardware. This leads to placing upper bounds on certain values in the system, such as array indices and the maximum number of process instances that may be executing simultaneously. Once these constraints are added, additional fault tolerance functionality can be added to handle the situations where these limits are reached.

One may also want to examine the manipulation of large data structures. Since SDL has copy semantics, whenever data is assigned to another variable, passed as a formal parameter to processes, procedures, or operators, or conveyed as a signal parameter from one process to another, a large performance overhead may be incurred due to data copying. To avoid this penalty, one may want to take careful advantage of the references that are available as part of the SDL2000 standard, and that may be available as tool-specific extensions.

2.3   Reverse-Engineering Code

Do not reverse engineer the architecture of an SDL model from C code. The structure of the model should be derived from requirements. Legacy code usually has grown in complexity through evolution, and its structure most likely contains numerous implementation idiosyncrasies, making it difficult to extract a clean, flexible foundation for future development. We have seen models where the number of states in a process was significantly reduced when its overall behavior was revisited from a requirements perspective rather than being based on the implementation that had catered too many other details.

2.4   Unused Signals and Sorts

Only signals and sorts that are used should be included in the model. If the signals and sorts are created from an externally controlled specification that cannot be changed (e.g., a protocol description document), there are two solutions:

- Have a process explicitly consume the unused signals. This solution is acceptable as a temporary measure when the actual functionality associated with a signal has yet to be filled in. This may be the case early in the design phase.
- Generate only the signals and sorts needed in the first place. It is often possible to automatically generate only those signals and sorts needed in a model. This method will ensure consistency between the model and the external protocol specifications.

2.5   Exception Handling

There are several types of errors and exceptions that can occur outside of the realm of the model that, in themselves, make no sense to the model. Examples of this type of exceptions are: memory allocation failures, signal decode failures, callback function or platform API errors, platform signals such as SIGERR, etc. These exceptions can occur, in effect, at random times during the execution of the model. To handle these conditions, SDL2000 has added exception handling. However, tool support for this mechanism is limited.

Exception Signals. It is not always an option to simply use signals in place of exceptions. For example, it would not be useful to try to create a signal to indicate an out-of-memory exception since there is no more memory to create the signal. To handle exceptions, either a customer code generator can be used, or modifications can be made to the existing code generators. The modeler should, however, define exception signals for individual exceptions where they make sense. For example, a signal handler thread may inject a specific signal into the model for each system interrupt that it encounters. This is also useful to allow the modeler to explicitly raise an exception by sending the signal to handle, for example, an error code returned by an external function.

Exception States. The mechanism that we have used for general exception handling is to have the modeler specify in the SDL model how the application will handle an exception. This is done on a per-process basis by adding specially named states with continuous signals to each process. The conditions on these continuous signals are ignored since they are only placeholders to allow a syntactically correct state. The details of the transition are customized for each situation, and the generated code ties its exception handling mechanism directly to these states.

2.6   Data Marshaling

Typically, the underlying representation of data used within a model is different than that used by code outside the model. This is an issue when the model needs to exchange data with external entities such as parameters of signals to or from the environment. Data encoding and decoding (also known as packing and unpacking, or collectively as marshaling [1]) is common to most applications. For several reasons, marshaling should not be represented directly in a model:

- SDL does not provide appropriate operations for data marshaling. For example, trying to represent low-level bit manipulation algorithms is cumbersome. Implementation languages such as C have the appropriate operators.
- The format of the external data is independent of the behavior of the model.
- Trying to share existing data format header files with the model can be problematic. Unless the headers were written in SDL, translating them and keeping them synchronized with the model is difficult. In addition, as previously mentioned, one should include only those definitions that are actually used.

 – Dispatching on signals with nested data types usually makes for very confusing SDL models. The decision graphs that result as the various nested conditional fields of the input are decoded make for intricate combinations of SDL transitions that are difficult to follow and understand. Only the abstracted data should be used.

Most such external data handling should be done outside the model, with appropriate signals being sent into or received from the model for further processing.

A typical example of this is the handling of an incoming data stream consisting of bit-encoded messages that make up a protocol. First, the bit streams are parsed using C routines, often in a thread dedicated to a communications channel. This results in the extraction of individual messages and their data values. Next, separate SDL signals are created for each message, and the signals are injected into the SDL model.

2.7   Testing

Test the model, but do not rely on testing tools (e.g., a model verifier or a simulator) or the code generation process to catch all dynamic errors. Many problems may be masked in the testing, especially if the underlying implementation language is C.

Examples of errors that may not be caught if they occur are accessing an array or string element out of bounds, data subrange mismatches, and uninitialized variables.

3   SDL Recommendations

We present guidelines in this section that are specific to individual constructs in SDL. Examples are mostly in SDL'96 syntax as that is the most common for tool support.

3.1   Case Sensitivity

Since many implementation languages are case sensitive, it is important to assume case sensitivity for modeling. Even if the modeling tool allows varying case for SDL keywords, be consistent so that the problems associated with model searching, metrics reporting, reviewing, etc., are minimized.

3.2   SDL Sorts and Generators

This section focuses on practical guidelines for using the SDL-specific sorts, giving examples of typical issues that occur both in the models themselves and in the implementation of the models.

Subrange Compatibility. With any sort that restricts the range of its parent sort, problems during assignments can occur. For example, consider the following declarations:

```
SYNONYM max index = 10;
SYNTYPE index = Natural CONSTANTS 1 : max ENDSYNTYPE;
```

```
DCL n Natural, i index;
```

If the assignment i := n occurs in the model, it may not be possible to tell whether or not the value in n will actually fit in i. Assignments across sorts with potentially incompatible data values such as this should be avoided whenever possible.

A similar but perhaps more insidious problem can occur when using loops. Consider the following SDL fragment based on the example above:

```
TASK i := 1;
loop_top: DECISION i <= max;
  (true): /* loop body stmt */;
          TASK i := i + 1; JOIN loop_top;
  else: JOIN loop_break;
loop_break:
```

By a consistent interpretation of the sort information, there are two problems with the loop. First, the increment expression i + 1 will take on the value 11 (max + 1), and then attempt to assign the value back to i. This value is clearly outside of the allowable range. The second problem is that the loop condition itself could be legitimately optimized away by a code generation system. By the definition above, i is always less than or equal to max. The Boolean condition, then, can be replaced by true, which corresponds to an infinite loop. The simplest way to solve the problem is to always check the condition at the end of the loop, and then only increment and go back to the top of the loop if there is more to do. For example:

```
TASK i := 1;
loop_top: /* loop body */
DECISION i < max;
  (true): TASK i := i + 1; JOIN loop_top;
  else: JOIN loop_break;
loop_break:
```

Note that the Z.100 specification is a bit counter-intuitive on what should happen for Integer subranges. The Z.100 definition of syntypes (Section 5.3.1.9 in SDL'96, Section 12.1.9.4 in SDL2000) does *not* place a restriction on a syntype that the range condition must fit within the parent sort. Without this restriction, the specification allows misleading definitions such as:

```
SYNTYPE parent = Integer CONSTANTS 1 : 10 ENDSYNTYPE;
SYNTYPE child = parent CONSTANTS 100 : 200 ENDSYNTYPE;
```

Size Constraints. As part of the ASN.1 extensions in Z.105 [2, 4], some aggregate sorts such as String may be given bounds on minimum and maximum lengths. When supported by the modeling tool, the size bounds should be given for these sorts and generators (`String`, `Charstring`, `Powerset`, `Bag`, `Octet_string`, `Bit_string`). The final implementation can be chosen to be more efficient. Without size bounds, it must be assumed that a sort can contain an arbitrarily large number of elements, which is the worst-case assumption in terms of the allowable implementation.

If the minimum is set to greater than zero, beware of trying to build a String element by element, or of trying to initialize the String to `EMPTY`. It may be better to set the minimum size to zero and then to check the final size explicitly.

Time Literals. The origin of time has no definition in SDL, and varies from platform to platform. All uses of time should be relative to the `NOW` expression.

Time Operators. Manipulating `Time` values directly is typically not needed. A possible exception is determining relative timing of events. However, appropriate care must be taken to ensure expectations of time resolution are realistic.

Time and Duration Precision. Values of `Time` and `Duration` in SDL have decimal places, but this may be extremely difficult to implement on a real platform. It is best to use only integer-like values of time and duration within a model.

Real Comparisons. Although `Real` numbers in SDL are defined over the rational numbers, `Real` arithmetic is not precise using fixed-precision arithmetic (as with float or double in C). It cannot be guaranteed that two seemingly equal floating point numbers will actually be equal in the final implementation. For example, the folowing comparison, while true in SDL, may not evaluate to true when implemented:

```
0.1 = ((1.0 / 30.0) * 3.0)
```

If such a comparison is needed, then use an expected accuracy. For example:

```
SYNONYM epsilon Real = 0.0001;
PROCEDURE near;
  FPAR IN a Real, IN b Real; RETURNS Boolean;
  START; RETURN Fix((a - b) / epsilon) = 0;
ENDPROCEDURE;
```

High-Precision Real Values. Make sure that `Real` literals are given with a realistic precision, and be careful when creating values with operations such as `1.0 / 3.0`, which cannot be exactly represented in a finite (no less realistic) number of bits.

Large Integer and Natural Values. SDL `Integer` and `Natural` numbers must stay within the size limits of a realistic implementation used by a target compiler. Be wary of assumptions made about what a particular C compiler may support. For example, in C there is no universal standard on what number of bits correspond to the types int or long int, and some compilers do not even support long long int.

It would be better if, for a given target compiler, the modeler were to create a set of definitions that map sorts to various bit sizes. For example:

```
SYNTYPE unsigned_16_bit = Integer CONSTANTS 0:65535 ENDSYNTYPE;
```

These sorts can then be equated to the available types in the implementation. These sorts should be used whenever there is doubt or confusion about what value ranges are allowed for an Integer. Also, the sort Natural should be used instead of Integer whenever the data values will be non-negative. Not only does this give additional information to the reader, it allows larger values to be stored.

ERROR Expressions and Terms. If an ERROR expression or term is encountered in the execution of a model, the future behavior of the model is undefined. Error recovery should be implemented explicitly based on the condition that triggers the error as described previously.

Choice Sorts and Partial Initialization. As part of SDL2000 and the ASN.1 extensions in Z.105, the Choice sort is available. This sort is not the same as a union in C, however. The selection of the contained sort must be explicit, and implicit casting is not supported.

A common problem can occur when one has a Choice type containing structures:

```
NEWTYPE ch Choice
  aa struct1;
  bb othertype;
ENDNEWTYPE;

NEWTYPE struct1 STRUCT
  f1 Natural;
  f2 Natural;
ENDNEWTYPE;

DCL var ch;
```

The problem occurs with assignments such as the following:

```
TASK var!aa!f1 := 5;
```

If the variable is uninitialized before the assignment, or is the bb choice, it does not have a tag of the aa choice. However, in order for the f1 field to exist in the choice, the choice type must be aa. It is common practice in implementations (as well as part of the correct semantics) to check to see if the choice has type aa in order to know whether or not it has to reset the value.

The proper way to accomplish the above is to assign the choice value as a whole, which sets the tag without having to check it first:

```
TASK var!aa := (. 5, 10 .);
```

3.3   SDL Components

These guidelines focus on the features of SDL that are not directly sort-related.

Naming. SDL is quite flexible in what can constitute an identifier, including non-alphanumeric characters. In order to be able to preserve the identifiers as they exist in the SDL model (which greatly aids in the understanding of the implementation code), some care should be used in creating SDL identifiers.

We strongly suggest the use of only proper C-style syntax for identifiers. Note that SDL does not allow an identifier to begin or end with an underscore character (although some modeling tools allow it), so some external procedures may not be able to be called directly.

Numbers should not be used as variable names, labels, etc. Identifiers containing numbers as well as other non-numeric characters are acceptable, but using only numbers is not. For example:

```
TASK call_911 := true; /* this is okay */
TASK 911 := true;      /* this is legal, but not okay */
```

C does not allow overloading of identifiers, so the same name should not be used for more than one external entity in the SDL model. External entities include external procedures, external operators, synonyms, sorts, and literals derived from external code, and signals and channels that go to or come from the environment.

Identifiers that clash with a C keyword cannot be left unchanged in the final code. We recommend that they not be used for the sake of readability of the generated code. In addition, be careful about naming operators or procedures with names that already exist as standard C library functions, e.g., `free`, `raise`, `putc`, etc.

NODELAY Components. In SDL'96, channels, remote variables, and remote procedures can be marked as `NODELAY`. In most realistic implementation, the concept of delay versus no delay has no meaning. Systems do what they do as fast as they can. This feature is deprecated in SDL2000.

Unbounded Process Instances. A process definition may implicitly state that an infinite number of process instances may be created. This will happen if one does not explicitly specify the maximum number in the process definition header. While this in itself is not a problem, only a finite number of processes can really be created. It may be difficult to determine the real upper bound for resource allocation purposes during implementation.

Always provide an explicit maximum number in a process definition header, and provide the default initial value of one for completeness. For values other than one, the use of synonyms for maximum and initial values is strongly encouraged.

Nondeterministic Decisions. Decision constructs which use the `ANY` or the informal text forms should be avoided since they indicate nondeterminism, and the behavior of the model is subsequently undefined. Alternative: Do not use ANY or informal text as a decision question, and always use valid, non-overlapping decision conditions instead of informal text. Create enough answer parts and possibly an ELSE part to make sure that all possible outcomes of the decision question are covered.

ANY Expressions. The ANY expression introduces nondeterminism and should not be used in most cases. Instead, select a single value from the sort. If a random value is needed, an external procedure can be written to return one. There are two cases, however, in which it makes sense to use a nondeterministic value, both related to situations where the data value cannot affect the model:

- Giving a value to a parameter that will not be used. Processes, procedures, and operators can have parameters. It may be that the return value or another parameter indicates the validity of a parameter. When a parameter is indicated to be invalid, it does not matter what its value is since it should never be used. For example:

```
PROCEDURE next_digit;
   FPAR IN/OUT d Character; RETURNS Boolean;
   START; DECISION d;
      ('0' : '8') : TASK d := chr(num(d) + 1); RETURN true;
      ('9') :       TASK d := '0'; RETURN true;
      ELSE :        TASK d := ANY(Character); RETURN false;
   ENDDECISION;
ENDPROCEDURE;
```

- Giving a value to a structure field or choice field or a signal parameter that the model will not use. In general, a field or parameter that is never used in a model should be removed completely. There are cases, however, where the fields or parameters are constrained externally. For example, a structure may be derived from one that is defined in an external C header file, or a parameter of a signal may be dictated by an external protocol. In these cases, the ANY expression can be used to indicate that the value is not used in the model.

Viewed Variables. SDL allows a variable in one process to be manipulated by another process. This feature is enabled by the REVEALED and VIEWED keywords, and is accessed using the VIEW keyword. In a sense, this allows global variables with varying scopes. This feature is deprecated in SDL2000.

Information should be explicitly passed between processes using signals or shared through imported / exported variables. Note that a positive implication of not having shared variables is that continuous signals do not require a busy-wait semantics.

THIS in a Context that is not Type-based. The type-based keyword THIS used in a procedure call should only be used with a procedure that is inherited.

While other uses may be technically correct (the keyword is optional in this case and has no effect), they indicate that there is perhaps a misunderstanding about their use.

Informal Text. When informal text is encountered in a model, it means that the future behavior of the model is undefined because the semantics of the informal text are user-defined. Typically, informal text is initially put into a model to indicate information that will be filled in later. As such, it should not be in the completed model. Comments should be used in place of informal text.

Nondeterministic Signal Sends. In SDL, the architecture of interconnecting signal routes and channels is normally used to guide a signal from a sending process to a receiving process. However, there are times when this is insufficient to determine a unique destination process instance. For these cases, a signal route, channel, gate, process identifier, or process instance identifier may be specified as part of the output statement to steer the signal to a unique destination. When a unique destination process instance can be determined for the output statement, the signal is delivered to that process. When a unique process cannot be determined, one of three cases applies:

- If the signal can traverse more than one path and each path terminates in a different process instance, one arbitrary process connected to those paths will be chosen to receive the signal. This is a form of nondeterminism and should not be used.
- If the signal encounters more than one process instance at the end of a path because multiple instances of the receiving process have been created, then one arbitrary process instance will be chosen to receive the signal. This also is a form of nondeterminism and should not be used.
- One may wish to broadcast the signal to multiple routes. In this case, use the VIA ALL form of output, and the signal will be broadcast to the routes specified as if multiple separate outputs were used. This use is acceptable since there is no nondeterminism in choosing the initial path, but it would not be sufficient if the path branches later (in another block) or terminates in multiple process instances.

If a signal can be on more than one route from a process, do one of the following:

- Explicitly specify the desired signal path using the VIA form of output and specifying either a signal route, channel, or gate.
- Explicitly specify the desired receiving process using the TO form of output and specifying either a process identifier or a Pid value.
- Broadcast the signal using VIA ALL.
- If a signal destination goes to more than one process instance, explicitly specify the desired receiving process using TO and a Pid value.

A related case is if an input channel is receiving a signal, but there is more than one possible receiver process and it is not possible to determine which process will actually receive the signal. This is a form of nondeterminism.

Spontaneous Transitions. A spontaneous transition allows a transition between states without requiring any input signals. The activation of a spontaneous transition is independent of the presence of any signals in the input port of the process. There is also no implied priority between normal transitions and spontaneous transitions. Spontaneous transitions therefore represent nondeterministic behavior. If one needs to make a transition without waiting for an input signal, a continuous signal can be used.

Ambiguous Continuous Signals. If the value of the Boolean expression is true for more than one continuous signal, a nondeterministic choice is made as to which transition will be taken. For example:

```
STATE SomeState;
  PROVIDED v1 > 4; /* transition 1 */
  PROVIDED v1 < 6; /* transition 2 */
```

Instead, add priorities to the overlapping continuous signals or make them non-overlapping. For example:

```
STATE SomeState;
  PROVIDED v1 > 4; PRIORITY 1; /* transition 1 */
  PROVIDED v1 < 6; PRIORITY 2; /* transition 2 */
```

Automatically Discarded Signals. SDL semantics state that a signal sent to a process is discarded if the state machine does not explicitly handle the signal in the current state. While this case may be acceptable, it may also indicate a missed requirement. It would be better to have an asterisk input explicitly indicating the desire to discard or specially handle all other signals.

Parameterized Timers with a Large or Infinite Index. Timers may be parameterized by a sort. In effect, parameterized timers allow the specification of an infinite number of timers. While this is not inherently a problem, in reality only a finite number of timers can be active. It may be difficult to determine the real upper bound for resource allocation purposes during implementation.

If it is helpful to have timers parameterized by a sort, but that sort has an infinite number of literals (e.g., **Integer**), then create a new sort that is a restricted subrange of the original and parameterize the timer by the new sort. For example, replace:

```
TIMER delay(Integer);
```

with:

```
SYNONYM MaxTimers Integer = 10;
SYNTYPE TimerNumber = Integer
  CONSTANTS 1 : MaxTimers
ENDSYNTYPE;
TIMER delay(TimerNumber);
```

If there will only be a very small number of timers, consider using separate timers instead of a single parameterized one which, in most implementations, will need to become separate timers anyway.

Complex Ground Expressions. SDL allows ground expressions to be arbitrarily complex (e.g., when used for the default value of a sort). This makes sense from a syntactic perspective, but the developer must be able to easily determine the appropriate value to use in the implementation code. Whenever possible, the use of ground expressions should be limited to simple operations on literals or synonyms, such as `max + 1`.

4   Performance Considerations

While it is important not to overconstrain an implementation of a model, it is also important not to make an efficient implementation difficult, either. This section discusses some considerations that will facilitate an efficient implementation.

Large Data Structures. Although SDL2000 supports references, SDL'96 has copy semantics. At signal sends, assignments, and procedure and operator parameters that are not `IN/OUT`, a copy must be made of the original data. Make sure that all the data that is copied really needs to be. For example, do not pass entire structures around when only a single field is needed.

Variables declared at the process level can also be a problem. There is no such concept in SDL as a transition-local variable. That means that the data in a variable that is used only in a single transition may be kept around even when it is not needed. Consider the use of a procedure or operator if a large temporary variable is needed.

Recursive Procedures. By the semantics of SDL, a procedure called from a process has full access to the input queue of the calling process. While this in itself does not cause a problem, it can force the system to save a tremendous amount of state information during context switches. This can disallow some powerful forms of optimization and makes it difficult to create an efficient implementation.

A recursive procedure that does not access the input queue of the process does not cause any problems and can be freely used. For a procedure which does access the input queue of the process, it is best to think of it as merely a convenient way to refer to some functionality that will be expanded in place within the calling state machine (similar to a macro).

Note, however, that if the most natural expression for an algorithm is through recursion, then it can be used. The designer must weigh the performance penalty in the generated code (in terms of time and dynamic memory) against the maintainability and clarity of the specification.

Invalid Pid Values. It is recommended that signals only be sent to processes that exist. That is, it should always be true that when a signal is sent to a process, either:

- the process is a static process, or
- the logic of the model ensures that if a process does not exist, the signal is not sent.

If the above conditions hold, then the implementation can be more efficient. If the conditions do not hold, then the model is relying on the SDL semantics of throwing a signal away if the receiver does not exist or the Pid is Null. In this case, a check for the existence of the receiver must be included everywhere in the code and the code becomes noticeably larger and slower.

Output to an Unreachable Pid Value. If an OUTPUT statement sends a signal directly to a Pid that does not correspond to a reachable process (that is, there are no signal routes which can take the signal from the sender to the designated receiver), the semantics of SDL states that the signal should be discarded. While this mechanism will allow the execution of the system to continue, there are two problems:

- Handling this special case, which should be rare, requires an extra check on all signal sends. This check takes time and requires a larger executable.
- This situation almost certainly indicates a design error.

One should try to ensure that this situation never happens in the model.

External Procedures. Some operations are inherently difficult in SDL, and are extremely time consuming. In these cases, it is often better to call out to external procedures. For example, converting a Charstring containing a hexadecimal value into an Integer value is difficult in SDL and could be better done with a call to sprintf from the C library.

Exported Variables. The semantics of SDL requires that a copy of exported / imported variables be kept. The exporting process makes changes to a local variable and then explicitly exports it. The export operation copies the local copy to the visible one. For large data values, this can be an extremely inefficient operation. For example, profiling on a product model indicated that approximately 20% of the total execution time was being spent in this copy operation. Under two conditions, this overhead can be eliminated in the implementation:

- Processes within a single SDL system are synchronous (e.g., through data passing). In this case, the processes can be interleaved. The restriction then only has to be that the update of the variable by the exporting process is atomic, such as can be achieved by surrounding the code with a mutex lock.
- The exporting process updates the variable in such a way that the contained value is always consistent. For example, if the exported variable is a structure with two fields whose values must be consistent, both fields are always updated together. This update also needs to be an atomic operation.

If these conditions hold true, the exported variable can be implemented as a global variable. Note that there is also a deadlock possibility with exported variables, which can be eliminated by making the exporting process static or by explicitly ensuring that the exporting process must exist at the time of the corresponding import.

Sort Inheritance. In implementation languages that do not support inheritance, it can be very inefficient to implement a sort declared using this feature of SDL. The naïve solution of copying all operations can lead to large amounts of pointless code.

Dynamic Lists. In the absense of additional information, it must be assumed that list-like sorts, generators, and parameterized sorts (`String`, `Charstring`, `Powerset`, and any similar Z.105 or tool-specific extensions) can contain an arbitrarily large number of elements, which is the worst-case assumption in terms of the allowable implementation. Even the `Array` generator (or parameterized sort – we will only use the term "generator" here, but the discussion is equally applicable to parameterized sorts), which one can easily set to a bounded size by providing a suitable index sort, may be very wasteful of space if only a small fraction of the potential values are ever used at one time.

For an efficient implementation, one must be free to choose an appropriate concrete data type, and one must have sufficient information to be able to make the choice. Specifications typically require the use of a sort that allows hash-table functionality. That is, one wants to be able to access some data value through a domain value (or "index"). In SDL, this mapping is created through the `Array` generator. A common use is a mapping of call identifiers with the Pid value of the process that is handling them. However, there are two major problems with using the `Array` generator:

- Size bounds are needed to efficiently implement the functionality in the generated code. Most often, the maximum number of mappings to be stored in the map is significantly less than the size of the domain sort. Along with a size bound, the implementer needs an indication of how "dense" the mapping is (i.e., the maximum number of elements that can be in the mapping versus how many there typically are). This information is rarely apparent from the model itself, and is often controlled by external factors. From this information, it can be determined how to efficiently implement the generated sort (e.g., as a sparse array, a hash table, a regular array, etc.).
- SDL does not provide a convenient way to determine if a mapping is contained in the `Array`. That is, does a given index correspond to a valid value?

Another common requirement is for more than one domain sort in a given map. For example, one may need to know a region identifier and a cell identifier to be able to map a call to its location. While this can be achieved through the creating of an intermediate structure sort that has these two fields, that leads to the creation of auxiliary sorts which are not really required. Similarly, one may need multiple values stored for a single domain value.

Because of these restrictions, a separate `Map` generator or parameterized sort should be defined. At a minimum, the `Map` should allow the explicit specification of the domain sorts, range sorts, the maximum number of values, and the typical number of values.

Typical operations include adding a value, deleting a value, updating a value, retrieving a value, clearing all values, iteration over the mappings, determining if the map is empty, determining if a value is in the map, and returning the number of elements in the map.

Consistent Sort Operations. It is important to be consistent in the way that a particular abstract operation on a sort is used in the model. For example, one could always build up a String with the // operator. This consistency makes performance tuning easier and can isolate common cases for special implementations. To make special implementations even easier, any frequently used set of operations should be isolated in a separate procedure or operator.

Charstring Literals and Enumerations. Do not use a `Charstring` literal when an enumerated sort would be more appropriate. For example, do not use:

```
SYNONYM signal_err Charstring   = 'Signal error';
SYNONYM range_err Charstring    = 'Range error';
SYNONYM transmit_err Charstring = 'Transmit error';
```

when the following can be used instead:

```
NEWTPYE error_indicator
  LITERALS signal_err, range_err, transmit_err
ENDNEWTYPE;
```

5   Platform Interfaces

On a real system, the implementation code must be well behaved with the platform, platform libraries, and the rest of the applications executing on the system. This section discusses some considerations to make such an implementation easier.

Interfacing with External Types. When an SDL sort must interface with an external data type, it is crucial that they match exactly. This interface occurs at external procedure and operator calls (parameter types and return types), external synonyms, and the parameters of signals to and from the environment.

For example, when calling an external C function that has a *long int* parameter, the SDL sort of the actual parameter must have exactly the same number of bits as the C function expects. This number of bits is platform and compiler dependent. This problem is made intractable is the same SDL sort is used for example, to interface to an *int* parameter which has a different number of bits.

An enumerated sort in SDL'96 is not the same as *enum* in C, which is, for all practical purposes equivalent to an integer. In SDL'96, there is no direct correspondence or conversion between enumerated types and `Integer` types. However, see the definition of a "named number" in SDL2000.

A `Choice` sort in SDL (the Z.105 ASN.1 extension) is different from a *union* in C in an important way. The union type provides an implicit cast mechanism. No such mechanism exists in SDL. A `Choice` sort allows only one of the choices to exist in the variable at a given time. One cannot write the data as one sort and read it as another, as can be done in C.

A Charstring in SDL is not equivalent to *char* *in C. The C data structure is not auto-allocated, and the end-of-string indicator is a NULL character. As SDL Charstring can grow as needed, and NULL characters can be contained within the Charstring. The auto-allocation causes extra problems when it is not clear which entity is responsible for allocating and freeing the memory.

Incompatible Interface Types. It is common for two external interfaces to have different specifications for essentially the same data. For example, one external specification may declare a cell identifier to be a 32-bit unsigned integer, while another one may declare the same data as an octet string of length four. One should handle these different formats at the external marshaling interface since it would be inefficient to directly convert the values where needed in the model.

References. When using references at external interfaces, be aware of who is responsible to allocating and freeing the associated memory.

Asynchronous External Events. External events such as interrupts must be handled in external code, typically a separate thread, and translated into signals that are injected into the model.

Callback Functions. There is no easy way to make an SDL procedure or operator be visible to the external environment and still preserve the execution semantics of SDL. Because of this, if an external API requires a callback function, write it outside of the model, execute it in its own thread, and translate the return values into a signal.

Initializing External Global Memory. In some cases, an external procedure requires that a global variable be initialized before the procedure can be called. However, there is no equivalent in SDL to an extern declaration in C for variables, and there are no truly global variables in SDL itself. In order to initialize the global variable, create an external C function that only sets the variable to the proper value. This function can then be declared as an external procedure in SDL and called as necessary.

Preprocessor Directives. In C code, a preprocessor directive such as #DEFINE is a purely lexical substitution. In contrast, an SDL SYNONYM must have a sort and is syntactically restricted. To use common definitions, one must translate definitions from header files such as:

```
#DEFINE MAX_CALLS 10
```

into a value of an appropriate sort in SDL such as:

```
SYNONYM MAX_CALLS Natural = 10;
```

6   Portability Issues

One of the benefits of modeling is maintaining the proper abstraction so that the model can be implemented on any platform. We discuss here some of the issues that can affect portability.

6.1   Tool-Specific Extensions

As much as is practical avoid tool-specific extensions that limit the conformance of the model to the Z.100 standard. For example, tools may provide ways to escape into the underlying implementation language directly in the model, pre-initialize all memory to zero (whether or not this is a legal value for the sort), provide special sorts, provide special ways to represent binary, octal, or hexadecimal values, etc.

Not only do these extensions limit the use of add-on tools such as metrics applications, they can force a team to stay with a specific vendor unless they are willing to invest considerable effort in porting. We have seen both of these situations occur more than once within product models.

6.2   Target-Specific Implementation Assumptions

Do not assume any particular machine size for references. In particular, do not try to masquerade an unsigned integer sort of seemingly appropriate size as a reference. For example, do not use a 32-bit unsigned integer where one would normally use a reference merely because references happen to be 32 bits wide on the target. Embedding implementation information causes several problems. For example:

- It severely limits the portability of the model. If the model ever does need to be ported, then it is hard to track down and correctly update all such information. It is also very difficult to identify and analyze the effect such knowledge had during creation of the model, and whether any influenced areas need to also be altered.
- This practice of sort interchange can be very confusing during analysis and usually leads to defects that are very difficult to track down.
- These sort interrelationships inhibit the application of many optimization techniques.

7   Conclusions

We have presented guidelines for making practical use of SDL for design. The guidelines presented here should not be taken as a comment on SDL in general. The focus of the paper, and the experience on which it is based, is on design and subsequent application generation. Many of the features discussed here (e.g., stating a maximum number of process instances) may be perfectly valid for requirements analysis, protocol modeling, etc. Much of the process of creating a design model from an analysis model entails refining the model by removing unwanted features (e.g., nondeterminism) and adding detail (e.g., a maximum number of process instances).

These guidelines are based on what is required to deploy a fully functional application that meets given requirements for performance, code size, platform interfaces, error handling, etc. Using these guidelines, product groups have been able to successfully deliver large telecommunications applications on time and with a reduced defect rate. By carefully balancing portability and reuse concerns with ease of implementation, the product groups have been able to achieve the promised benefits of model-driven engineering.

While the guidelines in this paper have been collected over several years and many projects, large subsets of the guidelines have been applicable to each project. As such, formulating these guidelines as patterns and antipatterns and providing tool support in the form of design checking tools and pattern applicators would allow them to be consistently applied.

References

1. Dietz, P., Weigert, T., WeilF.: Formal Techniques for Automatically Generating Marshalling Code from High-Level Specifications. Second IEEE Workshop on Industrial Strength Formal Specification Techniques, Boca Raton, USA, October 1998.
2. ITU-T: Recommendation X.680 (07/02) Information technology - Abstract Syntax Notation One (ASN.1): Specification of basic notation. International Telecommunication Union, Geneva, 2002.
3. ITU-T: Recommendation Z.100 (08/02) Specification and Description Language (SDL). International Telecommunication Union, Geneva, 2002.
4. ITU-T: Recommendation Z.105 (07/03), SDL combined with ASN.1 modules (SDL/ASN.1). International Telecommunication Union, Geneva, 2003.
5. Telelogic AB: Tau 4.5 SDL Suite, 2003.

Validating Wireless Protocol Conformance Test Cases

Paresh Jain and Amresh Nandan

TATA Consultancy Services (TCS),
D4, Sector-3, NOIDA-201301, India
{paresh.jain, amresh.nandan}@tcs.com

Abstract. This paper shares our experiences in using SDL to unit test TTCN-2 scripts written for the conformance testing of 3G UMTS protocols. The tool used in this assignment was Telelogic Tau^{TM}, which provided a way of bridging SDL and TTCN-2. Telelogic calls this feature "co-simulation", which allows testing SDL applications using TTCN without the need for writing target adaptation, environment, and encoding and decoding parts. This paper describes how the co-simulation feature was used the other way around, i.e., to check TTCN protocol conformance test cases. The work was carried out to test a TTCN test suite for inter system handover protocol conformance (3G to 2G). The experiment successfully demonstrates the capabilities of co-simulation and its benefits in developing TTCN test cases, particularly when target test equipments are under development.

1   Introduction and Motivation

In the 3G UMTS domain, 3GPP controls and implements the development of conformance scripts from specification to implementation. This implementation is in the form of Tree and Tabular Combined Notation (TTCN 2.0) [5] scripts, and test equipment manufacturers use these scripts on their test systems to test the user equipment (UE) or Network Entities. This whole development cycle involves contributions from ETSI, test manufacturers, network and UE manufacturers, as well as other institutions involved in these activities. In one of the experiments, which we performed, the script for Inter System Handover between UMTS and GSM [2] was under development. As part of the TTCN development team, it was brought to our attention that the development of hardware (target test system) would take time and so the TTCN test suite could not be tested right away. There were two alternatives: one was to wait until the target test system was ready, the other was to find an approach to test the test cases before the target test system got ready for use. As scripts for testing the inter system handover were still raw and since the script development team was not confident about their correctness, a brainstorming session was carried out and it was highlighted that there were two aspects of scripts correctness to be tested. One aspect was to test correctness and completeness of protocol state machines,

D. Amyot and A.W. Williams (Eds.): SAM 2004, LNCS 3319, pp. 290–300, 2005.

and the other was to test the identification of incorrect parameters used in the test cases. Further, it was noticed that the TTCN script development tools could detect most of the syntactical defects, but as these tools were still evolving, some of these defects might not be detected at compile time and might cause major problems at run time. Subsequently, it was assumed that there were lots of problems with the test suite, which could be detected before the target system was ready.

A *test harness* was required to be developed which could test the scripts. There were two options to develop the harness: one option was to develop it in C/C++, and the other was to develop it in SDL. A quick comparison was carried out and SDL won over the C/C++ application as detailed further in Section 3.

Several tools [8] and their features were discussed and it was found that Telelogic Tau [12] provides a feature called "co-simulation", which can bridge the signaling between TTCN and SDL without any need for writing target adaptation parts, environments, etc. Telelogic Tau provides this feature to test any SDL system using the TTCN scripts but we decided to use this feature the other way round. As TTCN scripts were supposed to be tested for the state flow and incorrect parameters, it was decided to write a small SDL system, which would simulate the UMTS and GSM protocol stack for UE side and system simulator (SS) configuration. The idea was to provide a responsive system for TTCN scripts so that all the TTCN script test paths could be tested [3]. One great advantage of co-simulation based testing was that it could generate Message Sequence Charts (MSC), which proved to be an important instrument in detecting problems.

After the decision of including co-simulation in the script development process, there was a significant change in the development cycle. Traditionally, directly after development and review of test scripts, the latter were integrated with the Target Adaptation part (Figure 1). This process involved detecting all the problems during Target Testing.

In the new process (Figure 2), co-simulation was introduced as part of unit testing of TTCN scripts. This was helpful in detecting problems related to exe-

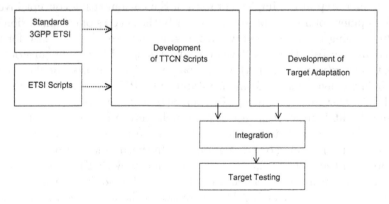

Fig. 1. Typical development lifecycle for 3G conformance scripts

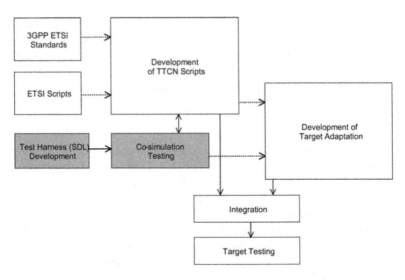

Fig. 2. Development lifecycle for 3G conformance scripts with co-simulation

cutions of test paths, protocol correctness, and other errors, which could not be detected during Target Testing.

The rest of the paper is organised as follows: Section 2 presents the architecture, design, and implementation of the concept. Several key differences in host testing methods are given in Section 3. In Section 4, we discuss the results generated out of this exercise, as well as the merits and drawbacks of this approach. We provide our conclusions in Section 5.

2   Implementation

2.1   Co-simulation Testing Architecture

The very first step in the implementation of the co-simulation concept involved the development of a small prototype to verify the success of co-simulation testing. Prototyping results were very encouraging and provided the base for steps involved in the Test Harness development. A single PIXIT file (protocol implementation extra information) was prepared, which was used for the access of protocol implementation conformance statements (PICS) and PIXIT parameters from TTCN abstract test suite (ATS) and SDL test harness.

Typically at high level, a test system architecture consists of a TTCN abstract test suite (compiled and converted to an executable test suite with target adaptor modules) running on test equipment. In the absence of target test equipment, we used the SDL test harness to communicate with TTCN ATS using the co-simulation feature of Telelogic Tau. The ASN.1 module with message data structures imported in TTCN ATS was reused without any modification in the SDL model as well.

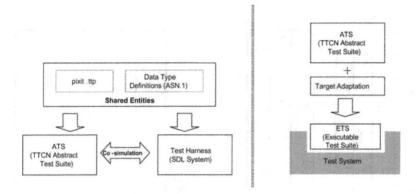

Fig. 3. (a) Entities involved in co-simulation testing, (b) testing of ATS with target

Data types in TTCN scripts, which were not defined in ASN.1 notation [1], were mapped to corresponding data types in SDL. Figure 3(a) shows the entities involved in the testing of scripts with co-simulation whereas Figure 3(b) shows the entities involved in the target testing of ATS.

2.2   Test Harness

The design of a SDL test harness was done with the goal of testing a UTRAN to GSM handover test case and thus the SDL system was designed by taking UMTS and GSM protocol systems into consideration [6]. The SDL system diagram contained UTRAN (UMTS terrestrial Radio Access Network) and GERAN (GSM/EDGE Radio Access Network) blocks, which were representing system simulator (SS) as well as user equipment (UE).

Both UTRAN and GERAN blocks contained processes to handle protocol messages and test case logic. Each block has procedures to handle SS configuration messages coming from the TTCN test suite and appropriate responses for each of them with logical conditioning. The UTRAN block has procedures for accepting system information messages, RRC connection, location update procedure and call set up procedure. The GERAN block has procedures for successful as well as unsuccessful completion of inter-system handover steps as defined in the 3GPP test specification [2]. A separate block was included in the model for reading PICS and PIXIT parameters. This block also handles initiating UTRAN and GERAN processes as well as high-level procedures for test cases.

After the development of this test harness, integration testing was carried out with the TTCN ATS. There were some minor changes carried out in the test harness. The test process generated run-time errors if there were problems with the ATS, so the script was corrected and testing was continued. This whole process caught a substantial amount of defects, which would have had a larger impact in the target-testing phase. These figures are discussed in Section 4. A sample MSC generated using this testing approach is shown in Figure 5.

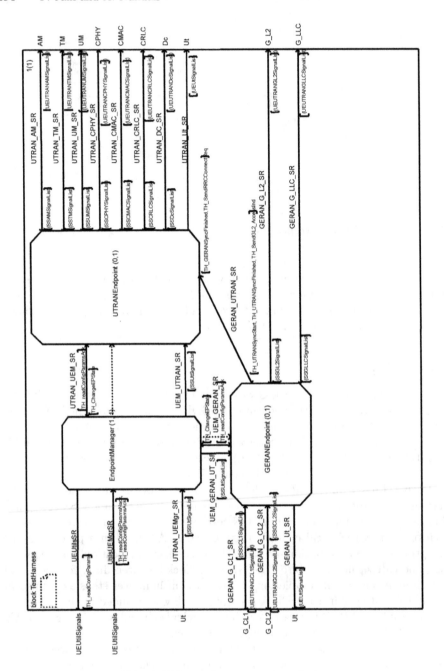

Fig. 4. SDL test harness system design

An important point to be noted here is that TTCN test suites developed as per 3GPP test specifications cannot be used directly for co-simulation. This

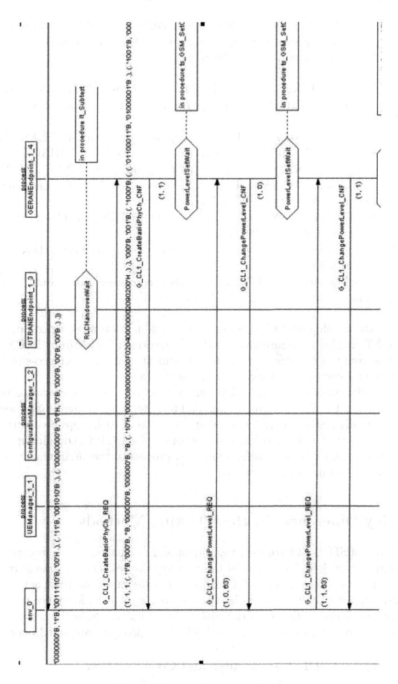

Fig. 5. Message Sequence Chart

is because certain TTCN data types cannot be recognized by SDL and certain modifications are required in the TTCN test suite before co-simulation.

These changes however do not affect the protocol conformance nature of the test suite and can be reverted back after host testing. A list of co-simulation specific changes in the test suite is listed below:

- The PICS and PIXIT files, which form part of the ATS, are consolidated as one .ttp file (pixit.ttp) for the purpose of co-simulation (this is a tool requirement).
- SDL does not recognize the HEXSTRING data type, thus all HEXSTRING data types in pixit.ttp file have been changed to OCTETSTRING.
- Co-simulation does not allow specifying the length of any PICS and PIXIT variable. This can be handled by defining simple types in TTCN and referring them as user-defined types in pixit.ttp file.
- Values for a BITSTRING, IA5STRING and OCTETSTRING data types go between quotes (e.g., '00100110').
- SDL cannot recognize the value '-' as a constraint parameter, these should be replaced with '*'.
- TTCN ASPs with Meta PDU type in their constraint lists should be redefined and constraints should also be modified.

After the development of a test harness, co-simulation was carried out using Telelogic Tau. The procedure involves the generation of C code from TTCN ATS as well as from the SDL test harness model, and the generation of a co-simulator executable for each one of them using Telelogic Tau.

Co-simulation produces three different types of reports from execution of the test cases, i.e., TTCN report (containing all test steps, assignments and message transfer details), SDL report (containing execution of each step, procedure and message transfer details) and Message Sequence Chart (MSC, containing graphical sequences of message transfer from each process to the environment, which is ATS in this case, and vice-versa).

3   Key Differences in Host Testing Methods

As a result of SDL test harness development and testing using co-simulation, we observed certain key differences in the two approaches, i.e., co-simulation and C/C++ test harness approach. These differences are important to be noted while deciding an approach to perform host testing of protocol conformance test cases as they can directly impact on the cost and schedule of the activities involved. Key advantages and disadvantages of both the approaches are listed below.

Advantages of SDL Test Harness and Co-simulation

- SDL enables faster test harness development.
- Co-simulation gives graphical logging in the form of Message Sequence Charts during testing, which allows easier verification of messages exchanged between the ATS and the test harness.

- Development and testing is independent of external components such as encoders/decoders (CODECs), adaptation libraries, and communication mechanism modules.
- In 3G conformance test cases, a large percentage of test steps are reused and so test harness developed in SDL can reuse processes and procedures for different test cases. This reduces the development effort and the complexity of the harness when a large number of test cases are to be developed.

Disadvantages of SDL Test Harness and Co-simulation

- Data types are shared between the harness and the ATS in the form of ASN.1 files. This does not allow testing of C/C++ data structures (which would be used finally after integration with target adaptor modules).
- Development of a SDL test harness requires additional SDL skilled resources and training on co-simulation.
- Costs of SDL and co-simulator licenses are very high and the required expenditure may not be justified in case of small projects.

Advantages of Using a C/C++ Test Harness

- C/C++ test harnesses enable the testing of additional components (such as adaptor libraries and CODECs), which are required on the target system, while ATS testing. This helps reducing the overall testing period of the target test system.
- Since this approach does not need any external tools (except a suitable compiler for development using C/C++, which is required in every approach), there is no additional license cost involved.

Disadvantages of Using a C/C++ Test Harness

- This approach requires more development effort and time.
- This approach does not provide graphical logging in the form of MSCs, and the user needs to verify everything using TTCN's text-based logging.
- A reliable and tested communication mechanism needs to be developed for communication between the harness and the ATS.
- Additional components such as adaptor libraries and CODECs need to be developed and tested (at least partially) for use with the C/C++ test harness.

4   Results

One of the important factors to be observed in this exercise was the effort required for test cases development [10] and testing using co-simulation as compared to the use of traditional test harness methodologies. Based on exercises done in the past, where a test harness was written using C++ to check TTCN test cases, the activities and effort required in each activity [11] could be compared with that of the co-simulation approach. The activities involved and effort

Effort Required (Person Days)

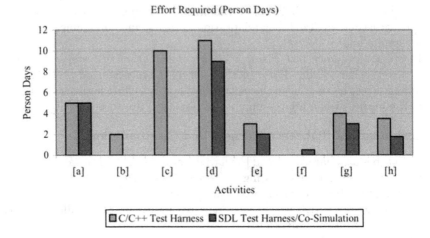

Fig. 6. Comparative Effort Chart

required in writing, analyzing and debugging TTCN test cases are the same for both methodologies, however the efforts required for writing test harnesses, testing and enhancing a test harness significantly differ. Using an example of typical UTRAN to GSM test case of medium complexity, the activities and effort required are as listed and charted below:

Activities:

[a] Design of test harness
[b] Development of communication mechanism between TTCN test suite and test harness (e.g., socket)
[c] Development of message encoders and decoders
[d] Development of test case
[e] Implementation of error and boundary conditions
[f] Development of PICS & PIXIT files for test harness
[g] Testing
[h] Addition of other similar test cases to the test harness (with logical conditioning for test cases selection).

From Figure 6, we can conclude that development of a C or C++ test harness with capability to test one test case required nearly 45% more effort than what was required when using TTCN-SDL co-simulation. The real benefit comes when lots of test cases are to be implemented in the test harness and SDL reusability makes it nearly 50% less effort consuming.

Further data was collected to compare the number of errors detected in TTCN ATS at different stages of development. In this exercise manual review of test suite was carried out while SDL test harness was under development. The stages of development and number of errors found during them are summarized in Table 1.

Table 1. Number of errors detected per development stage

No.	Development stage and activity	Errors
1.	Analysis (in Telelogic Tau) of TTCN-2 ATS	7
2.	Manual review of ATS with respect to 3GPP test specification and core specifications	14
3.	Host testing using co-simulation	9
	Total	30

Thus nearly 30% of the errors found before target testing were detected during co-simulation, and these were errors which could not get detected during manual review of the test suite.

From this activity, it can be comfortably said that a comprehensive SDL test harness can potentially bring out most types of errors in the ATS. Some of the key errors detected during testing by method of co-simulation are as listed below.

- In some cases, standard protocol procedures were not followed as per the specifications. Using the test harness, the flow of test cases was corrected.
- Table References were missing in several PICS/PIXIT parameter tables.
- In a few test steps such as ts_GSM_SS_CellRelease, the indentation of rows was logically incorrect.
- In some of the test steps where timers were being used, the cancel timer step was missing for the timer started earlier in other test steps.
- A few test case variables were not initialized properly or not at all.
- There was no handling of else / otherwise conditions for some parameters where certain logical conditions were false.

5   Conclusion

We conclude that SDL-TTCN co-simulation can be a very useful methodology for testing protocol conformance test suites developed using TTCN-2, when target test equipments are still under development or not available at all. The test harness development using SDL takes significantly less effort and time compared to conventional programming languages. The complexity of a SDL test harness is considerably less than that of C/C++ test harness, and reusability is very high. Further use of a co-simulation approach in testing enables the development of fairly stable test suites in shorter time periods, which can be readily tested on target test equipments when they are ready. Fairly refined test suites allow testing of target test systems as well and aids in faster product development.

References

1. 3GPP: User Equipment (UE) conformance specification; Part 3: Abstract Test Suites (ATSs) (Release 1999). 3rd Generation Partnership Project, TS 34.123-3, V0.0.0 (2000-03).

2. 3GPP: Technical Specification Group Terminals; User Equipment (UE) conformance specification; Part 1: Protocol conformance specification (Release 1999). 3rd Generation Partnership Project, TS 34.123-1, V3.5.0 (2001-09).

3. Alkhodre, A., Babau, J.-P., Schwarz, J.-J.: Preparing SDL code generation for real-time embedded systems modeling. IEEE Real-Time Embedded System Workshop, December 2001.

4. ETSI: Methods for Testing and Specification (MTS); Protocol and profile conformance testing specifications - The Tree and Tabular Combined Notation (TTCN) style guide. ETSI ETR 141, ETSI TC-MTS Reference: DTR/MTS-00020, October 1994. http://portal.etsi.org/edithelp/pdf/141_r1.pdf

5. ITU-T: Recommendation X.292 (05/02) OSI conformance testing methodology and framework for protocol Recommendations for ITU-T applications - The Tree And Tabular Combined Notation (TTCN). International Telecommunication Union, Geneva, 1998.

6. ITU-T: Recommendation Z.100 (08/02) Specification and Description Language (SDL). International Telecommunication Union, Geneva, 2002.

7. Mansurov, N., Chernov, A.V., Ragozin, A.S.: Industrial strength code generation from SDL. Cavalli, A.R., Sarma, A. (Eds.) Proc. 8th International SDL Forum, Evry, France, September 1997. Elsevier, 415–430.

8. Pohjolainen, P.: Software Testing Tools. University of Kuopio, Finland, March 2002. http://www.cs.uku.fi/research/Teho/SoftwareTestingTools.pdf

9. Saracco, R., Smith, J.R.W., Reed, R.: Telecommunications Systems Engineering Using SDL. New York, North-Holland, 1989.

10. TCS: Software Development Process Handbook. Tata Consulting Services.

11. TCS: Software Estimation Guidelines Ver. 2.0. Tata Consultancy Services, TCS-iQMS-103, January 2003.

12. Telelogic AB: Tau v4.4 User's Guide, http://www.telelogic.com.

Author Index

Lecture Notes in Computer Science

For information about Vols. 1–3284

please contact your bookseller or Springer